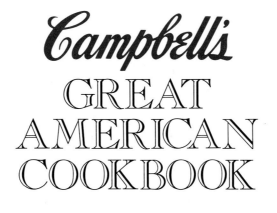

Campbell's
GREAT AMERICAN COOKBOOK

Traditional Stuffed Turkey, Mulled Cider, Brussels Sprouts and Chestnuts, Strawberry Shortcake, New England Clam Chowder, Giblet Gravy

Campbell's
GREAT AMERICAN COOKBOOK

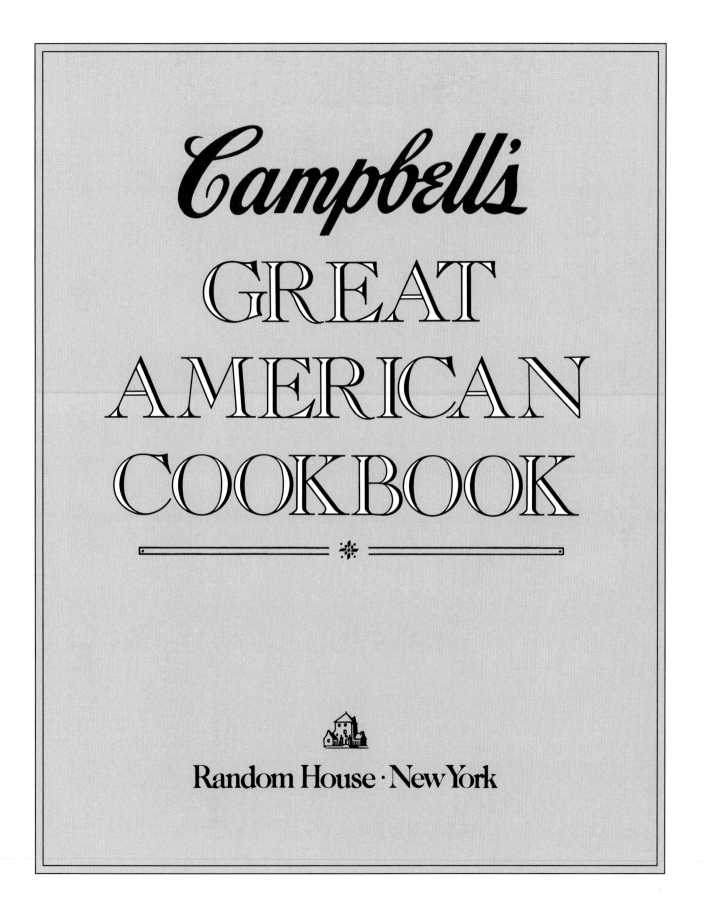

Random House · New York

What is American cooking? We explored that question in depth as we compiled this exciting new cookbook. We found that American food is the product of the American people—rich and poor, urban and rural, natives and immigrants from around the world. All these people worked to make life better, to improve on what they found, to incorporate the customs of faraway places into the fabric of the growing nation. We examined the cooking of todays's Americans from coast to coast and back through centuries of our history. And we discovered that the American cuisine is ever-changing, from region to region, from season to season. We at Campbell's are proud to be a part of the fascinating story of American food, and we are pleased to bring you this chronicle of good cooking in America.

Zoe Coulson
Vice President, Campbell Soup Company

The book was prepared by the Publications Center of the Campbell Soup Company, Camden, NJ 08101. Betty Cronin, Director; Flora Szatkowski, Editor; Louise Martineau, Recipe Coordinator; Kathleen Callan, Carolyn Maynes and Patricia Wade, Home Economists. Photographer, Richard Jeffery; Food Stylist, Lucy Wing and Accessories Stylist, Yvonne McHarg.

Cover Photographer, William R. Houssell; Food Stylist, Marianne Langan, and Accessories Stylist, Lynn Wilson.

Illustrator, Earl Herche; Designer, Amy Lamb.

✳ CONTENTS ✳

Asparagus Quiche, Spaghetti Primavera, Fried Potato Skins, Challah, White Sangría

GREAT AMERICAN COOKING

The story of American cooking is a chronicle of millions of American cooks in kitchens of every size and description. It is an American Indian cooking beans in a pit . . . a Colonial woman baking bread in a brick oven . . . a cowboy cook preparing a stew on the trail . . . a European-trained chef directing a staff in presenting a classic menu . . . an immigrant seeking comfort in familiar foods in a strange land . . . a farm wife putting up jars of preserves . . . a hostess sampling new dishes for a party . . . a single working parent trying to provide quick, economical, nutritious food for growing children. The food of America belongs to no one person more than another.

American cooking is a cuisine of the people. As varied as the population, it takes in the food of the rich and the poor, the urban and the rural. Most of all, it is a tribute to the American home cook, who learned to adapt to inadequate supplies and other challenges, and who never lost interest in exploring new ways to use familiar foods nor the curiosity to experiment with new foods and new combinations.

Today's American food has its roots in the American Indian tradition, for it was the Indians who first learned to use the native foods, such as chocolate, corn and peppers, that are now such an important part of our food heritage.

Although we tend to think of them as wandering hunters, Indians actually had a grasp of sound agricultural practices, such as fertilizing, crop rotation and irrigation. They knew how to preserve meats and vegetables for the winter and they were skilled at cooking foods over a fire or baking foods in a pit lined with red-hot rocks. They had not yet developed cooking pots that could withstand fire, so they boiled foods in tightly woven baskets by dropping heated stones into the liquid.

The Indians taught the early colonists a great deal about raising and preparing the native foods, and the colonists also had much to teach the Indians. The Europeans showed the Indians how to domesticate animals for milk, eggs and meat. They brought European foods to combine with the Indian foods, and iron cooking pots to use over a fire.

Spanish explorers were the first Europeans to travel to Florida and the Southwest, and their culture became the major European influence in those regions. Among contributions from Spain were citrus fruits and livestock, but the Spanish also were important for exporting many native American foods to Europe.

They did more exploring than settling, though, so their influence is less obvious in American cooking than that of the British or other colonists. Spanish missionaries were responsible for improving agriculture and for beginning the California wine industry. They also had a great share in integrating European and American Indian styles of cooking.

The colonists in the East learned much from the Indians, but they also continued trying to duplicate the foods they had known in their homes. They planted European crops and imported recipes and equipment from their native lands. For cookie baking, they brought traditional molds; for serving soup, they brought heirloom tureens; and for all types of foods, they brought the family recipes that helped them feel at home in the New World.

There were many years of struggle and hardship before the standard of living began to improve. The wealthy acquired servants, fine china and crystal for serving elaborate meals patterned after European cuisine. The working classes returned to many of their favorite Old World foods as soon as they were able—wheat bread rather than corn bread, trifle rather than Indian pudding.

Meanwhile, exploration of the western parts of the country continued, and whole families moved to settle the frontiers. Like the early colonists, they faced periods of hardship when crops were poor or supplies from the East did not arrive, and they learned to make do with the little they had. As the frontier moved farther west, more pioneers followed. Many of these pioneers were part of an enormous wave of immigration during the nineteenth century. Tales of fabulous wealth in America drew people from all walks of life to the New World.

Although different nationalities scattered across the continent, they often settled together with others of their homeland—Irish in Boston, Polish in Chicago, Scandinavians in the upper Midwest, Germans in Pennsylvania and the Midwest, Italians in large Eastern cities. These were certainly not the only regions where the immigrants settled, but these areas helped keep the various cuisines alive in the United States.

At the same time, Asian immigrants were arriving on the West Coast. Many of them worked on the transcontinental railway project, and some settled along the railroad in other parts of the West.

By the beginning of the twentieth century few frontiers were left to explore in America. Improved transportation made more and more foods available to people all across the continent, and the canning process preserved foods to make storage easier. The variety gave American cooks more choices and expanded their cooking horizons.

The American food industry stepped onto this scene with a world of inventive products designed to make life easier. There were soft drinks, canned milk, condensed soups, chocolate bars and packaged gelatin. Later came frozen foods of all descriptions; packaged mixes for making biscuits, cakes and other baked goods; and refrigerated doughs and prepared foods.

Why all the packaged foods? Women began to enter the work force in great numbers, and homes that had employed servants to cook and serve no longer could afford that luxury. The convenience offered by processed foods appealed to the American homemaker.

In the 1980s a new trend in food is evident. Today's Americans, newly aware of the relationship between nutrition and health, are showing an interest in preparing fresh, simple foods. Since 1970 our use of fresh fruits and vegetables has increased every year.

We will not give up our conveniences. We bake bread, but we buy much more than we bake. We prepare whole meals, but use prepared sauces, seasoning mixtures and salad dressings. For most of us, time is an important factor, no matter how much we like to cook.

We are experimenting with more new products, both processed foods and exotic fruits and vegetables from around the world. Improved technology allows us to keep foods longer, while transportation brings it to us more quickly. The microwave oven, food processor and other advanced equipment simplify many preparation chores. A cook can now prepare a whole meal in the time it once took a farm wife to chase down a chicken and wring its neck.

Restaurants have awakened to the joys of American food. Regional restaurants are springing up all over the country, ones that make the most of local specialties like crawfish, wild rice and persimmons instead of mimicking the classic European cuisines. They are proud of our American cuisine and wonderful American ingredients.

Food in American homes and restaurants is constantly changing, with fads and trends dictated by fashion or economics, health concerns or nostalgia, taste or appearance. We delight in the simple foods our mothers made, but we enjoy new creations, too.

For this book we have assembled a sampling of all the kinds of food Americans cook and eat, with recipes from all periods in our nation's history. Every recipe has its story, whether it was created by a chef in a fancy restaurant or by a busy mother trying to stretch time and money; these stories are included to show the recipes in context, to make you smile or to let you in on some American trivia. The dishes are among the best America has to offer, and they are meant to be enjoyed by you, your family, your friends and future generations of American cooks.

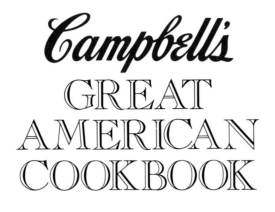

Campbell's
GREAT
AMERICAN
COOKBOOK

Deviled Nuts, Curry Fruit Popcorn, Sesame Cheese Sticks/Cheese Sticks, Olive Pinwheels

APPETIZERS AND SNACKS

An appetizer at the start of a meal is a sign of affluence. Our early settlers didn't need to have their appetites stimulated; as a matter of fact, they often served heavy puddings as first courses, hoping they would satisfy hunger and leave the scarce meat and vegetables to more moderate appetites.

But as America grew richer, its dining became more formal. The upper classes dined European-style, with complicated meals that began with appetizers of oysters or other seafood and went on to soups before reaching the main course. Housekeeping books show that Thomas Jefferson, an admirer of French and Italian cuisine, served lavish, multicourse dinners at Monticello.

Appetizer food reached the masses early in the nineteenth century when the free lunch, a custom from the Far West, spread over the country. Saloon keepers laid out counters of ham, beans, seafood, cheese, bread and fruits, particularly salty dishes that encouraged customers to buy more beer. Many students and bachelors relied on the free-lunch counter for their main meal of the day.

At the same time as the free-lunch counter was introducing snack foods to the populace, Scandinavian immigrants were bringing over the tradition of the smorgasbord. A smorgasbord table presented all the dishes for a meal at once—hot and cold fish, meats, vegetables, pickles, breads, cheeses, casseroles and sweets. The guests filled their own plates, quenching their thirst with aquavit.

These two traditions—the free lunch and the smorgasbord—helped establish that most-American tradition, the cocktail party. Cocktail parties evolved during and after Prohibition, at a time when a new informal style was developing, and when households no longer had domestic help for more formal entertaining.

A cocktail party requires food that can be eaten standing up with a minimum of silverware and china. A whole category of foods has been developed to fit these requirements, foods such as miniature sandwiches and canapés, tiny stuffed pastries, dips and spreads, cheese balls, and sausages eaten from a cocktail pick. These have almost completely replaced the knife-and-fork appetizers of Europe. They also have brought about a revolution in disposable dishes, flatware and napkins. And once again, young Americans—students and people starting out—have been known to make their dinner at the cocktail party table.

❈ Buffalo Chicken Wings

These spicy fried chicken wings originated in Buffalo, New York, where they are served by the bucketful in restaurants and bars. Celery, carrots and blue cheese dressing always accompany the wings, and mugs of cold beer moderate their fiery heat.

BEGIN: 1 HOUR AHEAD   24 PIECES

2   pounds chicken wings
    Salad oil
1   tablespoon Louisiana hot pepper sauce
¼   cup butter or margarine, melted
    Blue Cheese Dressing (see page 185)
    Celery sticks
    Carrot sticks

1. Cut tips off wings (save for soup). Split each wing at joint into 2 pieces.

2. In 4-quart saucepan, heat 2 inches salad oil to 375°F. Lower wings into oil. Fry 15 minutes or until very tender. Drain on paper towels.

3. Meanwhile, in large bowl, stir together hot pepper sauce and butter until well blended. Add chicken wings; toss gently to coat well.

4. To serve: Arrange chicken in bucket or on platter. Serve with Blue Cheese Dressing for dipping, celery and carrot sticks.

BROILED BUFFALO CHICKEN WINGS: Prepare as above but broil chicken wings instead of frying. Arrange chicken pieces on rack in broiler pan. Brush with salad oil. Broil 6 inches from heat 25 to 30 minutes or until crisp, turning occasionally. Proceed as in step 3.

TIP: Add more hot pepper sauce to make spicier wings.

❈ Oysters Rockefeller

Created at Antoine's in New Orleans, Oysters Rockefeller was named when a diner commented that it tasted as rich as Rockefeller. The original probably had no spinach, but took its green color from celery, green onions and fresh herbs. It also contained a dash of absinthe, which today's cooks may replace with anisette or Pernod.

BEGIN: 30 MINUTES AHEAD   6 SERVINGS

2   tablespoons butter or margarine
3   green onions, finely chopped
¼   cup finely chopped celery
1   cup chopped spinach
¼   cup chopped parsley
¼   teaspoon salt
    Generous dash hot pepper sauce
¼   cup dried bread crumbs
    Rock salt
24 small oysters on the half shell
    Grated Parmesan cheese
2   slices bacon, partially cooked and diced
    Lemon halves
    Parsley sprigs

1. In 1-quart saucepan over medium heat, in hot butter, cook green onions and celery until tender. Stir in spinach, parsley, salt and hot pepper sauce; cook until spinach is heated through, stirring occasionally. Add bread crumbs; toss to combine.

2. Place enough rock salt in bottom of large shallow baking pan to keep oysters in shell from tipping over. Place oysters in shell in baking pan; spoon spinach mixture over oysters. Sprinkle with cheese and bacon.

3. Bake at 425°F. 10 minutes or until edges of oysters are curled. Serve with lemon and garnish with parsley.

Oysters Rockefeller, Shrimp Cocktail

❀ Shrimp Cocktail

Shrimp cocktail, served with a horseradish-flavored to-mato sauce, is popular far from either American ocean, as well as on the coasts. In areas where fresh crab is available, the same sauce accompanies chunks of crab.

BEGIN: EARLY IN DAY

¾ cup ketchup
1 tablespoon prepared horseradish
1 tablespoon lemon juice
1 teaspoon Worcestershire
   Dash hot pepper sauce
   Steamed shrimp, chilled

In small bowl, combine all ingredients except shrimp; mix well. Cover; chill thoroughly. Serve with shrimp. Yields ¾ cup sauce.

CRAB COCKTAIL: Prepare as above but substitute crabmeat for shrimp.

❀ Pigs in Blankets

The name "hot dog" began at the New York Polo Grounds, where vendors called their sausages "red hots." Sports cartoonist Tad Dorgan created a new character in honor of the sandwich—a dachshund nestled in a bun —and the hot dog was born. Another nickname, pigs in blankets, describes the sausages (pigs) in blankets of pastry.

BEGIN: 1 HOUR AHEAD   40 APPETIZERS

   Pastry for 2-Crust Pie (see page 256)
   Prepared mustard
1 pound small cocktail frankfurters (about 40)
1 egg, beaten
1 tablespoon water

1. Prepare pastry. Roll pastry to 12- by 12½-inch rectangle. Spread lightly with mustard. Cut pastry into forty 3- by 1¼-inch strips.

2. Preheat oven to 425°F. Wrap each frankfurter with pastry strip, pinching ends together. Place seam side down on baking sheet. In cup, combine egg with water. Brush over pastry.

3. Bake 12 minutes or until golden.

TIP: Substitute frankfurters cut into 2-inch pieces for cocktail frankfurters.

❋ Spanakopitas

Spanakopitas are a contribution of the Greek community in America. Phyllo, the thin dough that makes the delicate pastry for this appetizer, also is used for making dessert pastries such as baklava, and frozen phyllo can be found in supermarkets and gourmet shops. It may be spelled in many ways, so look for phyllo, filo, fillo or phylo.

BEGIN: 1½ HOURS AHEAD   24 APPETIZERS

2   tablespoons olive or salad oil
1   small onion, finely chopped
1   teaspoon dill weed, crushed
1   package (10 ounces) frozen chopped
        spinach, thawed and drained
6   ounces feta cheese, crumbled
1   egg, beaten
¼   teaspoon pepper
¼   pound phyllo (about 6 sheets)
½   cup butter or margarine, melted

1. In 2-quart saucepan over medium-high heat, in hot oil, cook onion and dill until onion is tender, stirring occasionally. Add spinach; cook 5 minutes more or until all liquid is evaporated. Remove from heat. Stir in feta cheese, egg and pepper.

2. With knife, cut phyllo lengthwise into 3-inch-wide strips. Place on waxed paper; cover with a damp towel to prevent drying.

3. Working with one phyllo strip at a time, brush strip with melted butter; place 1 tablespoon spinach mixture at one end of strip. Fold one corner of strip diagonally over filling so short edge meets long edge, forming a right angle.

4. Continue folding over until you reach end of strip, making a triangular package. Repeat with remaining phyllo strips, butter and spinach mixture, and proceed as in steps 3 and 4.

5. Preheat oven to 425°F. Place triangles on jelly-roll pan; brush with butter. Bake 15 minutes or until lightly browned. Serve warm.

❋ Fried Cheese

Cheese is wonderful deep-fried: crisp on the outside, molten and creamy on the inside. Harder cheese, such as Cheddar, may be cut into bite-sized pieces for frying, but softer cheeses such as Camembert and Brie can be fried whole, so that the natural rind keeps the cheese intact.

BEGIN: 30 MINUTES AHEAD   8 SERVINGS

1   egg
2   tablespoons milk
¾   cup dried bread crumbs
1   pound firm cheese, well chilled and cut
        into 1-inch cubes
¼   cup all-purpose flour
    Salad oil
    Pear and apple slices or seedless grapes

1. In pie plate, beat egg with milk; place crumbs on waxed paper. Coat cheese with flour. Dip cheese in egg to coat; then coat with crumbs.

2. In 4-quart saucepan, heat 2 inches oil to 375°F. Fry a few pieces at a time until coating is lightly browned, turning occasionally. Drain on paper towels.

3. To serve: Arrange cheese on serving plate with fruit; serve at once.

TIP: Choose a firm cheese such as Cheddar, fontina, mozzarella, provolone, Colby or Muenster.

FRIED CAMEMBERT OR BRIE: Prepare as above but omit flour and substitute *2 packages (4½ ounces each) round Camembert or Brie cheese* for the cheese; do not cut cheese into cubes. In skillet, heat 1 inch oil to 375°F. Fry 1 cheese at a time until coating is lightly browned, turning once.

Spanakopitas, Nachos, Fried Camembert

❖ Nachos

This combination of corn chips, cheese and chilies first became popular in Mexican restaurants, whose customers soon realized that Nachos are easy to make at home. A native Mexican cook would use leftover tortillas, cutting them into bite-sized pieces and frying them in oil or lard until crisp.

BEGIN: 30 MINUTES AHEAD   8 SERVINGS

1   bag (8 ounces) tortilla chips
4   cups shredded Monterey Jack cheese (1
     pound)
1   can (4 ounces) green chilies, drained,
     seeded and chopped
1   medium onion, chopped

1. Preheat oven to 350°F. Place ¼ of the tortilla chips on each of 2 ovensafe platters or baking sheets.

2. In medium bowl, toss cheese, chilies and onion to mix. Sprinkle ¼ of the cheese mixture over chips on each platter. Top with remaining chips and cheese mixture.

3. Bake 5 minutes or until cheese is melted. Serve at once.

TO MICROWAVE: Prepare as above in steps 1 and 2, but assemble on 2 microwave-safe platters. Microwave each platter on HIGH 2 minutes or until cheese is melted.

❋ Rumaki

Rumaki—chicken livers and water chestnuts wrapped in bacon—reached the American public from Japan by way of Hawaii. Islanders arrange hot rumaki around a "pupu fire," which can be hot coals in a hibachi or a warming candle placed in a hollowed pineapple. Barbecued ribs, chicken wings, fried shrimp, won tons, meatballs and fruit also may be included on the "pupu tray."

BEGIN: EARLY IN DAY   36 APPETIZERS

1   pound chicken livers, each cut in half
¼   cup soy sauce
¼   cup dry sherry
1   small clove garlic, minced
½   teaspoon ground ginger
1   can (8 ounces) whole water chestnuts, drained and halved
1   pound sliced bacon, halved crosswise and partially cooked

1. In medium bowl, combine first 5 ingredients. Cover; chill at least 6 hours, turning occasionally. Drain.

2. Wrap each bacon piece around water chestnut half and chicken liver half; secure with toothpick. Repeat with remaining pieces. Place on rack in broiler pan.

3. Broil 4 inches from heat until liver is cooked, turning frequently.

❋ Fried Potato Skins

A recent innovation in finger food is fried potato skins, cut into strips, fried crisp and served with dips or filled with cheese, sour cream or guacamole. Save the pulp for making hashed browns or mashed potatoes.

BEGIN: 1½ HOURS AHEAD   4 SERVINGS

4   large baking potatoes
    Salad oil
¼   cup all-purpose flour
    Salt

1. Wash and dry potatoes; rub lightly with oil. Place in shallow pan. Bake at 450°F. 45 minutes or until fork-tender; cool.

2. Cut potatoes in half lengthwise; scoop out pulp, leaving ¼-inch shell (reserve pulp for another use). Cut skins lengthwise into 1-inch strips. Dip skins in flour to coat.

3. In 4-quart saucepan, heat 2 inches oil to 375°F. Fry a few skins at a time 2 minutes or until lightly browned. Drain on paper towels. Repeat with remaining skins.

4. To serve: Arrange hot skins on serving plate; sprinkle with salt.

TO MICROWAVE: Wash and dry potatoes; rub lightly with oil. Prick skins of potatoes before cooking. Place on microwave-safe dish. Microwave on HIGH 20 to 22 minutes or until done, turning occasionally. Let stand 2 minutes. Proceed as in step 2.

TIP: Serve with Guacamole (see page 13) or grated Parmesan cheese, if desired.

❋ Hot Cheese Canapés

The word canapé *harks back to the old French, meaning a covering for a bed: hence, a covering for bread. So simple, the recipe for this delicious hot* canapé *can be found in fund-raising cookbooks all over the country.*

BEGIN: 15 MINUTES AHEAD   24 APPETIZERS

1   cup mayonnaise
½   cup grated Parmesan cheese
½   cup sliced green onions
½   teaspoon Worcestershire
24 melba toast rounds

1. In small bowl, combine first 4 ingredients; mix well. Spread mixture over melba toast. Place on rack in broiler pan.

2. Broil 4 inches from heat until lightly browned. Serve warm.

✢ Stuffed Mushrooms

Mushroom caps are attractive edible containers for such tasty fillings as crab, sausage and cheese. Choose fresh, medium-sized mushrooms small enough to be eaten in one bite, but large enough to hold a good amount of filling.

BEGIN: 2 HOURS AHEAD   90 MUSHROOMS

2   pounds medium mushrooms
¼   cup butter or margarine
2   tablespoons finely chopped green onion
1   clove garlic, minced
1   cup shredded natural Swiss or Cheddar cheese
½   cup dried bread crumbs
2   tablespoons chopped parsley
½   teaspoon salt

1. Remove stems from mushrooms; chop stems. Set mushroom caps and stems aside.

2. In 10-inch skillet over medium-high heat, in hot butter, cook mushroom stems, green onion and garlic until tender. Remove skillet from heat; stir in cheese, crumbs, parsley and salt. Preheat oven to 450°F.

3. Fill mushroom caps with crumb mixture. Place mushrooms on a jelly-roll pan. Bake 10 minutes or until mushrooms are very hot.

CRAB-STUFFED MUSHROOMS: Prepare as above but omit cheese. Add *1 can (6 ounces) crabmeat, drained and picked over; 1 beaten egg; 2 tablespoons dry sherry* and *2 tablespoons mayonnaise* to skillet along with bread crumbs.

ITALIAN-STYLE STUFFED MUSHROOMS: Prepare as above but substitute *1 cup shredded mozzarella cheese* for Swiss cheese. Add *½ teaspoon basil leaves, crushed,* and *½ teaspoon oregano leaves, crushed,* along with bread crumbs. Sprinkle mushrooms with *2 tablespoons grated Parmesan cheese* just before baking.

SAUSAGE-STUFFED MUSHROOMS: Prepare as above but omit butter. Cook *½ pound fresh pork sausage* with chopped mushrooms, onion and garlic, stirring to break up meat.

✢ Cheese Sticks

Crisp, cheesy pastry sticks are fun snacks for all types of gatherings. The rich dough also makes a good pastry to wrap around olives for bite-sized Olive Puffs. Try the recipe with both cheeses; they produce quite different results.

BEGIN: 1 HOUR AHEAD   60 STICKS

1   cup all-purpose flour
¼   teaspoon cayenne pepper
1½ cups shredded Cheddar or natural Swiss cheese
½   cup butter or margarine
1   teaspoon Worcestershire

1. In large bowl, stir together flour and cayenne until mixed. With pastry blender or 2 knives used scissor-fashion, cut in cheese and butter until mixture resembles coarse crumbs. Sprinkle with Worcestershire. Using hands, work dough until mixture holds together. Shape into a ball.

2. Preheat oven to 425°F. On lightly floured surface, roll pastry to 10- by 12-inch rectangle. Cut into 4- by ½-inch strips. Transfer strips to baking sheets.

3. Bake 6 to 8 minutes until golden; cool on wire racks.

SESAME CHEESE STICKS: Prepare as above but sprinkle dough rectangle with *1 tablespoon sesame seeds* before cutting into strips. Press lightly into dough with rolling pin.

OLIVE PUFFS: Prepare dough as above in step 1. Drain *50 pimento-stuffed olives.* Wrap about 1 teaspoon dough around each olive to cover completely. Place wrapped olives on baking sheet. Bake at 400°F. 12 to 15 minutes until golden. Serve warm or cool.

TIP: Freeze unbaked Olive Puffs for later use. Bake frozen puffs at 400°F. 18 to 20 minutes until golden.

❋ Tarragon Marinated Mushrooms

Raw mushrooms can be simply washed and added to a tray of crudités for dips, or they can be marinated overnight to make delicious cold nibbles. When served as a sit-down appetizer, the mushrooms are often sliced before marinating and served on a bed of salad greens; whole, they make a splendid food for spearing on a cocktail pick. Be sure to include marinated mushrooms in an Italian antipasto.

BEGIN: DAY AHEAD   8 SERVINGS

1½ cups olive or salad oil
½   cup white wine vinegar
1   tablespoon tarragon leaves, crushed
1   teaspoon salt
½   teaspoon pepper
3   cloves garlic, minced
1   pound small whole mushrooms

1. In large bowl, combine first 6 ingredients until well mixed. Stir in mushrooms. Cover; refrigerate overnight, stirring once or twice.

2. To serve: Drain mushrooms. Arrange mushrooms on serving plate; spear with cocktail picks. Yields 4 cups.

TIP: Use this marinade for other vegetable appetizers such as carrot sticks, green pepper strips, green beans or cauliflowerets. Cook vegetables in boiling water just until tender-crisp; drain well. Marinate overnight.

❋ Olive Pinwheels

Tea sandwiches have been a hallmark of many social occasions, especially card parties, showers and teas, but they also are appropriate for cocktail parties and receptions. Creative caterers and homemakers have discovered many ways to make these sandwiches attractive; they can look like checkerboards, pinwheels and other fancy shapes, and even the fillings are pretty.

BEGIN: DAY AHEAD   63 APPETIZERS

1   jar (7 ounces) small pimento-stuffed
      olives, drained
1   package (8 ounces) cream cheese,
      softened
½   cup finely chopped walnuts or pecans
9   slices whole wheat bread

1. Finely chop enough olives to make ½ cup. Reserve remaining whole olives.

2. In small bowl with mixer at medium speed, beat cream cheese until fluffy; beat in chopped olives and nuts.

3. Trim crusts from bread; flatten bread slightly with rolling pin. Spread each slice with cheese mixture. Place a row of whole olives on one end of each bread slice. Roll up each slice jelly-roll fashion around olives. Cover with damp towel. Refrigerate overnight.

4. To serve: Cut each roll into seven ½-inch slices. Arrange on serving plate.

❉ Deviled Eggs

No picnic or Fourth of July celebration is complete without a plate of Deviled Eggs. The addition of anchovies, bacon or olives makes a more elegant mouthful, but they're simply delicious stuffed with traditional mustard-flavored yolks.

BEGIN: 1 HOUR AHEAD   12 APPETIZERS

6   hard-cooked eggs
¼   cup mayonnaise
1   teaspoon prepared mustard
     Salt
     Pepper
     Paprika

1. Shell eggs; slice in half lengthwise. Gently remove yolks; place in small bowl. With fork, finely mash yolks. Stir in mayonnaise, mustard, salt and pepper to taste.

2. Pile yolk mixture into egg white centers. Cover; refrigerate until serving time. Sprinkle with paprika.

ANCHOVY DEVILED EGGS: Prepare as above but omit salt and add *1 tablespoon anchovy paste* to egg yolk mixture. Garnish with anchovy fillets, if desired.

BACON DEVILED EGGS: Prepare as above but add *2 slices bacon, cooked and crumbled,* to egg yolk mixture.

OLIVE DEVILED EGGS: Prepare as above but add *2 tablespoons finely chopped pimento-stuffed olives* to egg yolk mixture. Garnish with sliced olives.

❉ Cream Puff Appetizers

Tiny cream puff pastries with savory fillings make a welcome addition to any appetizer assortment. When you add shredded cheese to the dough, the resulting pastries are delicious enough to serve without a filling.

BEGIN: EARLY IN DAY   50 APPETIZERS

1   cup water
½   cup butter or margarine
⅛   teaspoon salt
1   cup all-purpose flour
4   eggs
3   cups Egg Salad (see page 182) or
     Seafood Salad (see page 182)

1. Preheat oven to 425°F. In 2-quart saucepan over medium heat, heat water, butter and salt until boiling. Add flour all at once. With wooden spoon, vigorously stir until mixture forms a ball and leaves side of pan. Remove from heat.

2. Add eggs, one at a time, beating well after each addition until smooth. Cool slightly. Drop by teaspoonfuls 2 inches apart onto baking sheet.

3. Bake 30 minutes or until puffed and dry. Cool thoroughly.

4. *About 1 hour before serving:* With sharp knife, cut tops off cream puffs; fill each with about 1 tablespoon salad. Replace tops; refrigerate until serving time.

CHEESE PUFFS: Prepare dough as above, but add *¾ cup shredded natural Swiss or Gruyère cheese* along with flour. Proceed as above. Serve hot, or cool and fill with choice of filling.

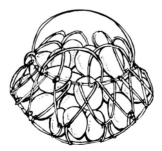

❉ Hot Crab Dip

The appetizer buffet is a good place to offer foods that are more expensive than everyday fare; because the items are served in small quantities, a little goes a long way. And because there is usually a selection of hors d'oeuvres and dips, a costly dish can be offset by a less expensive one. Try the elegant but easy bread basket as a container for this luscious hot crab dip.

BEGIN: 45 MINUTES AHEAD

2	packages (8 ounces each) cream cheese, softened
½	cup mayonnaise
¼	cup dry white wine
2	green onions, chopped
2	cloves garlic, minced
½	teaspoon Worcestershire
2	cans (6 ounces each) crabmeat, drained and picked over
¼	cup chopped pimentos
	Crackers or fresh vegetables

1. In small bowl with mixer at medium speed, beat cream cheese until smooth and fluffy. Gradually beat in mayonnaise, wine, green onions, garlic and Worcestershire until smooth and well blended. Stir in crab and pimentos. Turn mixture into 1-quart casserole.

2. Bake at 350°F. 20 minutes or until very warm, stirring once. Stir before serving. Serve with crackers or vegetables. Yields 3½ cups.

TO MICROWAVE: Prepare as above in step 1 but turn mixture into 1-quart microwave-safe casserole; cover. Microwave on HIGH 4 to 5 minutes until very warm, stirring twice. Stir before serving.

CRAB DIP IN BREAD BASKET: Prepare as above, but do not turn crab mixture into casserole. Slice top off *2-pound round loaf wheat or rye bread.* Scoop out center of loaf to make a basket (reserve center to make bread crumbs for another use). Place bread loaf on baking sheet; fill center with crab mixture. Bake at 350°F. 45 minutes or until very warm.

Cheese Ball, Crab Dip in Bread Basket

TIP: To use a 1-pound bread loaf for dip, fill bread basket with only part of the dip. After most of dip is eaten, heat remaining dip and refill bread.

CLAM DIP: Prepare as above but omit wine, green onions, crab and pimentos. Drain *2 cans (6½ ounces each) minced clams;* reserve juice. Beat *⅓ cup clam juice* and *½ teaspoon prepared horseradish* into cream cheese along with mayonnaise. Stir in drained clams. Refrigerate until serving time. Serve cold.

❋ Cheese Ball

A cheese ball is easy to prepare and provides a showcase for fine American cheeses. Domestic Cheddar varieties include Wisconsin, New York, Vermont and Oregon cheeses in mild to extra-sharp. Try one of the excellent American blue cheeses the next time you prepare this recipe.

BEGIN: 3 HOURS AHEAD OR EARLY IN DAY

1   package (8 ounces) cream cheese,
      softened
2   cups shredded Cheddar cheese, at room
      temperature
¼   cup chopped parsley
2   tablespoons finely chopped green onion
1   tablespoon Worcestershire
1   cup finely chopped walnuts or almonds
      Crackers or fresh vegetables

1. In small bowl with mixer at medium speed, beat cream cheese and Cheddar cheese until smooth and fluffy. Beat in parsley, green onion and Worcestershire. Refrigerate 30 minutes.

2. Shape mixture into a ball. Roll in nuts to coat. Serve immediately, or wrap and refrigerate until 2 hours before serving time; let stand at room temperature 2 hours before serving. Serve with crackers or vegetables.

BLUE CHEESE BALL: Prepare as above but add ½ *cup crumbled blue cheese* along with other cheeses.

❋ Beef Jerky

Native Americans had two forms of dried meat that were essential to their way of life. The first, pemmican, was a mixture of dried meat, fat and cherries or berries, all pounded together. The second was jerky, thin strips of meat that were salted or dipped in brine, then hung to dry in the sun or near a fire. Both jerky and pemmican helped Indians, explorers and pioneers through many a long journey and hard winter. Today jerky is savored by hikers and campers on the trail and by snackers at parties.

BEGIN: EARLY IN DAY

1   pound boneless beef round steak
1½ teaspoons garlic salt
½   teaspoon pepper

1. Freeze meat 1 hour to firm (makes slicing easier); trim and discard fat from steak. Cut steak into very thin slices.

2. Place strips in single layer on wire rack in jelly-roll pan. Sprinkle with garlic salt and pepper.

3. Bake at 200°F. about 6 hours until beef is dry. Cool; store in covered container in refrigerator. Yields ½ pound.

❋ Guacamole

In Mexico, Guacamole is a salad, a sauce for tacos and other entrées and a filling for hors d'oeuvres. But in the Southwestern United States, no party is complete without a bowl of this dip, fiery hot or more delicately seasoned, accompanied with tortilla chips for dipping. If you like it hot, add more chilies or include some hot pepper sauce.

BEGIN: 30 MINUTES AHEAD

2   medium avocados
1   small tomato, finely chopped
1   tablespoon grated onion
1   tablespoon chopped, seeded canned
      green chilies
1   tablespoon lemon juice
      Dash garlic powder
      Tortilla chips or potato chips

1. Cut each avocado in half; remove seed. Scoop out pulp into a bowl; with fork, mash avocado. Add remaining ingredients except tortilla chips; stir until well mixed.

2. To serve: Turn mixture into serving bowl; surround with tortilla chips for dipping. Serve immediately. Yields 2½ cups.

❋ Cereal Snack Mix

Ready-to-eat breakfast cereal was first developed by Dr. J. H. Kellogg for patients at a sanitorium in Battle Creek, Michigan. The dry cereal provided the healthy nutritional value of whole grains, and required a certain amount of chewing, which Dr. Kellogg believed to be necessary for good health. The American public quickly took up this cereal, perhaps for health reasons, but also because it was easier to prepare and less expensive than traditional breakfasts. Mrs. Kellogg made a piecrust with crushed cereal, beginning a trend of using cereals as a recipe ingredient.

BEGIN: 1 HOUR AHEAD

½   cup butter or margarine
2   tablespoons Worcestershire
½   teaspoon garlic powder
    Dash hot pepper sauce
1   can (3 ounces) chow mein noodles
2   cups toasted oat cereal
2   cups bite-sized shredded corn cereal
1   cup pretzel rings
1   cup toasted peanuts or cashews

1. Preheat oven to 300°F. In 13- by 9-inch baking pan, place butter. Heat in oven until butter is melted. Stir in Worcestershire, garlic powder and hot pepper sauce. Add chow mein noodles, cereals, pretzels and peanuts; toss to coat well.

2. Bake 30 minutes or until lightly browned, stirring occasionally. Cool; store in tightly covered container. Yields 7½ cups.

❋ Cheesy Buttered Popcorn

Indians discovered popping corn's unusual reaction to heat; and both the Indians and the settlers found many ways to use the fluffy kernels. Our forefathers served it as a breakfast cereal with milk, made soup from it, used it to thicken stews, made a boiled dessert pudding of it, used it as a base for confections, garnished other foods with it and strung it on threads for adorning Christmas trees.

BEGIN: 15 MINUTES AHEAD

¼   cup butter or margarine
1   teaspoon basil leaves, crushed
½   teaspoon oregano leaves, crushed
½   teaspoon garlic salt
10 cups popped corn
¼   cup grated Parmesan cheese

1. In small saucepan over medium heat, melt butter; stir in basil, oregano and garlic salt.

2. In large bowl, pour butter mixture over popped corn. Sprinkle with cheese; toss to coat well. Serve immediately. Yields 10 cups.

CINNAMON SUGAR POPCORN: Prepare as above but omit basil, oregano, garlic salt and Parmesan. Stir *½ teaspoon ground cinnamon* into butter; sprinkle buttered popcorn with *¼ cup sugar* and *¼ teaspoon salt.*

CURRY FRUIT POPCORN: Prepare as above but omit basil, oregano, garlic salt and Parmesan. Stir *1 teaspoon curry powder* into butter. Add *1 cup salted peanuts* and *1 cup raisins* to buttered popcorn; toss to combine. Salt to taste.

❋ Chicken Liver Pâté

Whether you call it pâté or chopped liver, this is one of the best ways ever to serve liver. Our version resembles the Jewish classic, chopped liver, with its hard-cooked eggs and onion. But Jewish cooks prefer the flavor of chicken fat for cooking the onion and livers.

BEGIN: EARLY IN DAY

½   cup butter or margarine
1   pound chicken livers
1   medium onion, chopped
2   hard-cooked eggs, cut up
2   tablespoons brandy
½   teaspoon salt
⅛   teaspoon pepper
    Chopped parsley
    Crackers

1. In 10-inch skillet over medium-high heat, in hot butter, cook chicken livers and onion until chicken livers are tender but still pink inside, stirring often; place in blender container. Cover.

2. At low speed, blend mixture until smooth, stopping blender occasionally and scraping sides with rubber spatula. Add eggs, brandy, salt and pepper; blend until smooth.

3. Spoon mixture into a small bowl. Cover; refrigerate until serving time.

4. To serve: Mound pâté on serving plate. Garnish with parsley; surround with crackers. Yields 2 cups.

❋ Deviled Nuts

The American continent is rich in nut trees. The Indians boiled nuts to make a kind of milk for drinking and cooking; they added ground nuts to breads and stews. And they enjoyed nuts as we do today, roasted or raw, right from the shell or with a few seasonings.

BEGIN: 1 HOUR AHEAD

2 tablespoons butter or margarine
3 cups pecan halves, walnut halves or whole almonds
2 tablespoons Worcestershire
1 tablespoon chili powder
1 teaspoon garlic salt
¼ teaspoon cayenne pepper

1. Preheat oven to 300°F. In 13- by 9-inch baking pan, place butter. Heat in oven until butter is melted. Add nuts and Worcestershire; toss to coat well.

2. Bake 30 minutes or until nuts are toasted, stirring occasionally. Sprinkle with chili powder, garlic salt and cayenne; toss to mix well. Cool; store in tightly covered container. Yields 3 cups.

CURRIED NUTS: Prepare as above but omit Worcestershire and chili powder; add *1 tablespoon curry powder* along with garlic salt.

SPICY NUTS: Prepare as above but omit Worcestershire, chili powder, garlic salt and cayenne. Stir *1 teaspoon ground cinnamon, ¼ teaspoon ground allspice* and *¼ cup sugar* into butter before adding nuts.

❋ Green Onion Dip

A dip served with chips or raw vegetables has become almost indispensable party fare. It can be as simple as onion soup mix stirred into sour cream—one of the most popular of all time—or as elegant as expensive caviar. Set the tone of the dip by the dippers you serve with it. Carrots and celery are always welcome, but why not add other vegetables such as cherry tomatoes, raw mushrooms, cauliflower, broccoli, turnips, green beans, asparagus and snow pea pods?

BEGIN: EARLY IN DAY

½ cup sour cream
½ cup mayonnaise
¼ cup finely chopped green onions
1 tablespoon Worcestershire
1 small clove garlic, minced
  Potato chips or fresh vegetables

In small bowl, combine first 5 ingredients; stir until well mixed. Cover; refrigerate several hours or overnight to blend flavors. Serve with chips or vegetables. Yields 1 cup.

DILL DIP: Prepare as above but substitute *2 teaspoons dill weed, crushed,* for Worcestershire and reduce green onions to 2 tablespoons.

SPINACH DIP: Prepare as above but stir in *1 package (10 ounces) frozen chopped spinach, thawed and well drained.*

Oyster Stew, Okra Gumbo, Pumpkin Soup

SOUPS

Soup has been a part of world cuisine almost as long as fire has been known to man. Even before they learned to make fireproof pottery, ancient cooks prepared soups in animal skins or seashells over an open fire. Because there were no spoons before the Middle Ages, the custom was to sip soup from a bowl, or to dip bread into it. This method of eating was known as *sop* or *sup,* and the word later became "soup."

The first soups made on this continent were created centuries ago by native Americans. They filled watertight wooden, leather or wicker vessels with food chunks and liquid, then added white-hot stones to heat the soup. Or they made soup in gutted buffalo carcasses or stomachs, cooked over a low fire. Later, they learned to make pottery containers that could withstand the fire's heat.

Indian soups tended to be concoctions of available foods. It was the Indians who made the first soups of native American beans, corn and pumpkins, combined with game and seafood. When the colonists arrived with their large iron kettles, soup was already an important food for the Indians.

Besides their superior cooking pots, the colonists added ingredients from their native lands to American soup: domesticated beef, chicken, a variety of garden vegetables, grains and pasta. Often they would cook large pieces of meat and vegetables in a pot with liquid, then serve the liquid separately as a broth. Other times, the soup kettle was a catchall for a few bits of meat and vegetables that made a flavorful vegetable soup.

The colonists had a homemade version of bouillon cubes made by boiling veal and pork bones until the liquid became a gelatinous gluelike substance. The mixture, which they called "pocket soup," could be dried and carried along by travelers, then eaten as a snack or used as a base for a later soup.

Through the centuries each group of immigrants brought its own foods and cooking methods to make the soup pot a symbol of the American spirit, the melting pot. With corn, chilies and tomatoes from the Americas, beef and pork from Europe, spices from the East and okra from Africa, such bold soups emerged as Gumbo and Chili Soup, as well as new American soups such as Pumpkin Soup.

In 1897 the world of soup was revolutionized when the American firm that later became the Campbell Soup Company introduced commercially canned condensed soups. Homemakers learned that they could have quality soups quickly and economically from these flavorful canned products. Dehydrated and frozen soups followed later, giving cooks new ways to shortcut soup preparation.

American soups today run the spectrum from simple to complicated; from light to hearty. Soup can be an appetizer, a meal in itself or a fortifying snack. The soups in this chapter are a cross section of the ones Americans eat today, influenced by many cuisines, but with a definite American flair.

❋ Chestnut Soup

Chestnut trees grew abundantly in the New World, providing native Americans and European settlers with chestnuts for soups, stuffings, sweets and even for grinding into flour for breads. During the first part of this century a blight wiped out American chestnut trees. Since then, many have been replaced by Oriental chestnuts. An autumn favorite, chestnuts are used in Thanksgiving turkey stuffing, and for a creamy Chestnut Soup to begin the Thanksgiving meal.

BEGIN: 2 HOURS AHEAD   12 SERVINGS

1   **pound chestnuts**
3½ **cups chicken broth**
2   **tablespoons butter or margarine**
1   **carrot, diced**
1   **stalk celery, sliced**
1   **small onion, finely chopped**
2   **cups heavy cream**
     Dash white pepper

1. With sharp knife, cut an X through shell of each chestnut. In 4-quart saucepan, place chestnuts; add water to cover. Over medium-high heat, heat to boiling. Reduce heat to low. Cover; simmer 20 minutes. Drain; cool. Peel and discard all skin from chestnuts.

2. Return chestnuts to pan; add broth. Over medium-high heat, heat to boiling. Reduce heat to low. Cover; simmer 30 minutes or until chestnuts are soft.

3. Meanwhile, in 10-inch skillet over medium heat, in hot butter, cook carrot, celery and onion until tender; set aside.

4. In covered blender container at low speed, blend ⅓ of the chestnuts and ⅓ of the broth with vegetables until very smooth. Return to saucepan. Repeat with remaining chestnuts and broth. Stir in cream and pepper. Heat just to boiling, stirring constantly. Yields 7 cups.

❋ Corn Chowder

During the food shortages of World War I, corn chowder became known as "Mock Clam Chowder." Corn chowder varies across the country. The Indians made it with dried corn. The Pennsylvania Dutch add tiny dumplings known as "rivels." In the South, the soup is enriched with egg yolks and cream. And Midwesterners prepare it this way, although the use of crackers for thickening is characteristic of New England.

BEGIN: 1 HOUR AHEAD   6 SERVINGS

6   **unsalted soda crackers, finely crushed**
2   **cups milk**
¼   **cup diced salt pork**
1   **medium onion, chopped**
2   **cups diced potatoes**
2   **cups corn kernels**
1   **cup water**
½   **teaspoon salt**
⅛   **teaspoon white pepper**
     Generous dash paprika

1. Soak crackers in 1 cup milk; set aside.

2. In 4-quart saucepan, over medium heat, fry salt pork until crisp. With slotted spoon, remove pork; set aside. Pour off all but 1 tablespoon drippings. In hot drippings, cook onion until tender.

3. Stir in remaining 1 cup milk, potatoes, corn, water, salt, pepper and paprika. Over high heat, heat to boiling. Reduce heat to low. Cover; simmer 20 minutes or until potatoes are fork-tender. Stir in reserved soaked crackers; heat through.

4. To serve: Ladle soup into bowls; garnish with salt pork. Yields 6 cups.

QUICK CORN CHOWDER: Prepare as above but omit crackers, water and salt; reduce milk to ¾ cup. Substitute *1 can (10 ¾ ounces) condensed cream of potato soup* for fresh potatoes and *1 can (16 ounces) cream-style golden corn* for fresh corn. Heat all ingredients just to boiling.

Corn and Tomato Soup

❄ Corn and Tomato Soup

Corn and tomato soup is at least 100 years old. As with so many classic American recipes, this one combines two New World crops to produce an original creation. The introduction of canning in the early 1800s made it possible to enjoy this summer soup even in the winter.

BEGIN: 1 HOUR AHEAD   6 SERVINGS

2   **tablespoons butter or margarine**
1   **medium onion, chopped**
2   **cans (10¾ ounces each) condensed chicken broth**
2   **cups corn kernels**
2   **cups chopped tomatoes**
1   **bay leaf**
    Generous dash pepper
1   **cup milk**

1. In 3-quart saucepan over medium-high heat, in hot butter, cook onion until tender, stirring often.

2. Stir in broth, corn, tomatoes, bay leaf and pepper. Over high heat, heat to boiling. Reduce heat to low. Cover; simmer 25 minutes. Discard bay leaf. Stir in milk; heat through. Yields 6 cups.

WINTER CORN AND TOMATO SOUP: Prepare as above but substitute *1 can (16 ounces) whole kernel corn* for fresh corn and *1 can (16 ounces) tomatoes, chopped,* for tomatoes.

❋ Pumpkin Soup

Long before the colonists arrived, the Indians used pumpkins and other squashes in meaty soups and stews. The colonists added dairy products and European cooking methods to make more sophisticated, creamy pumpkin soups.

BEGIN: 30 MINUTES AHEAD   6 SERVINGS

¼   cup butter or margarine
1   medium onion, chopped
1   can (16 ounces) pumpkin
1   can (10¾ ounces) condensed chicken
      broth
3   cups milk
½   teaspoon salt
⅛   teaspoon ground nutmeg
      Generous dash sugar
      Generous dash white pepper
      Croutons

1. In 3-quart saucepan over medium-high heat, in hot butter, cook onion until tender, stirring often.

2. Stir in pumpkin, broth, milk, salt, nutmeg, sugar and pepper. Heat just to boiling, stirring constantly.

3. To serve: Ladle soup into bowls; garnish with croutons. Yields 6½ cups.

❋ Beef Broth Printanier

This springtime vegetable soup is similar to the one brought to the United States by the French governess who looked after Thomas Jefferson's children.

BEGIN: 30 MINUTES AHEAD   8 SERVINGS

2   cans (10½ ounces each) condensed beef
      broth
2   soup cans water
½   cup carrot cut into julienne strips
½   cup green pepper cut into julienne strips
⅓   cup diagonally sliced green onions
½   cup sliced cherry tomatoes

1. In 2-quart saucepan over high heat, heat all ingredients except tomatoes to boiling.

2. Reduce heat to low. Cover; simmer 10 minutes or until vegetables are tender-crisp, stirring occasionally. Add tomatoes; heat through. Yields 6 cups.

❋ Virginia Peanut Soup

Virginia Peanut Soup is an American version of an African soup, made almost exclusively in the South. George Washington Carver once served businessmen an entire meal made from peanuts, beginning with his version of peanut soup.

BEGIN: 45 MINUTES AHEAD   6 SERVINGS

2   tablespoons butter or margarine
¼   cup finely chopped onion
¼   cup finely chopped celery
2   tablespoons all-purpose flour
1¾ cups chicken broth
1   cup creamy peanut butter
3   cups milk
      Chopped peanuts

1. In 3-quart saucepan over medium-high heat, in hot butter, cook onion and celery until tender. Add flour; stir together until smooth. Gradually stir in broth; cook until mixture boils, stirring constantly.

2. In covered blender container at low speed, blend ½ of the broth mixture at a time until smooth. Return to saucepan.

3. With wire whisk, blend in peanut butter. Stir in milk. Over medium heat, heat just to boiling.

4. To serve: Ladle soup into bowls; garnish with chopped peanuts. Yields 6 cups.

✳ Mushroom Soup

Before the arrival of Europeans, native Americans were enjoying many varieties of mushrooms. Wild mushrooms grow in American woods and along river banks, but only during a few weeks each year. Cultivated mushrooms, quite different from the wild ones, allow us to enjoy mushrooms year-round.

BEGIN: 30 MINUTES AHEAD   4 SERVINGS

2   tablespoons butter or margarine
2   tablespoons thinly sliced green onions
1   can (10¾ ounces) condensed cream of
      mushroom soup
¼   pound whole mushrooms
2   tablespoons dry sherry (optional)
      Generous dash pepper
¾   cup heavy cream
      Sliced mushrooms

1. In 3-quart saucepan over medium-high heat, in hot butter, cook onions until tender, stirring often. Stir in soup, whole mushrooms, sherry and pepper.

2. In covered blender container at medium speed, blend soup mixture until smooth. Return mixture to saucepan; gradually stir in cream. Over low heat, heat through, stirring constantly.

3. To serve: Ladle soup into bowls; garnish with sliced mushrooms. Yields 2½ cups.

✳ Onion Soup Gratinée

Before Europeans came to the New World, Indians were well acquainted with many types of wild onions. Jacques Marquette, the seventeenth-century French Jesuit explorer, was saved from starving by eating onions he found in the Great Lakes region. Onions may also be responsible for the name of the largest city on the Great Lakes; "Chicago" comes from the Indian word for strong or powerful. According to legend, the name was given to the city because of the abundance of onions in the area.

BEGIN: 1¼ HOURS AHEAD   6 SERVINGS

¼   cup butter or margarine
4   cups sliced onions
3   cans (10½ ounces each) condensed beef
      broth
2   soup cans water
⅛   teaspoon pepper
1   teaspoon Worcestershire
6   slices French bread, toasted
3   cups shredded Swiss cheese

1. In 4-quart saucepan over medium-high heat, in hot butter, cook onions until tender. Stir in broth, water, pepper and Worcestershire. Over high heat, heat to boiling. Reduce heat to low. Cover; simmer 30 minutes. Preheat oven to 425°F.

2. Ladle soup into six 12-ounce ovensafe bowls; place 1 slice toasted bread on surface of soup in each bowl. Sprinkle ½ cup cheese onto each toasted bread slice in soup.

3. Bake 10 minutes or just until cheese is melted. Yields 8 cups.

FRENCH ONION SOUP FOR TWO: In 1-quart saucepan over medium-high heat, heat *1 can (10½ ounces) condensed French onion soup* and *1 soup can water* to boiling, stirring occasionally. Toast *2 slices French bread.* Ladle soup into two 12-ounce ovensafe bowls; top with toasted bread and *1 cup shredded Swiss cheese.* Bake at 425°F. 10 minutes or just until cheese is melted.

❋ Old-Fashioned Pea Soup

American Indians knew how to grow and dry beans, but Europeans brought peas and lentils to this country. Colonial pea soup had meat and vegetables added to it daily, changing its character from day to day. The "Pease Porridge" really might have been served hot, cold or "in the pot, nine days old."

BEGIN: DAY AHEAD   6 SERVINGS

1	package (16 ounces) dry green or yellow peas
1	ham bone with meat
2	medium onions, chopped
1	teaspoon salt
½	teaspoon pepper

1. Soak peas in 8 cups water overnight; drain.

2. *About 2 hours before serving:* In 5-quart Dutch oven over high heat, heat 6 cups water, peas and remaining ingredients to boiling. Reduce heat to low. Cover; simmer 1½ hours or until peas are tender.

3. Remove bone; cool until easy to handle. Cut meat from bone; discard bone. Cut meat into bite-sized pieces; return to soup. Heat. Yields 8 cups.

SPLIT PEA SOUP: Prepare as above but substitute *1 package (16 ounces) dry green or yellow split peas* for whole peas and add *1 cup chopped celery, 1 cup sliced carrots, 2 tablespoons chopped parsley, ¼ teaspoon ground nutmeg* and *1 bay leaf.* Discard bay leaf before serving.

LENTIL SOUP: Prepare as above but substitute *1 package (16 ounces) dry lentils* for peas, and do not soak lentils in water. Add *1 cup diced celery; 1 cup diced carrots; 1 large clove garlic, minced; ¼ cup tomato paste; 2 tablespoons wine vinegar; 1 bay leaf* and increase water to 7 cups. Discard bay leaf before serving.

Old-Fashioned Pea Soup

TIP: Soak peas the quick way: Add peas to boiling water, allowing 4 cups water for each cup dry peas. Over high heat, heat to boiling; boil 2 minutes. Remove from heat. Cover; let stand 1 hour. Drain and prepare as above.

✳ U.S. Senate Bean Soup

Many politicians have been involved in the folklore surrounding U.S. Senate Bean Soup. Although Senator Henry Cabot Lodge, Sr., is credited with originating the soup, Senators Dubois of Idaho and Nelson of Minnesota are said to be responsible for passing a resolution requiring that the soup be served every day in the Senate dining room.

BEGIN: DAY AHEAD   8 SERVINGS

1   **cup dry pea (navy) beans**
1   **ham bone with meat**
2   **medium onions, finely chopped**
2   **cups chopped celery**
2   **medium potatoes, mashed (1¼ cups)**
1   **clove garlic, minced**
1   **tablespoon chopped parsley**
     Salt
     Generous dash pepper

1. Soak beans in 4 cups water overnight; drain.

2. *About 3 hours before serving:* In 4-quart saucepan over high heat, heat beans, bone and 6 cups water to boiling. Reduce heat to low. Cover; simmer 1½ hours or until beans are tender.

3. Add remaining ingredients. Simmer, uncovered, over low heat 30 minutes or until flavors are blended.

4. Remove bone; cool until easy to handle. Cut meat from bone; discard bone. Cut meat into bite-sized pieces; return to soup. Simmer, uncovered, until desired consistency. Yields 8 cups.

TIP: Soak beans the quick way: Add beans to boiling water, allowing 4 cups water for each cup dry beans. Over high heat, heat to boiling; boil 2 minutes. Remove from heat. Cover; let stand 1 hour. Drain and prepare as above.

✳ Black Bean Soup

Black beans were introduced to the Americas by Spanish explorers. In areas of Spanish influence such as Florida and Louisiana, black beans are served with rice to make a hearty meal. Add some crushed red pepper or extra cayenne to this elegant appetizer soup to give it the flavor of the Southwest.

BEGIN: DAY AHEAD   8 SERVINGS

1   **cup dry black beans**
½   **cup diced salt pork**
2   **medium onions, chopped**
1   **carrot, diced**
1¾   **cups chicken broth**
½   **teaspoon marjoram leaves, crushed**
½   **teaspoon thyme leaves, crushed**
¼   **teaspoon salt**
1   **bay leaf**
     Dash cayenne pepper
¼   **cup dry sherry**
2   **hard-cooked eggs, chopped**
1   **lemon, sliced**

1. Soak beans in 4 cups water overnight; drain.

2. *About 2 hours before serving:* In 4-quart saucepan over high heat, heat beans, 4 cups water, salt pork, onions, carrot, broth, marjoram, thyme, salt, bay leaf and cayenne to boiling. Reduce heat to low. Cover; simmer 1½ hours or until beans are tender. Discard bay leaf.

3. In covered blender container at low speed, blend ½ of the soup mixture at a time until smooth. Return to saucepan; heat. Stir in sherry.

4. To serve: Ladle soup into bowls; garnish with eggs and lemon slices and serve with additional sherry. Yields 7 cups.

❇ Baked Bean Soup

The Pilgrims learned from the Indians how to cook beans slowly with a bit of salt meat for flavoring. The settlers would start the beans on Friday night or Saturday morning for Saturday's supper, then serve the remaining beans for breakfast or lunch on Sunday to avoid breaking the Sabbath. What was left of the beans was diluted and served as Baked Bean Soup.

BEGIN: 45 MINUTES AHEAD   4 SERVINGS

1¾ cups Boston Baked Beans (see page 141)
      or 1 can (16 ounces) home style beans
2   cups water
1   tablespoon butter or margarine
2   tablespoons finely chopped onion
1   tablespoon all-purpose flour
      Generous dash pepper

1. In covered blender container at high speed, blend beans and water until smooth; set aside.

2. In 2-quart saucepan over medium-high heat, in hot butter, cook onion until tender. Add flour; stir together until smooth.

3. Gradually stir in bean mixture and pepper. Heat to boiling. Reduce heat to low. Cover; simmer 15 minutes or until flavors are blended. Yields 3½ cups.

❇ Irish Potato Soup

The white potato from South America came to North America by way of Europe, where it had a hard time gaining acceptance. It was thought to be poisonous, to cause leprosy and to be fit only for animals. Although such notable farmers as Thomas Jefferson planted potatoes in America, the vegetable was slow to be accepted by the general population until the Irish immigrations of the eighteenth and nineteenth centuries.

BEGIN: 1 HOUR AHEAD   4 SERVINGS

2   tablespoons butter or margarine
1   large onion, finely chopped
⅛   teaspoon thyme leaves, crushed
4   medium potatoes, cubed
1   cup water
1   teaspoon salt
3   cups milk
      Chopped parsley

1. In 3-quart saucepan over medium-high heat, in hot butter, cook onion with thyme until onion is tender.

2. Stir in potatoes, water and salt; heat to boiling. Reduce heat to low. Cover; simmer 20 minutes or until potatoes are fork-tender.

3. With electric mixer at low speed, beat mixture until smooth. Gradually add milk, stirring constantly. Over low heat, heat just to boiling, about 10 minutes, stirring occasionally.

4. To serve: Ladle soup into bowls; garnish with chopped parsley. Yields 5 cups.

❇ Chicken Soup with Matzo Balls

Chicken soup is part of many cuisines; the starchy garnish of the soup often signals its origin. Rice is typical of Greek and Indian soups; dumplings and noodles are common to many European cuisines; won tons are the Oriental version of dumplings. The matzo balls in this soup are prepared in Jewish communities all over the world. Matzo balls are unleavened, as required by Passover dietary laws.

BEGIN: EARLY IN DAY   8 SERVINGS

1   5-pound stewing chicken, cut up
8   cups water
2   onions, cut up
2   carrots, cut up
2   stalks celery, cut up
¼   cup chopped parsley
2   teaspoons salt
1   teaspoon dill weed, crushed
⅛   teaspoon pepper
      Matzo Balls*

1. In 6-quart Dutch oven over medium-high heat, heat all ingredients except Matzo Balls to boiling. Reduce heat to low. Cover; simmer 3 hours or until chicken is fork-tender.

2. Remove chicken; cool until easy to handle. Cut chicken from bones; discard skin and bones. Cut chicken into bite-sized pieces; set aside. Strain broth through sieve and return to pot; discard vegetables. Skim off fat.

3. Stir in reserved chicken. Add Matzo Balls to soup. Over medium-high heat, heat just to boiling. Season to taste. Yields 10 cups broth.

CHICKEN-NOODLE SOUP: Prepare as above through step 2 but omit Matzo Balls. Over medium-high heat, heat to boiling. Stir in *½ package (8-ounce size) wide egg noodles.* Reduce heat to low. Simmer, uncovered, 8 minutes. Stir in reserved chicken. Heat just to boiling. Season to taste.

CHICKEN-RICE SOUP: Prepare as above through step 2 but omit Matzo Balls. Stir in *½ cup raw regular rice.* Over medium-high heat, heat to boiling. Reduce heat to low. Cover; simmer 25 minutes or until rice is tender. Stir in reserved chicken. Heat just to boiling. Season to taste.

*Matzo Balls

1   **cup matzo meal**
½   **cup water**
⅓   **cup rendered chicken fat, cooled, or melted butter or margarine**
4   **eggs, beaten**
1½ **teaspoons salt**
    Dash white pepper

1. In medium bowl, combine all ingredients; mix well. Cover; chill at least 1 hour.

2. *45 minutes before serving:* In 5-quart Dutch oven over high heat, heat 3 quarts water to boiling. Reduce heat to medium.

3. With wet hands, shape chilled matzo mixture into 1-inch balls. Drop into boiling water. Cover; simmer 25 to 30 minutes until done. With slotted spoon, remove balls. Serve with hot chicken soup. Yields 24 balls.

❋ Brunswick Stew

Everyone agrees that Brunswick Stew is the most Southern of dishes, whether it originated in Brunswick, Georgia, Brunswick County, North Carolina, or Brunswick County, Virginia. Some purists insist that it is not authentic without rabbit or squirrel meat, but most of today's cooks use chicken. The vegetables are certain to include tomatoes, lima beans and corn.

BEGIN: 3 HOURS AHEAD   12 SERVINGS

½   **cup diced salt pork**
2   **pounds chicken parts**
8   **cups water**
3   **medium potatoes, diced**
3   **medium onions, chopped**
1   **can (28 ounces) tomatoes, chopped**
2   **cups corn kernels or 1 can (16 ounces) whole kernel golden corn**
1   **package (10 ounces) frozen lima beans**
1   **tablespoon Worcestershire**
½   **teaspoon salt**
¼   **teaspoon pepper**

1. In 6-quart Dutch oven over high heat, heat salt pork, chicken and water to boiling. Reduce heat to low. Cover; simmer 45 minutes or until chicken is fork-tender.

2. Remove chicken; cool until easy to handle. Cut chicken from bones; discard bones and skin. Cut chicken into bite-sized pieces; return to soup.

3. Stir in remaining ingredients. Reduce heat to low. Simmer, uncovered, 1 hour or until flavors are blended. Yields 16 cups.

OKRA SOUP: Prepare as above but add *1 pound okra, sliced,* to the vegetables.

❋ Beef-Barley Soup

The United States is second only to the Soviet Union in barley production, but most American barley is used for animal feed or for brewing beer and whiskey. Today's Americans are probably most familiar with barley in soups, where its nutty flavor and chewy texture add substance and character to the broth. The word "pearled" applies to barley that has had its outer hull removed.

BEGIN: 4 HOURS AHEAD   6 SERVINGS

2	beef shank cross cuts, each cut about 1 inch thick
1	stalk celery, cut up
1	parsnip, cut up
1	carrot, cut up
8	cups water
1	medium onion, finely chopped
2	cups chopped mushrooms
¼	cup pearled barley
2	tablespoons butter or margarine
2	tablespoons all-purpose flour
2	teaspoons salt
¼	teaspoon pepper
1	tablespoon chopped parsley or chopped fresh dill weed

1. In 6-quart Dutch oven over medium-high heat, heat beef, celery, parsnip, carrot and water to boiling. Reduce heat to low. Cover; simmer 2 hours or until meat is fork-tender.

2. Remove meat; cool until easy to handle. Cut meat from bones; discard bones. Cut meat into bite-sized pieces; set aside. Strain broth and return to pot; discard vegetables. Skim off fat.

3. Stir in onion, mushrooms and barley. Over medium-high heat, heat to boiling. Reduce heat to low. Cover; simmer 1 hour or until barley is tender.

4. In small saucepan over medium heat, melt butter. Stir in flour, salt and pepper; cook until lightly browned, stirring occasionally. Stir in about 1 cup of the beef broth mixture. Cook until mixture boils.

5. Return flour mixture to soup. Heat to boiling. Add reserved meat; heat through. Season to taste. Garnish with parsley or dill. Yields 7 cups.

❋ Turkey-Vegetable Soup

Today's improved transportation and preservation techniques make it possible to have virtually any combination of vegetables available any time of year in almost every part of the country. Enjoy this turkey soup with its spring peas and summer tomatoes during any season.

BEGIN: 1¼ HOURS AHEAD   6 SERVINGS

1	tablespoon butter or margarine
1	medium onion, chopped
1	medium carrot, sliced
½	cup sliced celery
¼	teaspoon thyme leaves, crushed
5	cups chicken or turkey broth
1	can (8 ounces) tomatoes, cut up
½	cup fresh or frozen peas
½	cup diced yellow squash
1	cup diced cooked turkey
¼	cup raw regular rice

1. In 5-quart Dutch oven over medium-high heat, in hot butter, cook onion, carrot, celery and thyme until just tender, stirring occasionally.

2. Stir in broth, tomatoes, peas, squash and turkey. Over high heat, heat to boiling. Reduce heat to low. Cover; simmer 20 minutes.

3. Add rice. Cover; simmer 20 minutes more or until rice is tender. Yields 6 cups.

Turkey-Vegetable Soup, Vegetable-Beef Soup

❋ Vegetable-Beef Soup

The variety of vegetables in today's vegetable soup would have astonished the early settlers in this country, who were limited to whatever was in season or in storage at that time. In spring and summer fresh leeks, asparagus and lettuce might fill the soup pot, while root vegetables such as carrots, turnips and onions would dominate a winter one.

BEGIN: 4 HOURS AHEAD   8 SERVINGS

2   tablespoons salad oil
2   pounds beef shank cross cuts, each cut
        about 1 inch thick
1   large onion, cut up
½   cup cut-up celery tops
1   sprig parsley
1   bay leaf
1   tablespoon salt
¼   teaspoon pepper
8   cups water
1   can (16 ounces) tomatoes, cut up
2   stalks celery, sliced
2   medium carrots, diced
2   medium potatoes, diced
1   cup corn kernels or 1 can (8 ounces)
        whole kernel corn
1   cup green beans cut into ½-inch pieces
        or baby lima beans
½   teaspoon thyme leaves, crushed

1. In 6-quart Dutch oven over medium-high heat, in hot oil, cook beef until well browned, turning occasionally. Add onion, celery tops, parsley, bay leaf, salt, pepper and water. Heat to boiling. Reduce heat to low. Cover; simmer 2 hours or until meat is fork-tender.

2. Remove meat; cool until easy to handle. Cut meat from bones; discard bones. Cut meat into bite-sized pieces; set aside. Strain broth through sieve and return to pot; discard vegetables. Skim off fat.

3. Add cut-up meat and remaining ingredients to broth. Heat to boiling. Reduce heat to low. Cover; simmer 30 to 40 minutes until vegetables are tender. Yields 11 cups.

❄ Hearty Vegetable Soup

Many farm kitchens had a "perpetual soup" on the back of the stove, changing daily as this or that was added to the soup. Today's cooks have a different kind of perpetual soup pot in canned soups and broths, to which they can add bits of leftover meat and vegetables to create hearty, whole-meal soups.

BEGIN: 1½ HOURS AHEAD   8 SERVINGS

2   tablespoons salad oil
1   onion, chopped
2   stalks celery, sliced
1   clove garlic, minced
2   cups shredded cabbage
2   medium carrots, sliced
2   tablespoons chopped parsley
1   teaspoon basil leaves, crushed
4   cups water
2   cans (10½ ounces each) condensed beef
      broth
2   cups tomato juice
1   can (20 ounces) cannellini (white kidney
      beans)
2   small zucchini, sliced
½   cup uncooked small shell or elbow
      macaroni
    Grated Parmesan cheese

1. In 6-quart Dutch oven over medium-high heat, in hot oil, cook onion, celery and garlic until vegetables are tender. Stir in cabbage, carrots, parsley, basil, water, broth and tomato juice. Heat to boiling. Reduce heat to low. Cover; simmer 15 minutes.

2. Stir in beans, zucchini and macaroni. Over high heat, heat to boiling. Reduce heat to low; simmer, uncovered, 15 minutes until macaroni and vegetables are tender, stirring occasionally. Pass Parmesan cheese to spoon over each serving. Yields 12 cups.

❄ Philadelphia Pepperpot

This meal-in-itself soup has its origins in Philadelphia. The story goes that the Continental Army was quartered at Valley Forge, when General Washington ordered a sustaining meal for his troops to ward off hunger and boost morale. One local farmer donated tripe and another gave some peppercorns. To these meager beginnings, the cook added scraps of meat and vegetables and created the first pepperpot. It became so popular that it was sold by Philadelphia street vendors in the 1800s.

BEGIN: 4 HOURS AHEAD   4 SERVINGS

½   pound honeycomb tripe
1   pound veal shank
1   teaspoon black peppercorns
6½ cups water
2   tablespoons butter or margarine
2   medium onions, sliced
½   cup chopped celery
¼   cup chopped green pepper
1   cup diced potatoes
1½ teaspoons marjoram leaves, crushed
1½ teaspoons thyme leaves, crushed
1   teaspoon salt
⅛   teaspoon crushed red pepper
2   tablespoons all-purpose flour

1. Wash and scrub tripe thoroughly. In 4-quart saucepan over high heat, heat tripe, veal shank, peppercorns and 6 cups water to boiling. Reduce heat to low. Cover; simmer 2 hours or until meat is fork-tender. Strain broth; set aside. Discard peppercorns.

2. Cool bone and tripe until easy to handle. Cut meat from bone; cut meat and tripe into ¼-inch pieces; set aside.

3. In same saucepan over medium-high heat, in hot butter, cook onions, celery and green pepper until tender. Add reserved broth, meat, tripe, potatoes and seasonings. Over high heat, heat to boiling. Reduce heat to low. Cover; simmer 20 minutes or until potatoes are fork-tender.

4. In cup, blend flour with remaining ½ cup water until smooth. Gradually stir flour mixture into simmering soup. Cook until mixture boils, stirring constantly. Yields 5 cups.

❋ Albóndigas

Albóndigas is the Spanish word for meatball, and for a Mexican soup. The meatballs are traditionally cooked by dropping them into boiling broth; the rice in the meatballs cooks while the meatballs simmer.

BEGIN: 1 HOUR AHEAD   6 SERVINGS

½   **pound ground beef**
½   **pound ground pork**
¼   **cup raw regular rice**
1   **egg, beaten**
½   **teaspoon salt**
⅛   **teaspoon pepper**
3½ **cups beef broth**
1   **can (8 ounces) tomato sauce**
1   **small onion, chopped**
1   **clove garlic, minced**

1. In medium bowl, combine first 6 ingredients; mix well. Shape mixture into about fifty ½-inch meatballs.

2. In 3-quart saucepan over high heat, heat remaining 4 ingredients to boiling.

3. Add meatballs to broth mixture; heat to boiling. Reduce heat to low. Cover; simmer 30 minutes. Yields 6 cups.

❋ Chili Soup

Chili is a staple of Tex-Mex cuisine, with a following that has elevated the dish to a national pastime. Chili cooks debate whether chili should be hot or mild, thin or thick, made with beans or without, made with ground beef, stew beef, or even without meat at all. Chili can be as thick as a stew or souplike, as this one is.

BEGIN: 45 MINUTES AHEAD   6 SERVINGS

½   **pound ground beef**
1   **medium onion, chopped**
1   **clove garlic, minced**
1   **can (16 ounces) pinto or kidney beans**
1   **can (16 ounces) tomatoes, chopped**
2   **cups water**
2   **teaspoons chili powder**
½   **teaspoon salt**
¼   **teaspoon ground cumin**
⅛   **teaspoon pepper**
1   **bay leaf**

1. In 4-quart saucepan over medium-high heat, cook ground beef, onion and garlic until meat is browned and onion is tender, stirring to break up meat. Pour off fat.

2. Stir in remaining ingredients; heat to boiling. Reduce heat to low. Cover; simmer 15 minutes or until flavors are blended. Discard bay leaf. Yields 7 cups.

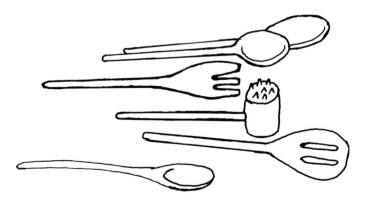

❄ Knockwurst Chowder

The German flavor in this robust soup comes from knock-wurst, caraway seed and cabbage. Knockwurst is a smoked sausage made from pork and beef that is similar to the frankfurter, but plumper and more garlicky.

BEGIN: 45 MINUTES AHEAD   6 SERVINGS

2   tablespoons butter or margarine
1   pound knockwurst or frankfurters, cut
        into bite-sized pieces
2   cups diagonally sliced carrots
¼   teaspoon caraway seed
2   cans (10¾ ounces each) condensed
        cream of celery soup
1   soup can milk
1   soup can water
2   cups shredded cabbage

1. In 3-quart saucepan over medium heat, in hot butter, cook knockwurst and carrots with cara-way until meat is browned. Stir in remaining in-gredients. Over high heat, heat to boiling.

2. Reduce heat to low. Cover; simmer 10 min-utes or until cabbage is tender-crisp, stirring oc-casionally. Yields 7½ cups.

❄ Picadillo Soup

Picadillo, the Mexican version of meat hash, begins with ground or chopped cooked meat, and is flavored with onions, chili, tomatoes and garlic. Raisins, olives and almonds are often included.

BEGIN: 30 MINUTES AHEAD   6 SERVINGS

2   tablespoons salad oil
½   pound ground beef
1   medium onion, chopped
1   clove garlic, minced
2   cans (11¼ ounces each) condensed chili
        beef soup
2   soup cans water
1   cup cooked rice
1   can (8 ounces) tomatoes, chopped
2   teaspoons chili powder
¼   teaspoon sugar
¼   cup sliced pitted ripe olives

Knockwurst Chowder, Picadillo Soup

1. In 3-quart saucepan over medium-high heat, in hot oil, cook beef, onion and garlic until meat is browned and onion is tender, stirring to break up meat; pour off fat. Stir in remaining ingredi-ents except olives. Over high heat, heat to boil-ing.

2. Reduce heat to low. Cover; simmer 10 min-utes to blend flavors, stirring occasionally. Add olives. Yields 6½ cups.

❊ New England Clam Chowder

New Englanders contend that chowder should never contain tomatoes; in 1939 Maine's legislature passed a bill prohibiting the use of tomatoes in that state's chowder. The debate had political overtones, when one politician contended that the addition of the red tomato was an attempt on the part of "the reds" to undermine their most hallowed tradition.

BEGIN: 1 HOUR AHEAD   6 SERVINGS

1   quart shucked hard-shell clams with
      liquor reserved
¼   pound salt pork, diced
2   medium onions, chopped
6   medium potatoes, diced
⅛   teaspoon white pepper
2   cups milk
2   tablespoons butter or margarine

1. Strain and measure clam liquor, adding water to make 2 cups; set aside. Chop clams; set aside.

2. In 4-quart saucepan over medium heat, fry salt pork until crisp. With slotted spoon remove pork; set aside. Over medium-high heat, in hot drippings, cook onions until tender.

3. Stir in potatoes, pepper and reserved clam liquor; heat to boiling. Reduce heat to low. Cover; simmer 20 minutes or until potatoes are fork-tender.

4. Meanwhile, in small saucepan over medium heat, heat milk until tiny bubbles form around edge *(do not boil)*. Add with butter and clams to potato mixture. Over low heat, simmer 5 minutes.

5. To serve: Ladle soup into bowls; garnish with salt pork. Yields 7½ cups.

❊ Manhattan Clam Chowder

What Manhattan and New England clam chowders have in common are clams, onions, potatoes and either salt pork or bacon. But Manhattan chowder is a vigorous red soup made with tomatoes and herbs. Despite its name, Manhattan Clam Chowder is as popular in Connecticut and Rhode Island as it is in New York City.

BEGIN: 1½ HOURS AHEAD   6 SERVINGS

1   pint shucked hard-shell clams with liquor
      reserved
6   slices bacon, diced
1   cup chopped onions
½   cup finely chopped carrots
½   cup finely chopped celery
1   teaspoon thyme leaves, crushed
1   teaspoon marjoram leaves, crushed
¼   teaspoon pepper
1½ cups diced potatoes
1   can (16 ounces) tomatoes, chopped
1   bay leaf
1   tablespoon chopped parsley

1. Strain and measure clam liquor, adding water to make 2½ cups; set aside. Chop clams; set aside.

2. In 4-quart saucepan over medium heat, fry bacon until almost crisp. Pour off all but 2 tablespoons drippings. In hot drippings, cook onions, carrots, celery, thyme, marjoram and pepper until tender.

3. Stir in clam liquor, potatoes, tomatoes, bay leaf and parsley. Heat to boiling. Reduce heat to low. Cover; simmer 20 minutes or until potatoes are fork-tender.

4. Stir in clams. Over low heat, simmer 5 minutes. Discard bay leaf. Yields 7½ cups.

❋ Fish Chowder

Good, plain food was the rule for New England Puritans, who believed that simplicity in living was a form of worship. Their thrifty cooks found soup a good way to make the most of the bounty of the sea. Fish chowders usually contained salt pork, onions, milk and whatever fish was plentiful and inexpensive.

BEGIN: 1½ HOURS AHEAD   6 SERVINGS

½   cup diced salt pork
2   medium onions, thinly sliced
4   medium potatoes, diced
½   teaspoon salt
⅛   teaspoon white pepper
1   large bay leaf
2   cups water
1½ pounds cod, cut into chunks
2   cups milk
2   tablespoons butter or margarine

1. In 4-quart saucepan over medium heat, fry salt pork until crisp. Pour off all but 2 tablespoons drippings. With slotted spoon, remove pork; set aside.

2. Over medium-high heat, in hot drippings, cook onions until tender. Stir in potatoes, salt, pepper, bay leaf and water. Heat to boiling. Reduce heat to low. Cover; simmer 20 minutes until potatoes are fork-tender.

3. Add fish; heat to boiling. Reduce heat to low. Cover; simmer 5 to 10 minutes until fish flakes easily when tested with fork. Discard bay leaf. Add milk and butter; heat.

4. To serve: Ladle soup into bowls; garnish with salt pork. Yields 8 cups.

❋ Cioppino

As Italian as Cioppino sounds, it is a San Francisco original, a combination of West Coast seafood with Italian seasonings. There is much speculation about the origins of the name. Is it a corruption of "chip in," what fishermen did with their catches, or is it from a Genoese dialect?

BEGIN: 2½ HOURS AHEAD   8 SERVINGS

¼   cup olive oil
2   medium onions, chopped
1   green pepper, chopped
1   cup sliced mushrooms
2   cloves garlic, minced
½   cup chopped parsley
1   can (16 ounces) tomatoes, chopped
1   can (6 ounces) tomato paste
2½ cups water
1   quart mussels, well scrubbed
1   cup dry red wine
1½ pounds striped bass, cut into chunks
1   pound medium shrimp, shelled and
        deveined
½   pound cooked crabmeat, picked over

1. In 5-quart Dutch oven over medium-high heat, in hot oil, cook onions, green pepper, mushrooms and garlic until tender.

2. Stir in parsley, tomatoes, tomato paste and water. Reduce heat to low. Cover; simmer 15 minutes.

3. Meanwhile, in 3-quart saucepan over medium-high heat, steam mussels in wine about 5 minutes or until shells open. Remove mussels in shells to bowl. Discard any unopened mussels. Strain cooking liquid.

4. Add cooking liquid, bass, shrimp and crabmeat to vegetables in Dutch oven. Cover; simmer 15 minutes. Arrange mussels in soup mixture; heat. Yields 11 cups.

TIP: Substitute well-scrubbed hard-shell clams in shells for all or part of mussels.

✳ Crab Soup

Soups made from crab vary from region to region. Near the Gulf of Mexico, the soup has a Creole influence with onions, garlic, tomatoes and cayenne. Around the Chesapeake Bay, it is a spicy vegetable soup rich with chunks of blue crab. The West Coast version includes chili powder, green pepper and pieces of Dungeness or King crab. Perhaps the best known of all is She-Crab Soup from Charleston, South Carolina, where only female crabs are used because of their delectable roe. If female crabs are unavailable, Southern cooks add crumbled hard-cooked egg yolks as a substitute for the roe.

BEGIN: 30 MINUTES AHEAD   6 SERVINGS

2 tablespoons butter or margarine
3 tablespoons all-purpose flour
4 cups milk
½ pound cooked crabmeat, picked over
¼ cup dry sherry
1 teaspoon Worcestershire
½ teaspoon salt
¼ teaspoon ground mace
¼ teaspoon grated lemon peel
   Dash cayenne pepper

1. In 3-quart saucepan over medium heat, melt butter. Add flour; stir together until smooth. Gradually stir in milk; cook until mixture boils, stirring constantly.

2. Stir in remaining ingredients. Heat just to boiling. Yields 5 cups.

Cioppino

✳ Oyster Stew

Not really a stew, this is a thin, creamy soup full of oysters, which can be made quickly in a saucepan or a chafing dish. It is often the specialty of the man of the house, prepared with much ceremony on Christmas Eve in households with English ancestry. The mania for oysters and oyster stew in the mid-1800s prompted two East Coast men to invent the perfect crackers to serve with the shellfish—oyster crackers.

BEGIN: 30 MINUTES AHEAD   4 SERVINGS

1   **pint shucked oysters with liquor reserved**
2   **tablespoons butter or margarine**
     Generous dash white pepper
1   **cup half-and-half**
1   **cup milk**
     Oyster crackers

1. Into 2-quart saucepan, strain 1 cup oyster liquor. Add oysters, butter and pepper. Over low heat, cook oysters until the edges curl.

2. In small saucepan over medium heat, heat half-and-half and milk until tiny bubbles form around the edge *(do not boil).* Add to oyster mixture.

3. To serve: Ladle soup into bowls; garnish with oyster crackers. Yields 4 cups.

✳ Gumbo

Gumbo, a specialty of Louisiana's Creole cooks, is a mixture of French, Spanish, African and American Indian influences. It starts with a French roux made by browning fat and flour. The Spanish influence emerges in the spices and seasonings in the dish. Africans contributed okra. From the Chocktaw and Houma Indians came filé powder, made from the leaves of the sassafras plant. Other ingredients in gumbo can include chicken, ham, shrimp, oysters, crab and sausage.

BEGIN: 1½ HOURS AHEAD   6 SERVINGS

¼   **cup salad oil**
¼   **cup all-purpose flour**
1   **medium onion, chopped**
1   **medium green pepper, chopped**
1   **clove garlic, minced**
1   **tablespoon chopped parsley**
½   **teaspoon thyme leaves, crushed**
1   **pound cooked ham, diced**
1   **pound medium shrimp, shelled and deveined**
1   **can (8 ounces) tomatoes, chopped**
4   **cups water**
1   **teaspoon salt**
⅛   **teaspoon pepper**
1   **bay leaf**
1   **tablespoon filé powder**
     Hot cooked rice

1. In 5-quart Dutch oven over medium heat, in hot oil, slowly cook flour until dark brown but not burned, about 8 minutes, stirring constantly.

2. Stir in onion, green pepper, garlic, parsley and thyme; cook until onion is tender, stirring occasionally.

3. Add ham, shrimp, tomatoes, water, salt, pepper and bay leaf; heat to boiling. Reduce heat to low. Cover; simmer about 30 minutes or until flavors are blended. Remove from heat; discard bay leaf. Stir in filé powder.

4. To serve: Scoop rice into bowls; ladle soup over rice. Yields 8 cups.

OKRA GUMBO: Prepare as above but add *½ pound okra, sliced,* along with ham and omit filé powder.

❊ Snapper Soup

Snapper Soup, or Snapping Turtle Soup, is claimed by Philadelphians, Creole cooks, and by those from the Chesapeake region. In 1893 a private jury was appointed to decide which version was best. The Philadelphia contingent insisted that cream was essential; Marylanders argued that it should consist of a clear broth seasoned with sherry. Maryland won, and this soup follows their recommendations.

BEGIN: 45 MINUTES AHEAD   6 SERVINGS

⅓ **cup all-purpose flour**
½ **teaspoon salt**
⅛ **teaspoon pepper**
1 **cup cooked turtle meat, cut into bite-sized pieces**
¼ **cup salad oil**
1 **medium onion, chopped**
1 **clove garlic, minced**
½ **teaspoon thyme leaves, crushed**
1 **bay leaf**
2 **cans (10½ ounces each) condensed beef broth**
2 **soup cans water**
1 **tablespoon lemon juice**
½ **cup dry sherry**
1 **hard-cooked egg white, diced**

1. In small bowl, combine first 3 ingredients. Coat turtle meat with seasoned flour. Reserve remaining flour.

2. In 4-quart saucepan over medium-high heat, in hot oil, cook turtle meat, onion, garlic, thyme and bay leaf until onion is tender.

3. Stir in broth, water and lemon juice. Over high heat, heat to boiling. Reduce heat to low. Cover; simmer 15 minutes. Discard bay leaf.

4. In cup, blend reserved flour mixture with sherry until smooth. Gradually stir flour mixture into simmering soup. Cook until mixture boils, stirring constantly. Stir in egg white. Yields 6 cups.

❊ Vichyssoise

Don't be fooled by the name—Vichyssoise is an American creation. This coolly sophisticated soup was first served at the Ritz-Carlton in New York City in 1910. Chef Louis Diat named it for the French town of Vichy because it resembles a French potato and leek soup; Diat's inspiration was to serve it cold.

BEGIN: EARLY IN DAY   8 SERVINGS

¼ **cup butter or margarine**
4 **leeks, chopped (white part only)**
1 **medium onion, sliced**
5 **medium potatoes, peeled and sliced**
2 **cans (10¾ ounces each) condensed chicken broth**
1½ **soup cans water**
2 **cups heavy cream**
   Chopped chives

1. In 4-quart saucepan over medium-high heat, in hot butter, cook leeks and onion until tender.

2. Stir in potatoes, broth and water. Over high heat, heat to boiling. Reduce heat to low. Cover; simmer 30 minutes or until potatoes are very tender.

3. In covered blender container at low speed, blend ⅓ of the soup mixture at a time until smooth.

4. Pour into large bowl; stir in cream. Cover; chill until serving time, at least 6 hours.

5. To serve: Ladle soup into chilled bowls; garnish with chopped chives. Yields 7½ cups.

QUICK VICHYSSOISE: Prepare as above, but omit potatoes, condensed broth, water and heavy cream. In step 2, stir in *3 cans (10¾ ounces each) condensed potato soup* and *1 can (14½ ounces) ready-to-serve chicken broth.* Heat to boiling. Blend mixture as directed in step 3. Gradually add *1 cup milk*; blend until smooth. Pour into large bowl; stir in *1 cup light cream.* Chill and garnish as above.

TIP: Clean the sand out of leeks by halving them lengthwise, then rinsing under cold water.

✳ Borscht

Borscht was brought to this country from Poland, Russia and the Ukraine. The word borscht comes from the Slavic barszcz, *which means beet, but not all recipes for borscht include beets. Some recipes call for cabbage, some for* kvas, *a slightly fermented liquid made from beets or rye bread.*

BEGIN: EARLY IN DAY   4 SERVINGS

1 **pound beets with tops**
1 **medium onion, sliced**
5 **cups water**
2 **tablespoons sugar**
1 **teaspoon sour salt**
2 **eggs**
   Sour cream

1. Trim beets, leaving 2 inches of tops and roots attached. Rinse beets under cold running water, being careful not to damage skins.

2. In 3-quart saucepan over high heat, heat beets, onion and water to boiling. Reduce heat to low. Cover; simmer 30 to 60 minutes or until fork-tender (depending on maturity and size of beets). Cool.

3. With slotted spoon, remove beets from liquid; reserve liquid. Peel beets and cut into julienne strips. Return to liquid mixture in saucepan. Stir in sugar and sour salt. Over high heat, heat to boiling. Reduce heat to low. Cover; simmer 10 minutes. Cool soup to lukewarm.

4. In small bowl with fork, beat eggs. Stir into soup. Cover; chill until serving time, at least 6 hours.

5. To serve: Ladle soup into bowls; garnish with sour cream. Yields 4 cups.

TIP: Substitute ¼ cup lemon juice and 1 teaspoon salt for 1 teaspoon sour salt.

✳ Gazpacho

America's first regional cookbook, The Virginia Housewife, *was printed in 1824. In it, author Mary Randolph included a recipe for Gazpacho, which she identified as a Spanish salad. In her recipe, bread, tomatoes, cucumbers and onion were layered in a bowl, then covered with tomato juice flavored with mustard oil. Today, gazpacho is a term used for an uncooked vegetable soup, featuring tomatoes, cucumbers and onions seasoned with oil and vinegar.*

BEGIN: EARLY IN DAY   4 SERVINGS

1 **small onion, cut up**
1 **cucumber, peeled, seeded and cut up**
1 **small green pepper, cut up**
2 **cloves garlic**
3 **tablespoons wine vinegar**
2 **tablespoons olive oil**
1 **tablespoon lemon juice**
¼ **teaspoon oregano leaves, crushed**
3 **cups tomato juice**

1. In covered blender container at high speed, blend all ingredients except tomato juice, ⅓ at a time, until smooth.

2. Pour mixture into large bowl; stir in tomato juice. Cover; chill until serving time, at least 6 hours.

3. To serve: Ladle soup into bowls; garnish with additional chopped vegetables. Yields 4½ cups.

TIP: Add salt and cayenne to taste, if desired.

❉ Cold Cucumber Soup

Cold soups are refreshing summer appetizers. Many are merely chilled versions of hot soups, but others, such as this Cold Cucumber Soup, were created to be served cold.

BEGIN: EARLY IN DAY   8 SERVINGS

3   cucumbers, peeled
2   tablespoons butter or margarine
¼   cup sliced green onions
1   teaspoon dill weed, crushed
3½   cups chicken broth
1½   cups water
⅛   teaspoon white pepper
2   tablespoons cornstarch
     Sour cream

1. Halve cucumbers lengthwise; scoop out and discard seeds. Cut cucumbers into chunks. In 3-quart saucepan over medium-high heat, in hot butter, cook green onions until tender.

2. Stir in cucumbers and dill; cook 1 minute more. Add broth, 1 cup water and pepper. Heat to boiling. Reduce heat to low. Cover; simmer 15 minutes or until cucumbers are tender.

3. In covered blender container, blend ⅓ of the broth mixture at a time until smooth.

4. Return to saucepan. In cup, combine remaining ½ cup cold water with cornstarch. Stir into soup. Over medium-high heat, heat to boiling, stirring occasionally. Cover; chill until serving time, at least 6 hours.

5. To serve: Ladle soup into bowls; garnish with sour cream. Yields 6 cups.

Gazpacho, Cold Cucumber Soup

Grilled Peppered Steak, Oven-Barbecued Ribs, Lamb Kabobs

MEATS

Before the Europeans came, North American Indians depended on game animals for meat in their diets. The South American Indians had domesticated guinea pigs, dogs, llamas and alpacas, and used them for food after the animals were too old for other uses. But Europeans brought cattle, sheep and pigs—livestock raised especially for food—to the New World, causing great changes in the way future Americans would eat.

Cattle (in limited numbers) were brought with the earliest Spanish explorers. Pigs, goats and sheep followed shortly afterward. The Indians quickly adopted European methods of raising livestock, cooking and preserving the meat in the same way that they had the buffalo, deer and squirrels.

Pork was the most important meat in the Colonial diet. Pigs were easier to transport across the Atlantic than larger animals, and they could find their own food, living off fallen nuts in the dense forests. The wild boars that became so numerous in the heartland are descendants of European pigs. The Pennsylvania Dutch were said to use "everything but the oink" in foods such as sausages and scrapple or in nonfood products made from hides and bristles. Southern plantation owners ate "high on the hog," while their slaves made the most of the less-desirable hocks, snouts, ears, chitterlings and spareribs.

It wasn't until the nineteenth century that beef began to rival pork in the American diet, and only in the twentieth century did beef consumption pass pork consumption. But it is beef that is remembered in the history books and folklore of the United States, through the legendary cowboys and cattle drives of the nineteenth century.

Texas longhorns were wild cattle that had descended from Spanish stock. Although their meat was not the choicest, the animals had adapted to the harsh climate and geography of the Southwest, and were capable of survival where other cattle would have perished.

With cattle free for the taking, vast lands free for the grazing, and no need to buy feed or provide shelter, Western stockmen were able to sell cattle at a fraction of the cost of Eastern cattle. They could drive the animals across hundreds of miles to get them to the more lucrative Midwestern and Eastern markets.

The beginning of the twentieth century brought an end to the cowboy era. Fences were erected across the cattle trails and land became too valuable to use for wandering herds. Beef cattle today are raised in feed lots, with grain diets that give American beef a worldwide reputation for excellence.

The abundance of livestock and grazing lands in America have made Americans a population of meat-eaters. Americans eat more meat per person than any other people in the world, consuming about one third of the world's meat supply. The American favorite is beef, followed closely by pork, with veal and lamb finishing third and fourth. Although the amount of red meat in the American diet has shown a slight decline, it remains the focal point of more meals than any other food.

❉ Pot Roast

Pot roast is a favorite main dish for cooks from all parts of the world, because it needs little attention from the cook and can be adapted to most tastes. The typical pot roast is a simple, hearty roast flavored with salt, pepper, onion and vegetables. To vary the roast, some cooks add herbs or fruit, or use a flavorful cooking liquid such as beer, wine or soup.

BEGIN: 4 HOURS AHEAD   12 SERVINGS

1	4-pound beef round or chuck pot roast
¼	cup all-purpose flour
1	teaspoon salt
¼	teaspoon pepper
2	tablespoons salad oil
2	large onions, sliced
1	clove garlic, minced
1	bay leaf
1½	cups water
6	medium potatoes, quartered
6	carrots, cut into 2-inch pieces

1. Trim and discard any excess fat from roast. On waxed paper, combine flour, ½ teaspoon salt and pepper; coat roast with mixture. Reserve remaining flour mixture.

2. In 6-quart Dutch oven over medium-high heat, in hot oil, cook roast until evenly browned on all sides. Remove roast from Dutch oven, reserving drippings. Over medium-high heat, in drippings, cook onions and garlic until tender.

3. Return roast to Dutch oven; add remaining ½ teaspoon salt, bay leaf and 1¼ cups water. Over high heat, heat to boiling. Reduce heat to low. Cover; simmer 2½ hours or until meat is nearly tender, turning occasionally and adding more water as needed. Add potatoes and carrots. Cover; simmer 40 minutes more until meat and vegetables are fork-tender.

4. Remove roast, potatoes and carrots to platter; keep warm. Discard bay leaf. In cup with fork, stir together reserved flour mixture and remaining ¼ cup water. Stir into simmering liquid in pot.

Cook until mixture boils, stirring constantly. Season to taste with salt and pepper. Spoon some gravy over roast; pass remaining gravy.

FRUITED POT ROAST: Prepare as above but omit garlic, bay leaf, potatoes and carrots; substitute *apple cider* for water. Prepare as above in steps 1 through 3, but simmer roast 3 hours. Stir in *1 cup dried apricots, 1 cup dried prunes, 1 teaspoon ground cinnamon* and *¼ teaspoon ground cloves.* Cover; simmer 15 minutes more. Proceed as above in step 4.

BEER POT ROAST: Prepare as above but substitute *1 can (12 ounces) beer* for water.

BURGUNDY POT ROAST: Prepare as above but omit sliced onions and substitute *dry red wine* for water. Add *24 peeled small white onions* along with carrots. Ten minutes before roast is done, stir in *1 pound small whole mushrooms.*

HERBED POT ROAST: Prepare as above but add *1 teaspoon thyme leaves, crushed,* and *½ teaspoon marjoram leaves, crushed,* along with the bay leaf.

SOUPER POT ROAST: Prepare as above but omit salt, onions, garlic and bay leaf. Substitute *1 can (10½ ounces) condensed French onion, golden mushroom or cream of mushroom soup* for the first 1¼ cups water.

OVEN POT ROAST: Prepare as above in steps 1 and 2. Place browned roast with cooked onions and garlic in ovensafe pot; add remaining ½ teaspoon salt, bay leaf and 1¼ cups water to roast. Cover; bake at 325°F. 3 hours. Add potatoes and carrots; cover. Bake 30 to 45 minutes more until meat and vegetables are fork-tender. On rangetop thicken gravy as in step 4.

TIP: Any roast from the beef round or chuck can be pot-roasted, including arm roast, shoulder roast, eye roast, 7-bone roast, rump roast and cross rib roast. The time allowed in this recipe is sufficient for most roasts, but if yours is very thick, you may need extra time; if it is less than 2 inches thick, the time may be reduced.

❈ Carpetbag Steaks

Recipes for tender steaks stuffed with oysters crop up in regional cookbooks all over the country, and even in Australia. It's no wonder, since the flavors complement each other so well.

BEGIN: 30 MINUTES AHEAD　　　4 SERVINGS

4　beef tenderloin (filet mignon) steaks,
　　each cut 1½ inches thick
4　tablespoons butter or margarine
½　pint shucked oysters, drained
2　tablespoons sliced green onion
2　tablespoons chopped parsley
　　Dash pepper

1. With sharp knife, form pocket in meat by cutting horizontally through each steak almost to the other side.

2. In 10-inch skillet over medium-high heat, in 2 tablespoons hot butter, cook oysters just until edges curl, stirring occasionally. Remove from heat.

3. Stuff oysters into pockets in steaks. Secure openings with toothpicks. In same skillet over medium-high heat, in remaining 2 tablespoons hot butter, cook steaks 10 to 14 minutes until browned on both sides, turning once. Remove steaks to platter; keep warm.

4. Reduce heat to medium; add green onion, parsley and pepper to skillet. Cook 1 minute; spoon over steaks. Serve immediately.

❈ Grilled Peppered Steak

Where did steak cuts get their unusual names? Porterhouse was named after the public houses of the late 1700s where this cut was a frequent offering; the inns were known as porterhouses because they served a dark ale called porter. Delmonico steak takes its name from the famous Delmonico restaurant of the 1800s. A T-shaped bone is responsible for the name of T-bone steak. According to legend, a beef loin steak was dubbed Sir Loin by a delighted King Charles II in the mid-seventeenth century, but most historians agree that sirloin actually is a corruption of surlonge, *French for "top of the loin."*

BEGIN: 1 HOUR AHEAD　　　8 SERVINGS

1　2-pound boneless beef sirloin steak, cut
　　1½ inches thick
2　tablespoons peppercorns
¼　cup butter or margarine, softened
1　tablespoon chopped parsley
1　tablespoon lemon juice

1. Prepare grill for barbecuing. Trim and discard excess fat from steak; slash fat on edges to prevent curling.

2. With mortar and pestle or rolling pin, slightly crush peppercorns. Rub pepper into both sides of steak.

3. Grill over medium coals 6 to 10 minutes on each side until desired doneness.

4. Meanwhile, in small bowl, combine butter, parsley and lemon juice.

5. To serve: Spoon butter mixture over steak; cut steak into thin slices or serving-sized portions.

TO BROIL: Prepare as above, but place steak on rack in broiler pan; broil about 4 inches from heat 6 to 10 minutes on each side.

TIP: Peppercorns can also be crushed in a covered blender.

TIP: Other steaks that may be prepared in this way include porterhouse, T-bone and tenderloin.

New England Boiled Dinner, Horseradish Sauce

✻ New England Boiled Dinner

To free the New England cook for other household work, salted beef and vegetables were combined in a large pot and hung over an open fire to boil most of the day. Naturally the ingredients varied according to what was in the pantry, but the pot usually held such easily stored vegetables as potatoes, onions, carrots, cabbage, squash, turnips, rutabagas and dry beans. Beets are often cooked in a separate pot to serve with this filling dish. Save leftover meat and potatoes to make Corned Beef Hash or Red Flannel Hash.

BEGIN: 2½ HOURS AHEAD   8 SERVINGS

1 **3-pound corned beef brisket**
16 **small white onions, peeled**
8 **small potatoes, peeled**
8 **medium carrots, halved crosswise**
1 **rutabaga or 2 turnips, peeled and cut**
   into wedges
1 **medium head cabbage, cut into wedges**
   Prepared mustard
   Horseradish Sauce*

1. In 6-quart Dutch oven, place corned beef and enough water to cover. Over high heat, heat to boiling. Reduce heat to low. Cover; simmer 1½ hours or until meat is nearly tender.

1. Freeze steak 1 hour to firm (makes slicing easier); trim and discard any excess fat from steak. Cut steak into very thin slices; set aside. In small bowl with fork, stir together broth, soy sauce, cornstarch, sugar, ginger and pepper; set aside.

2. In 10-inch skillet or wok over high heat, in hot oil, cook carrot and garlic, stirring quickly and frequently (stir-frying) about 3 minutes or until tender-crisp. Add green pepper; stir-fry 2 minutes more. With slotted spoon, remove vegetables to a bowl.

3. To skillet, add beef strips; stir-fry 3 to 5 minutes until browned. Add water chestnuts and green onions; stir-fry 1 minute. Add cooked vegetables; stir-fry 1 minute more.

4. Stir broth mixture; gradually stir into hot mixture in skillet. Cook until mixture boils, stirring constantly. Stir in tomato wedges; serve immediately over rice. Yields 5 cups.

TIP: Substitute 2 teaspoons grated fresh ginger root for ground ginger.

❋ Chuck Wagon Stew

The chuck wagon was the center of life on the famous cattle drives of the late nineteenth century. Named for its inventor, Charles (Chuck) Goodnight, it was loaded with the essential foodstuffs for the long journey from Texas to northern markets. Cooking on the trail presented special problems. All the food had to be packed into the wagon, so the cook had to use imagination to vary a diet consisting largely of bread, beans and beef. Stews were frequently on the menu, served with sourdough bread, biscuits or cornmeal dumplings.

BEGIN: 3 HOURS AHEAD   6 SERVINGS

1½	**pounds beef for stew**
½	**cup all-purpose flour**
1	**teaspoon chili powder**
¼	**teaspoon cayenne pepper**
½	**teaspoon salt**
4	**slices bacon**
1	**small onion, chopped**
1	**medium green pepper, chopped**
1	**stalk celery, chopped**
1	**clove garlic, minced**
1	**can (28 ounces) tomatoes, chopped**
1	**cup water**
1	**teaspoon oregano leaves, crushed**
½	**teaspoon sugar**
½	**cup yellow cornmeal**
1	**teaspoon baking powder**
⅛	**teaspoon salt**
¼	**cup milk**
1	**egg, beaten**
1	**tablespoon butter or margarine, melted**

1. Cut beef into 1-inch pieces. In paper bag, combine ¼ cup flour, chili powder, cayenne and ½ teaspoon salt. Add meat a few pieces at a time; close bag and shake to coat. Repeat with remaining meat. Reserve remaining flour mixture.

2. In 5-quart Dutch oven over medium heat, cook bacon until crisp; remove bacon, reserving drippings in pan. Drain bacon on paper towels; crumble and set aside.

3. Over medium-high heat in bacon drippings, cook meat until browned on all sides. With slotted spoon, remove meat to bowl, reserving drippings. In drippings, cook onion, green pepper, celery and garlic until tender. Stir in reserved flour mixture.

4. Gradually stir in tomatoes, water, oregano and sugar. Over medium heat, cook until mixture boils, stirring constantly. Return meat to Dutch oven. Reduce heat to low. Cover; simmer 2 hours, stirring occasionally.

5. In medium bowl, stir together cornmeal, baking powder, ⅛ teaspoon salt and remaining ¼ cup flour. Add milk, egg and butter; stir just until smooth. Stir in reserved bacon. Drop batter by rounded tablespoonfuls onto simmering stew. Cover; simmer 15 minutes more without lifting lid. Yields 6 cups.

❋ Sukiyaki

Sukiyaki is thought of as a traditional Japanese dish, but its history only goes back a short time in that ancient cuisine, because meat was forbidden in the Buddhist religion. An American statesman was the first to have a cow slaughtered for food in Japan in 1856. In 1872 Japan's emperor sampled beef for the first time, and the country immediately broke with its vegetarian tradition. One Japanese historian suggested that eating beef signaled an "advanced state of civilization." If Sukiyaki was prepared before this revolution in food habits, it probably was made for Europeans. The traditional method of cooking Sukiyaki is unlike some other stir-fried foods, in that each ingredient is kept separate during cooking.

BEGIN: 1½ HOURS AHEAD   4 SERVINGS

1	pound boneless beef sirloin steak
½	cup beef broth
⅓	cup soy sauce
1	tablespoon sugar
2	tablespoons salad oil
2	stalks celery, cut into ½-inch pieces
4	green onions, cut into 1-inch pieces
2	cups sliced mushrooms
1	can (8 ounces) bamboo shoots, drained and sliced
4	cups spinach, torn into pieces
	Hot cooked rice

1. Freeze steak 1 hour to firm (makes slicing easier); trim and discard any excess fat from steak. Cut steak into very thin slices; set aside. In cup, combine broth, soy sauce and sugar; set aside.

2. In 10-inch skillet or wok over high heat, in hot oil, cook celery and green onions, stirring quickly and frequently (stir-frying) about 3 minutes, keeping vegetables separate. Push vegetables to sides of skillet or wok.

3. Add mushrooms and bamboo shoots; stir-fry 2 minutes or until all vegetables are tender-crisp, keeping vegetables separate. Push vegetables to sides.

4. Add meat to center of pan; stir-fry 3 minutes or until just done. Pour broth mixture over all. Add spinach. Cook 2 minutes more until spinach is wilted. Serve immediately over rice. Yields 4 cups.

❋ Old-Fashioned Meat Loaf

The versatility of ground beef has made it the single most popular form of beef in this country. Because it can be made into stir-frys, soups, stews and sandwiches as well as patties, balls and loaves, it is featured in thousands of recipes, many of them improvised by home cooks. Meat loaf is one dish that has been endlessly varied to suit a family's taste, budget and schedule.

BEGIN: 2 HOURS AHEAD   6 SERVINGS

1	pound ground beef
½	pound ground pork
½	cup crushed saltines
¼	cup milk
1	egg, slightly beaten
1	large onion, finely chopped
1	clove garlic, minced
2	tablespoons Worcestershire
2	tablespoons ketchup
½	teaspoon salt
1	teaspoon dry mustard
¼	teaspoon pepper

1. In large bowl, thoroughly mix all ingredients. In 12- by 8-inch baking pan, shape meat into 8- by 4-inch loaf. Drizzle with additional ketchup.

2. Bake at 350°F. 1¼ to 1½ hours until done. Let stand 5 minutes; spoon off fat.

COUNTRY MEAT LOAF: Prepare as above but add *½ cup finely shredded carrot* with all ingredients.

HERBED MEAT LOAF: Prepare as above but add *¼ cup chopped parsley, ¼ teaspoon basil leaves, crushed,* and *¼ teaspoon oregano leaves, crushed,* with all ingredients.

❋ Best-Ever Meat Loaf

Canned soup has been used in meat loaves since the early 1950s. Because the seasonings are in the soup, this recipe requires few ingredients and makes a delicious meat loaf with flavorful gravy. Try it with each of the soups for a different flavor each time.

BEGIN: 2 HOURS AHEAD   8 SERVINGS

1   can (10¾ ounces) condensed cream of
       mushroom, golden mushroom or
       tomato soup
2   pounds ground beef
½   cup dried bread crumbs
1   small onion, finely chopped
1   egg, slightly beaten
1   teaspoon salt
⅓   cup water

1. In large bowl, thoroughly mix ½ cup soup, beef, bread crumbs, onion, egg and salt. In 12-by 8-inch baking pan, firmly shape meat into 8-by 4-inch loaf.

2. Bake at 350°F. 1¼ to 1½ hours until done. Spoon off fat, reserving 2 to 3 tablespoons drippings.

3. In 1-quart saucepan over medium-high heat, heat remaining soup, water and reserved drippings to boiling, stirring occasionally. Spoon over meat loaf.

MEAT LOAF WELLINGTON: Prepare as above but bake loaf only 1 hour. Spoon off fat. Separate *1 package (8 ounces) refrigerated crescent dinner rolls.* Place triangles crosswise over top and down sides of meat loaf, overlapping slightly. Bake 15 minutes more until golden.

FROSTED MEAT LOAF: Prepare as above but bake loaf only 1 hour. Spoon off fat. Spread *3 cups hot, seasoned mashed potatoes* over loaf; sprinkle with *½ cup shredded Cheddar cheese.* Bake 15 to 30 minutes more until meat is done.

❋ Salisbury Steak

A seasoned hamburger without a bun is often known as Salisbury Steak. The name comes from a turn-of-the-century doctor who championed eating ground beef as a curative for such diverse maladies as rheumatism, gout, tuberculosis and arteriosclerosis. Although there aren't many people who would make that claim today, there are still quite a few who enjoy Salisbury Steak.

BEGIN: 45 MINUTES AHEAD   6 SERVINGS

1   can (10¾ ounces) condensed golden
       mushroom soup
1½ pounds ground beef
½   cup dried bread crumbs
¼   cup finely chopped onion
1   egg, slightly beaten
⅓   cup water

1. In medium bowl, thoroughly mix ¼ cup soup, beef, bread crumbs, onion and egg; firmly shape into 6 patties.

2. Over medium heat, heat 10-inch skillet until very hot. Add patties; cook 3 to 4 minutes on each side until browned. Pour off fat.

3. Stir remaining soup and water into skillet. Cover; cook over low heat 20 minutes or until done, stirring occasionally.

Texas Chili, Bean and Beef Burritos, Chimichangas, Salsa Cruda, Cheese and Chili Enchiladas

❋ Texas Chili

Many Texans maintain that true chili contains only meat, chilies, herbs and spices, while others insist on tomatoes and beans. Still others disagree about the size of the meat pieces and the cooking time. To settle such debates, chili cooking contests have proliferated, particularly in the Southwest. Perhaps the most prestigious of these takes place every November in Terlingua, Texas: the World Championship Chili Cook-Off, the final showdown of preliminary winners and the climax of the chili cook-off season.

BEGIN: 3 HOURS AHEAD   8 SERVINGS

3 **pounds beef for stew**
2 **tablespoons salad oil**
4 **medium onions, chopped**
4 **cloves garlic, minced**
⅓ **to ½ cup chili powder**
2 **tablespoons ground cumin**
1 **teaspoon salt**
1 **can (8 ounces) tomato sauce**
3 **cups water**
    Hot pepper sauce
    Shredded Cheddar cheese
    Sliced green onions

1. Cut beef into ½-inch pieces. In 4-quart saucepan over medium-high heat, in hot oil, cook meat until browned on all sides. With slotted spoon, remove meat to bowl, reserving drippings. In drippings, cook onions, garlic, chili powder, cumin and salt until onions are tender.

2. Return meat to saucepan; stir in tomato sauce and water. Over high heat, heat to boiling. Reduce heat to low. Cover; simmer 1½ to 2 hours until meat is fork-tender. Season to taste with hot pepper sauce.

3. To serve: Ladle into bowls; garnish with cheese and green onions. Yields 6 cups.

CHILI WITH BEANS: Prepare as above but substitute *2 pounds ground beef* for beef cubes and add *2 cans (16 ounces each) pinto beans, drained,* along with tomato sauce.

❈ Bean and Beef Burritos

With the interest in Mexican food increasing all across the country, Americans are becoming acquainted with more than just tacos and enchiladas. Among other dishes, burritos and chimichangas are gaining popularity. A well-seasoned beef mixture is combined with refried beans and cheese and wrapped in a tortilla for burritos (little donkeys); the burritos may be fried to make crispy chimichangas.

BEGIN: 3 HOURS AHEAD   6 SERVINGS

1½ **pounds beef for stew or pork for stew**
1   **large onion, chopped**
2   **cloves garlic, minced**
1   **can (4 ounces) green chilies, drained, seeded and chopped**
1   **teaspoon salt**
1½ **teaspoons oregano leaves, crushed**
1   **teaspoon ground cumin**
¼   **teaspoon pepper**
1   **cup water**
2   **cups Refried Beans (see page 140) or 1 can (16 ounces) refried beans**
12 **8-inch flour tortillas**
2   **cups shredded Cheddar or Monterey Jack cheese**
    Sour cream
    Salsa Cruda*

1. Cut beef or pork into ½-inch pieces. In 2-quart saucepan over high heat, heat meat and next 8 ingredients to boiling. Reduce heat to low. Cover; simmer 2 hours or until meat is fork-tender. Uncover; over high heat, cook until *most* of liquid evaporates, stirring often. Remove from heat.

2. Spoon heaping tablespoon beans on center of one tortilla. Top with about 3 tablespoons meat mixture and about 3 tablespoons shredded cheese. Fold left and right sides of tortilla over mixture; fold in ends. Repeat with remaining tortillas, beans, meat mixture and cheese. On baking sheet, arrange filled tortillas seam side down; cover with foil.

3. Bake at 350°F. 15 minutes or until hot. Serve warm; garnish with sour cream and Salsa Cruda.

CHIMICHANGAS: Prepare as above in steps 1 and 2. In 10-inch skillet over medium-high heat, in ½ inch hot *salad oil,* cook filled tortillas, a few at a time, 2 to 3 minutes on each side until lightly browned. Drain on paper towels. Garnish with sour cream and Salsa Cruda.

TIP: If tortillas are dry or crack when you fold them, heat before filling to make them pliable. Wrap in foil and bake at 325°F. 10 minutes. Or, briefly dip tortillas, one at a time, into hot oil in small skillet.

*Salsa Cruda

An all-purpose sauce in Mexican and Southwestern homes, Salsa Cruda is also a staple in Mexican restaurants. It is served as a dip for tortilla chips and a sauce for all sorts of main dishes, in much the same way as ketchup is served in American homes. The sauce varies with the cook; it may have more or less onions, peppers or seasonings.

2   **medium tomatoes, cut up**
1   **small onion, quartered**
2   **pickled jalapeño peppers, cut up**
1   **tablespoon chopped fresh coriander leaves**
½   **teaspoon salt**

In covered blender container at low speed, blend all ingredients until chopped. Refrigerate until serving time. Yields 1 cup.

❋ Stuffed Green Peppers

Green peppers, also known as bell peppers and sweet peppers, are native to the Western Hemisphere. They are mild, sweet members of the family that includes the hot chilies associated with Latin American cooking. In the United States they have become an important ingredient in casseroles, stews, salads and sandwiches, but also perform as attractive edible containers in a typically American entrée, Stuffed Green Peppers.

BEGIN: 1½ HOURS AHEAD   6 SERVINGS

6   large green peppers
1   pound ground beef
¼   cup finely chopped onion
1   cup cooked rice
1   can (15 ounces) tomato sauce
1   tablespoon Worcestershire
½   teaspoon salt
½   teaspoon basil leaves, crushed
½   cup shredded Cheddar cheese

1. With sharp knife, slice tops off green peppers; discard seeds and membranes. Finely chop pepper tops to make ½ cup; set aside.

2. In 10-inch skillet over high heat, heat 1 inch water to boiling. Add pepper shells cut side down. Reduce heat to low. Cover; simmer 5 minutes. Remove from heat. Drain peppers on paper towels. Empty water from skillet; dry skillet.

3. In same skillet over medium-high heat, cook beef, onion and chopped green pepper until meat is browned and vegetables are tender. Pour off fat. Stir in rice, 1 cup tomato sauce, Worcestershire, salt and basil. Heat to boiling; remove from heat.

4. Spoon meat mixture into pepper shells. In 10-by 6-inch baking dish, place stuffed peppers upright. Pour remaining tomato sauce over peppers. Cover with foil.

5. Bake at 350°F. 30 minutes. Uncover; sprinkle each pepper with cheese. Bake 10 minutes more.

❋ Tamale Pie

To make a tamale, Mexicans spread a dough made from corn (masa) over a corn husk, add a filling of meat or beans, roll the husk up like a jelly roll and steam the packet. Americans have adapted this wonderful flavor combination into an easy-to-prepare one-dish meal, Tamale Pie. A longstanding favorite in the Southwest, it has become popular in other parts of the country.

BEGIN: 1½ HOURS AHEAD   6 SERVINGS

2½   cups water
2   tablespoons butter or margarine
1½   teaspoons salt
¾   cup yellow cornmeal
1   pound ground beef or fresh pork
     sausage
1   large onion, chopped
1   large green pepper, chopped
1   tablespoon chili powder
1   clove garlic, minced
1   can (8 ounces) tomato sauce
1   can (16 ounces) whole kernel golden
     corn, drained
½   cup sliced pitted ripe olives
     Dash pepper

1. In 2-quart saucepan over high heat, heat water, butter and 1 teaspoon salt to boiling. Slowly add cornmeal, stirring constantly. Reduce heat to low. Simmer, uncovered, 10 minutes, stirring often.

2. Meanwhile, in 10-inch skillet over medium-high heat, cook meat, onion, green pepper, chili powder and garlic until meat is browned and onion is tender. Pour off fat. Stir in tomato sauce, corn, olives, pepper and remaining ½ teaspoon salt. Heat to boiling. Reduce heat to low. Simmer, uncovered, 5 minutes. Turn mixture into 2-quart casserole. Spoon cornmeal mixture over meat.

3. Bake at 375°F. 30 to 35 minutes until topping is set.

❋ Spaghetti and Meatballs

Nearly every cuisine has its own version of meatballs, from delicate Swedish meatballs to spicy Mexican ones. Perhaps the best-known kind in this country are Italian-style meatballs with tomato sauce served over spaghetti. Or enjoy these tasty meatballs on a sandwich roll with cheese.

BEGIN: 2½ HOURS AHEAD   8 SERVINGS

1½ pounds ground beef
¼   cup dried bread crumbs
¼   cup grated Parmesan cheese
¼   cup finely chopped onion
¼   cup milk
1   egg, slightly beaten
2   tablespoons chopped parsley
½   teaspoon oregano leaves, crushed
½   teaspoon salt
¼   teaspoon pepper
2   tablespoons salad oil
8   cups Tomato Spaghetti Sauce (see page 131) or 2 jars (32 ounces each) spaghetti sauce
     Hot cooked spaghetti

1. In large bowl, combine first 10 ingredients; mix thoroughly. With hands, firmly shape into 1-inch meatballs.

2. In 4-quart saucepan over medium heat, in hot oil, cook meatballs, ¼ at a time, until browned on all sides; spoon off fat. Return all meatballs to saucepan; pour spaghetti sauce over meatballs. Over high heat, heat to boiling. Reduce heat to low. Cover; simmer 15 minutes.

3. To serve: Arrange hot spaghetti on large platter. Ladle meatballs and sauce over spaghetti.

MEATBALL SANDWICHES: Use ingredients as above but omit spaghetti and use only 2 cups spaghetti sauce. Prepare meatball mixture as above but shape into 24 meatballs. Cook meatballs in 10-inch skillet. Spoon meatballs and sauce onto *6 split 7-inch-long bread rolls.* Top meatballs with *sliced provolone cheese.*

❋ Porcupine Meatballs

These interesting meatballs appeal to children of all ages. The grains of rice in the meat mixture swell as the meatballs cook, causing them to stick out of the meat like porcupine quills, hence the name.

BEGIN: 1½ HOURS AHEAD   6 SERVINGS

1   can (10¾ ounces) condensed tomato soup
1   pound ground beef
1   egg, slightly beaten
¼   cup raw regular rice
¼   cup finely chopped onion
¼   teaspoon salt
     Dash pepper
1¼ cups water
1   teaspoon prepared mustard
1   clove garlic, minced

1. In medium bowl, combine ¼ cup soup, beef, egg, rice, onion, salt and pepper; mix well. With hands, firmly shape into 24 meatballs.

2. In 10-inch skillet over medium heat, cook meatballs until browned on all sides. Spoon off fat. Stir in remaining soup, water, mustard and garlic. Heat to boiling. Reduce heat to low. Cover; simmer 35 minutes or until rice in meatballs is done, stirring frequently. Yields 4 cups.

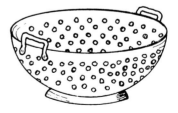

❄ Bierocks

A popular fast-food choice in Middle America, Bierocks are savory filled buns with a German influence. A filling of ground beef, onions and cabbage is wrapped in a yeast dough and baked.

BEGIN: 3 HOURS AHEAD   10 SERVINGS

½   recipe White Bread (see page 190) or 1 loaf (16 ounces) frozen white bread dough
1   pound ground beef
4   cups shredded cabbage
2   medium onions, chopped
1   teaspoon salt
½   teaspoon pepper
⅛   teaspoon garlic powder
1   teaspoon Worcestershire
1   egg, beaten

1. Prepare bread dough as directed in recipe for White Bread through step 3, or thaw frozen bread dough.

2. Meanwhile, in 5-quart Dutch oven over medium-high heat, cook beef, cabbage and onions until meat is browned and vegetables are tender, stirring often to break up meat. Continue cooking until most of liquid is evaporated. Drain off fat. Stir in salt, pepper, garlic powder and Worcestershire. Remove from heat; cool to room temperature.

3. Grease 2 jelly-roll pans. Divide bread dough into 10 equal pieces. On floured surface, roll each piece to a 6-inch round. Spoon about ½ cup meat mixture onto center of each dough round; bring up edges over meat, pressing together firmly to seal. Place on prepared jelly-roll pans; cover and let rise in warm place 20 minutes. Brush dough with beaten egg.

4. Bake at 375°F. 20 minutes or until golden. Cool slightly before serving.

CHEESE BIEROCKS: Prepare as above, but add *2 cups shredded Cheddar cheese* to meat mixture before filling dough.

TIP: When using White Bread recipe, prepare through step 3. Use half of the recipe for Bierocks and bake other half as directed in White Bread recipe.

❄ Creamed Dried Beef

Dried meat has been made in America since the Indians made jerky by drying buffalo or venison meat. Colonists followed the Indians' example, but they dried beef in the European manner, using a good deal of salt and cutting the meat thin. Dried beef has been important because it travels well, is light in weight and needs no refrigeration. U.S. military personnel are familiar with this simple but delicious breakfast, lunch or dinner dish, known as Creamed Dried Beef or Frizzled Beef.

BEGIN: 30 MINUTES AHEAD   4 SERVINGS

1   jar (5 ounces) dried beef
¼   cup butter or margarine
¼   cup all-purpose flour
¼   teaspoon pepper
2   cups milk
2   tablespoons chopped parsley
4   slices toast or 4 baked potatoes

1. Rinse dried beef with cold water; cut into strips. In 10-inch skillet over medium-high heat, in hot butter, cook beef about 3 minutes or until edges curl. Add flour and pepper; stir together until smooth.

2. Gradually stir in milk. Cook until mixture boils, stirring constantly. Cook 1 minute more. Stir in parsley.

3. To serve: Spoon over toast or split baked potatoes. Yields 2¾ cups.

❋ Corned Beef Hash

Hash is a dish of leftovers that takes on the character of the region where it's made. Simple Roast Beef Hash can be found all across the nation. In the Southwest, you'll find it flavored with chilies and olives. Red Flannel Hash with beets and corned beef is the New England version; thrifty Yankees insist that it is mostly beets, with small amounts of meat and potatoes.

BEGIN: 45 MINUTES AHEAD   4 SERVINGS

2   cups finely chopped cooked corned beef
2   cups finely chopped cooked potatoes
1   small onion, chopped
¼   teaspoon pepper
¼   cup butter or margarine
¼   cup milk

1. In large bowl, combine corned beef, potatoes, onion and pepper; toss to mix well.

2. In heavy, 10-inch skillet over medium-high heat, heat butter. Add corned beef mixture to skillet; press down with spatula to form an even layer. Pour milk evenly over top. Cook 10 minutes or until lightly browned on bottom. Reduce heat to medium; cook 5 minutes more or until well browned.

3. With spatula, turn mixture over in large pieces; press down with spatula. Cook 5 to 10 minutes more until browned.

RED FLANNEL HASH: Prepare as above but add *1 cup chopped cooked beets* along with potatoes.

ROAST BEEF HASH: Prepare as above but substitute *2 cups coarsely ground cooked roast beef* for corned beef, *¼ cup salad oil* for butter and *½ cup beef drippings* for milk. Add *1 teaspoon Worcestershire* and *½ teaspoon salt* to meat mixture.

CHICKEN HASH: Prepare as above but substitute *2 cups finely chopped cooked chicken* for corned beef and *½ cup light cream* for milk and add *½ teaspoon salt* to meat mixture.

❋ Liver and Onions

Long before researchers isolated and identified vitamins, doctors knew that certain diseases could be successfully treated with specific foods. For example, scurvy disappeared with citrus fruits, and night blindness improved when liver was eaten. The liver of an animal is its storehouse of vitamins, so liver is an excellent source of those nutrients. Of all the ways to prepare liver, cooking it with onions and bacon is the most popular in America.

BEGIN: 45 MINUTES AHEAD   4 SERVINGS

4   slices bacon
2   large onions, thinly sliced
1   pound beef liver, cut ¼ inch thick
3   tablespoons all-purpose flour
2   tablespoons salad oil

1. In 10-inch skillet over medium heat, fry bacon until crisp; remove bacon, reserving 2 tablespoons drippings in pan. Drain bacon on paper towels.

2. In drippings, cook onions 10 to 15 minutes until very tender, stirring often. Remove onions to platter; keep warm.

3. Cut liver into 4 portions; coat liver with flour. In same skillet over medium-high heat, in hot oil, cook liver 4 minutes or until browned on both sides, turning once. Place liver on onions; top each piece with a bacon slice.

Braised Beef Tongue

✳ Braised Beef Tongue

BEGIN: DAY AHEAD   12 SERVINGS

Variety meats are too often overlooked by American cooks. As a category, they tend to be high in nutrition and relatively inexpensive. In our more rural days, we used these meats more often, for it was necessary to make the most of every part of an animal. Tongue can be purchased fresh, canned, corned or smoked in supermarkets and butcher shops. The smoked tongue is usually braised, then served warm or cold with a peppy sauce. It is also a favorite meat for sandwiches and salads.

1   2½-pound smoked beef tongue
1   cup dry white wine
1   onion, chopped
1   carrot, cut up
1   stalk celery, cut up
1   clove garlic, halved
½   teaspoon thyme leaves, crushed
½   teaspoon peppercorns
      Watercress
      Prepared mustard
      Prepared Horseradish*

1. In 5-quart Dutch oven, place tongue and water to cover. Over medium-high heat, heat to boiling. Reduce heat to low. Cover; simmer 15 minutes. Drain tongue; rinse.

2. In same Dutch oven, place tongue, 4 cups water, wine, onion, carrot, celery, garlic, thyme and peppercorns. Over medium-high heat, heat to boiling. Cover; simmer 2 hours or until tongue is fork-tender. Cool tongue in liquid.

3. When cooled, remove tongue from pan, reserving broth. With sharp knife, remove and discard gristle and bone from base of tongue. Discard skin. Place tongue in large bowl.

4. Strain reserved broth over tongue in bowl; discard vegetables and bones. Cover; refrigerate at least 6 hours or until well chilled.

5. To serve: Remove tongue from broth; thinly slice tongue. Garnish with watercress. Serve with mustard and Prepared Horseradish.

*Prepared Horseradish

As with many familiar seasonings, horseradish was first used as a medicine for curing stomach and respiratory ailments. Today horseradish serves as a piquant relish with fresh, smoked or cured meats and luncheon meats. Once a tedious, tear-producing process, grating horseradish has become an easy task with the help of a food processor or blender.

1   **pound fresh horseradish, peeled and cut into 1-inch pieces**
1¼ **cups white vinegar**

1. In food processor with metal blade, process horseradish until finely chopped.

2. Carefully place mixture in jar; add vinegar. Cover jar tightly; store in refrigerator. Yields 2 cups.

TIP: Blender method: In covered blender container at medium speed, blend ½ of the horseradish and ½ of the vinegar until horseradish is finely chopped. Carefully place mixture in jar; repeat.

❋ Pork Roast with Corn Bread Stuffing

In the nineteenth-century West, cattle was king, but on Southern plantations the pig reigned. For several weeks each year plantation life centered on the butchering of the estate's hogs. Although much of this meat was destined for preservation in the smokehouse, fresh pork was abundant. With its typically Southern corn bread stuffing, this flavorful roast is a good example of fine Southern cooking.

BEGIN: 4 HOURS AHEAD   10 SERVINGS

1   **5-pound pork loin center rib roast**
½   **cup butter or margarine**
1   **large onion, chopped**
1   **stalk celery, finely chopped**
1   **teaspoon thyme leaves, crushed**
½   **teaspoon rubbed sage**
3½ **cups coarsely crumbled corn bread**
½   **cup chopped walnuts**
¼   **cup chicken broth or water**
    Salt

1. *Ask butcher to crack backbone of roast between ribs.* With sharp knife, cut pockets between ribs in meaty side of roast, about ¾ of the way through roast.

2. In 10-inch skillet over medium-high heat, in hot butter, cook onion, celery, thyme and sage until tender. Stir in corn bread and walnuts; toss to combine. Stir in chicken broth.

3. Stuff corn bread mixture into pockets in roast. Sprinkle roast with salt and tie with string, securing pockets together. In roasting pan, place roast stuffed side up. Insert meat thermometer into thickest part of meat, not touching bone or stuffing.

4. Roast at 325°F. 2½ to 3 hours until thermometer reads 170°F. Let stand 15 minutes before carving.

TIP: One package (8½ ounces) corn bread mix, prepared as label directs, yields 3½ cups corn bread crumbs.

❈ Stuffed Pork Chops

Pork chops are a favorite family meat because they are an easy-to-handle size that cooks, quickly, and can be prepared in many different ways. Thick pork chops become an elegant main dish when they are stuffed with an apple-and-sage-flavored dressing.

BEGIN: 2 HOURS AHEAD   6 SERVINGS

2   tablespoons butter or margarine
1   small onion, chopped
1   stalk celery, chopped
1   medium apple, peeled, cored and diced
2   cups dried bread cubes
½   cup apple juice
½   teaspoon salt
½   teaspoon rubbed sage
⅛   teaspoon pepper
6   pork loin rib chops, each cut 1½ inches thick
2   tablespoons salad oil

1. In 10-inch skillet over medium-high heat, in hot butter, cook onion, celery and apple until tender. Stir in bread cubes, apple juice, salt, sage and pepper. Remove from heat.

2. With sharp knife, trim and discard excess fat from edges of pork chops. Make a pocket in each chop by cutting horizontally through each chop almost to the bone. Stuff bread mixture into pockets; secure openings with toothpicks.

3. In same skillet over medium-high heat, in hot oil, cook chops, 3 at a time, until browned on both sides, turning once. In 13- by 9-inch baking pan, arrange pork chops. Cover with foil.

4. Bake at 325°F. 1 hour or until chops are fork-tender. Arrange on platter; spoon pan juices over.

❈ Stuffed Crown Roast of Pork

Sometimes the way a food is presented makes a big difference in its reception. A crown roast of pork is cut from the same portion of the animal as pork chops, yet it is a far more elegant dish. The center is often filled with new potatoes, Brussels sprouts, vegetable purées or a simple garnish of greens or fruit. Here it is stuffed with an herbed fruit dressing, then flamed to make an even more impressive entrée. Plan ahead when you serve this roast; you may have to order it from your market a few days in advance.

BEGIN: 4 HOURS AHEAD   8 SERVINGS

1   6-pound pork crown roast (12 to 16 small ribs)
3   slices bacon
½   cup sliced green onion
¼   cup finely chopped celery
2   cups orange juice
¼   cup chopped parsley
½   cup chopped dried apricots
¼   teaspoon thyme leaves, crushed
⅛   teaspoon pepper
1   package (8 ounces) herb-seasoned stuffing mix
½   cup chopped toasted almonds
1   jar (12 ounces) apricot preserves
4   tablespoons brandy
    Celery leaves
    Preserved kumquats

1. In roasting pan, place roast, bones pointing up. Cover bone tips with small pieces of foil. Insert meat thermometer into thickest part of meat, not touching bone or fat. Roast at 325°F. 1½ hours.

2. Meanwhile, in 10-inch skillet over medium heat, fry bacon until crisp. Remove bacon, reserving drippings in pan. Drain bacon on paper towels. Crumble bacon; set aside. In hot drippings, cook green onion and celery until tender. Stir in orange juice, parsley, apricots, thyme and pepper. Over high heat, heat to boiling. Reduce heat to low. Cover; simmer 5 minutes.

3. In large bowl, combine stuffing mix, nuts and bacon. Pour orange juice mixture over; toss to mix well. Spoon stuffing into center of roast, mounding it high. Cover stuffing with foil. Roast 1 hour more. Remove foil from stuffing.

4. In small saucepan over medium-high heat, heat apricot preserves and 2 tablespoons brandy; brush over roast. Roast 30 minutes more or until thermometer reads 170°F. Brush with preserves every 10 minutes; reserve ¼ cup preserves.

5. Remove roast from oven; let stand 15 minutes for easier carving. Place on serving platter; surround with celery leaves and kumquats. Remove foil from bones. Heat reserved preserves mixture; pour remaining 2 tablespoons brandy over preserves mixture. Ignite; pour over roast.

TIP: Before roasting, place a triple thickness of foil the same diameter as the roast under the meat to make transfer of roast easier.

TIP: Cut ends off preserved kumquats and scoop out center with a melon baller. Use to garnish ends of bones.

Stuffed Crown Roast of Pork

❋ Breaded Pork Chops

Americans prepare many meats by coating them with crumbs and frying them. This may be a throwback to pioneer and cowboy times, when most meat was cooked in a cast-iron skillet over a fire. The cooks might coat the meat with cracker crumbs or crumbs from dried bread before frying. These pork chops are coated with seasoned crumbs, then browned and cooked slowly to produce flavorful, tender chops.

BEGIN: 1½ HOURS AHEAD   6 SERVINGS

4	tablespoons salad oil
2	medium onions, thinly sliced
6	pork loin chops, each cut ½ inch thick
1	egg
2	tablespoons milk
½	teaspoon salt
¾	cup Italian-seasoned dried bread crumbs
2	tablespoons water

1. In 10-inch ovensafe skillet over medium-high heat, in 2 tablespoons hot oil, cook onions until tender. Remove from pan; set aside.

2. With sharp knife, trim and discard excess fat from edges of pork chops. In pie plate, beat egg, milk and salt; place crumbs on waxed paper. Coat chops with egg mixture, then with crumbs.

3. In same skillet, in remaining 2 tablespoons hot oil, cook chops, 3 at a time, until well browned on both sides. Pour off fat. Return all chops to skillet; top with reserved onions. Add water; cover.

4. Bake at 350°F. 45 minutes or until meat is fork-tender.

❋ Oven-Barbecued Ribs

A distinctly American style of cooking is the "soul food" developed by Southern blacks. The soul food dish known to the largest number of Americans is barbecued ribs. Originally the ribs were cooked slowly over coals and tended by plantation cooks with their spicy sauces. Often the ribs were flavored with the smoke from green hickory sticks or chips. To enjoy the ribs even during stormy weather, this method was developed to reproduce the fine barbecue flavor in the oven.

BEGIN: 2½ HOURS AHEAD   6 SERVINGS

6	pounds pork spareribs
¼	cup butter or margarine
2	large onions, chopped
2	cloves garlic, minced
1½	cups ketchup
½	cup lemon juice or vinegar
¼	cup Worcestershire
½	cup packed brown sugar
1	teaspoon pepper
½	teaspoon hot pepper sauce

1. Place ribs in 8-quart Dutch oven, cutting to fit if necessary. Add cold water to cover ribs. Over high heat, heat to boiling. Reduce heat to low. Cover; simmer 1 hour or until fork-tender. Drain ribs.

2. In 2-quart saucepan over medium heat, in hot butter, cook onions and garlic until tender. Stir in remaining ingredients except ribs; heat to boiling. Reduce heat to low. Cover; simmer 5 minutes.

3. Place ribs in roasting pan. Spoon ½ of the sauce evenly over ribs. Bake at 400°F. 45 minutes or until glazed, turning occasionally and basting with remaining sauce. Yields 3 cups sauce.

BARBECUED RIBS: Prepare as above through step 2. Cut ribs into serving portions. Grill over medium coals 30 minutes or until glazed, turning occasionally and basting with sauce.

❋ Ribs and Sauerkraut

To turn crisp cabbage into flavorful sauerkraut, it is salted and pressed in a crock with a weighted plate. Sometimes sauerkraut is flavored with caraway seed, dill or juniper berries. Whether the kraut is homemade or commercial, home cooks often season it with apples, onions and bay leaves.

BEGIN: 2½ HOURS AHEAD   4 SERVINGS

1   **jar (32 ounces) sauerkraut, drained and rinsed**
2   **medium onions, sliced and separated into rings**
2   **medium apples, diced**
½   **teaspoon caraway seed**
¼   **teaspoon pepper**
1   **bay leaf**
2   **pounds pork country-style ribs**

1. In 12- by 8-inch baking dish, combine sauerkraut, onions, apples, caraway seed, pepper and bay leaf. Spread mixture evenly in pan. Arrange spareribs in a single layer over sauerkraut mixture. Cover tightly with foil.

2. Bake at 325°F. 1½ hours. Uncover ribs; bake 30 minutes more or until fork-tender. Discard bay leaf.

❋ Breaded Pork Tenderloins

The pork tenderloin is a lean, tender cut from the pork loin. It is often roasted or braised, but in the important pork-producing area of the Midwest, the tenderloin is sliced, pounded, breaded and fried to make these delicious cutlets. On the menu in restaurants all over the Midwest, they are also called pork fritters.

BEGIN: 30 MINUTES AHEAD   4 SERVINGS

1   **¾-pound pork tenderloin**
¼   **cup all-purpose flour**
1   **egg**
2   **tablespoons milk**
½   **teaspoon salt**
⅛   **teaspoon pepper**
¾   **cup dried bread crumbs**
¼   **cup salad oil**

1. Slice pork tenderloin crosswise into 4 pieces. On cutting board with meat mallet, pound each slice to ¼-inch thickness.

2. Place flour on waxed paper; in pie plate, beat egg, milk, salt and pepper. Place crumbs on another sheet of waxed paper. Using tongs dip each pork slice into flour, then egg mixture, then crumbs to coat well.

3. In 10-inch skillet over medium-high heat, in hot oil, cook pork slices about 10 minutes until well browned and fork-tender, turning once.

TENDERLOIN SANDWICHES: Prepare as above, but serve each pork slice on a *toasted sandwich bun* with *lettuce, tomato* and *mayonnaise* to taste.

TIP: If you don't have a meat mallet, you can use the dull edge of a French knife to pound meat.

❋ Corn and Sausage Casserole

Corn and Sausage Casserole is a country dish that probably evolved from the puddings so popular with the English colonists. Once they began using native corn to replace wheat flour in their puddings, it was bound to turn up in other dishes. One English dish known as Toad-in-the-Hole was made with sausage and a popoverlike batter; it may have been the inspiration for this thoroughly American dish.

BEGIN: 1½ HOURS AHEAD   6 SERVINGS

1   **pound fresh pork sausage**
1½   **cups soft bread crumbs**
2   **eggs, beaten**
1   **can (16 ounces) cream-style golden corn**
½   **cup milk**
¼   **teaspoon pepper**

1. In 10-inch skillet over medium-high heat, cook sausage until browned, stirring to break up meat. Pour off fat. Stir in 1 cup bread crumbs and remaining ingredients. Turn mixture into 1½-quart casserole; top with remaining ½ cup crumbs.

2. Bake at 350°F. 55 to 60 minutes until set.

❋ Sweet and Sour Pork

One of the first foods Americans adopted from Chinese cuisine was Sweet and Sour Pork. Pork pieces are deep-fried, then cooked in a sauce of vinegar, sugar and soy sauce. The Chinese also use a similar method for fish, shrimp and chicken, but in America it usually is pork.

BEGIN: 2 HOURS AHEAD   8 SERVINGS

1   egg
1¾ cups chicken broth
½   cup cornstarch
     Peanut or salad oil
2   pounds boneless pork shoulder or loin,
         cut into ½-inch pieces
1   large green pepper, cut into strips
2   carrots, thinly sliced
1   clove garlic, minced
½   cup vinegar
¼   cup sugar
2   tablespoons soy sauce
1   can (20 ounces) pineapple chunks
3   tablespoons cornstarch
     Hot cooked rice

1. In small mixing bowl with rotary beater, beat egg until frothy. Beat in ¼ cup chicken broth and ½ cup cornstarch until smooth.

2. In 4-quart saucepan, heat 2 inches oil to 375°F. Dip pork cubes in egg mixture to coat; fry a few pork cubes about 3 minutes or until crisp. Drain on paper towels. Repeat with remaining pork cubes.

3. In 10-inch skillet or wok over medium-high heat, in 2 tablespoons hot oil, cook green pepper, carrots and garlic until tender-crisp, stirring often. Stir in remaining 1½ cups chicken broth, vinegar, sugar and soy sauce. Over high heat, heat to boiling. Reduce heat to low; simmer 2 minutes.

4. Meanwhile, drain pineapple, reserving liquid. In cup, stir pineapple liquid into 3 tablespoons cornstarch until smooth. Stir cornstarch mixture into vegetable mixture. Cook 2 minutes or until thickened, stirring constantly.

5. Add pineapple chunks and fried pork to skillet; heat. Serve over rice. Yields 7 cups.

❋ Pinwheel Pork Loaf

Meat loaves usually feature beef, but pork is another choice. This loaf is a variation on the theme of pork and sauerkraut: ground pork is spread with sauerkraut, then rolled up to make an attractive dish with flavors blended throughout.

BEGIN: 1½ HOURS AHEAD   8 SERVINGS

1½ pounds ground pork
½   cup dried bread crumbs
½   cup chopped onion
1   egg, slightly beaten
½   teaspoon salt
½   teaspoon Worcestershire
⅛   teaspoon pepper
1   jar (16 ounces) sauerkraut, rinsed,
         drained and chopped
½   teaspoon caraway seed
4   slices bacon, halved crosswise

1. In large bowl, combine first 7 ingredients; mix thoroughly. On waxed paper, pat into 12- by 8-inch rectangle.

2. In medium bowl, combine sauerkraut and caraway. Spread sauerkraut evenly over meat. Roll meat up jelly-roll fashion, starting at narrow edge. In 12- by 8-inch baking dish, place roll seam side down. Arrange bacon slices crosswise over loaf.

3. Bake at 350°F. 1¼ hours or until bacon is done and all pinkness disappears from meat. Spoon off fat. Slice to serve.

❋ Stuffed Cabbage Rolls

Immigrants from all over Europe, particularly Poland, Germany and Hungary, brought recipes for stuffed cabbage rolls to America. The best-known version is a pork and rice combination with a sweet and sour tomato sauce. Another fine recipe has a similar filling, but a smooth sour cream sauce.

BEGIN: 1½ HOURS AHEAD   6 SERVINGS

12   **large cabbage leaves**
     Boiling water
1   **pound ground pork**
1   **small onion, finely chopped**
1   **cup cooked rice**
1   **teaspoon prepared mustard**
1   **teaspoon salt**
     Dash pepper
1   **can (16 ounces) tomatoes, chopped**
2   **tablespoons brown sugar**
2   **tablespoons vinegar**
½   **teaspoon ground allspice**
¼   **cup cold water**
2   **tablespoons cornstarch**

1. In 5-quart Dutch oven, cover cabbage with boiling water; let stand 10 minutes. Drain well.

2. Meanwhile, in large bowl, thoroughly mix pork, onion, rice, mustard, ½ teaspoon salt and pepper. Place about ¼ cup meat mixture onto each cabbage leaf. Fold in sides to enclose meat mixture and roll up. Secure with toothpicks. In same Dutch oven, place cabbage rolls seam side down.

3. In medium bowl, combine tomatoes, brown sugar, vinegar, allspice and remaining ½ teaspoon salt; pour over cabbage rolls. Over medium-high heat, heat to boiling. Reduce heat to low. Cover; simmer 30 minutes or until meat is done. With slotted spoon, remove cabbage rolls to platter and discard toothpicks; keep warm.

4. In cup, stir ¼ cup cold water into cornstarch. Add cornstarch mixture to simmering tomato liquid. Cook until mixture boils, stirring constantly. Spoon sauce over cabbage rolls.

SOUR-CREAMED CABBAGE ROLLS: Prepare as above in steps 1 and 2. Omit tomatoes, brown sugar, vinegar, ½ teaspoon salt and ¼ cup water. Pour *1¾ cups chicken broth* over cabbage rolls; sprinkle with allspice. Cover; simmer 30 minutes until done. Remove cabbage rolls to platter; keep warm. In small bowl, stir cornstarch into *1 cup sour cream.* Stir sour cream mixture into broth. Cook just until mixture boils, stirring constantly. Spoon over cabbage rolls. Sprinkle with *paprika* before serving.

❋ Country-Style Sausage

More than any other group of immigrants, the Germans brought the art of sausage making to America; then Americans developed their own varieties. The most characteristic American sausage is seasoned with sage and shaped without casings into patties. It's easy to make sausage at home with no more equipment than a food grinder. Like generations of sausage makers, you can develop your own recipe for fresh sausage by changing the amounts of the ingredients here or adding more seasonings such as garlic, thyme, coriander, anise and parsley.

BEGIN: 1½ HOURS AHEAD   30 PATTIES

4   **pounds boneless pork shoulder, cut into 1-inch pieces**
¾   **pound pork fat**
1   **tablespoon rubbed sage**
4   **teaspoons salt**
2   **teaspoons pepper**
½   **teaspoon ground nutmeg**
¼   **teaspoon cayenne pepper**
     Water

1. With food grinder, using coarse blade, grind pork with pork fat into large bowl. Add sage, salt, pepper, nutmeg and cayenne; mix well. Grind mixture again. Shape into patties 3 inches in diameter and ½ inch thick. Refrigerate or freeze until needed.

2. *About 20 minutes before serving:* In 10-inch skillet over medium heat, cook a few patties at a time with 1 tablespoon water 15 to 20 minutes until no pinkness remains, turning once. Repeat with remaining patties. Yields 4½ pounds.

TIP: Store sausage in refrigerator no more than 2 days, in freezer up to 3 months.

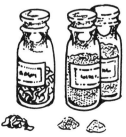

✳ Sausages with Apples

Sausage has been made in America as long as there has been pork for making it. The smoking process, along with spices and salt, helped preserve meat long after the animal was slaughtered. Today, with refrigeration available everywhere, smoking is used more for adding flavor than for preservation.

BEGIN: 30 MINUTES AHEAD   4 SERVINGS

1   **package (12 ounces) smoked sausage links**
2   **tablespoons butter or margarine**
2   **medium apples, cored and cut into wedges**
2   **tablespoons brown sugar**
¼   **cup water**
½   **teaspoon ground cinnamon**

1. In 10-inch skillet over medium heat, cook sausages 5 minutes until browned on all sides, turning often. Pour off fat. Remove sausages to platter; keep warm.

2. In same skillet over medium heat, in hot butter, cook apples 5 to 7 minutes until tender-crisp, turning occasionally. Stir in sugar, water and cinnamon; cook 1 minute more, stirring to coat apples.

3. Add apples to platter with sausages; spoon pan juices over.

✳ Cheese and Chili Enchiladas

To make enchiladas, tortillas are wrapped around a filling and covered with sauce. This recipe is a Mexican standard: the tortillas are stuffed with cheese and onion, then smothered in a chili sauce made with chorizo, a spicy pork sausage.

BEGIN: 1 HOUR AHEAD   6 SERVINGS

½   **pound chorizo sausage**
2   **teaspoons chili powder**
2   **cloves garlic, minced**
1   **can (15 ounces) tomato sauce**
1   **can (8 ounces) tomatoes, chopped**
1   **can (4 ounces) green chilies, drained, seeded and chopped**
½   **teaspoon ground coriander**
12   **6-inch tortillas**
4   **cups shredded Monterey Jack or Cheddar cheese (1 pound)**
¾   **cup chopped onion**

1. Remove sausage from casing. In 10-inch skillet over medium-high heat, cook sausage, chili powder and garlic until meat is browned, stirring to break up meat. Pour off fat. Stir in tomato sauce, tomatoes, green chilies and coriander. Heat to boiling. Reduce heat to low. Cover; simmer 5 minutes or until slightly thickened. Remove from heat. Into 13- by 9-inch baking dish, pour 1 cup sauce.

2. Dip one tortilla into remaining sauce to coat. Place tortilla on work surface; top with ¼ cup cheese and 1 tablespoon onion. Roll up tortilla around filling. In prepared baking dish, place tortilla seam side down. Repeat with remaining tortillas, cheese and onion, reserving 1 cup cheese. Pour remaining sauce over tortillas. Cover with foil.

3. Bake at 350°F. 20 minutes. Uncover; top with remaining 1-cup cheese. Bake, uncovered, 5 minutes more.

TIP: If you cannot find Mexican-style chorizo at your market, substitute ½ pound ground pork, ½ teaspoon ground cumin, ¾ teaspoon salt and ¼ teaspoon pepper.

❅ Beans and Franks

Perhaps the best-known beans in the United States are Boston Baked Beans, but other regions of the country have their own favorites. In the Midwest, tomatoes or tomato ketchup add color and flavor to the beans. Sausage or frankfurters turn the beans into a hearty meal. If you start with canned beans, it also becomes a speedy one.

BEGIN: 45 MINUTES AHEAD   6 SERVINGS

2   tablespoons butter or margarine
1   large onion, chopped
1   small green pepper, chopped
2   cans (16 ounces each) pork & beans in
       tomato sauce
¼   cup maple-flavored syrup
¼   cup ketchup
2   tablespoons prepared mustard
1   pound frankfurters, cut into 1-inch
       pieces
½   cup shredded Cheddar cheese

1. In 3-quart saucepan over medium-high heat, in hot butter, cook onion and green pepper until tender.

2. Stir in pork & beans, syrup, ketchup, mustard and franks. Heat to boiling. Reduce heat to low; simmer, uncovered, 20 minutes or until beans are slightly thickened, stirring occasionally. Sprinkle with cheese. Yields 6 cups.

❅ Traditional Baked Ham

American country-style hams have become famous all over the world. American pigs, fed on the peanuts that grow so well in the New World, produce hams with their own distinctive character. American curing methods also differ from the European ones; our hams are dry-cured with salt, then aged and smoked, unlike the European hams, which are cured in salt water.

BEGIN: 2½ HOURS AHEAD   12 SERVINGS

1   5-pound fully cooked smoked rump or
       shank half ham
     Whole cloves
½   cup packed brown sugar
2   tablespoons vinegar
1   teaspoon dry mustard
1   teaspoon grated orange peel
     Pineapple slices
     Pecan halves

1. On rack in roasting pan, place ham, fat side up. With sharp knife, score fat into ¾-inch squares. Stud center of each square with whole clove. Insert meat thermometer into thickest part of meat, not touching bone or fat. Bake at 325°F. 1 hour.

2. In bowl, combine sugar, vinegar, mustard and orange peel. Remove ham from oven; arrange pineapple slices and pecan halves over ham. Spoon sugar mixture over ham.

3. Bake 45 minutes more or until thermometer reads 140°F. Let stand 10 minutes before carving.

BAKED CANNED HAM: Substitute *3-pound canned ham* for smoked ham. Score ham fat into ¾-inch squares; stud each with whole clove. Insert meat thermometer. Proceed as above in steps 2 and 3.

BAKED COUNTRY HAM: Substitute *10- to 12-pound cook-before-eating Smithfield ham or country ham* for smoked ham. *Day before serving:* Place ham, skin side down, in large, deep roasting pan; cover with water. Soak 12 hours or overnight. *About 5 hours before serving:* Discard water; scrub ham. Rinse; place in roasting pan. Cover ham with more water. Over high heat, heat to boiling. Reduce heat to low. Cover; simmer 20 minutes per pound or until bone on small end feels loose. Place ham on rack in roasting pan; discard water. Bake at 325°F. 20 minutes. Remove skin; trim fat, leavingabout¼-inch layer fat. Score fat into ¾-inch squares; stud each with whole clove. Proceed as above in step 2; bake 30 minutes or until ham is glazed.

❋ Hocks and Black-Eyed Peas

Black-eyed peas were brought to America in the late 1600s by African slaves carrying the seeds from their old homes. Many of the slaves had small gardens, where they grew vegetables for their own use. After the plantation owners were served the choicest parts of an animal, the slaves were given the leftovers; that's how cuts such as pork hocks and chitterlings became the basis for what we now classify as soul food. Hocks and Black-Eyed Peas shows how good this humble food could taste.

BEGIN: 4 HOURS AHEAD   4 SERVINGS

4   smoked pork hocks (about ¾ pound
       each)
8   cups water
1½ cups dry black-eyed peas
1   large onion, sliced
3   tablespoons chopped parsley
1   teaspoon ground cumin
⅛   teaspoon cayenne pepper

1. In 6-quart Dutch oven, combine hocks and water. Over high heat, heat to boiling. Reduce heat to low. Cover; simmer 2 hours.

2. Stir black-eyed peas into hock mixture. Add onion, parsley, cumin and cayenne.

3. Over high heat, heat to boiling. Reduce heat to low. Cover; simmer 1½ hours or until hocks are fork-tender and peas are tender, stirring occasionally and adding more water as needed.

TIP: Substitute 1 can (10¾ ounces) condensed chicken broth for 1 cup water.

❋ Ham and Swiss Cheese Crêpes

Like other food fads, the crêpe craze has left its mark on American cooking. During the 1970s crêpe pans and cookbooks were favorite Christmas and wedding gifts, and most restaurants offered at least one variety of crêpe. Although the fervor has subsided, crêpes have become a staple element in American food. Here they enclose ham and cheese, making an elegant meal of that all-American combination.

BEGIN: 1½ HOURS AHEAD   6 SERVINGS

¼   cup butter or margarine
1   small onion, finely chopped
1   stalk celery, finely chopped
¼   cup all-purpose flour
2   cups milk
2   tablespoons chopped parsley
2   tablespoons dry white wine (optional)
2   cups chopped cooked ham
2   cups shredded natural Swiss cheese
12 Crêpes*
     Paprika

1. In 2-quart saucepan over medium-high heat, in hot butter, cook onion and celery until tender. Stir in flour until well combined. Gradually add milk; cook until mixture boils, stirring constantly. Stir in parsley and wine. Remove from heat.

2. In medium bowl, combine ham and 1 cup cheese. Stir in ½ cup sauce mixture. Spoon about ¼ cup ham mixture onto each crêpe; roll up. In 13- by 9-inch baking dish, arrange crêpes seam side down. Pour remaining sauce over crêpes; sprinkle with remaining 1 cup cheese and paprika.

3. Bake at 350°F. 15 to 20 minutes until crêpes are heated through and cheese is melted.

*Crêpes

4 eggs
2 cups milk
1½ cups all-purpose flour
1 teaspoon salt
 Salad oil

1. In large bowl with wire whisk, beat eggs, milk, flour, salt and 2 tablespoons oil until smooth.

2. In 8-inch crêpe pan over medium-high heat, heat 1 teaspoon oil. Pour about 3 tablespoons batter into pan, tilt pan to coat bottom. Cook until top is just set and underside is lightly browned. With spatula, lift edge of crêpe all around; shake pan gently so crêpe will come loose.

3. With pancake turner, turn crêpe over. Cook a few seconds. Place cooked crêpe onto wire rack to cool. Repeat with remaining batter to make 24 crêpes, adding more oil to pan as needed.

❊ Schnitz und Knepp

Typical of hearty Pennsylvania Dutch cookery, Schnitz und Knepp is made with the delicious hams produced by the butchers of that region. It is a dish of ham simmered with dried apples (schnitz), *then topped with fluffy dumplings* (knepp).

BEGIN: DAY AHEAD   8 SERVINGS

2 cups dried apples
1 3-pound fully cooked smoked ham, rump (butt) portion
2 tablespoons brown sugar
2 cups all-purpose flour
1 tablespoon baking powder
¼ teaspoon salt
1 cup milk
1 egg
2 tablespoons butter or margarine, melted

1. In small bowl, cover apples with water; let stand overnight.

2. *About 3 hours before serving:* In 6-quart Dutch oven over high heat, heat ham, brown sugar and 6 cups water to boiling. Reduce heat to low. Cover; simmer 2 hours.

3. Stir in apples and their liquid. Cover; simmer 20 minutes or until apples are tender.

4. Meanwhile, in medium bowl with fork, combine flour, baking powder and salt. In small bowl, beat together milk, egg and melted butter; slowly stir into flour until soft dough forms.

5. Remove ham to platter; keep warm. Drop dough by heaping tablespoonfuls onto simmering ham broth. Cover tightly; simmer 20 minutes without lifting cover.

6. To serve: With slotted spoon, remove apples and dumplings from broth; arrange on platter with ham. Spoon some broth over all.

❊ Ham Loaf

Nearly two thirds of American pork is either smoked or made into sausage; the remaining one third is sold fresh (unsmoked). Both smoked and fresh pork are used in this delicious meat loaf. The ham dominates the flavor, while fresh pork adds moistness and binding to the loaf.

BEGIN: 2 HOURS AHEAD   8 SERVINGS

1 pound ground smoked ham
1 pound ground pork
1½ cups soft bread crumbs
⅓ cup finely chopped onion
2 tablespoons finely chopped green pepper
½ teaspoon dry mustard
2 eggs
½ cup milk
½ cup packed brown sugar
¼ cup vinegar
 Dash ground cloves

1. In large bowl, combine first 8 ingredients; mix well. Spoon mixture into 9- by 5-inch loaf pan, packing mixture lightly into pan.

2. In cup, combine brown sugar, vinegar and cloves; mix well. Spoon over unbaked ham loaf.

3. Bake at 350°F. 1½ hours or until meat is done. Let stand 10 minutes; drain and invert onto warm platter.

❈ Broiled Ham and Sweet Potatoes

Southern hams are the best-known American hams, boasting the famous Smithfield and other Virginia hams as well as varieties from the other Southern states. Another Southern favorite, the sweet potato, was often teamed with ham in a favorite combination for fast meals as well as more formal holiday presentations. This quick-to-fix supper dish has the charm of the South, but only a fraction of the trouble and cooking time of a whole ham.

BEGIN: 30 MINUTES AHEAD   4 SERVINGS

1   smoked ham center slice, cut ¾ inch thick (about 1 pound)
½   cup orange marmalade
¼   cup orange juice
2   tablespoons butter or margarine
¼   teaspoon ground cloves
1   can (17 ounces) vacuum-packed sweet potatoes
4   orange slices

Hocks and Black-Eyed Peas, Broiled Ham and Sweet Potatoes, Sausages with Apples

1. Cut ham slice into 4 portions, discarding bone, if present.

2. In small saucepan, stir together marmalade, orange juice, butter and cloves. Over medium-high heat, heat mixture to boiling, stirring constantly. Remove from heat.

3. On rack in broiler pan, arrange ham pieces and sweet potatoes. Brush with marmalade mixture. Broil 4 inches from heat 10 minutes, turning ham and potatoes often and brushing with marmalade mixture. Place orange slices on ham, brush with marmalade mixture. Broil 3 minutes more.

❋ Roast Leg of Lamb

Lamb is meat from a six- to twelve-month-old lamb. In America, lamb is preferred to mutton, which is meat from sheep more than one year old; Europeans like the stronger flavor of mutton.

BEGIN: 4 HOURS AHEAD   8 SERVINGS

1   **5-pound whole lamb leg**
¼   **cup Dijon mustard**
1   **clove garlic, minced**
½   **cup Italian-seasoned dried bread crumbs**

1. On rack in roasting pan, place lamb, fat side up. In small bowl, combine mustard and garlic. Spread evenly on all meat surfaces. Sprinkle with bread crumbs. Insert meat thermometer into thickest part of meat, not touching bone or fat.

2. Roast at 325°F. until thermometer reads 140°F. for rare (1½ to 2 hours); 160°F. for medium (2 to 2½ hours); or 170°F. for well done (2½ to 3 hours). Let stand 15 minutes before carving.

❋ Grilled Butterflied Lamb

Outdoor cooking came to be known as barbecuing after the Spanish word barbacoa, *their name for the pit that Indians filled with hot coals and used for grilling meat and fish. Today, Americans barbecue meats of every description, from ground beef to the finest steaks and roasts. When the bone is removed from a leg of lamb and the meat is flattened to an even thickness, this roast cooks like a thick steak.*

BEGIN: DAY AHEAD   10 SERVINGS

1   **6- to 7-pound whole lamb leg, boned and butterflied**
1   **clove garlic, halved**
½   **cup fresh mint leaves, chopped**
1   **tablespoon lemon juice**
½   **teaspoon pepper**
¼   **cup butter or margarine**
½   **teaspoon salt**
½   **teaspoon thyme leaves, crushed**

1. On cutting board, lay lamb out flat. Rub cut surface with garlic; sprinkle with mint leaves, lemon juice and pepper. Roll up meat jelly-roll fashion. Cover; refrigerate overnight.

2. *About 1¼ hours before serving:* Prepare grill for barbecuing. In small saucepan over medium heat, melt butter; stir in salt and thyme. Unroll meat. Lay meat flat on grill over slow coals. Brush with butter mixture. Cook 35 to 40 minutes until lamb is desired doneness, turning often and brushing with butter mixture.

TO BROIL: Prepare as above but lay meat flat on rack in broiler pan; broil meat 6 inches from heat 35 to 40 minutes or until desired doneness, turning often and brushing with butter mixture.

Seasoned Lamb Chops, Broiled Lamb Patties with Dill Sauce

❋ Seasoned Lamb Chops

In early cookbooks, meat nearly always meant a large quantity: a 14- to 16-pound round of beef, a 15-pound piece of veal. The larger households of the time may have accounted for these amounts, and the fact that Americans of that era had great appetites produced by their active lives. Today's smaller families want smaller cuts of meat, such as steaks and chops, that cook quickly and produce no leftovers. This quick meal can be prepared in the same amount of time for one or six people just by changing the number of chops you buy.

BEGIN: 15 MINUTES AHEAD   6 SERVINGS

1 tablespoon chopped parsley
1 tablespoon salad oil
1 tablespoon lemon juice
1 tablespoon soy sauce
1 clove garlic, minced
1 teaspoon ground ginger
6 lamb loin chops, each cut ¾ inch thick

1. In small bowl, combine first 6 ingredients. On rack in broiler pan, arrange chops; brush with parsley mixture.

2. Broil 4 inches from heat 10 minutes or until desired doneness, turning chops once and brushing with parsley mixture occasionally.

✳ Broiled Lamb Patties with Dill Sauce

People in the sheep-raising parts of the Mediterranean regions have many ways to cook ground lamb. They add it to Moussaka, a lamb and eggplant casserole; they use it for stuffing grape leaves and other vegetables; and they make savory meatballs to eat plain or in sandwiches. Lamb patties seem to be an American invention, like hamburgers and Salisbury steak.

BEGIN: 45 MINUTES AHEAD   6 SERVINGS

1½ **pounds ground lamb**
¼ **cup finely chopped onion**
¼ **cup chopped parsley**
¼ **cup crushed saltines**
1 **egg, slightly beaten**
1 **clove garlic, minced**
½ **teaspoon salt**
6 **slices bacon**
¼ **cup sour cream**
¼ **cup mayonnaise**
1 **teaspoon dill weed, crushed**
  Dash pepper

1. In large bowl, thoroughly mix lamb, onion, parsley, crumbs, egg, garlic and salt. Shape mixture into 6 patties, each about 1 inch thick.

2. On rack in broiler pan, arrange bacon slices; broil 4 inches from heat until partially cooked. Wrap one bacon slice around edge of each lamb patty; secure with toothpick. Place patties on same rack in broiler pan.

3. Broil 6 minutes. Turn; broil 6 to 7 minutes more or until patties are of desired doneness. Discard toothpicks.

4. Meanwhile, in small saucepan over medium heat, heat sour cream, mayonnaise, dill and pepper just until hot.

5. To serve: Arrange patties on serving plate; spoon sauce over each. Yields ½ cup sauce.

TIP: It may be necessary to use more than one slice of bacon for each patty, depending on the type of bacon you use.

✳ Lamb Kabobs

Shish kabobs are said to have originated in what is now Turkey, where cubes of meat were threaded onto swords and cooked over a fire. The Turks probably were not the only people to think of spearing quick-cooking cubes of meat, but the name comes from the Turkish words shish *for skewer and* kebap *for roast meat. The word has come to include all types of foods that are cut up and cooked on skewers: meats, vegetables and even fruits.*

BEGIN: EARLY IN DAY   4 SERVINGS

½ **cup dry red wine**
⅓ **cup olive or salad oil**
1 **tablespoon lemon juice**
2 **cloves garlic, minced**
1 **teaspoon salt**
½ **teaspoon pepper**
½ **teaspoon basil leaves, crushed**
1 **pound boneless lamb shoulder or leg,**
  cut into 1½-inch pieces
8 **medium mushrooms**
1 **green pepper, cut into 1-inch squares**
1 **large onion, cut into 8 wedges**
4 **cherry tomatoes**

1. In large bowl, combine first 7 ingredients. Stir in lamb. Cover; refrigerate 4 hours or overnight, stirring occasionally.

2. *About 1 hour before serving:* Prepare grill for barbecuing. Drain lamb, reserving marinade. On four 18-inch skewers, thread lamb alternately with mushrooms, green pepper and onion.

3. On grill over medium coals, arrange skewers; cook 15 to 20 minutes until lamb is desired doneness, turning often and basting with marinade. Place one cherry tomato on each skewer; serve at once.

TO BROIL: Prepare as above but place kabobs on rack in broiler pan; broil 6 inches from heat 15 minutes or until desired doneness, turning often and basting with marinade.

TIP: To prevent splitting, pour boiling water over mushrooms. Let stand 1 minute; drain.

❋ Curried Lamb

In India, curry was prepared as long as 5,000 years ago, and Indian cooks still prepare their own by mixing cloves, cinnamon, ginger, chilies, turmeric, coriander and cumin. In America, curry powder is blended by manufacturers. We get curries from two sources: the English who ruled India and, more recently, Indian immigrants to America. Lamb is one traditional choice for curries because climate and religious taboos make beef and pork scarce in India.

BEGIN: 2½ HOURS AHEAD   6 SERVINGS

2   tablespoons butter or margarine
1½ pounds lamb for stew, cut into 1-inch
      pieces
3   medium onions, sliced
2   tablespoons curry powder
2   tablespoons all-purpose flour
1   teaspoon salt
1   teaspoon ground ginger
½   teaspoon ground cinnamon
¼   teaspoon pepper
1   cup chicken broth
2   apples, peeled, cored and cut into thin
      wedges
     Hot cooked rice
½   cup peanuts or cashews

1. In 10-inch skillet over medium heat, in hot butter, cook lamb until browned on all sides. Remove meat from pan, reserving drippings.

2. In drippings, cook onions and curry powder until onions are tender. Stir in flour, salt, ginger, cinnamon and pepper; stir together until smooth. Gradually stir in chicken broth. Cook until mixture boils, stirring constantly. Stir in reserved meat; heat to boiling. Reduce heat to low. Cover; simmer 1 hour or until lamb is nearly tender.

3. Stir in apples. Cover; simmer 10 minutes more or until lamb and apples are fork-tender.

4. To serve: Spoon lamb mixture over rice; sprinkle with peanuts. Yields 4½ cups.

❋ Braised Lamb Shanks

The Spaniards introduced sheep to the Southwest of this country. During the growth of the cattle industry, conflicts often arose between cattle raisers and shepherds over who would be allowed to use these vast lands for grazing. Because sheep can survive on sparse grasses, they have endured in that area of the country. This recipe reflects the Southwestern influence with its spicy barbecue flavor and the coffee that cowboy cooks often added to their stews.

BEGIN: 2½ HOURS AHEAD   4 SERVINGS

¼   cup salad oil
4   lamb shanks (about 4 pounds)
2   medium onions, sliced
2   stalks celery, sliced
1   clove garlic, minced
1   can (8 ounces) tomato sauce
1   cup brewed coffee
2   tablespoons lemon juice
1   tablespoon Worcestershire
2   teaspoons sugar
1   teaspoon celery seed
½   teaspoon salt
½   teaspoon oregano leaves, crushed
¼   teaspoon dry mustard
¼   teaspoon pepper
1   bay leaf

1. In 5-quart Dutch oven over medium-high heat, in hot oil, cook lamb shanks until browned on all sides. Remove shanks from Dutch oven. Pour off all but 2 tablespoons drippings.

2. In drippings, cook onions, celery and garlic until tender. Stir in remaining ingredients; heat to boiling. Return lamb shanks to pot. Reduce heat to low. Cover; simmer 1½ to 2 hours until shanks are fork-tender.

3. Remove shanks to platter; keep warm. Skim fat from liquid. Over high heat, boil cooking liquid 5 minutes until slightly thickened. Discard bay leaf. Spoon sauce over shanks.

❄ Irish Stew

Irish Stew, by tradition, is made in the springtime, the only time that lamb used to be available. Delicate lamb was teamed with spring vegetables—baby new potatoes, tiny onions and peas. Unlike many stews, Irish Stew has no thickener, so the gravy is light and fresh tasting.

BEGIN: 2½ HOURS AHEAD   8 SERVINGS

2   pounds lamb for stew, cut into 1-inch
        pieces
2   cups water
2   teaspoons salt
¼   teaspoon pepper
1   teaspoon rosemary leaves, crushed
1   bay leaf
16   small new potatoes, peeled or 8 medium
        potatoes, peeled and halved
6   medium carrots, sliced
1   small turnip, peeled and cubed
16   small white onions
2   cups peas or 1 package (10 ounces)
        frozen peas
2   tablespoons chopped parsley

1. In 5-quart Dutch oven over medium-high heat, heat lamb, water, salt, pepper, rosemary and bay leaf to boiling. Reduce heat to low. Cover; simmer 1 hour.

2. Stir in potatoes, carrots, turnip and onions. Over medium-high heat, heat to boiling. Reduce heat to low. Cover; simmer 45 minutes. Stir in peas and parsley; simmer 10 minutes more or until meat and vegetables are fork-tender. Discard bay leaf. Yields 12 cups.

❄ Shepherd's Pie

Shepherd's Pie was first made by baking leftover lamb, gravy and mashed potatoes together. Pleased diners insisted on having the dish even when there were no leftovers, so a ground-meat version also has become popular all over the country.

BEGIN: 30 MINUTES AHEAD   4 SERVINGS

2   tablespoons butter or margarine
2   cups cubed cooked lamb or beef
1   large onion, chopped
2   stalks celery, thinly sliced
2   tablespoons all-purpose flour
½   cup beef broth
2   teaspoons Worcestershire
2   cups hot, seasoned mashed potatoes

1. In 10-inch skillet over medium heat, in hot butter, cook lamb, onion and celery until vegetables are tender, stirring often. Stir in flour. Gradually add beef broth. Cook until mixture boils, stirring constantly. Stir in Worcestershire. Turn meat mixture into 10- by 6-inch baking dish. Spread mashed potatoes over mixture.

2. Bake at 450°F. 10 minutes or until potatoes are lightly browned.

TIP: Prepare as above but substitute *1 pound ground lamb or beef* for cubed meat; omit butter and increase *beef broth to 1 cup.* Cook meat with onion and celery as above; drain off fat. Proceed as above.

❊ Veal Stew

Veal is the tender, pale meat of young calves less than 3 months old. Cooks all over the world make veal stews. Some of the best known are from Hungary, with paprika and sour cream; from Italy, with tomatoes and lemon peel; and this American stew, an adaptation of a French blanquette.

BEGIN: 2½ HOURS AHEAD   8 SERVINGS

1   medium onion, chopped
1   carrot, chopped
1   stalk celery, chopped
2   whole cloves
1   bay leaf
1   teaspoon thyme leaves
¼   teaspoon peppercorns
2   pounds veal for stew, cut into 1½-inch
        pieces
1   teaspoon salt
3   cups water
1   pound small white onions
¼   cup butter or margarine
2   cups whole small mushrooms
¼   cup all-purpose flour
2   egg yolks
1   tablespoon lemon juice
⅛   teaspoon ground nutmeg

1. Prepare *bouquet garni:* Place onion, carrot, celery, cloves, bay leaf, thyme and peppercorns on 12-inch cheesecloth square. Pull up corners; tie with string.

2. In 5-quart Dutch oven, combine veal, salt, *bouquet garni* and water. Over medium-high heat, heat to boiling. Reduce heat to low. Cover; simmer 1¼ hours or until veal is nearly tender.

3. Stir in onions. Cover; simmer 15 minutes more or until onions are fork-tender. Discard *bouquet garni.* With ladle, remove 2 cups broth; set aside.

4. In 3-quart saucepan over medium heat, in hot butter, cook mushrooms 5 minutes or until tender. Add flour; stir together until blended. Gradually stir in 2 cups reserved broth. Heat to boiling, stirring constantly. Reduce heat to low; simmer 2 minutes. Stir into veal mixture. Remove 1 cup gravy; set aside.

5. In small bowl with fork, beat egg yolks. Gradually stir 1 cup reserved gravy into yolks; return to stew. Stir in lemon juice and nutmeg; heat through but do not boil. Makes 7 cups.

❊ Veal Birds

Veal Birds were a specialty in Colonial times. Also known as Veal Partridges or Mock Birds, they are slices of veal pounded and rolled up around a filling. This recipe, with its simple crumb filling and wine gravy, is as elegant as any.

BEGIN: 1½ HOURS AHEAD   6 SERVINGS

1½   pounds veal cutlets, cut about ¼ inch
        thick (6 large or 12 small cutlets)
½   cup butter or margarine
1   large onion, chopped
1   clove garlic, minced
2   cups soft bread crumbs
¼   teaspoon salt
½   teaspoon dill weed, crushed
⅛   teaspoon pepper
¼   cup all-purpose flour
1   cup dry white wine or water

1. Cut veal into 12 portions if necessary. On cutting board with meat mallet, pound each veal piece until slightly flattened.

2. In 10-inch skillet over medium heat, in ¼ cup hot butter, cook onion and garlic until tender. Stir in bread crumbs, salt, dill and pepper. Divide mixture among veal pieces; pat mixture evenly over veal. Roll up from short end, jelly-roll fashion. Secure with toothpicks. Coat with flour.

3. In same skillet over medium heat, in remaining ¼ cup hot butter, cook veal until lightly browned on all sides. Pour wine over veal. Reduce heat to low. Cover; simmer 30 minutes until veal is fork-tender. Remove veal to platter; discard toothpicks. Stir additional water into pan juices to thin, if necessary. Serve with veal.

TIP: Smaller pieces of veal cutlet may be pounded together to make a larger piece.

❉ City Chicken

At least three veal dishes have been inspired because veal can duplicate the flavor of other meats. One is the Italian Vitello Tonnato (veal with tuna sauce). A second is the mock turtle soup that was common 100 years ago. Early in this century, when chicken was scarcer and more expensive than veal, veal stood in for the poultry in City Chicken. Although the tables have turned and veal is now the more expensive meat, City Chicken is a delicious reminder of other times.

BEGIN: 2 HOURS AHEAD   8 SERVINGS

1   pound boneless veal shoulder, cut into
        1½-inch cubes
1   pound boneless pork, cut into 1½-inch
        cubes
1   egg
2   tablespoons milk
½   teaspoon salt
¼   teaspoon pepper
¾   cup finely crushed saltines
⅓   cup butter or margarine
1   cup chicken broth
2   tablespoons all-purpose flour
¼   cup water

1. Thread veal and pork alternately onto eight 6-inch skewers, pushing pieces close together. In pie plate, beat egg, milk, salt and pepper. Place cracker crumbs on waxed paper. Dip skewered meat into egg mixture; coat with crumbs.

2. In 10-inch skillet over medium heat, in hot butter, cook ½ of the skewered meat about 4 minutes until browned on all sides, turning occasionally. Remove from pan; repeat with remaining meat. Return all meat to skillet. Pour chicken broth over meat; heat to boiling. Reduce heat to low. Cover; simmer 45 to 50 minutes until meat is tender. Remove skewered meat to platter; keep warm.

3. In cup, stir together flour and water until smooth. Stir into pan juices; cook until mixture boils, stirring constantly. Serve pan juices with meat.

❉ Grillades with Grits

Generally served for breakfast or brunch, Grillades with Grits is a hearty morning meal from the Creole cuisine. The characteristic vegetables and seasonings—green pepper, celery, garlic and cayenne—are simmered with the veal or beef to make a lively sauce. Like many regional specialties, this dish varies with the cook who prepares it. If you like your food extra spicy, add more cayenne or put a bottle of Louisiana pepper sauce on the table.

BEGIN: 2½ HOURS AHEAD   6 SERVINGS

1½ pounds veal or beef round steak, cut ½
        inch thick
6   tablespoons all-purpose flour
¼   cup lard or salad oil
2   medium onions, chopped
1   large green pepper, chopped
2   medium tomatoes, peeled and chopped
1   stalk celery, chopped
2   cloves garlic, minced
1¾ cups beef broth
1   bay leaf
1   teaspoon salt
½   teaspoon thyme leaves, crushed
¼   teaspoon pepper
⅛   teaspoon cayenne pepper
     Hot cooked grits

1. Cut steak into 6 portions. Coat with 2 tablespoons flour. In 10-inch skillet over medium-high heat, in hot lard, cook steaks until browned on both sides. Remove steaks from skillet.

2. To drippings in skillet, add remaining 4 tablespoons flour. Reduce heat to low. Cook about 15 minutes until mixture turns deep brown, stirring often. Stir in onions, green pepper, tomatoes, celery and garlic. Cook until vegetables are tender, stirring often.

3. Stir in broth, bay leaf, salt, thyme, pepper and cayenne. Over high heat, heat to boiling. Reduce heat to low. Return steaks to skillet. Cover; simmer 1½ hours or until meat is fork-tender, stirring occasionally.

4. To serve: Place grits on large platter; arrange steaks on grits. Spoon sauce over steaks.

Southern-Fried Chicken with Cream Gravy, Prune-Stuffed Duckling, Chicken Pie

POULTRY

Poultry has been a part of American tradition since Benjamin Franklin proposed the wild turkey as the symbol of the new nation. Herbert Hoover tied poultry to the American way of life in 1928 when he promised to work toward an economy where there would be "a chicken in every pot." Contemporary American food writer Calvin Trillin continues the poultry controversy with his tongue-in-cheek campaign to have the Thanksgiving turkey replaced with platters of Spaghetti Carbonara.

Our continent held a large variety of game birds before the Europeans arrived. Native Americans trapped wild turkeys, ducks, geese, quails, larks, pigeons, partridges and sea gulls. They roasted the birds over open fires or buried them in the embers, often flavoring them with herbs, vegetables and fruits.

The early colonists brought chickens along for their extended ocean voyages. The hens laid eggs during the trip; when they were too old to lay, they were stewed for dinner. Their descendants provided food for the colonies and for later generations of Americans.

The settlers enjoyed game birds, too. Both wild and domestic fowl were roasted on spits or stewed in cast-iron kettles in kitchen fireplaces. A fruit or bread stuffing often was added to make the dish go farther.

The changing American scene has reduced our once-plentiful supply of game. Passenger pigeons, which numbered in the billions, were an easy target for hunters before the birds became extinct around 1900. Several varieties of ducks also have disappeared. Other bird populations, such as the wild turkey, have greatly diminished.

In contrast, the production of domestic fowl has increased. Poultry farmers breed chickens and turkeys for high yields and tender flesh. Their efforts also have produced the Cornish hen, a bird that provides only one or two servings, perfect for today's smaller families.

There was a time when chicken was expensive, and less-costly veal was cooked to make it taste like chicken. With efficient production methods, the cost of serving poultry has dropped. Although they still appear on elegant menus, chicken and turkey are staple foods for economical family meals. Just recently, with the new interest in low-fat cooking, they have become even more popular.

New equipment has introduced new ways of cooking poultry. In the nineteenth century, ovens were improved, making roasting a common cooking method and encouraging the creation of many stuffings. Microwave ovens and slow cookers give the twentieth-century cook even more options for cooking poultry.

❈ Traditional Stuffed Turkey

The Thanksgiving feast we celebrate today is very different from the legendary first Thanksgiving of 1621, but the spirit of the day has endured through the centuries. President Lincoln first made Thanksgiving an annual national holiday in 1863; since then we have celebrated it as a time for giving thanks, feasting, family reunions and the beginning of the Christmas season. Although many historians believe that turkey was not a part of the original Thanksgiving menu, today it is hard to imagine Thanksgiving without a turkey.

BEGIN: 6 HOURS AHEAD   18 TO 20 SERVINGS

1   pound fresh pork sausage
½   cup butter or margarine
2   large apples, peeled, cored and chopped
1   medium onion, chopped
½   cup chopped celery
½   cup water
4   cups crumbled corn bread or 1 package (8 ounces) corn bread stuffing mix
½   cup coarsely chopped pecans
¼   cup chopped parsley
½   teaspoon poultry seasoning
1   18- to 20-pound frozen ready-to-stuff turkey, thawed
½   cup butter or margarine, melted
    Salt
    Pepper
    Giblet Gravy*

1. In 10-inch skillet over medium heat, cook sausage until browned, breaking apart with fork. Stir in ½ cup butter, apples, onion and celery; cook until celery is tender, about 5 minutes, stirring occasionally. Add water; heat to boiling. Remove from heat. In large bowl, combine meat mixture with corn bread, pecans, parsley and poultry seasoning. Stir until well mixed.

2. Remove giblets and neck from inside turkey and reserve for gravy. Rinse turkey with running cold water; drain well. Spoon some stuffing lightly into neck cavity. Fold neck skin over stuffing; skewer closed. With turkey breast side up, lift wings up toward neck, then fold under back of bird to balance it.

3. Spoon remaining stuffing lightly into body cavity. Fold skin over opening; skewer closed. Tie legs or fasten under metal clip. On rack in roasting pan, place turkey breast side up. Brush skin with melted butter. Sprinkle with salt and pepper. Insert meat thermometer into thickest part of meat between breast and thigh, not touching bone.

4. Roast uncovered at 325°F. 4 to 4½ hours until thermometer reads 180°F. or thickest part of drumstick feels soft when pressed between thumb and forefinger protected by paper towels. Baste occasionally with pan drippings. When skin turns golden, cover loosely with tent of foil. Begin checking for doneness after 3 hours cooking time. Toward end of roasting, remove foil; brush turkey with drippings.

5. Remove turkey from oven; let stand 20 minutes for easier carving. Serve with Giblet Gravy.

*Giblet Gravy

BEGIN: 2½ HOURS AHEAD

    Reserved giblets and neck from turkey
½   cup chopped celery
½   cup chopped onion
1   teaspoon salt
    Water
    Pan drippings from roast turkey
6   tablespoons all-purpose flour

1. While turkey is roasting, in 2-quart saucepan combine giblets, neck, celery, onion and salt. Add water to cover; over high heat, heat to boiling.

2. Reduce heat to low. Cover; simmer 1 to 2 hours until giblets are tender. With slotted spoon, remove neck and giblets. Strain broth; discard celery and onion. Chop neck meat and giblets; set aside.

3. In large bowl with mixer at low speed, beat potatoes with onion mixture until fluffy. Beating at medium speed, add bread cubes, eggs, parsley, salt, thyme, marjoram and pepper; beat until well mixed.

4. Remove neck and giblets from inside goose (use giblets and neck for broth if desired). Discard fat from body cavity. Rinse goose with running cold water; drain well. With goose breast side up, lift wings up toward neck, then fold under back of bird to balance it.

5. Spoon stuffing lightly into body cavity. Fold skin over opening; skewer closed. Tie legs; with fork, prick skin. On rack in roasting pan, place goose breast side up. Insert meat thermometer into thickest part of meat between breast and thigh, not touching bone.

6. Roast uncovered at 350°F. about 2½ hours until thermometer reads 190°F. or thickest part of drumstick feels soft when pressed between thumb and forefinger protected by paper towels. Baste with pan drippings and spoon off fat occasionally during roasting.

7. Remove goose from oven; let stand 15 minutes for easier carving.

POTATO DRESSING: Prepare stuffing as above in steps 1 through 3. Spoon stuffing into buttered 1½-quart casserole; dot with *1 tablespoon butter or margarine.* Bake at 350°F. 35 minutes.

TIP: If you purchase a frozen goose, thaw it before stuffing.

❄ Prune-Stuffed Duckling

Ducks were so abundant in the early days of the nation that it didn't take a crack shot to bag several in a single day. One tall tale that has come down from the Northern frontier involves Paul Bunyan, the giant lumberjack, and his blue ox, Babe. The story tells how Bunyan and Babe captured an entire flock of ducks in a large piece of canvas, then brought them back to camp to make a monumental meal featuring fried, stewed, fricasseed and baked duck with plenty of duck gravy.

BEGIN: 4 HOURS AHEAD   4 SERVINGS

1	**5-pound duckling**
½	**cup butter or margarine**
½	**cup chopped celery**
½	**cup chopped onion**
1	**cup pitted prunes, coarsely chopped**
1	**teaspoon slivered orange peel**
½	**cup chopped peeled orange**
2½	**cups herb-seasoned stuffing mix**
1	**cup water**
¼	**teaspoon ground nutmeg**
⅛	**teaspoon ground cloves**
½	**teaspoon salt**
⅛	**teaspoon pepper**

1. Remove giblets and neck from inside duckling. Chop giblets; set aside (use neck for broth if desired). Rinse duck with running cold water; drain well.

2. In 10-inch skillet over medium-high heat, in hot butter, cook celery and onion with chopped giblets until tender. Stir in prunes, orange peel and chopped orange. Remove from heat. Stir in stuffing mix, water, nutmeg and cloves.

3. Spoon some stuffing lightly into neck cavity. Fold neck skin over stuffing; skewer closed. With duckling breast side up, lift wings up toward neck, then fold under back of bird to balance it.

4. Spoon remaining stuffing lightly into body cavity. Fold skin over opening; skewer closed. Tie legs; with fork, prick skin. On rack in roasting pan, place duckling breast side up. Sprinkle with salt and pepper. Insert meat thermometer into thickest part of meat between breast and thigh, not touching bone.

5. Roast uncovered at 325°F. 2 to 2½ hours until thermometer reads 185°F. or thickest part of drumstick feels soft when pressed between thumb and forefinger protected by paper towels. Baste with pan drippings and spoon off fat occasionally during roasting.

6. Remove duck from oven; let stand 15 minutes for easier carving.

❊ Wild Rice-Stuffed Capon

A capon is a neutered rooster, larger than a roasting hen, with more white meat and a reputation for better flavor. In this recipe, the capon is stuffed with one of the most American of foods, wild rice.

BEGIN: 5 HOURS AHEAD   8 SERVINGS

¼   cup butter or margarine
2   cups sliced mushrooms
1   large onion, chopped
1   cup raw wild rice
1¾ cups chicken broth
½   cup water
1   tablespoon chopped parsley
½   teaspoon rubbed sage
1   6- to 8-pound capon
2   tablespoons butter or margarine, melted
    Salt
    Pepper

1. In 10-inch skillet over medium-high heat, in ¼ cup hot butter, cook mushrooms and onion until tender, stirring occasionally.

2. Meanwhile, wash rice thoroughly in warm water; drain well. To skillet, add rice, broth, water, parsley and sage. Over high heat, heat to boiling. Reduce heat to low. Cover; simmer 40 minutes or until rice is tender.

3. Remove giblets and neck from inside capon (use giblets and neck for broth if desired). Rinse capon with running cold water; drain well. Spoon some stuffing lightly into neck cavity. Fold neck skin over stuffing; skewer closed. With capon breast side up, lift wings up toward neck, then fold under back of bird to balance it.

4. Spoon remaining stuffing lightly into body cavity. Fold skin over opening; skewer closed. Tie legs. On rack in roasting pan, place capon breast side up. Brush with melted butter. Sprinkle with salt and pepper. Insert meat thermometer into thickest part of meat between breast and thigh, not touching bone.

5. Roast uncovered at 325°F. 3 to 4 hours until thermometer reads 180°F. or thickest part of drumstick feels soft when pressed between thumb and forefinger protected by paper towels. Baste occasionally with pan drippings. When skin turns golden, cover loosely with tent of foil. Begin checking for doneness after 2½ hours cooking time. Toward end of roasting, remove foil; brush capon with drippings.

6. Remove capon from oven; let stand 15 minutes for easier carving.

❊ Mushroom Stuffing

There are two schools of thought about the consistency of stuffing. One camp insists on a moist stuffing, one that is roasted inside a bird, where it can absorb the juices while the bird cooks; the other prefers a dry, even crusty version, baked in a separate pan. Enjoy Mushroom Stuffing both ways.

BEGIN: 30 MINUTES AHEAD   9 SERVINGS

⅓   cup butter or margarine
1   cup sliced mushrooms
½   cup chopped celery
⅓   cup chopped onion
1   can (10¾ ounces) condensed chicken
        broth
1   package (8 ounces) herb-seasoned
        stuffing mix
1   egg, slightly beaten
2   tablespoons chopped parsley

1. In 10-inch skillet over medium-high heat, in hot butter, cook mushrooms, celery and onion until tender, stirring occasionally. Add chicken broth; heat to boiling. Remove from heat.

2. Stir in stuffing mix, egg and parsley. Use to stuff chicken, turkey or capon. Yields 4 cups.

BAKED MUSHROOM SQUARES: Prepare as above but spoon into buttered 8- by 8-inch baking dish. Bake at 350°F. 20 minutes or until hot and set. Cut into squares to serve.

❄ Glazed Cornish Hens

Although the Cornish game hen takes its name from the county of Cornwall in England, it is an American bird. A cross between the Plymouth rock hen from America and the Cornish rock rooster of England, the bird is a relatively recent creation. It may be broiled, fried or braised, but most often it is roasted.

BEGIN: 1½ HOURS AHEAD   4 SERVINGS

4   **1-pound Cornish game hens**
4   **small white onions, quartered**
4   **sprigs parsley**
¼   **cup butter or margarine, melted**
1   **teaspoon salt**
¼   **teaspoon paprika**
⅛   **teaspoon pepper**
⅓   **cup honey**
⅓   **cup orange marmalade**
⅓   **cup orange juice**
2   **large oranges, peeled and sliced**

1. Remove giblets and neck from inside Cornish hens (use giblets and neck for broth if desired). Rinse hens with running cold water; drain well. With hens breast side up, lift wings up toward neck, then fold under backs of birds to balance them.

2. Place onions and parsley into cavities. Tie legs. On rack in roasting pan, place hens breast side up. Brush with melted butter. Sprinkle with salt, paprika and pepper.

3. Roast uncovered at 350°F. 45 minutes. Baste occasionally with pan drippings.

4. Meanwhile, in small bowl, combine honey, marmalade and orange juice. Brush over hens; roast 10 minutes more. Add oranges to roasting pan. Baste hens and oranges with honey mixture. Roast 10 to 15 minutes more or until hens are fork-tender; baste occasionally with honey mixture.

5. To serve: Arrange hens on platter with orange slices.

Glazed Cornish Hens

❄ Chicken Liver-Rice Stuffing

Stuffings made with rice are popular in the South, where rice is an important food and cash crop. This traditional rice stuffing is flavored with chicken livers; with the addition of gizzards and hot peppers or pepper sauce, the stuffing becomes Dirty Rice, a Cajun classic that can be used as a stuffing or as an entire meal.

BEGIN: 1 HOUR AHEAD   6 SERVINGS

¼   **cup butter or margarine**
½   **pound chicken livers, coarsely chopped**
1   **cup chopped mushrooms**
1   **cup chopped onions**
½   **cup chopped celery**
1   **cup raw regular long-grain rice**
3½ **cups chicken broth**
¼   **teaspoon poultry seasoning**

1. In 10-inch skillet over medium heat, in hot butter, cook chicken livers until browned, stirring occasionally. Stir in mushrooms, onions and celery; cook until tender, stirring occasionally.

2. Add rice, broth and seasoning; heat to boiling. Reduce heat to low. Cover; simmer 30 minutes or until rice is tender. Use to stuff chicken or small turkey. Yields 4 cups.

DIRTY RICE: Prepare as above but add *½ pound chicken gizzards, finely chopped,* with chicken livers. Add *1 teaspoon hot pepper sauce* with seasoning.

❄ Sweet Potato Dressing

Another stuffing characteristic of the South is Sweet Potato Dressing. African slaves brought yams to the New World while, at the same time, the similar sweet potato made its way to the United States from Latin America. Today the vegetables are used interchangeably in breads, casseroles, pies and puddings, many of them first produced by the Southern slaves.

BEGIN: 1½ HOURS AHEAD   8 SERVINGS

⅓   **cup butter or margarine**
½   **cup finely chopped carrot**
½   **cup finely chopped onion**
⅓   **cup chopped celery with leaves**
2   **cups hot mashed sweet potatoes**
2   **eggs, beaten**
2   **cups coarse soft bread crumbs**
1   **teaspoon grated orange peel**
2   **oranges, peeled and chopped**
½   **teaspoon salt**
¼   **teaspoon ground nutmeg**

1. Butter 1½-quart casserole. In 2-quart saucepan over medium-high heat, in hot butter, cook carrot, onion and celery until tender.

2. In large bowl with mixer at high speed, beat potatoes with eggs until fluffy. With spoon, stir in carrot mixture and remaining ingredients. Spoon dressing into prepared casserole.

3. Bake at 350°F. 30 minutes or until hot. Serve with poultry. Yields 6 cups.

TO MICROWAVE: In 1½-quart microwave-safe casserole, combine butter, carrot, onion and celery; cover. Microwave on HIGH 5 to 7 minutes until tender, stirring occasionally. In large bowl with mixer at high speed, beat potatoes with eggs until fluffy. With spoon, stir in remaining ingredients. Stir potato mixture into carrot mixture in casserole; cover. Microwave on HIGH 8 to 10 minutes until hot.

❋ Southern-Fried Chicken with Cream Gravy

If there is one chicken dish that inspires more controversy than any other, it is fried chicken. Cooks disagree about the coating (flour, crumbs or batter), the fat (salad oil, bacon fat, chicken fat, butter or lard), how to make the gravy (if any) and even how to cut up the chicken. But despite the disagreement, there are few Americans who don't enjoy a plate of fried chicken. Our recipe seasons the chicken only with salt and pepper, then makes gravy from thickened pan drippings and milk. It's a simple method that might have been used centuries ago.

BEGIN: 1½ HOURS AHEAD 4 TO 6 SERVINGS

½ cup all-purpose flour
1 teaspoon salt
¼ teaspoon pepper
2 pounds chicken parts
¼ cup bacon drippings or salad oil
1½ cups milk or light cream
1 tablespoon chopped parsley
   Hot cooked rice

1. In paper bag, combine flour, salt and pepper. Add chicken a few pieces at a time. Close bag and shake to coat chicken. Repeat with remaining chicken pieces. Reserve 2 tablespoons flour mixture.

2. In 10-inch skillet over medium-high heat, in hot bacon drippings, cook chicken pieces until well browned on all sides, turning frequently. Reduce heat to low. Cover; cook about 35 minutes until chicken is fork-tender, turning pieces occasionally. Uncover during last few minutes to crisp skin. Remove chicken pieces to warm platter; keep warm.

3. To make gravy: Pour off all but 2 tablespoons drippings from skillet; blend in 2 tablespoons reserved flour mixture. Over medium heat, cook until golden, stirring and scraping bits loose from skillet.

4. Gradually stir in milk; heat to boiling, stirring constantly. Cook 1 minute more. Stir in parsley and season to taste with additional salt and pepper.

5. To serve: Spoon gravy over chicken; serve remaining gravy over rice.

❋ Crispy Fried Chicken

This second recipe for fried chicken makes a spicy chicken with a crisp, light coating, much like the fried chicken popular at take-out stands all over the country. Home cooks like this version for picnics or other times when the chicken is served cold.

BEGIN: DAY AHEAD 4 TO 6 SERVINGS

1½ cups all-purpose flour
½ cup Italian salad dressing
2 pounds chicken parts
1 teaspoon baking powder
1 teaspoon paprika
½ teaspoon rubbed sage
¼ teaspoon salt
¼ teaspoon pepper
1 cup buttermilk
   Salad oil

1. In small bowl, combine ½ cup flour and Italian salad dressing to make a paste. Spread mixture all over chicken pieces to coat. Cover; refrigerate overnight.

2. *About 1½ hours before serving:* In pie plate, combine remaining 1 cup flour, baking powder, paprika, sage, salt and pepper. In another pie plate, place buttermilk. Dip chicken pieces in buttermilk, then in flour mixture.

3. In 10-inch skillet over medium-high heat, in ½ inch hot oil, cook chicken pieces until browned on all sides, carefully turning once. On wire rack in jelly-roll pan, arrange chicken pieces in single layer.

4. Bake at 350°F. 50 to 60 minutes until chicken is fork-tender.

✳ Oven-Fried Chicken with Mushroom Sauce

Oven-frying is easy, avoiding the close watching and spattering that can occur on the range-top. Variations for this method coat the chicken with crumbs made from bread, crackers, corn flakes, potato chips, or with cornmeal or flour.

BEGIN: 1½ HOURS AHEAD   4 TO 6 SERVINGS

½ cup all-purpose flour
½ teaspoon salt
⅛ teaspoon pepper
1 3- to 3½-pound broiler-fryer, cut up
2 tablespoons butter or margarine
½ cup sliced mushrooms or 1 can (4
   ounces) sliced mushrooms, drained
½ cup chicken broth
2 tablespoons lemon juice
1 tablespoon Worcestershire

1. In paper bag, combine flour, salt and pepper. Add chicken a few pieces at a time. Close bag and shake to coat chicken. Repeat with remaining chicken pieces.

2. In 13- by 9-inch baking dish, arrange chicken skin side up. Dot with butter. Bake at 350°F. 45 minutes.

3. Combine remaining ingredients. Pour over chicken. Bake 30 minutes more or until chicken is fork-tender, basting occasionally.

✳ Chicken Fricassee

A fricassee is a hearty, home-style chicken stew. A white fricassee starts with a well-seasoned stewed chicken and broth that is enriched with egg yolks and cream. This brown version begins by browning the chicken pieces, then making a creamy stew with mushrooms.

BEGIN: 2 HOURS AHEAD   4 TO 6 SERVINGS

½ cup all-purpose flour
1 teaspoon salt
¼ teaspoon pepper
2 pounds chicken parts
2 tablespoons salad oil
2 cups sliced mushrooms
½ cup chopped onion
½ cup chopped celery
2 tablespoons chopped parsley
2 cups water
½ cup heavy cream
1 tablespoon lemon juice (optional)
   Hot cooked rice

1. In paper bag, combine flour, salt and pepper. Add chicken a few pieces at a time. Close bag and shake to coat chicken. Repeat with remaining chicken pieces. Reserve ¼ cup flour mixture.

2. In 10-inch skillet over medium-high heat, in hot oil, cook chicken pieces until well browned on all sides, turning frequently. Pour off fat.

3. Add mushrooms, onion, celery, parsley and water. Over medium-high heat, heat to boiling. Reduce heat to low. Cover; simmer 1 hour or until chicken is fork-tender. Remove chicken to warm platter; keep warm.

4. In cup, stir cream into reserved flour mixture until smooth; gradually stir into pan juices. Over medium heat, heat to boiling, stirring constantly. Cook 1 minute more; stir in lemon juice. Pour sauce over chicken; serve with rice.

❄ Chicken with Dumplings

One of those classic homespun dishes that need no adorn-ment is Chicken with Dumplings, a favorite recipe for using hens whose laying days were over. Slow simmering tenderized the tough old birds, then a dumpling dough was added to the savory broth. This recipe is still enjoyed today, although stewing chickens are less common than they once were.

BEGIN: 2½ HOURS AHEAD   8 SERVINGS

1   **5-pound stewing chicken**
3   **stalks celery, sliced**
2   **carrots, sliced**
1   **onion, chopped**
2   **bay leaves**
2½   **teaspoons salt**
¼   **teaspoon pepper**
5   **cups water**
1½   **cups all-purpose flour**
1   **tablespoon baking powder**
1   **tablespoon chopped parsley**
½   **cup milk**
1   **egg**

1. Remove neck and giblets from inside chicken; cut chicken into serving pieces. Rinse under run-ning cold water. In 6-quart Dutch oven, combine chicken, neck, giblets, celery, carrots, onion, bay leaves, 2 teaspoons salt and pepper; add water. Over high heat, heat to boiling. Reduce heat to low. Cover; simmer 1½ hours or until chicken is fork-tender. Spoon off most of fat. Discard bay leaves.

2. Meanwhile, in medium bowl with fork, com-bine flour, baking powder, parsley and remain-ing ½ teaspoon salt. In small bowl with fork, mix milk and egg; slowly stir into flour mixture until soft dough forms.

3. Drop dough by heaping tablespoonfuls onto simmering chicken. Cover tightly; cook 20 min-utes without lifting cover.

4. To serve: Spoon chicken and dumplings into serving dish; spoon some of pan juices over.

❄ Chicken with Noodles

American families of German ancestry cooked old hens in a flavorful broth with plenty of homemade noodles. The Pennsylvania Dutch (who came from Germany, not from Holland) prepare a similar dish they call "potpie." It is a chicken stew cooked with noodles that have been cut into squares rather than strips.

BEGIN: 4 HOURS AHEAD   8 SERVINGS

    Homemade Noodles (see page 130)
1   **5-pound stewing chicken, cut up**
1   **onion, halved**
2   **cloves**
2   **stalks celery with tops, cut up**
1   **tablespoon salt**
8   **cups water**
2   **carrots, shredded**

1. Prepare Homemade Noodles, but do not cook.

2. In 6-quart Dutch oven, combine chicken, onion studded with cloves, celery, salt and water. Over high heat, heat to boiling. Reduce heat to low. Cover; simmer 1½ hours or until chicken is fork-tender. Discard onion pieces and celery.

3. Remove chicken from broth; cool until easy to handle. Remove meat from bones; discard skin and bones. Cut meat into bite-sized pieces; set aside. Spoon off and discard fat from broth.

4. Over high heat, heat broth to boiling; add noodles and carrots. Reduce heat to low; simmer 10 minutes or until noodles are tender. Add chicken pieces to noodle mixture; heat through.

5. To serve: With slotted spoon, serve chicken and noodles into bowls. Yields 12 cups.

TIP: 5 pounds of your favorite chicken parts can be substituted for the whole chicken.

CHICKEN POTPIE: Prepare Homemade Noodles, but cut rolled-out dough into 2-inch squares in-stead of long strips; proceed as in step 2.

❊ Glorified Chicken

In the early 1960s this simple recipe was developed, using canned soup to make cooking easy without sacrificing flavor. Recipes for Glorified Chicken appeared in advertisements, labels, cookbooks, magazines and newspapers, sometimes with additional seasonings and sometimes in this basic form. A modern-day classic, it has been adapted for new equipment and can be prepared in the microwave oven, slow-cooker and pressure cooker.

BEGIN: 1½ HOURS AHEAD   4 TO 6 SERVINGS

2   **tablespoons salad oil**
2   **pounds chicken parts**
1   **can (10¾ ounces) condensed cream of mushroom or golden mushroom soup**

1. In 10-inch skillet over medium-high heat, in hot oil, cook chicken pieces until browned on all sides. Pour off fat.

2. Stir in soup. Reduce heat to low. Cover; simmer 45 minutes or until chicken is fork-tender, turning occasionally.

OVEN GLORIFIED CHICKEN: In 12- by 8-inch baking dish, arrange chicken pieces skin side down. Drizzle with *2 tablespoons melted butter or margarine.* Bake at 375°F. 20 minutes. Turn chicken skin side up; bake 20 minutes more. In small bowl, stir soup; spoon over chicken. Bake 20 minutes more or until chicken is fork-tender. Stir sauce before serving.

TO MICROWAVE: Use ingredients as above, but omit oil and remove skin from chicken. In 12- by 8-inch microwave-safe baking dish, arrange chicken with thickest pieces toward the edge of dish; cover loosely. Microwave on HIGH 8 to 10 minutes until chicken is no longer pink, turning dish occasionally. Turn chicken pieces over. Pour soup over chicken, stirring into drippings. Microwave, uncovered, on HIGH 8 to 10 minutes until chicken is fork-tender, turning dish and stirring sauce occasionally.

❊ Barbecued Chicken

Outdoor cooking is a way of life for Americans in the summer. The barbecue varies with the part of the country. In New England, there are clambakes; in the Southeast, pork barbecue with peppery vinegar sauce. Southwestern barbecues feature beef. And at Hawaiian luaus, suckling pig is served with Polynesian-style sauce. Chicken barbecues are popular all across the country.

BEGIN: EARLY IN DAY   8 SERVINGS

1   **cup salad oil**
½   **cup lemon juice**
½   **cup sliced green onions**
2   **tablespoons chopped parsley**
2   **cloves garlic, minced**
1   **teaspoon salt**
½   **teaspoon paprika**
½   **teaspoon hot pepper sauce**
¼   **teaspoon pepper**
2   **3-pound broiler-fryers, quartered**

1. For marinade, in medium bowl, combine all ingredients except chickens. In 13- by 9-inch baking dish, pour marinade over chickens. Cover; marinate in refrigerator 4 hours or overnight.

2. *About 1½ hours before serving:* Prepare grill for barbecuing. Remove chicken from marinade; reserve marinade.

3. Grill chicken pieces over medium coals 1 hour, turning often and basting with marinade.

TIP: Give chicken a smoky flavor by using hickory or mesquite chips. Soak chips in water 1 hour before grilling, then sprinkle over coals. Grill chicken as above, adding more chips to coals after 30 minutes. If using covered grill, close cover for more smoky flavor.

❊ Teriyaki Chicken

Teriyaki entered American cuisine from Japan by way of Hawaii. The teriyaki marinade, which makes a shiny glaze, varies in seasonings but always includes soy sauce and wine. The Japanese use rice wine, either mirin *or* sake, *but in the United States, sherry often is substituted.*

BEGIN: DAY AHEAD   4 TO 6 SERVINGS

½   **cup soy sauce**
¼   **cup sugar**
¼   **cup dry sherry**
¼   **cup salad oil**
1   **tablespoon grated fresh ginger root or**
     ¾ **teaspoon ground ginger**
2   **cloves garlic, minced**
2   **pounds chicken parts**

1. In 13- by 9-inch baking dish, combine soy sauce, sugar, sherry, oil, ginger root and garlic. Place chicken in marinade; cover and refrigerate overnight, turning pieces occasionally.

2. *About 45 minutes before serving:* Remove chicken from marinade; reserve marinade. On rack in broiler pan, place chicken pieces skin side down.

3. Broil 6 inches from heat 35 to 45 minutes until chicken is fork-tender, basting chicken with marinade and turning occasionally with tongs.

BAKED TERIYAKI CHICKEN: Prepare as above in step 1, but place chicken skin side up in 13- by 9-inch baking dish. Bake at 375°F. 60 minutes or until fork-tender, basting chicken with marinade occasionally.

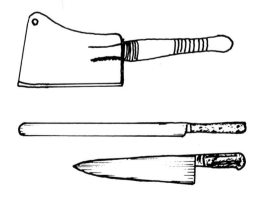

❊ Chicken Tetrazzini

Although the name sounds Italian, Chicken Tetrazzini is a thoroughly American dish created in San Francisco early in this century in honor of the great coloratura Luisa Tetrazzini. This version has become popular as an elegant last-minute dish for company meals.

BEGIN: 1 HOUR AHEAD   6 SERVINGS

¼   **cup butter or margarine**
1   **cup sliced mushrooms**
1   **small onion, chopped**
¼   **cup all-purpose flour**
½   **teaspoon salt**
1¾   **cups chicken broth**
1   **cup light cream**
2   **tablespoons dry sherry**
2   **cups cubed cooked chicken or turkey**
¼   **cup chopped pimentos**
2   **tablespoons chopped parsley**
8   **ounces spaghetti, cooked and drained**
½   **cup grated Parmesan cheese**

1. In 2-quart saucepan over medium-high heat, in hot butter, cook mushrooms and onion until tender. Stir in flour and salt until blended. Gradually stir in chicken broth. Cook until mixture boils, stirring constantly. Stir in cream, sherry, chicken, pimentos and parsley; heat until just boiling, stirring often. Remove from heat.

2. In 12- by 8-inch baking dish, spread spaghetti. Pour chicken mixture over spaghetti. Top with cheese. Bake at 450°F. 15 minutes or until cheese is golden.

EASY TETRAZZINI: Use ingredients as above but use only 2 tablespoons butter or margarine and omit flour, salt, chicken broth and cream. In 2-quart saucepan over medium-high heat, heat *only 2 tablespoons butter or margarine.* In butter, cook mushrooms and onion until tender. Stir in *2 cans (10¾ ounces each) condensed cream of chicken soup, 1 cup water* and sherry; heat through. Stir in chicken, pimentos and parsley; heat until just boiling, stirring often. Remove from heat. Proceed as in step 2.

✳ Country Captain

No one can agree on why this dish is named Country Captain. One mid-nineteenth century cookbook says it was created by a captain in British-controlled India. The fact that the dish is popular in the South gives credence to another story—that it was first prepared in Georgia with ingredients brought by a captain in the spice trade. A third tale says that no captain was involved at all; rather "captain" is a misunderstanding of the word "capon."

BEGIN: 1½ HOURS AHEAD   4 TO 6 SERVINGS

¼ **cup all-purpose flour**
1 **teaspoon salt**
⅛ **teaspoon pepper**
2 **pounds chicken parts**
2 **tablespoons butter or margarine**
1 **can (16 ounces) stewed tomatoes**
1 **cup sliced mushrooms**
1 **large green pepper, cut into 1-inch pieces**
½ **cup chopped onion**
¼ **cup raisins**
1 **clove garlic, minced**
1 **teaspoon curry powder**
¼ **teaspoon thyme leaves, crushed**
2 **tablespoons cold water**
1 **tablespoon cornstarch**
¼ **cup toasted slivered almonds**
   Hot cooked rice

1. In paper bag, combine flour, salt and pepper. Add chicken a few pieces at a time. Close bag and shake to coat chicken. Repeat with remaining chicken pieces.

2. In 10-inch skillet over medium heat, in hot butter, cook chicken pieces until well browned on all sides, turning frequently. Pour off fat.

3. In bowl, combine tomatoes, mushrooms, green pepper, onion, raisins, garlic, curry and thyme. Add to chicken; heat to boiling. Reduce heat to low. Cover; simmer 30 minutes or until chicken is fork-tender. Remove chicken pieces to warm platter; keep warm.

4. In cup, blend water into cornstarch until smooth. Stir into mixture in skillet. Over medium heat, heat to boiling, stirring constantly. Cook 1 minute more.

5. To serve: Pour sauce over chicken; garnish with almonds. Serve with rice.

Country Captain

❊ Georgia Chicken Bake

Georgia peaches and pecans combine with corn bread, another Southern favorite, to make a sophisticated stuffing for chicken breasts. The stuffing is tucked under the chicken's skin to absorb some of the juices and make an attractive serving.

BEGIN: 1½ HOURS AHEAD   6 SERVINGS

¼ **cup butter or margarine**
¼ **cup sliced green onions**
1   **can (16 ounces) sliced peaches**
¼ **cup chopped pecans or toasted almonds**
2   **cups corn bread stuffing mix**
3   **medium whole chicken breasts, split**
2   **tablespoons butter or margarine**
1   **cup orange juice**
1   **tablespoon cornstarch**
½ **cup halved seedless green grapes**
1   **tablespoon slivered orange peel**
⅛ **teaspoon ground cinnamon**
    Chopped parsley

1. In 3-quart saucepan over medium-high heat, in ¼ cup hot butter, cook green onions until tender, stirring occasionally. Meanwhile, drain peaches, reserving syrup. Add water to peach syrup to make 1 cup. Chop enough peaches to make ½ cup; reserve remaining peach slices. Add peach liquid, chopped peaches, pecans and stuffing mix to green onions; toss to mix well. Remove from heat; set aside.

2. With fingers, separate skin from breasts at one end to make a pocket. Spoon stuffing evenly into each pocket. Pull skin over stuffing; secure with toothpick, if necessary. Place breasts in 13-by 9-inch baking dish. Dot with remaining 2 tablespoons butter.

3. Bake at 325°F. 45 minutes or until chicken is fork-tender.

4. Meanwhile, in small saucepan, combine orange juice and cornstarch. Over medium heat, heat to boiling, stirring constantly. Add remaining peaches, grapes, orange peel and cinnamon. Heat to boiling. Reduce heat to low. Simmer 5 minutes.

5. To serve: Spoon fruit sauce over chicken; garnish with parsley.

TIP: To use fresh peaches, poach 4 peaches as directed in steps 1 and 2 of Peach Melba (see page 229). Slice peaches; substitute peaches and 1 cup poaching liquid for canned peaches and their syrup.

Georgia Chicken Bake

❋ Chicken Kiev

In this dish from the city of Kiev in the Ukraine, flattened chicken breasts are wrapped around chilled butter, then fried. The butter melts in its casing of crisp, fried chicken, and when the diner cuts into it, warm butter spurts out onto a bed of rice or kasha.

BEGIN: 4 HOURS AHEAD   6 SERVINGS

¾ **cup butter or margarine, softened**
2 **tablespoons chopped chives**
1 **tablespoon chopped parsley**
½ **teaspoon salt**
⅛ **teaspoon pepper**
3 **large whole chicken breasts, skinned, boned and split**
¼ **cup all-purpose flour**
1 **egg**
1 **tablespoon milk**
½ **cup dried bread crumbs**
   Salad oil
   Hot cooked rice or kasha

1. In small bowl, combine butter, chives, parsley, salt and pepper. On waxed paper, shape mixture into 6-inch-long roll; freeze 30 minutes.

2. Meanwhile, with smooth side of meat mallet, pound each chicken breast until ¼ inch thick.

3. Cut butter into six 1-inch rounds. Place one round in center of each piece of chicken. Roll up, enclosing butter completely. Secure with toothpicks.

4. Place flour on waxed paper; beat egg and milk in pie plate. Place crumbs on another sheet of waxed paper. Coat rolls with flour, then egg, then crumbs. In 13- by 9-inch baking dish, place rolls in single layer. Cover; refrigerate at least 2 hours.

5. In 4-quart saucepan, heat 2 inches oil to 350°F. Lower 3 rolls into oil. Fry 8 to 10 minutes until chicken is firm and browned. Do not pierce with fork. Drain on paper towels. Repeat with remaining chicken. Discard toothpicks; keep chicken warm in oven while frying remainder. Serve with rice or kasha.

OVEN CHICKEN KIEV: Prepare as above in steps 1 through 4. In 10-inch skillet over medium heat, in ½ inch hot oil, cook chicken until browned on all sides, turning frequently. Place chicken in 13- by 9-inch baking dish. Bake at 325°F. 20 minutes or until chicken feels firm when pressed with fork.

❋ Chicken à la King

Chicken à la King, a favorite choice for luncheon menus, is also a good way to use up leftover chicken. A comforting nineteenth-century dish, its origins are unknown. Some say the name is a corruption of Chicken à la Keene, and that it was created in London. Others say it began at the Brighton Beach Hotel in New York, and was named for a family in the hotel business named King.

BEGIN: 1 HOUR AHEAD   4 SERVINGS

2 **tablespoons butter or margarine**
1 **cup sliced mushrooms**
½ **cup green pepper strips**
¼ **cup sliced green onions**
1 **can (10¾ ounces) condensed cream of chicken soup**
⅓ **cup milk**
1½ **cups cubed cooked chicken**
2 **tablespoons chopped pimento**
2 **tablespoons dry sherry**
4 **baked patty shells or toast**

1. In 2-quart saucepan over medium heat, in hot butter, cook mushrooms, green pepper and onions until tender, stirring occasionally.

2. Stir in soup and milk. Add chicken and pimento; heat just to boiling, stirring occasionally. Stir in sherry.

3. To serve: Spoon chicken mixture into patty shells or over toast. Yields 4 cups.

❋ Arroz con Pollo

Arroz con Pollo is the Spanish name for chicken with rice. In Spain, the rice is cooked with chicken and vegetables, and seasoned with saffron. In Florida, with its Cuban and Puerto Rican influences, Arroz con Pollo might include olives, sweet peppers and capers. The Mexican Arroz con Pollo that is served in the Southwest is flavored with chilies and tomatoes.

BEGIN: 1½ HOURS AHEAD   4 TO 6 SERVINGS

1   3½-pound broiler-fryer, cut up
1   teaspoon salt
⅛   teaspoon pepper
⅛   teaspoon paprika
¼   cup olive oil
1   cup sliced mushrooms
1   medium onion, chopped
1   large clove garlic, minced
3½ cups chicken broth
1   can (28 ounces) tomatoes, chopped
½   teaspoon oregano leaves, crushed
¼   teaspoon saffron, crushed
1   bay leaf
2   cups raw regular long-grain rice
1   package (10 ounces) frozen peas
¼   cup pimento strips

1. Season chicken with salt, pepper and paprika. In 5-quart Dutch oven over medium-high heat, in hot oil, cook chicken pieces, a few at a time, until browned on all sides; set aside.

2. Over medium heat, in hot drippings, cook mushrooms, onion and garlic until onion is tender, stirring occasionally. Stir in broth, tomatoes, oregano, saffron and bay leaf; heat to boiling.

3. Add rice and chicken. Reduce heat to low. Cover; simmer 30 minutes or until chicken is almost fork-tender. Add peas and pimento; cook 15 minutes more or until chicken is fork-tender. Discard bay leaf.

Arroz con Pollo

❋ Chicken Pie

Meat and poultry pies were popular among colonists from England. Some were made of whole stuffed birds in pastry; in others, the pastry enclosed sliced or chopped poultry in gravy, seasoned with vegetables, chestnuts, mushrooms, herbs, wine and spices. Some pies were even sweetened. One popular variation included oysters, and today makes an elegant dish for entertaining.

BEGIN: 2 HOURS AHEAD   6 TO 8 SERVINGS

¼ cup butter or margarine
1½ cups sliced celery
1   cup sliced carrots
1   cup chopped onions
1¼ cups all-purpose flour
1¾ cups chicken broth
3   cups cooked chicken or turkey, cut into
        1-inch pieces
½   cup heavy cream
¼   cup chopped parsley
½   teaspoon poultry seasoning
⅛   teaspoon pepper
¾   teaspoon salt
½   teaspoon baking powder
⅓   cup butter or margarine
1   egg yolk
1   to 2 tablespoons cold water

1. In 4-quart saucepan over medium-high heat, in ¼ cup hot butter, cook celery, carrots and onions until tender, stirring occasionally.

2. Stir in ¼ cup flour until blended. Gradually stir in broth; cook until mixture boils, stirring constantly. Stir in chicken, cream, parsley, poultry seasoning, pepper and ½ teaspoon salt. Spoon chicken mixture into 12- by 8-inch baking dish.

3. Preheat oven to 425°F. In medium bowl, combine remaining 1 cup flour, remaining ¼ teaspoon salt and baking powder. With pastry blender or 2 knives used scissor-fashion, cut in remaining ⅓ cup butter until mixture resembles coarse crumbs.

4. Stir in egg yolk. Add cold water, mixing lightly with fork until pastry just holds together. With hands, shape pastry into ball.

5. On lightly floured surface, roll pastry to 14- by 10-inch rectangle. With knife, cut slashes or design in center of rectangle. Place pastry loosely over filling.

6. With kitchen shears, trim edge, leaving 1-inch overhang; fold overhang under. Make a high stand-up edge; flute edge.

7. Bake 25 minutes or until crust is golden.

CHICKEN-OYSTER PIE: Prepare as above but add *1 pint shucked oysters, drained and halved,* along with the chicken.

❋ Creamy Chicken Casserole

The casserole has become a staple of American cuisine, especially for such occasions as potluck dinners, family reunions and church suppers. Most casseroles are composed of meat, a starchy ingredient and a flavorful sauce to make a hearty, often thrifty, meal that can be prepared ahead.

BEGIN: 1 HOUR AHEAD   8 SERVINGS

2   tablespoons butter or margarine
½   cup chopped onion
1   can (10¾ ounces) condensed cream of
        chicken soup
1   can (10¾ ounces) condensed cream of
        mushroom soup
1   cup milk
⅛   teaspoon pepper
3   cups cubed cooked chicken or ham
4   cups cooked noodles
½   cup shredded Cheddar cheese

1. In 4-quart saucepan over medium-high heat, in hot butter, cook onion until tender. Stir in soups, milk and pepper. Stir in chicken and noodles. Pour into 3-quart casserole.

2. Bake at 400°F. 25 minutes or until hot; stir. Sprinkle with cheese. Bake 5 minutes more or until cheese melts. Yields 8 cups.

To Microwave: In 3-quart microwave-safe casserole, combine butter and onion; cover. Microwave on HIGH 4 to 5 minutes until tender. Stir in soups, milk and pepper. Stir in chicken and noodles; cover. Microwave on HIGH 10 to 12 minutes until hot, stirring occasionally. Sprinkle with cheese; cover. Let stand 2 to 3 minutes until cheese is melted.

❋ Sunday Chicken Bake

Sunday Chicken Bake turns up in fund-raising cookbooks all over the country. Nearly everyone knows someone who claims to have created this rich, slow-cooking dish. One reason for its popularity is that a cook can put it into the oven before going to church, then return home to find it bubbling and ready to serve.

BEGIN: 4½ HOURS AHEAD   8 SERVINGS

1   jar (2½ ounces) sliced dried beef, rinsed
      and drained
4   whole chicken breasts, skinned, boned
      and split
1   can (10¾ ounces) condensed cream of
      mushroom soup
½   cup sour cream
4   slices bacon, halved crosswise and
      partially cooked
      Hot cooked rice
      Chopped parsley

1. Preheat oven to 300°F. In 12- by 8-inch baking dish, arrange beef in single layer. Place chicken on beef. In small bowl, combine soup and sour cream; mix well. Pour over chicken; top with bacon. Cover.

2. Reduce oven heat to 250°F. Bake chicken 2 hours. Uncover; stir soup mixture around edges of dish. Bake uncovered 2 hours more.

3. To serve: Serve chicken over rice. Spoon sauce over all; sprinkle with parsley.

Tip: To speed preparation: Bake covered dish at 325°F. 1 hour; uncover. Stir; bake 30 minutes more.

❋ Chicken Livers with Apples

For every chicken that's cooked, there's a chicken liver and gizzard left over. Many cooks will prepare these parts along with the chicken, but others save them to cook separately. There are many uses for the livers, such as middle-European chopped liver, French pâté, Oriental rumaki and Cajun dirty rice. This recipe accents American liver and onions with the sweet taste of apple.

BEGIN: 30 MINUTES AHEAD   2 TO 3 SERVINGS

2   tablespoons butter or margarine
1   small apple, peeled and diced
1   small onion, cut into wedges
½   pound chicken livers, each cut in half
1   tablespoon all-purpose flour
½   cup water
1   tablespoon dry sherry
1   tablespoon chopped parsley
¼   teaspoon salt
      Dash pepper
      Buttered toast or hot cooked rice
      Apple slices

1. In 10-inch skillet over medium-high heat, in hot butter, cook diced apple and onion until tender, stirring often. With slotted spoon, remove apple and onion to bowl.

2. In remaining butter in skillet, cook chicken livers about 5 minutes until done, stirring often. With slotted spoon, remove livers to bowl.

3. To drippings remaining in pan, stir in flour. Gradually stir in water. Stir in sherry, parsley, salt and pepper.

4. Over medium heat, heat to boiling, stirring constantly. Return livers, apple and onion to pan; cook 1 minute more. Serve over toast or rice. Garnish with apple slices.

❋ Chop Suey

Chop Suey is not Chinese, but an American dish that originated in the West. It probably was first prepared to resemble the food that many workers on the transcontinental railroad had eaten in their native China, but adapted to use readily available ingredients.

BEGIN: 1 HOUR AHEAD   6 SERVINGS

2   **tablespoons soy sauce**
2   **tablespoons cornstarch**
1¾ **cups chicken broth**
3   **tablespoons salad oil**
2   **cups shredded cabbage or Chinese cabbage**
1   **large onion, sliced**
2   **stalks celery, diagonally sliced**
2   **cups sliced mushrooms**
2   **cups cooked chicken or turkey cut into julienne strips**
2   **cups fresh or canned bean sprouts, drained**
½ **cup sliced water chestnuts**
    Hot cooked rice or chow mein noodles

1. In small bowl, blend soy sauce with cornstarch until smooth. Stir in chicken broth; set aside.

2. In 10-inch skillet or wok over high heat, in hot oil, cook cabbage, onion, celery and mushrooms, stirring quickly and frequently (stir-frying) about 3 minutes or until tender-crisp.

3. With slotted spoon, remove vegetables to bowl, leaving oil in skillet. To oil remaining in skillet, add chicken strips; stir-fry 3 minutes or until lightly browned. Add bean sprouts and water chestnuts; stir-fry 1 minute. Add cooked vegetables; stir-fry 1 minute.

4. Stir soy sauce mixture to mix; gradually stir into hot mixture in skillet and cook, stirring constantly until thickened. Serve immediately over rice or chow mein noodles. Serve with additional soy sauce. Yields 5 cups.

❋ Scalloped Turkey

Leftover turkey from the Thanksgiving or Christmas bird has inspired culinary creativity in casseroles, stir-frys, salads, soups and sandwiches. This layered casserole recaptures the holiday flavor for stuffing fanciers.

BEGIN: 1¾ HOURS AHEAD   8 SERVINGS

¼ **cup butter or margarine**
2   **stalks celery, chopped**
1   **large onion, chopped**
¼ **cup all-purpose flour**
1   **teaspoon salt**
½ **teaspoon rubbed sage**
¼ **teaspoon pepper**
1   **can (10¾ ounces) condensed chicken broth**
2½ **cups water**
4   **cups cubed cooked turkey or chicken**
1   **package (8 ounces) herb-seasoned stuffing mix**

1. In 3-quart saucepan over medium-high heat, in hot butter, cook celery and onion until vegetables are tender. Stir in flour, salt, sage and pepper until well blended. Stir in chicken broth and water. Over high heat, heat to boiling, stirring constantly. Remove from heat. Stir in turkey; set aside.

2. Prepare stuffing mix as label directs. Spoon ½ of the reserved turkey mixture into 13- by 9-inch baking dish. Top with ½ of the stuffing mixture. Repeat layers.

3. Bake at 325°F. 45 minutes or until golden.

❋ Chicken Divan

Many versions of Chicken Divan have appeared in cookbooks and restaurants since the turn of the century. It always includes chicken or turkey and broccoli; the sauce can change. Sometimes it is a Cheddar cheese sauce, sometimes a lemony Hollandaise, sometimes one made with mayonnaise or condensed soup.

BEGIN: 1 HOUR AHEAD   6 SERVINGS

¼ cup butter or margarine
1 cup chopped mushrooms
3 tablespoons all-purpose flour
½ teaspoon salt
1½ cups milk
1 tablespoon dry sherry
⅛ teaspoon ground nutmeg
1 pound fresh broccoli, cut into spears, or
    1 package (10 ounces) frozen broccoli
    spears, cooked and drained
1 pound cooked chicken or turkey meat,
    sliced or cubed
¼ cup grated Parmesan cheese or ½ cup
    shredded Cheddar cheese

1. In 2-quart saucepan over medium-high heat, in hot butter, cook mushrooms until tender. Stir in flour and salt until blended. Gradually stir in milk; cook until mixture boils, stirring constantly. Stir in sherry and nutmeg; set aside.

2. In 10- by 6-inch baking dish, place broccoli spears in single layer. Arrange chicken or turkey over broccoli. Pour mushroom mixture over all; sprinkle with cheese.

3. Bake at 450°F. 15 minutes or until hot.

SOUPER CHICKEN DIVAN: Prepare as above but omit first 4 ingredients and reduce milk to ¼ cup. In small bowl, stir together *1 can (10¾ ounces) condensed cream of mushroom soup,* the ¼ cup milk, sherry and nutmeg. Proceed as in step 2.

Chicken Divan, Chicken with Dumplings

Shrimp Jambalaya, Turbans of Sole, Trout Amandine, Sautéed Smelt

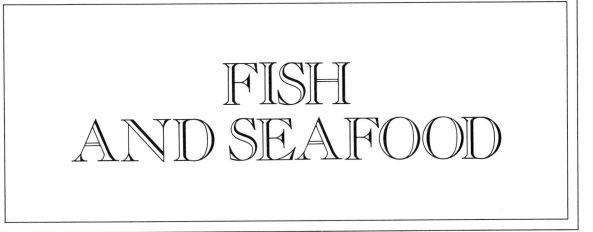

FISH AND SEAFOOD

America's lakes, rivers and coastlines have always boasted an abundance of fish. In Colonial days, the variety was stupendous; there were probably more types of fish at that time than at any other in our history. European fishermen traveled across the Atlantic to fish off the American coasts, then carried their catch back to Europe. Tales of the Colonial era tell of lobsters more than two feet long, in such abundance that they piled up on beaches after a storm. Other fish were so plentiful that Captain John Smith said that he thought he might catch them in a skillet.

American Indians made the most of this bounty, originating many of the fishing and cooking methods we use today. They cooked fish by the fire, often on planks propped up near the flames. They steamed seafood and used it in soups. Surplus fish was smoked for later consumption.

The Pilgrims were poor fishermen at first. They had not brought proper fishing gear with them from England, but they were able to gather some of the shellfish along the shores and catch eels with their hands.

The Indians taught them how to prepare a feast of seafood and vegetables, a forerunner of the New England clambake. To prepare one today, dig a shallow pit and line it with rocks. Build a fire in the pit and let it burn until the rocks are red hot. Sweep away the ashes, line the pit with wet rockweed, and then add your choice of clams, fish, lobsters, sausages, chicken, corn and potatoes. Cover everything with branches or a tarpaulin and wait an hour or so for it to be done.

A clambake is usually a community event. Other parts of the country have their own ways of preparing local specialties for such occasions, many with roots in the Indian tradition. There are fish fries in the South, crab feasts on the Atlantic and Gulf coasts, fish boils in the Wisconsin lake country and fish cookouts in California.

Our marine population has changed since the Europeans first reached these shores. No longer will you find two-foot-long lobsters on the beaches, or the bounty of oysters that made them so inexpensive. Pollution and unsound fishing practices have diminished the populations of fish and shellfish, but conservation practices are helping them recover. Fish farmers have developed ways of raising catfish, trout and other fish in controlled environments. And sport fishermen have stocked lakes and rivers with fish that never swam there before. That's how smelt and salmon came to live in the Great Lakes.

Americans eat more fish each year. As part of the move toward a healthier diet, many Americans have turned to low-calorie, low-fat fish as an alternative to meat. Cooked in traditional ways or by new methods, fish and seafood provide delicious, healthful meals.

✳ Shrimp-Stuffed Red Snapper

The red snapper is a fish that prefers the warm waters of the Gulf of Mexico and the South Atlantic. However, fresh snapper is now available in markets in all parts of North America. Red snapper is considered essential to a New Orleans bouillabaisse, as well as to various Florida fish stews. In northern states, it is more often baked, stuffed with seafood.

BEGIN: 1½ HOURS AHEAD   4 SERVINGS

2	1½-pound whole red snapper or sea bass, dressed
	Salt
	Pepper
¼	cup butter or margarine
⅓	cup finely chopped green onions
¾	cup finely chopped celery
½	pound shrimp, cooked, shelled, deveined and chopped
½	cup seasoned dried bread crumbs
½	cup sliced almonds
¼	cup dry white wine
1	egg, beaten
	Salad oil

1. Oil large shallow roasting pan. Sprinkle inside and outside of each fish with salt and pepper. Place fish in pan.

2. In 2-quart saucepan over medium-high heat, in hot butter, cook green onions and celery until vegetables are tender-crisp. Stir in shrimp, crumbs, almonds, wine and egg.

3. With spoon, lightly fill one fish cavity with ½ of the shrimp mixture. Skewer cavity closed with toothpicks. Brush fish with oil. Repeat with remaining fish and stuffing.

4. Bake at 350°F. 35 minutes or until fish flakes easily when tested with fork, brushing occasionally with oil.

5. With pancake turner, lift fish to warm platter. Remove toothpicks.

✳ Poached Salmon

It is said that Abigail Adams, wife of our second President, began the tradition of serving poached salmon with a creamy egg sauce on the Fourth of July. She served it with the seasonal new potatoes and green peas.

BEGIN: 1½ HOURS AHEAD   8 SERVINGS

8	cups water
4	cups dry white wine
1	large onion, coarsely chopped
1	celery stalk, cut up
1	carrot, sliced
5	parsley sprigs
2	bay leaves
½	teaspoon rosemary leaves, crushed
½	teaspoon thyme leaves, crushed
½	teaspoon salt
¼	teaspoon pepper
1	3-pound whole salmon, dressed
	Watercress
	Lemon slices
	Egg Sauce (see page 122) or Green Sauce*

1. In fish poacher or covered roasting pan (long enough for fish) with rack, over high heat, heat first 11 ingredients to boiling. Reduce heat to low. Cover; simmer 30 minutes.

2. Fold several thicknesses of cheesecloth to make a rectangle at least twice as wide and about 12 inches longer than fish. Center fish on cloth. Fold long sides of cloth over fish; tie knots in ends of cloth to secure fish. Lower salmon onto rack in simmering mixture; cover.

3. Over medium-low heat, simmer until fish flakes easily when tested with fork, allowing 10 minutes per inch of thickness at the thickest part. Cool slightly in broth. Remove fish from broth; carefully remove and discard skin.

4. To serve: Place salmon on platter; garnish with watercress and lemon slices. Serve warm with Egg Sauce or cold with Green Sauce.

*Green Sauce

This herb mayonnaise adds freshness to poached salmon, cold fish and poultry. It makes a fine dip for chips and raw vegetables as well.

¼ cup watercress, stems removed
¼ cup parsley sprigs, stems removed
¼ cup spinach torn into pieces
1 tablespoon chopped green onion
⅛ teaspoon chervil leaves, crushed
⅛ teaspoon tarragon leaves, crushed

4 cups boiling water
½ cup mayonnaise
½ cup sour cream or plain yogurt
Dash pepper

1. In sieve, combine first 6 ingredients. Pour boiling water over greens. Drain well.

2. In covered blender container at medium speed, blend greens with mayonnaise until smooth; turn into small bowl. Fold in sour cream and pepper. Cover; refrigerate until serving time. Yields 1 cup.

Poached Salmon, Green Sauce

✳ Wild Rice-Stuffed Northern Pike

The northern pike swims in the fresh waters of northern North America, where it is a favorite game fish. Sometimes known as "great northern" or simply "pike," the fish is especially popular in Minnesota, where it often is stuffed with another Minnesota specialty, wild rice.

BEGIN: 1½ HOURS AHEAD   4 SERVINGS

¼ cup raw wild rice
1¾ cups water
½ teaspoon salt
¼ cup raw regular long-grain rice
1 tablespoon butter or margarine
½ cup sliced mushrooms
¼ cup thinly sliced celery
1 green onion, sliced
¼ teaspoon thyme leaves, crushed
1 tablespoon chopped pimento
2 northern pike fillets (about 1½ pounds)
2 tablespoons butter or margarine, melted

1. Wash wild rice thoroughly in warm water; drain well.

2. In 3-quart saucepan over high heat, heat water to boiling. Stir in wild rice and salt. Reduce heat to low. Cover; simmer 25 minutes.

3. Stir in long-grain rice. Cover; simmer 20 minutes more or until all water is absorbed and rice is tender.

4. Meanwhile, in 10-inch skillet over medium-high heat, in 1 tablespoon hot butter, cook mushrooms, celery, onion and thyme until vegetables are tender. Stir in pimento. Add mixture to rice; toss to combine.

5. Place one fish fillet on rack in broiler pan. Spread rice mixture on fillet; top with second fillet. Brush with melted butter.

6. Bake at 350°F. 25 to 30 minutes until fish flakes easily when tested with fork.

TIP: If you have extra rice mixture, keep it warm, then serve with fish.

✳ Trout Meunière

Meunière is fish served with browned butter. It's even more elegant when almonds are added to the butter and toasted.

BEGIN: 45 MINUTES AHEAD   6 SERVINGS

¼ cup all-purpose flour
½ teaspoon salt
⅛ teaspoon pepper
½ cup milk
6 8-ounce whole brook or rainbow trout, pan-dressed
¼ cup salad oil
¼ cup butter or margarine
2 tablespoons lemon juice
2 tablespoons chopped parsley
   Lemon wedges

1. On waxed paper, combine flour, salt and pepper. Into pie plate, pour milk. Using tongs, dip trout in milk, then coat with flour mixture.

2. In 10-inch skillet over medium heat, in hot oil, fry fish, a few at a time, 4 minutes on each side or until fish flakes easily when tested with a fork.

3. With pancake turner, lift cooked fish onto warm platter; keep warm until all fish are cooked. Pour off all drippings from skillet; wipe skillet with paper towels.

4. In same skillet over medium heat, heat butter until golden brown. Stir in lemon and parsley; pour over fish. Garnish with lemon wedges.

TROUT AMANDINE: Prepare as above but add *½ cup sliced almonds* to butter in step 4. Cook until butter and almonds are golden brown. Proceed as above.

❀ Southern-Fried Catfish

In the South and parts of the Midwest, catfish is one of the most popular fish. Caught in local streams by the family angler, the catfish is coated with cornmeal and fried in an iron skillet or in a huge vat of hot fat for a community fish fry. Southerners accompany fried catfish with some type of corn bread (usually hush puppies) and coleslaw.

BEGIN: 45 MINUTES AHEAD   6 SERVINGS

6   **1-pound whole catfish, dressed**
1   **cup cornmeal**
2   **tablespoons all-purpose flour**
½   **teaspoon salt**
¼   **teaspoon pepper**
¼   **cup milk**
     Salad oil
     Hush Puppies (see page 207)

1. Skin fish; remove and discard head and tail. Set fish aside.

2. On waxed paper, combine cornmeal, flour, salt and pepper. Into pie plate, pour milk. Using tongs, dip each fish in milk, then coat well with cornmeal mixture.

3. In 10-inch skillet over medium heat, heat ½ inch oil to 375°F. Fry fish, a few at a time, 5 to 6 minutes on each side until fish flakes easily when tested with fork.

4. With pancake turner, lift cooked fish onto warm platter; keep warm until all fish are cooked. Serve with Hush Puppies.

TIP: To skin catfish: With sharp knife, slit skin all the way around fish just below head. Using pliers, grasp skin above back fin and pull away from body.

Southern-Fried Catfish, Hush Puppies, Creamy Coleslaw

❋ Sautéed Smelt

Smelt are little fish that thrive in the cold water of northern rivers and lakes. John Smith found smelt so abundant in New England that they could easily be scooped into baskets. In the West, Indians dried smelt, which had a high oil content, and burned it as a candle, giving the fish the nickname "candlefish." Today smelt are popular around the Great Lakes, Northeast and Northwest: usually they are deep-fried or sautéed.

BEGIN: 45 MINUTES AHEAD 4 SERVINGS

¼ cup all-purpose flour
¼ cup crushed saltines
¼ teaspoon salt
⅛ teaspoon pepper
⅛ teaspoon paprika
1 egg
1 tablespoon milk
1 pound smelt, pan-dressed
¼ cup salad oil
2 tablespoons butter or margarine
  Lemon wedges

1. On waxed paper, combine flour, crumbs, salt, pepper and paprika. In pie plate with fork, beat egg with milk. Using tongs, dip smelt, one at a time, into egg mixture, then coat with crumb mixture.

2. In 10-inch skillet over medium heat, heat oil and butter. Fry fish, a few at a time, 2 minutes on each side or until fish flakes easily when tested with fork.

3. With pancake turner, lift cooked fish onto warm platter; keep warm until all fish are cooked. Garnish with lemon wedges.

❋ Lemon-Buttered Flounder

The flounder is a flatfish, with the flatfish's fascinating anatomy. Born with normal features, its skull begins to twist after birth, and one eye migrates to the opposite side of the head, putting both eyes on the same side of the fish. These fish swim near the ocean floor, with both eyes looking up from a skin that camouflages them against the sand. The flatfish family, including flounder, sole, halibut and turbot, have a delicate flavor that is delicious in elaborate dishes or when prepared simply.

BEGIN: 15 MINUTES AHEAD 4 SERVINGS

¼ cup butter or margarine, melted
2 tablespoons lemon juice
¼ teaspoon salt
  Dash white pepper
1 pound flounder fillets
  Paprika
  Lemon wedges
  Parsley sprigs

1. In small bowl with fork, mix butter, lemon juice, salt and pepper. Place fillets on rack in broiler pan; brush with butter mixture.

2. Broil 4 inches from heat 6 to 8 minutes until fish flakes easily when tested with fork, occasionally basting with butter mixture.

3. To serve: With pancake turner, lift fillets onto warm plate; sprinkle with paprika. Garnish with lemon wedges and parsley.

LEMON-BUTTERED MONKFISH: Prepare as above but substitute *1 pound monkfish fillets* for flounder; broil 10 to 12 minutes until fish flakes easily when tested with fork.

TO MICROWAVE: In 12- by 8-inch microwave-safe baking dish, place butter. Microwave on HIGH 1 minute until melted. Stir in lemon juice, salt and pepper. Add fillets, turning to coat with butter mixture; cover. Microwave on HIGH 5 to 7 minutes until fish flakes when tested with fork, turning dish occasionally. Let stand 2 minutes before serving. Proceed as in step 3.

✳ Pompano en Papillote

The pompano is caught in the warm waters of the South Atlantic and Gulf of Mexico. The demand for it is so great that Northerners rarely have a chance to sample this delicious fish. The most famous way to cook it is as Pompano en Papillote, *created at Antoine's in New Orleans in honor of a balloonist—the paper package around the fish inflates during cooking to resemble a balloon.*

BEGIN: 1½ HOURS AHEAD · 6 SERVINGS

   Parchment paper
   Salad oil
1   carrot, sliced
1   stalk celery, sliced
2   green onions, sliced
2   cups water
1   cup dry white wine
1   bay leaf
3   peppercorns
¼   teaspoon salt
6   pompano or perch fillets (about 6 ounces each)
4   tablespoons butter or margarine
½   pound medium shrimp, shelled and deveined
1   cup sliced mushrooms
1   clove garlic, minced
1   tablespoon chopped chives (optional)
⅛   teaspoon thyme leaves, crushed
3   tablespoons all-purpose flour
¼   cup milk or light cream

1. Cut out 6 parchment hearts about 12 inches long by 15 inches wide. Oil lightly.

2. In 10-inch skillet over high heat, heat carrot, celery, onions, water, wine, bay leaf, peppercorns and salt to boiling. Reduce heat to low. Cover; simmer 5 minutes. Gently place 3 fish fillets in simmering liquid. Cover; simmer 5 minutes or until fish flakes easily when tested with fork. With slotted pancake turner, place one fish fillet on one half of each parchment heart; set aside. Repeat with remaining fillets. Strain poaching liquid; reserve 1 cup liquid.

3. In same skillet over medium-high heat, in 2 tablespoons hot butter, cook shrimp, mushrooms, garlic, chives and thyme 2 minutes. Divide mixture equally over fish fillets.

4. In same skillet over medium heat, heat remaining 2 tablespoons butter until melted. Add flour; stir together until smooth. Gradually stir in the 1 cup reserved poaching liquid; cook until mixture boils, stirring constantly. Stir in milk until smooth. Spoon sauce over prepared fish.

5. Fold other half of each parchment heart over fish. Starting at top, roll and crimp edges tightly together. Place on baking sheets.

6. Bake at 450°F. 8 to 10 minutes until paper is lightly browned.

7. To serve: With pancake turner, lift packets onto warm plates; slit paper.

Pompano en Papillote

❋ Crab-Stuffed Sole Fillets

Sole is valued for its white flesh and the delicate flavor that goes well with other foods. It is a favorite for stuffing with crab and other subtly flavored ingredients.

BEGIN: 1 HOUR AHEAD   4 SERVINGS

8   sole or other fish fillets (about 1½
      pounds)
2   tablespoons butter or margarine
¼   cup chopped celery
1   green onion, thinly sliced
½   pound cooked crabmeat, picked over
¼   cup dried bread crumbs
1   tablespoon chopped parsley
6   tablespoons mayonnaise
2   teaspoons prepared brown mustard
½   teaspoon Worcestershire
¼   teaspoon salt
      Dash pepper
      Lemon juice
      Paprika

1. Generously butter 13- by 9-inch baking pan. Arrange 4 fish fillets in pan; set aside.

2. In 2-quart saucepan over medium-high heat, in hot butter, cook celery and green onion until tender. Remove from heat. Stir in crab, bread crumbs, parsley, 2 tablespoons mayonnaise, 1 teaspoon mustard, Worcestershire, salt and pepper.

3. Spoon crabmeat mixture onto fillets in pan, mounding stuffing in center of each. Top each with one remaining fish fillet, joining edges. Brush fish with lemon juice.

4. Bake at 350°F. 10 minutes.

5. Meanwhile, in cup, combine remaining 4 tablespoons mayonnaise and remaining 1 teaspoon mustard. Spread evenly on fish fillets.

6. Bake 10 minutes more or until fish flakes easily when tested with a fork. Sprinkle with paprika before serving.

❋ Turbans of Sole

Sole is the fish of choice for these elegant spinach-filled "turbans" because its fillets are thin enough to shape easily. These may be made in small shapes for appetizers or larger ones for a main dish.

BEGIN: 1 HOUR AHEAD   4 SERVINGS

1½ pounds sole fillets
1   package (10 ounces) frozen chopped
      spinach, cooked and well drained
1   package (3 ounces) cream cheese, cubed,
      at room temperature
¼   cup milk
¼   teaspoon salt
¼   teaspoon chervil leaves or basil leaves
1   egg
¼   cup dried bread crumbs
¼   cup grated Parmesan cheese
      Hollandaise Sauce (see page 167)

1. Butter four 10-ounce custard cups. Line sides and bottoms with *thin* pieces of fish fillet (slice fillets horizontally if necessary), reserving about ¼ pound fish.

2. In covered blender container at high speed, blend spinach, cream cheese, milk, salt and chervil until almost smooth. Add egg; blend until *very* smooth, scraping sides of blender container occasionally. Stir in bread crumbs and Parmesan cheese.

3. Divide spinach mixture among prepared custard cups. Cover with remaining thin fish pieces.

4. Set custard cups in baking pan; place on oven rack. Add boiling water to baking pan to reach halfway up side of custard cups. Bake at 325°F. 35 minutes or until set in center. Remove cups from water bath.

5. Let stand 5 minutes. Drain excess liquid from fish. Invert onto serving platter. Serve with Hollandaise Sauce.

To Microwave: Prepare as above through step 3. Place custard cups in microwave oven. Microwave on HIGH 12 to 14 minutes until set in center, rearranging cups in oven twice. Proceed as in step 5.

Tip: To serve as an appetizer course, assemble turbans in six 5-ounce custard cups. Bake in conventional oven about 30 minutes.

Tip: For a different look, line only sides of custard cups with fish, leaving bottoms empty before filling with spinach mixture.

❉ Grilled Swordfish Steaks

Although cooking over a fire is one of the oldest ways to prepare fish, it is also one of the trendiest. A delicate marinade gives the fish a sparkling flavor; with the low-calorie fish, it is typical of the light eating Americans favor today.

BEGIN: 1 HOUR AHEAD   6 SERVINGS

1½ **pounds swordfish or other fish steaks, cut 1 inch thick**
¼ **cup salad oil**
2 **tablespoons lime or lemon juice**
2 **tablespoons chopped parsley**
1 **teaspoon dill weed, crushed**
¼ **teaspoon salt**
¼ **teaspoon pepper**

1. Cut fish steaks into 6 serving portions. Place in single layer in 10- by 6-inch baking dish.

2. In small bowl, combine remaining ingredients. Pour over fish. Cover; refrigerate 30 minutes, turning fish once.

3. Prepare grill for barbecuing.

4. *About 15 minutes before serving:* Drain fish, reserving marinade. Place fish on grill over medium coals. Cook about 15 minutes until fish flakes easily when tested with fork, turning once and basting often with marinade.

❉ Eastern Codfish Balls

Perhaps no food has been so disparaged yet so revered as the codfish. The fish owes its paradoxical reputation to its abundance and good drying quality. Because of this, it was a staple food for travelers as early as the sixteenth century. The cod was so vital to New England's eighteenth-century economy, that a statue of the fish was given a place of honor in the legislative chambers of Massachusetts; it is known to this day as the Sacred Cod.

BEGIN: DAY AHEAD   6 SERVINGS

1 **pound salt cod**
4 **medium potatoes, quartered**
2 **tablespoons butter or margarine**
1 **small onion, chopped**
½ **cup finely chopped celery**
2 **tablespoons chopped parsley**
1 **clove garlic, minced**
1 **egg**
⅛ **teaspoon white pepper**
    Salad oil

1. Soak cod in cold water several hours or overnight, changing water several times.

2. *One hour before serving:* In 3-quart saucepan, place potatoes. Add water to cover. Over high heat, heat to boiling. Reduce heat to low. Cover; simmer 20 minutes or until potatoes are fork-tender. Drain; mash until smooth. Set aside.

3. Meanwhile, in 10-inch skillet over medium-high heat, in hot butter, cook onion, celery, parsley and garlic until vegetables are tender.

4. Rinse cod in cold water; pat dry with paper towels. In large bowl with fork, flake fish. Stir in mashed potatoes, vegetables, egg and pepper. Shape mixture into 2-inch balls.

5. In 4-quart saucepan, heat 2 inches oil to 375°F. Fry cod balls, a few at a time, until golden on all sides. Drain on paper towels; keep warm. Yields 24 balls.

✳ Redfish Court-Bouillon

Redfish Court-Bouillon is one of the classic seafood dishes of New Orleans. Like many other Creole and Cajun specialties, it is a spicy, tomato-based dish with a hearty quality. Redfish, also known as red drum, channel bass and red bass, is the first choice, but red snapper, halibut and bluefish make good substitutes. Whatever fish you use, the traditional name for the stew remains Redfish Court-Bouillon.

BEGIN: 2 HOURS AHEAD   8 SERVINGS

½   **cup salad oil or bacon drippings**
½   **cup all-purpose flour**
2   **large onions, chopped**
2   **medium green peppers, chopped**
1   **stalk celery, chopped**
2   **cloves garlic, minced**
1   **can (16 ounces) tomatoes, cut up**
2   **cups water**
1   **cup dry red wine**
½   **cup sliced green onions**
2   **tablespoons chopped parsley**
1   **teaspoon salt**
¼   **teaspoon ground allspice**
¼   **teaspoon pepper**
⅛   **teaspoon cayenne pepper**
2   **bay leaves**
2   **pounds redfish, bluefish or other fish steaks**
1   **lemon, sliced**
    Hot cooked rice

1. In 5-quart Dutch oven over low heat, cook oil and flour about 15 minutes until mixture turns deep brown, stirring often. Stir in onions, green peppers, celery and garlic. Cook until vegetables are tender, stirring often.

2. Stir in tomatoes, water, wine, green onions, parsley, salt, allspice, pepper, cayenne and bay leaves. Over high heat, heat to boiling. Reduce heat to low; simmer, uncovered, 40 minutes or until mixture is thickened, stirring occasionally.

3. Cut fish into 8 serving pieces; add to tomato mixture along with lemon slices, covering fish with sauce. Simmer 15 to 20 minutes until fish flakes easily when tested with a fork, stirring occasionally. Discard lemon slices and bay leaves. Season to taste.

4. To serve: Spoon fish and sauce over rice in soup bowls. Yields 8 cups.

✳ Buttered Shad Roe

Shad roe is a welcome sign of spring for Americans on both coasts. From March until May, depending on the location, the adult shad swim from the ocean to warmer inland waters to spawn. At this time the female shad carries a pair of membrane sacs filled with roe, the delicious eggs of the fish. At one time these were included with the fish when you bought it, but the roe are now most often sold separately from the bony shad.

BEGIN: 30 MINUTES AHEAD   4 SERVINGS

2   **pairs (¾ pound each) shad roe**
⅛   **teaspoon salt**
    Generous dash pepper
¼   **cup butter or margarine**
2   **tablespoons chopped parsley**
1   **teaspoon chopped chives**
1   **tablespoon lemon juice**
    Bacon slices, crisply cooked
    Lemon wedges

1. Wash roe under cold water, being careful not to break membrane. Dry on paper towels. With sharp knife, separate membranes connecting the pairs. Sprinkle roe with salt and pepper.

2. In 10-inch skillet over medium heat, in hot butter, cook roe 6 minutes on each side or until golden. With spatula, remove roe to warm platter.

3. To drippings remaining in skillet, stir in parsley, chives and lemon juice; heat through. Pour over roe.

4. To serve: Garnish with crisp bacon slices and lemon wedges.

❋ Salmon Loaf

Until the second half of this century salmon was an abundant and inexpensive fish. In Colonial times, the earliest labor contracts of apprentices and indentured servants included clauses that limited the number of times they could be fed salmon each week. Salmon was so plentiful in America that one Northwestern explorer speculated that a man could cross a river on the backs of the closely packed salmon. Today's salmon population has been greatly diminished by pollution and overfishing, so it has become more expensive. But when you add bread crumbs and seasonings to make a salmon loaf, a salmon meal can still be moderate in cost.

BEGIN: 1½ HOURS AHEAD   6 SERVINGS

2   tablespoons butter or margarine
1   small onion, finely chopped
1   can (15 ounces) salmon
1¾ cups soft bread crumbs
½   cup mayonnaise
¼   cup milk
2   tablespoons lemon juice
1   tablespoon chopped parsley
2   eggs
½   teaspoon salt
⅛   teaspoon pepper
     Hollandaise Sauce (see page 167) or Egg
        Sauce (see page 122) (optional)

1. Grease 8- by 4-inch loaf pan. In 6-inch skillet over medium-high heat, in hot butter, cook onion until tender.

2. In large bowl, combine cooked onion with remaining ingredients except sauce; mix well. Spread into prepared pan.

3. Bake at 350°F. 50 to 60 minutes until set in center. Cool on wire rack 10 minutes. Serve with Hollandaise Sauce or Egg Sauce.

TUNA LOAF: Prepare as above but substitute *2 cans (7 ounces each) water-packed tuna, drained,* for the salmon.

TO MICROWAVE: Grease 1½-quart microwave-safe ring mold. In large microwave-safe bowl, combine butter and onion. Microwave on HIGH 2 to 2½ minutes until onion is tender. Stir in remaining ingredients except sauce; mix well. Spread into prepared dish. Microwave on HIGH 10 to 11 minutes until set, turning dish often. Cool on rack 10 minutes. Unmold; serve with Hollandaise Sauce or Egg Sauce.

❋ Perfect Tuna Casserole

Before World War I tuna was seldom served; it was available only at fresh fish markets. With the war's scarcity of meat, sardine canners began to put tuna in cans, and tuna casseroles became important in the American diet. A tuna casserole made with condensed soup has been popular for about 50 years. Although the meat scarcity is behind us, canned tuna has become one of the best-selling foods in the supermarket.

BEGIN: 1 HOUR AHEAD   4 SERVINGS

1   can (10¾ ounces) condensed cream of
        celery soup
¼   cup milk
1   can (7 ounces) tuna, drained and flaked
2   hard-cooked eggs, sliced
1   cup cooked peas
½   cup slightly crumbled potato chips

1. In 1-quart casserole, combine soup and milk. Stir in tuna, eggs and peas.

2. Bake at 350°F. 30 minutes or until hot; stir. Top with chips. Bake 5 minutes more.

TO MICROWAVE: In 1-quart microwave-safe casserole, combine soup and milk. Stir in tuna, eggs and peas; cover. Microwave on HIGH 7 to 8 minutes or until hot, stirring twice. Top with potato chips before serving.

✳ Shrimp Jambalaya

Jambalaya originated in Louisiana. Like a Spanish paella, it includes seafood, vegetables and rice to make a one-dish supper. The origin of the name is questionable. Some historians claim that it is named after the ham in the dish, from the Spanish jamon *or French* jambon; *others say it was the "jumble" of ingredients that gave it its name. As the second tale implies, the dish is made with whatever ingredients fall to hand, and it is rare to find two cooks making identical jambalaya.*

BEGIN: 2 HOURS AHEAD   8 SERVINGS

2   tablespoons salad oil
1½   cups finely chopped celery
2   green peppers, cut into ¼-inch strips
2   onions, finely chopped
2   cloves garlic, minced
¼   cup chopped parsley
½   teaspoon thyme leaves, crushed
½   pound cooked ham, cut into julienne
        strips
1¾   cups chicken broth
1   can (16 ounces) tomatoes, cut up
1   cup raw regular rice
1   teaspoon sugar
1   teaspoon salt
¼   teaspoon pepper
½   teaspoon hot pepper sauce
1   pound medium shrimp, shelled and
        deveined

1. In 5-quart Dutch oven over medium-high heat, in hot oil, cook celery, peppers, onions, garlic, parsley and thyme until vegetables are tender.

2. Stir in ham, broth, tomatoes, rice, sugar, salt, pepper and pepper sauce. Heat to boiling, stirring constantly. Reduce heat to low. Cover; simmer 20 minutes.

3. Stir in shrimp. Cook, uncovered, 8 to 10 minutes more or until rice is tender and all liquid is absorbed. Yields 9 cups.

SPICY SAUSAGE JAMBALAYA: Prepare as above but add *1½ pounds bulk sausage (Creole, andouille or Italian)* with vegetables in step 1. Drain off fat before adding remaining ingredients. Proceed as in steps 2 and 3 but substitute *1¾ cups beef broth* for chicken broth.

CHICKEN JAMBALAYA: Use ingredients as above but substitute *2 pounds chicken parts* for shrimp and drain tomatoes. In 5-quart Dutch oven over medium-high heat, in hot oil, cook chicken pieces, a few at a time, until browned on all sides. Remove chicken from Dutch oven. In drippings, over medium-high heat, cook celery, peppers, onions, garlic, parsley and thyme until tender. Return chicken to pot; stir in remaining ingredients. Heat to boiling, stirring often. Reduce heat to low. Cover; simmer about 30 minutes or until chicken is fork-tender.

✳ Shrimp Creole

The shrimp's name comes from its small size, but shrimp vary greatly in size. The tiniest Alaskan pinks come 180 to the pound, while one single Texas shrimp weighed in at 3 pounds. Most shrimp fall in between, with "medium" shrimp at about 30 per pound. The Gulf Coast produces a great deal of the shrimp we eat in America; it is also where this dish was created.

BEGIN: 2 HOURS AHEAD   6 SERVINGS

2   tablespoons salad oil
1   large onion, coarsely chopped
1   green pepper, coarsely chopped
1   stalk celery, thinly sliced
1   clove garlic, minced
1   can (16 ounces) tomatoes, chopped
1   bay leaf
½   teaspoon salt
⅛   teaspoon pepper
       Generous dash cayenne pepper
1½   pounds medium shrimp, shelled and
        deveined
       Hot cooked rice

1. In 4-quart saucepan over medium-high heat, in hot oil, cook onion, pepper, celery and garlic until vegetables are tender-crisp.

2. Stir in tomatoes, bay leaf, salt, pepper and cayenne. Heat to boiling. Reduce heat to medium. Simmer, uncovered, 20 minutes or until mixture is slightly thickened, stirring occasionally.

3. Stir in shrimp. Simmer 5 minutes more or until shrimp turn pink. Discard bay leaf. Serve with rice. Yields 4 cups.

❋ Szechuan Shrimp

Chinese food in America once was usually from the Cantonese region. Today, however, regional Chinese food is catching on, and one of the most popular is Szechuan, characterized by a spicy hotness; Szechuan Shrimp is no exception.

BEGIN: 45 MINUTES AHEAD   4 SERVINGS

¼   cup dry sherry
¼   cup ketchup
¼   cup chili sauce
¼   cup soy sauce
¼   cup rice wine or water
1   tablespoon sugar
4   teaspoons cornstarch
½   teaspoon salt
1   tablespoon salad oil
1   pound medium shrimp, shelled and
     deveined
3   green onions, diagonally sliced into
     ¼-inch pieces
3   cloves garlic, minced
2   tablespoons finely chopped fresh ginger
     root
½   teaspoon crushed red pepper
     Hot cooked rice

1. In small bowl, combine first 8 ingredients; mix well and set aside.

2. In wok or 10-inch skillet over high heat, in hot oil, cook shrimp, onions, garlic, ginger and red pepper 2 minutes or until shrimp is almost cooked, stirring constantly.

3. Stir in reserved sauce mixture. Heat to boiling. Serve with rice. Yields 3½ cups.

❋ Maryland-Style Crab Cakes

Blue crab is eaten along the East and Gulf coasts. The crabs are steamed or boiled with a spicy seasoning. Then, at tables draped with newspapers, happy eaters pick the succulent meat from the shells until they can eat no more. Another favorite way to serve the fine, sweet meat is to shred it and bind it with mayonnaise and crumbs to make crab cakes. Each cook has a favorite formula; many of these are family secrets. But the key to a great crab cake is starting with the very best crabmeat.

BEGIN: 30 MINUTES AHEAD   4 SERVINGS

1   pound cooked crabmeat, picked over
½   cup dried bread crumbs
½   cup mayonnaise
1   teaspoon dry mustard
1   teaspoon Worcestershire
½   teaspoon salt
¼   teaspoon white pepper
1   egg
2   tablespoons salad oil
     Lemon wedges

1. In large bowl with fork, break crabmeat into fine shreds. Stir in crumbs, mayonnaise, mustard, Worcestershire, salt, pepper and egg. Shape mixture into 8 patties.

2. In 10-inch skillet over medium heat, in hot oil, fry 4 patties at a time until golden on both sides, turning once. Serve with lemon wedges.

DEEP-FRIED CRAB CAKES: Prepare as above in step 1. In 4-quart saucepan, heat 2 inches oil to 375°F. Fry crab cakes, 2 at a time, until golden. Drain on paper towels.

TIP: For a browner exterior, coat crab cakes with additional dried bread crumbs before frying.

❊ Crab Imperial

The nation is blessed with many types of delectable crabs: The West Coast's Dungeness crab; the enormous King crab from colder Northwestern waters; blue and stone crabs from the East and Gulf regions; snow crabs from the colder waters of both coasts; and red and Jonah crabs from the deeper Atlantic. Crab Imperial is a favorite Chesapeake Bay treatment for crab, eaten alone or as a stuffing for fish or other seafood.

BEGIN: 1 HOUR AHEAD   8 SERVINGS

5	tablespoons butter or margarine
½	cup sliced green onions
1	tablespoon finely chopped green pepper
2	tablespoons all-purpose flour
1	tablespoon lemon juice
½	teaspoon salt
½	teaspoon dry mustard
½	teaspoon Worcestershire
1	cup milk
¼	cup mayonnaise
1	egg yolk
1	pound cooked crabmeat, picked over
1	tablespoon finely chopped pimento
¼	cup dried bread crumbs

1. Preheat oven to 400°F. Grease 1½-quart casserole.

2. In 1-quart saucepan over medium heat, in 4 tablespoons hot butter, cook onions and green pepper until tender. Add flour, lemon juice, salt, mustard and Worcestershire; stir together until smooth. Gradually stir in milk. Cook until mixture boils, stirring constantly. Remove from heat. Stir in mayonnaise.

3. In cup with fork, beat egg yolk; stir in ½ cup hot mixture. Add to saucepan, stirring constantly. Fold in crabmeat and pimento.

4. Pour mixture into prepared casserole; set aside. In small saucepan over medium heat, melt remaining 1 tablespoon butter; toss with bread crumbs. Sprinkle over casserole.

5. Bake 25 minutes or until mixture is hot.

❊ Lobster Thermidor

The law of supply and demand influences which foods are regarded as delicacies. The lobster, for instance, is one of today's most expensive and highly regarded foods, yet the colonists at Plymouth considered lobster a poor-man's food. At that time, the lobsters were so plentiful that they would be washed ashore in large piles after a storm. No one can argue that Lobster Thermidor is not a delicacy —it combines elegant ingredients in a lovely presentation. Our version is made with rock lobster, a crustacean from southern waters that is related to the New England lobster.

BEGIN: 1 HOUR AHEAD   4 SERVINGS

4	frozen rock lobster tails (6 ounces each), thawed and cooked
¼	cup butter or margarine
2	green onions, chopped
2	tablespoons all-purpose flour
½	teaspoon salt
½	teaspoon Dijon mustard
1½	cups light cream
¼	cup dry sherry
1	egg yolk
2	tablespoons chopped parsley
¼	cup buttered bread crumbs

1. With kitchen shears, cut away thin underside shell of each tail; gently pull meat from shell. Cut meat into 1-inch chunks; reserve meat and shells.

2. In 3-quart saucepan over medium heat, in hot butter, cook onions until tender. Add flour, salt and mustard; stir together until smooth. Gradually stir in cream and sherry; cook until mixture boils, stirring constantly.

3. In cup with fork, beat egg yolk; stir in small amount hot mixture. Add to saucepan, stirring constantly. Heat just to boiling. Add reserved lobster and parsley. Over low heat, cook until hot, stirring constantly. Fill lobster shells with mixture. Arrange shells in jelly-roll pan. Sprinkle with buttered bread crumbs.

4. Broil 4 inches from heat 2 minutes or until lightly browned.

TIP: To make buttered bread crumbs, combine 1 tablespoon melted butter or margarine with ¼ cup dried bread crumbs.

Lobster Thermidor

❋ Lobster Newburg

Lobster Newburg was created at Delmonico's in New York during the late nineteenth century. Most sources agree that the dish was named for Ben Wenberg, a sea captain and favored customer at the establishment. Later, after a disagreement between Captain Wenberg and Charles Delmonico, the name of the dish was changed from Lobster Wenberg to Lobster Newburg. This elegant sauce is often used with other seafood, such as crab, shrimp and scallops.

BEGIN: 45 MINUTES AHEAD   6 SERVINGS

¼   **cup butter or margarine**
2   **green onions, finely chopped**
1   **tablespoon all-purpose flour**
½   **teaspoon salt**
    Generous dash paprika
    Generous dash cayenne pepper
1½ **cups light cream**
2   **egg yolks**
1   **pound cooked lobster meat, cut into chunks**
2   **tablespoons dry sherry or Madeira**
    Patty shells or toast points

1. In 3-quart saucepan over medium-high heat, in hot butter, cook onions until tender. Add flour, salt, paprika and cayenne. Over medium heat, stir together until smooth.

2. Gradually stir in cream; cook until mixture boils, stirring constantly. Remove from heat; set aside.

3. In cup with fork, beat egg yolks slightly; stir in small amount of hot mixture. Add to saucepan, stirring constantly.

4. Add lobster and sherry; over low heat, cook until hot, stirring constantly. Do not boil. Serve over patty shells or toast points. Yields 3½ cups.

CRAB NEWBURG: Prepare as above but substitute *1 pound frozen King crab meat, thawed,* for lobster meat.

❊ Fried Oysters

Three types of oysters are found on American coasts. The most common is the Eastern oyster, from the Gulf and East coasts. Pacific and Olympia oysters grow on the West Coast. Some connoisseurs can distinguish not only the variety of oyster, but also the area where it is harvested. That is because the environment influences the flavor of the oysters more than the variety. One favorite way to prepare oysters is to fry them. To serve them Louisiana-style, pile fried oysters onto a loaf of French bread to make a po'boy.

BEGIN: 45 MINUTES AHEAD   4 SERVINGS

1½ cups finely crushed saltines
2   eggs
2   tablespoons milk
½   teaspoon celery salt
⅛   teaspoon pepper
1   quart shucked oysters, drained and
        patted dry
     Salad oil
     Lemon wedges

1. On waxed paper, place cracker crumbs. In pie plate with fork, beat together eggs, milk, celery salt and pepper. Using tongs, dip oysters, one at a time, into egg mixture; coat with crumbs. Let stand on waxed paper 10 minutes.

2. In 10-inch skillet over medium heat, in ½ inch hot oil, fry oysters, a few at a time, 5 to 7 minutes until lightly browned, turning once. Lift oysters onto warm platter; keep warm until all oysters are cooked. Serve with lemon wedges.

❊ Scalloped Oysters

When King Charles I divided Virginia and gave part to Lord Baltimore to govern, he placed the boundary on the western shore rather than in the center of the Potomac. Why? So Lord Baltimore's Maryland would control the rights to the rich crab and oyster beds on both sides of the river. Scalloped Oysters is a specialty of that region, made with the area's wonderful oysters.

BEGIN: 1 HOUR AHEAD   6 SERVINGS

½   cup butter or margarine
1   cup crushed saltines
1   cup soft bread crumbs
½   teaspoon Worcestershire
¼   teaspoon celery salt
⅛   teaspoon pepper
1   pint shucked oysters with liquor reserved
2   tablespoons light cream or milk

1. Butter 10- by 6-inch baking dish. In 2-quart saucepan over medium heat, melt butter. Stir in cracker and bread crumbs, Worcestershire, celery salt and pepper. Spoon ½ of the crumbs into prepared dish.

2. Drain oysters, reserving ½ cup liquor. Arrange drained oysters over crumbs. Top with remaining crumbs. Combine reserved oyster liquor and cream; pour over crumbs.

3. Bake at 400°F. about 25 minutes until heated through. Let stand 10 minutes before serving.

✳ Scallop Casseroles

The scallop has a long history in world culture as well as in cuisine. Pompeii's ruins were found to display the symbol of the scallop, and American Indians employed the shell in their rituals and dress. Today scallops are rarely seen in their shells. They are so perishable that the shells are removed aboard the fishing boats, and the scallops are immediately refrigerated. The pretty shells were often used as bowls in times past; many dishes that are now known as "scalloped" got their names because they were served in scallop shells.

BEGIN: 1 HOUR AHEAD   4 SERVINGS

1	pound bay scallops
¼	cup dry white wine
4	tablespoons butter or margarine
½	pound small whole mushrooms
½	cup sliced green onions
2	teaspoons chopped pimento
1	tablespoon chopped parsley
⅛	teaspoon pepper
2	tablespoons all-purpose flour
¼	cup grated Parmesan cheese
¼	cup half-and-half
2	cups soft bread crumbs

1. In 10-inch skillet over high heat, heat scallops and wine to boiling. Drain scallops, reserving liquid; set aside.

2. In same skillet over medium-high heat, in 2 tablespoons hot butter, cook mushrooms and green onions until tender. Stir in pimento, parsley, pepper and flour.

3. Gradually stir in reserved liquid and cook until mixture boils, stirring constantly. Add reserved scallops, Parmesan cheese and half-and-half. Heat through.

4. Divide mixture into four 8-ounce broilersafe casseroles or ramekins. In small saucepan over medium heat, melt remaining 2 tablespoons butter. Add bread crumbs; toss to coat well. Sprinkle crumbs over scallops.

5. Broil 4 inches from heat about 5 minutes until browned.

✳ Crawfish Etouffée

Crawfish are available in both fresh and salt waters of the United States. One favorite way to cook crawfish is to boil or steam them with spices and eat them right out of the shell, on newspaper-lined tables. For a more elegant presentation, prepare them in this well-seasoned stew from New Orleans.

BEGIN: 2 HOURS AHEAD   6 SERVINGS

5	pounds crawfish
¼	cup butter or margarine
2	tablespoons salad oil
2	tablespoons all-purpose flour
3	onions, chopped
½	cup chopped green onions
½	cup chopped green pepper
½	cup chopped celery
2	cloves garlic, minced
½	teaspoon hot pepper sauce
½	teaspoon salt
¼	teaspoon pepper
½	cup chicken broth or water
	Hot cooked rice

1. In 8-quart Dutch oven over high heat, heat 4 quarts water to boiling. Add crawfish; cook until fish turn deep red, stirring constantly. Drain. Remove and discard heads, reserving fat (yellow portion) from heads; peel and devein crawfish.

2. In 2-quart saucepan over medium heat, cook butter, oil, flour and crawfish fat about 10 minutes or until dark brown but not burned, stirring constantly. Stir in onions, green onions, green pepper, celery, garlic, hot pepper sauce, salt and pepper. Cook until vegetables are tender-crisp, stirring often.

3. Stir in crawfish and broth. Heat to boiling. Reduce heat to low. Cover; simmer 10 minutes. Serve over rice. Yields 4 cups.

SHRIMP ETOUFFÉE: Prepare as above but substitute *1½ pounds small shrimp in shells* for crawfish. In step 3, simmer only 2 minutes.

Seafood Tempura

❊ Seafood Tempura

Tempura is the term for Japanese fried food: Fish, shellfish and vegetables are coated with a light, delicate batter, then fried in oil. Use any combination of seafood and vegetables to suit your taste.

BEGIN: 1 HOUR AHEAD   6 SERVINGS

1   **cup all-purpose flour**
¼   **cup cornstarch**
2   **teaspoons baking powder**
2   **egg whites**
1   **tablespoon sesame oil**
1   **tablespoon soy sauce**
1½ **cups cold water**
    Salad oil
    Shrimp, sea scallops, fish fillets, sliced zucchini, parsley sprigs, mushrooms, asparagus

1. In medium bowl, combine flour, cornstarch and baking powder; mix well. Beat in egg whites, sesame oil, soy sauce and water until smooth. Cover; refrigerate 30 minutes. Gently stir batter.

2. In wok or 4-quart saucepan, heat 2 inches oil to 375°F. Dip seafood and vegetables into cold batter, coating well. Fry a few pieces at a time 2 to 5 minutes until desired doneness.

3. To serve: Serve tempura with small bowl of additional soy sauce for dipping. Yields 2½ cups batter.

TIP: Recipe makes enough batter to coat about 2 pounds fish and seafood plus an equal amount of vegetables.

❊ Steamed Mussels with Wine

Mussels were important to the early colonists and Indians and still are abundant in coastal waters. The Indians steamed them on red-hot rocks, while the colonists cooked theirs in pots. Today, mussels are usually steamed in a small amount of liquid, then served with the liquid in soup bowls with crusty bread to soak up the broth. This is a version of the classic mussel dish Moules Marinière.

BEGIN: 45 MINUTES AHEAD   2 SERVINGS

2   **pounds mussels**
2   **tablespoons butter or margarine**
1   **medium onion, finely chopped**
1   **shallot, finely chopped**
1   **clove garlic, minced**
2   **tablespoons chopped parsley**
¼   **teaspoon pepper**
½   **cup dry white wine**
    French bread

1. Scrub mussels thoroughly, cutting off beard portion. Rinse with cold water. Discard any mussels that remain open when tapped with finger.

2. In 5-quart Dutch oven over medium-high heat, in hot butter, cook onion, shallot and garlic until onion is tender. Stir in parsley, pepper and wine; add mussels. Heat to boiling. Reduce heat to low. Cover; simmer 5 to 8 minutes until all shells open.

3. To serve: Place mussels in soup bowls; spoon cooking liquid over mussels. Serve with bread.

TIP: Serve to 4 people as an appetizer.

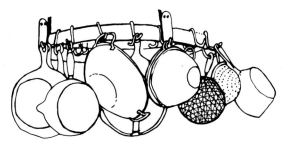

Eggs Florentine, Puffy Spanish Omelet, Macaroni and Cheese

EGGS AND CHEESE

Because they did not keep livestock, the American Indians used neither eggs nor cheese in their cooking. European colonists brought chickens for eggs, and cows for milk and cheese to the New World, and they have been a part of American food ever since.

The Germans who settled in the rich dairy country of Wisconsin were foremost among those who made cheese in the New World. They began by recreating the types of cheeses they knew. But they did create two completely American cheeses.

Emil Frey, a German-American, was trying to reproduce a German cheese in New York when he invented Liederkranz. Despite its German sound, the name comes from the choral society whose members first taste-tested it. And a Wisconsin cheesemaker of Swiss extraction invented brick cheese when he weighted the cheese with bricks to squeeze out the whey. Brick cheese even resembles a brick, with tiny holes throughout.

American dairymen have been able to produce excellent European-style cheeses, too. Some cheeses take on a slightly different character in different regions of the country. You can choose a fine New York Cheddar, Wisconsin Cheddar or the Cheddar from Oregon known as Tillamook. Other delicious American cheeses include California chèvres and Wisconsin blues.

You can be choosy with eggs, also. Although they are nutritionally equivalent to white eggs, brown eggs are preferred by some consumers. In some markets, you can buy eggs laid by organically fed or range-bred chickens.

We have usually had our eggs at breakfast and our cheese as snacks, but now that many Americans wish to reduce their meat consumption, both eggs and cheese are becoming popular as main-dish foods at any meal. Both provide a good dose of protein, as well as vitamins and minerals. Eggs and cheese are used together in casseroles, omelets and other dishes; these have proved especially valuable when meat and poultry were scarce and expensive.

When you try the egg and cheese recipes in this chapter, remember that there are other wonderful egg and cheese dishes in other parts of the book. Look through the appetizers and snacks, where you'll find Deviled Eggs, Cheese Ball, Fried Cheese and other good snacking foods. And don't overlook the dessert section with its luscious egg-and-cheese temptation, Cheesecake.

❋ Eggs Benedict

America's most elegant egg dish reportedly was created in New York City for a Mr. Benedict who had overindulged the night before. A combination of English muffins, Canadian bacon and Hollandaise sauce (a French name that means "Dutch sauce"), Eggs Benedict is an example of the cosmopolitan spirit of American cooking. Serve it for breakfast, lunch, brunch or supper.

BEGIN: 30 MINUTES AHEAD   4 SERVINGS

3   egg yolks, at room temperature
2   tablespoons lemon juice
⅛   teaspoon salt
    Dash cayenne pepper
½   cup butter or margarine, melted
2   English muffins, split
    Butter or margarine, softened
4   slices Canadian-style bacon or country
        ham
4   eggs
    Chopped parsley

1. In covered blender container at medium speed, blend egg yolks, lemon juice, salt and cayenne until smooth.

2. Remove center of cover (or cover). Continue blending, gradually adding ½ cup melted butter in a fine stream, until sauce is smooth and thickened. Pour into small bowl or top of double boiler; keep warm over hot water.

3. Spread each muffin half lightly with butter. Place buttered side up on broiler pan with bacon or ham alongside. Broil 4 inches from heat until muffins are golden and bacon is heated through. Keep warm.

4. Lightly grease a saucepan or deep skillet; add 1½ inches water. Over high heat, heat to boiling. Reduce heat to low. Break 1 egg into a saucer; gently slip egg into water. Repeat with remaining eggs; cook 3 to 5 minutes until desired doneness. Remove eggs from water with slotted spoon.

5. On heated platter, place muffin halves; top with bacon, then egg. Spoon sauce over all; garnish with parsley.

❋ Eggs Florentine

When you see "Florentine" in the name of a dish, expect a food made with spinach, often teamed with cheese and a creamy sauce. Serve this satisfying entrée with a fresh fruit compote, hot rolls and coffee to make an easy breakfast or brunch.

BEGIN: 1 HOUR AHEAD   6 SERVINGS

¼   cup butter or margarine
½   cup sliced mushrooms
¼   cup all-purpose flour
½   teaspoon salt
    Generous dash cayenne pepper
1½ cups milk
2   packages (10 ounces each) frozen
        chopped spinach, cooked and well
        drained
6   eggs
1   cup shredded Cheddar cheese

1. In 2-quart saucepan over medium heat, in hot butter, cook mushrooms until tender. Add flour, salt and cayenne; stir together until smooth. Gradually stir in milk; cook until mixture boils, stirring constantly. Stir in spinach; heat through.

2. Spread spinach mixture evenly in bottom of 12- by 8-inch baking dish. Make 6 indentations in spinach mixture; break eggs into depressions.

3. Bake at 350°F. 15 to 20 minutes until eggs are nearly done. Sprinkle with cheese; bake 3 minutes more or until eggs are desired doneness and cheese is melted.

SHORTCUT EGGS FLORENTINE: Prepare as above but substitute *1 can (10¾ ounces) condensed cream of celery soup* and *⅓ cup milk* for first 6 ingredients. In 2-quart saucepan, stir together soup and milk; over medium-high heat, heat to boiling. Stir in spinach; heat through. Proceed as in step 2.

TIP: To make individual servings, prepare as above in step 1. Spoon spinach mixture into 6 eight-ounce individual casseroles; make indentation in each. Break egg into each. Bake at 350°F. 10 to 15 minutes until eggs are nearly done. Sprinkle with cheese; bake 3 minutes more.

Huevos Rancheros

❋ Huevos Rancheros

Huevos Rancheros or ranch-style eggs come to us from Mexico and the American Southwest. Sometimes the eggs are poached in the sauce rather than fried; sometimes the cheese is Cheddar; and some cooks add garnishes such as avocado slices, sliced olives, chili strips and cilantro.

BEGIN: 45 MINUTES AHEAD   6 SERVINGS

3	tablespoons salad oil
½	cup chopped onion
¼	cup chopped green pepper
1	clove garlic, minced
2	canned green chilies, drained, seeded and chopped
2	tablespoons chopped cilantro leaves or parsley
½	teaspoon salt
2	cups chopped tomatoes or 1 can (16 ounces) tomatoes, chopped
6	6-inch corn tortillas
6	eggs
½	cup shredded Monterey Jack cheese

1. In 2-quart saucepan over medium-high heat, in 2 tablespoons hot oil, cook onion, green pepper, garlic, chilies, cilantro and salt until vegetables are tender. Stir in tomatoes; heat to boiling. Reduce heat to low. Simmer, uncovered, 20 minutes or until thickened, stirring often. Keep warm.

2. Wrap tortillas in foil. Heat at 325°F. 10 minutes or until just warm.

3. In 10-inch skillet over medium heat, in remaining 1 tablespoon hot oil, fry eggs to desired doneness.

4. To serve: Place warm tortilla on plate; top each with one egg. Spoon sauce over each egg; top with cheese. Serve immediately.

TIP: Cover eggs during frying for evenly cooked, sunny-side-up eggs.

❋ Saucy Baked Eggs in Toast Cups

These baked eggs are a good choice for a breakfast or brunch for guests. They are quickly assembled and cook unattended in their own toast cups while you prepare the rest of the menu. Accompany with asparagus or broccoli spears, mushrooms, ham, bacon, sausage or tomatoes.

BEGIN: 45 MINUTES AHEAD   8 SERVINGS

8   **Toast Cups***
1   **can (10¾ ounces) condensed cream of chicken soup**
⅓   **cup light cream**
½   **cup shredded natural Swiss cheese**
2   **tablespoons grated Parmesan cheese**
8   **eggs**

1. Prepare Toast Cups. In 2-quart saucepan, combine soup, cream and cheeses; mix well. Over medium-low heat, heat until cheese melts, stirring occasionally.

2. Break one egg into each Toast Cup in custard cup; spoon sauce over egg. Sprinkle with additional Parmesan cheese.

3. Bake at 350°F. 15 minutes or until eggs are desired doneness.

***TOAST CUPS:** Trim crusts from *8 thin slices white bread. Butter* 1 side of each bread slice. Press slices, buttered side down, into 6-ounce custard cups. Bake at 350°F. 10 minutes or until golden.

❋ Egg Sauce

In addition to being a simple main dish, Egg Sauce is traditionally served over fish (particularly poached salmon) in New England on Independence Day. Try it with plain cooked vegetables as well.

BEGIN: 30 MINUTES AHEAD   2 SERVINGS

2   **tablespoons butter or margarine**
2   **tablespoons all-purpose flour**
½   **teaspoon salt**
½   **teaspoon dry mustard**
⅛   **teaspoon paprika**
⅛   **teaspoon white pepper**
1½   **cups milk or half-and-half**
2   **hard-cooked eggs, sliced**
2   **tablespoons chopped parsley**
    Toast points

1. In 1-quart saucepan over medium heat, melt butter. Stir in flour, salt, dry mustard, paprika and pepper until smooth.

2. Gradually stir in milk; cook until mixture boils, stirring constantly. Gently stir in eggs and parsley. Serve over toast. Yields 1½ cups.

CHICKEN EGG SAUCE: Prepare as above but substitute *1¼ cups chicken broth* for milk and omit salt.

MUSHROOM EGG SAUCE: Prepare as above but add *½ cup sliced small mushrooms* to hot butter; cook until lightly browned. Proceed as above.

EGGS GOLDENROD: Prepare as above but separate egg yolks from whites; chop whites and add to sauce as above. Spoon sauce over toast. Force yolks through sieve; spoon over sauce.

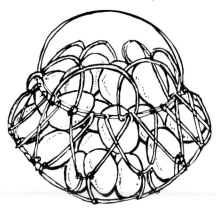

❋ Pickled Eggs

A favorite snack in bars and lunchrooms, pickled eggs are made by many ethnic groups. Scandinavians and Germans serve them at home, seasoned with caraway, ginger, allspice, celery seed and/or bay leaves.

BEGIN: 2 DAYS AHEAD   12 EGGS

2   cups white vinegar
1   tablespoon sugar
2   cloves garlic, halved
1   teaspoon salt
1   bay leaf
8   peppercorns
4   whole cloves
1   medium onion, sliced and separated into rings
12 hard-cooked eggs, cooled and shelled

1. In 2-quart saucepan, combine all ingredients except eggs. Over medium heat, heat just to boiling. Reduce heat to low; simmer 5 minutes.

2. Place eggs in 2-quart heatsafe jar with screw top. Pour pickling mixture over eggs. Cover; cool. Refrigerate at least 2 days.

❋ French Toast

French Toast entered American cuisine by way of the Creole cooks in Louisiana. There it was known by its French name Pain Perdu, *meaning lost bread, because it was made from stale bread that otherwise would have gone to waste. French Toast is made all over the world, and known by such names as Bombay Toast, German Toast, Rich Knights, Poor Knights and Nun's Toast.*

BEGIN: 15 MINUTES AHEAD   4 SERVINGS

3   eggs
1   cup milk or light cream
1   teaspoon sugar
¼   teaspoon salt
    Dash ground cinnamon or nutmeg
    Melted butter or margarine
8   slices white or whole wheat bread
    Maple syrup, honey or marmalade

1. In medium bowl, beat eggs, milk, sugar, salt and cinnamon until smooth.

2. Over medium-high heat, heat griddle or skillet. Brush griddle with melted butter.

3. Dip each bread slice into egg mixture until well saturated, turning to coat both sides; immediately place on hot griddle. Cook until browned on both sides, turning once and brushing griddle with more butter as needed. Serve with additional butter and syrup, honey or marmalade.

PAIN PERDU: Prepare as above but substitute *10 slices French bread cut ¾ inch thick* for white bread.

ORANGE FRENCH TOAST: Prepare as above but add *1 teaspoon grated orange peel* to egg mixture.

❋ Campbelled Eggs

You may have encountered this recipe tucked into egg cartons in the early 1950s. It's one of Campbell Soup Company's all-time most popular recipes, a great way to add flavor to everyday scrambled eggs. Try it with Campbell's Cheddar cheese, cream of celery, cream of mushroom and cream of chicken soups to make breakfast more interesting.

BEGIN: 15 MINUTES AHEAD   4 SERVINGS

1   can (10¾ ounces) condensed cream of chicken, celery, mushroom or Cheddar cheese soup
8   eggs, slightly beaten
    Dash pepper
2   tablespoons butter or margarine

1. In medium bowl, stir soup until smooth; beat in eggs and pepper.

2. In 10-inch skillet over medium heat, melt butter. Pour in egg mixture. As eggs begin to set, stir lightly so uncooked egg flows to bottom. Cook until set but still very moist; serve immediately. Yields 3 cups.

❊ Hangtown Fry

Why hangtown fry? One story tells of a condemned man who requested it for his last meal, hoping to delay the hanging by asking for hard-to-obtain eggs and oysters. Another tale has a gold miner who had struck it rich coming into Hangtown and ordering the most expensive food he could get. No one knows what he paid for that meal, but during the gold rush, eggs often were worth their weight in gold, and oysters probably cost at least as much.

BEGIN: 45 MINUTES AHEAD 8 SERVINGS

2	tablespoons all-purpose flour
9	eggs
1	cup crushed saltines
1	pint shucked oysters, drained and patted dry
½	pound sliced bacon
¼	cup milk
¼	cup grated Parmesan cheese
¼	cup chopped green onions
¼	cup chopped parsley
½	teaspoon salt
⅛	teaspoon pepper

1. Place flour on waxed paper; beat 1 egg in pie plate. Place crumbs on another sheet of waxed paper. Coat oysters in flour, then dip in egg, then coat with cracker crumbs.

2. In 10-inch skillet over medium heat, fry bacon until crisp. Remove bacon; set aside. Pour off all but 4 tablespoons drippings. In hot drippings, cook oysters until golden on both sides, turning once. Remove oysters; keep warm.

3. In medium bowl, combine remaining 8 eggs, milk, cheese, onions, parsley, salt and pepper. Pour into same skillet. As eggs begin to set, stir lightly so uncooked egg flows to bottom.

4. Cook until set but still very moist. Stir in oysters; cook 1 minute more. Serve with bacon.

❊ Puffy Spanish Omelet

According to legend, an ancient king of Spain stopped unexpectedly at the home of one of his subjects. His host cooked up a pan of eggs that delighted the king. "Quel homme leste!" (what a clever man), he said, and the dish became known as homme leste *or omelet.*

BEGIN: 45 MINUTES AHEAD 6 SERVINGS

4	tablespoons butter or margarine
1	medium green pepper, cut into strips
⅓	cup sliced celery
⅓	cup chopped onion
3	cups chopped tomatoes or 1 can (16 ounces) tomatoes, drained and chopped
¼	cup sliced pitted ripe olives (optional)
1	small clove garlic, minced
¼	teaspoon basil leaves, crushed
¾	teaspoon salt
⅛	teaspoon paprika
6	eggs, separated, at room temperature
¼	teaspoon cream of tartar
¼	cup water
½	cup shredded Monterey Jack cheese

1. In 2-quart saucepan over medium heat, in 2 tablespoons hot butter, cook green pepper, celery and onion until tender. Add tomatoes, olives, garlic, basil, ¼ teaspoon salt and paprika. Simmer 10 minutes; stir often. Cover; keep warm.

2. Preheat oven to 350°F. In large bowl with mixer at high speed, beat egg whites until foamy. Add cream of tartar; beat until stiff peaks form.

3. In small bowl with mixer at high speed, beat yolks with remaining ½ teaspoon salt and water until light and fluffy; carefully fold into beaten egg whites.

4. In ovensafe 10-inch skillet over medium heat, melt remaining 2 tablespoons butter. Pour egg mixture into skillet; cook about 2 minutes until underside of omelet is golden.

5. Place skillet in oven; bake 10 minutes or until surface is golden and springs back when pressed *lightly* with fingertip. Run spatula around side of skillet to loosen omelet. Spoon tomato mixture over omelet; sprinkle with cheese. Cut into 6 wedges. Serve at once.

❄ Western Omelet

Also known as a Denver, this omelet of eggs, ham, onions and peppers was probably created in a chuck wagon during the great cattle drives of the last century, when a "cookie" whipped up a quick, hearty meal for the cowboys. The cook may have been Chinese, as many were, and he may have simply prepared his version of eggs foo yung.

BEGIN: 30 MINUTES AHEAD   4 SERVINGS

3   tablespoons butter or margarine
1   cup diced cooked ham
⅓   cup chopped green pepper
¼   cup sliced green onions
6   eggs
2   tablespoons water
¼   teaspoon salt
⅛   teaspoon cayenne pepper
½   cup shredded Cheddar cheese

1. In 10-inch nonstick omelet pan over medium heat, in hot butter, cook ham, green pepper and onions until vegetables are tender.

2. In large bowl, beat eggs, water, salt and cayenne just to mix; stir into ham mixture. As eggs set around edge, lift edge, tilting skillet to allow uncooked egg mixture to run under omelet.

3. When omelet is set but still moist on surface, increase heat slightly to brown bottom. Remove from heat. Sprinkle cheese over omelet. Tilt pan away from you; using spatula, lift edge of omelet and quickly fold in half. Slide omelet onto warm plate; serve at once.

❄ Cheese Soufflé

Like the omelet, the soufflé is supposed to be difficult to prepare. But only two basic techniques are involved in the process. The first is making a smooth, thick sauce, and the second is folding it into beaten egg whites. To simplify the procedure, you can substitute a condensed soup for the sauce. The key to success with egg whites is to use a gentle hand for folding. One caution: have everyone seated at the table before you remove the soufflé from the oven. A few minutes' wait can mean the difference between a perfect soufflé and a deflated one.

BEGIN: 2 HOURS AHEAD   6 SERVINGS

¼   cup butter or margarine
¼   cup all-purpose flour
½   teaspoon salt
     Generous dash cayenne pepper
1½   cups milk
1   cup shredded sharp Cheddar cheese
6   eggs, separated, at room temperature

1. Cut piece of 12-inch-wide foil to fit around 2-quart soufflé dish and overlap about 2 inches; fold in half lengthwise. Carefully wrap foil strip around outside of dish so collar stands about 3 inches above rim. Fasten with tape.

2. In 2-quart saucepan over medium heat, melt butter. Add flour, salt and cayenne; stir together until smooth. Gradually stir in milk; cook until mixture boils, stirring constantly. Stir in cheese. Over low heat, heat until cheese melts, stirring constantly. Remove from heat; cool slightly. Preheat oven to 300°F.

3. In small bowl with mixer at high speed, beat egg yolks until thick and lemon-colored; gradually stir in cheese mixture.

4. In large bowl with mixer at high speed, using clean beaters, beat egg whites until stiff peaks form. Carefully fold cheese mixture into egg whites. Pour into prepared soufflé dish.

5. Bake 1¼ hours or until soufflé is browned. Remove collar; serve immediately.

EASY CHEESE SOUFFLÉ: Prepare as above but substitute *1 can (10¾ ounces) condensed cream of chicken soup* for first 5 ingredients. In 2-quart saucepan, stir soup until smooth. Proceed as in step 3.

❋ Rolled Soufflé

This soufflé shares the ingredients, method and elegance of the more traditional soufflé. But, instead of being baked in a soufflé dish, this one is prepared in a jelly-roll pan, then rolled up around a simple filling of cheese and bacon. The filling can change with the cook's whim, like the filling of an omelet.

BEGIN: 1 HOUR AHEAD   6 SERVINGS

1   **can (11 ounces) condensed Cheddar cheese soup**
6   **eggs, separated, at room temperature**
6   **slices bacon, cooked, drained and crumbled**
1¼ **cups shredded Cheddar cheese**

1. Oil 15½- by 10-inch jelly-roll pan; line with waxed paper, extending paper about 3 inches beyond pan on each end. Oil and lightly flour waxed paper. Line a large baking sheet with waxed paper. Preheat oven to 350°F.

2. In 2-quart saucepan over medium heat, heat soup, stirring occasionally. Remove from heat; cool slightly.

3. In small bowl with mixer at high speed, beat egg yolks until thick and lemon-colored; gradually stir in soup.

4. In large bowl with mixer at high speed, using clean beaters, beat egg whites until stiff peaks form; carefully fold soup mixture into egg whites. Spread evenly in prepared jelly-roll pan.

5. Bake 20 minutes or until set. Invert onto paper-lined baking sheet; with metal spatula, *gently* remove waxed paper from soufflé. Sprinkle soufflé with bacon and cheese.

6. With aid of waxed paper, roll up jelly-roll fashion, starting at narrow end. Transfer to ovensafe platter. Bake 5 minutes more or until cheese melts.

TIP: Rolled soufflé can be refrigerated, then reheated on ovensafe platter. Cover with foil; bake at 350°F. 20 minutes or until hot.

❋ Tomato Cheese Rabbit

Welsh rabbit is a humorous name for the cheese-ale dish made by Welshmen who came back from the hunt empty-handed. When the recipe reached America, tomatoes were added. This recipe has been known by a variety of names over the years: traditional names such as Tomato Cheese Rabbit and Tomato Rarebit, humorous names such as Blushing Bunny and Red Devil, and nonsense names such as Rum Tum Ditty, Rinktum Tiddy and Winkum.

BEGIN: 30 MINUTES AHEAD   4 SERVINGS

3   **slices bacon**
1   **medium onion, chopped**
1   **can (10¾ ounces) condensed tomato soup**
¼   **cup milk**
1   **cup shredded American cheese**
8   **slices white bread, toasted**

1. In 10-inch skillet over medium heat, fry bacon until crisp; remove and crumble. In bacon drippings, cook onion until tender.

2. Stir in soup, milk and cheese. Heat until cheese is melted, stirring often.

3. Spoon over toast. Sprinkle with crumbled bacon. Yields 1½ cups.

TO MICROWAVE: Arrange slices of bacon on microwave-safe rack placed in 12- by 8-inch microwave-safe dish. Microwave on HIGH 4 to 5 minutes until crisp; remove and crumble, reserving 2 tablespoons bacon drippings. In 1½-quart microwave-safe bowl, combine drippings and onion; cover. Microwave on HIGH 2 minutes or until onion is tender. Stir in soup, milk and cheese. Microwave on HIGH 3 to 4 minutes until cheese is melted, stirring once. Spoon over toast. Sprinkle with bacon.

✾ Wisconsin Cheese Fondue

When fondue became a popular party dish, it was natural for Americans to substitute Wisconsin Cheddar and domestic beer for the Swiss cheese and wine of European fondues. Pumpernickel and rye breads, common in the German- and Scandinavian-influenced Midwest, are particularly good with this creamy sauce.

BEGIN: 30 MINUTES AHEAD   6 SERVINGS

4   cups shredded Cheddar cheese (1 pound)
2   tablespoons cornstarch
½   teaspoon dry mustard
1   cup beer
1   teaspoon Worcestershire
     Pumpernickel or rye bread, cubed

1. In large bowl, toss cheese, cornstarch and mustard to coat cheese.

2. In 2-quart saucepan over low heat, heat beer and Worcestershire until hot, but not boiling.

3. With fork or wire whisk, gradually stir in cheese. Cook over low heat until cheese is melted and mixture is smooth and bubbling, stirring constantly. Pour into fondue pot for serving. Keep warm over low heat on fondue stand.

4. To serve: Let each person spear chunks of bread on long-handled fondue fork and dip into fondue. Yields 2¾ cups.

✾ Swiss Cheese Strata

A cheese strata can be put together the night before guests come for brunch, then baked while the rest of the menu is prepared. This elegant strata is made of Swiss cheese, wine and French bread, with a flavor reminiscent of a Swiss fondue.

BEGIN: EARLY IN DAY   6 SERVINGS

1   loaf stale French bread, cut into 1-inch
       cubes (8 cups)
1   can (11 ounces) condensed Cheddar
       cheese soup
1   soup can water
2   cups shredded natural Swiss cheese
4   eggs, beaten
⅓   cup dry white wine

1. Butter 12- by 8-inch baking dish. Arrange bread cubes evenly in prepared dish.

2. In medium bowl, combine remaining ingredients; mix well. Pour over bread. Cover; refrigerate at least 6 hours or overnight. Let stand at room temperature 1 hour. Uncover.

3. Bake at 350°F. 30 minutes or until set.

✾ Macaroni and Cheese

Thomas Jefferson was an adventurous eater who always returned from his travels with new foods, cooking techniques and seeds for his garden. He served macaroni pie at the White House while he was President, and he looked into ways of producing hollow macaroni. Jefferson enjoyed cheese with his noodles and macaroni, and may have enjoyed a macaroni and cheese dish like this one.

BEGIN: 1 HOUR AHEAD   6 SERVINGS

8   ounces elbow macaroni
¼   cup butter or margarine
¼   cup all-purpose flour
½   teaspoon salt
½   teaspoon dry mustard
¼   teaspoon white pepper
⅛   teaspoon hot pepper sauce
2½   cups milk
2   cups shredded sharp Cheddar cheese
     Shredded Cheddar cheese
     Tomato wedges

1. Cook macaroni in boiling water as label directs; drain. Butter 2-quart casserole or baking dish. Preheat oven to 350°F.

2. In 2-quart saucepan over medium heat, melt butter. Stir in flour, salt, mustard, pepper and hot pepper sauce until smooth. Gradually stir in milk; cook until mixture boils, stirring constantly. Stir in 2 cups cheese. Cook just until cheese is melted, stirring constantly. Add sauce to macaroni. Pour into prepared casserole. Top with additional shredded cheese.

3. Bake 30 minutes or until very hot. Garnish with tomato wedges.

Granola, Armenian Noodle-Rice Pilaf, Hoppin' John, Spaghetti Carbonara, All-American Lasagna

PASTA, GRAINS AND DRY BEANS

Grains and beans were among the first plants that man cultivated for food, and with good reason. They are a valuable yet inexpensive source of nutrients; they combine well with other foods; and they keep well in periods when there is no fresh food.

Before man cooked, he made pastes of grain pounded with water. When he learned to use fire, he baked these grain pastes on stones next to the fire, making flat breads that resembled tortillas and jonnycakes. Later, he preserved the pastes by drying them, then boiling them to make pasta.

Corn is the only grain native to North America. It was a diet mainstay of the Indians and became a staple for the colonists, too, before they could grow European wheat. The rest of the world refers to all grains by the word "corn" and says "maize" for our corn. The fact that in America "corn" means this one grain reflects its importance on this continent.

The Indians also used dry beans. They invented the beanhole style of cooking them, leaving beans to cook for days in a heated hole in the ground. For New England colonists, baked beans became a traditional Saturday night meal, and suppers of beans on the cattle trail are part of cowboy folklore.

The colonists did succeed in establishing European grains in America, as anyone who has seen our Midwestern wheatfields can testify. Rice was brought here by sea traders, and thrived along the Southern coast. By 1698, Virginia and South Carolina rice was being exported to England.

Noodles came with settlers from Europe, as well as with the Chinese. Today we enjoy noodles in dishes of many cuisines: German-style, in soups or with cottage cheese; Italian, with tomato and vegetable sauces; Chinese lo meins and all-American noodle casseroles.

Grains and beans are a major part of the American diet, all the more so since the health food movement. We eat them in some form all day long, from our morning cereals, through midday beans and franks, to the bread and rice on our supper table.

❊ Homemade Noodles

Noodles have a place in the cooking of many cultures: Italian food with its dozens of shapes and sauces, the noodles and spaetzle of central Europe, the wheat and rice noodles of Japan and China, and the potpies of our own Pennsylvania Dutch.

BEGIN: 3 HOURS AHEAD   8 SERVINGS

3	eggs
2	tablespoons milk
½	teaspoon salt
2	cups all-purpose flour
8	cups water or chicken broth

1. In medium bowl with fork, beat eggs, milk and salt until foamy. With wooden spoon, stir in flour to make a stiff dough. On floured surface, roll dough *very thin;* let stand 30 minutes or until dry enough to cut.

2. Sprinkle dough with flour; loosely roll up dough, jelly-roll fashion. With sharp knife, cut dough into ¼-inch slices. Unroll noodles and let dry 2 hours.

3. In 4-quart saucepan over high heat, heat water to boiling. Add noodles; cook about 10 minutes until tender. Drain; serve at once. Yields 7 cups.

❊ Noodles Romanoff

These cheese-smothered noodles originated in Eastern Europe and Russia, where they are often garnished with poppy seeds for a contrast in flavor and texture.

BEGIN: 1 HOUR AHEAD   6 SERVINGS

2	cups creamed cottage cheese
1	cup milk
1	cup sour cream
2	green onions, finely chopped
1	clove garlic, minced
1	teaspoon Worcestershire
½	teaspoon salt
⅛	teaspoon hot pepper sauce
	Dash pepper
8	ounces medium noodles, cooked and drained
½	cup grated Parmesan cheese or shredded Cheddar cheese

1. Butter 2-quart casserole. Preheat oven to 325°F. In large bowl, combine first 9 ingredients. Add noodles; toss together to mix well. Turn into prepared casserole.

2. Bake 20 minutes. Stir mixture gently; sprinkle with cheese. Bake 15 to 20 minutes more until hot. Yields 6 cups.

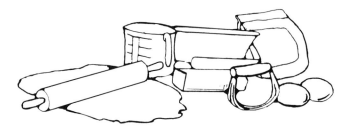

❊ Tomato Spaghetti Sauce

For many Americans, pasta is not spaghetti without a spicy tomato sauce. Sauces made with tomatoes are typical of the cuisine of southern Italy. When you hear Italian-Americans talk about spaghetti with "gravy," they don't mean a sauce made from meat drippings, but a tomato sauce like this one.

BEGIN: 2 HOURS AHEAD   8 SERVINGS

2   tablespoons olive or salad oil
2   large onions, chopped
3   cloves garlic, minced
2   cans (28 ounces each) tomatoes
2   cups water
1   can (12 ounces) tomato paste
2   bay leaves
2   teaspoons sugar
2   teaspoons oregano leaves, crushed
1   teaspoon salt
1   teaspoon basil leaves, crushed
½   teaspoon pepper
    Generous dash ground cloves

1. In 6-quart Dutch oven over medium-high heat, in hot oil, cook onions and garlic until tender.

2. Stir in remaining ingredients; heat to boiling. Reduce heat to low. Simmer, uncovered, 1½ hours or until sauce is desired consistency, stirring occasionally. Discard bay leaves. Yields 8 cups.

GROUND BEEF SPAGHETTI SAUCE: Prepare as above but cook *1 pound ground beef* with onion mixture in step 1, stirring to break up meat. Drain off fat before adding remaining ingredients.

SAUSAGE SPAGHETTI SAUCE: Prepare as above but cook *1 pound bulk Italian sausage* with onion mixture in step 1, stirring to break up meat. Drain off fat before adding remaining ingredients.

❊ All-American Lasagna

There are many ways to put together lasagna, but this is the way Americans prefer it—with layers of lasagna noodles, meat sauce and ricotta and mozzarella cheeses. (Many Italian recipes use a cream sauce instead of the ricotta.) Lasagna has become a crowd-pleaser in this country, a dish that everyone likes and that can be made ahead for a party. If you do not have time to prepare a homemade sauce, make Pantry-Shelf Lasagna, using a commercial spaghetti sauce.

BEGIN: 3 HOURS AHEAD   8 SERVINGS

3   eggs, beaten
1   container (32 ounces) ricotta cheese
½   cup grated Parmesan cheese
¼   cup chopped parsley
¾   teaspoon salt
¾   teaspoon pepper
4   cups Sausage Spaghetti Sauce (at left)
8   lasagna noodles, cooked and drained
3   cups shredded mozzarella cheese

1. In medium bowl, combine eggs, ricotta cheese, Parmesan cheese, parsley, salt and pepper; mix well. Set aside.

2. In 13- by 9-inch baking dish, spread 1 cup spaghetti sauce. Arrange 4 lasagna noodles on sauce. Top with ½ of the ricotta cheese mixture, ½ of the mozzarella cheese and ½ of the remaining sauce. Repeat layers. Sprinkle with additional Parmesan cheese.

3. Bake at 375°F. 35 to 40 minutes until heated through. Let stand 15 minutes before serving.

PANTRY-SHELF LASAGNA: In 3-quart saucepan over medium-high heat, cook *½ pound bulk Italian sausage* until browned, stirring to break up meat. Spoon off fat. Stir in *3 cups plain spaghetti sauce.* Heat to boiling. Reduce heat to low. Cover; simmer 10 minutes. Prepare as above but substitute this sauce for Sausage Spaghetti Sauce.

✳ Spaghetti Primavera

If there were a best-seller list for popular recipes, Spa-ghetti Primavera surely would have been included during the past few years. The vegetable and pasta combination appeals to the desire for fresh, healthy, quick foods. Yet a pasta concoction like this has been a staple in Italian homes for centuries, where this pasta-vegetable combina-tion is also called tutto giardino *or entire garden.*

BEGIN: 30 MINUTES AHEAD   6 SERVINGS

8   ounces thin spaghetti
1   tablespoon butter or margarine
1   tablespoon olive oil
4   green onions, diagonally sliced
1   clove garlic, minced
2   cups broccoli flowerets
1   small zucchini, thinly sliced
1   cup sliced mushrooms
3   tomatoes, diced
1   cup fresh or frozen peas, thawed
2   tablespoons chopped parsley
1   teaspoon salt
1   teaspoon Italian seasoning
⅛   teaspoon pepper
½   cup chicken broth
½   cup grated Parmesan cheese

1. Cook spaghetti as label directs; drain in colan-der and keep hot.

2. In 10-inch skillet over medium-high heat, heat butter and oil. Add green onions, garlic, broccoli, zucchini, mushrooms, tomatoes, peas, parsley, salt, Italian seasoning and pepper. Cover; cook 5 minutes or until vegetables are tender-crisp, stirring occasionally. Stir in chicken broth; heat through.

3. Toss vegetables with spaghetti; sprinkle with Parmesan cheese. Yields 7½ cups.

TIP: If you do not have Italian seasoning, use a mixture of thyme, basil and oregano leaves.

✳ Spaghetti Carbonara

The origin of this pasta served with bacon and eggs is obscure. One story suggests that it was created by Italian soldiers in the mid-1800s and named carbonara *after the fire used for cooking it. Many different versions have evolved—some with bacon or salt pork, others with Ital-ian sausage, prosciutto or American ham.*

BEGIN: 30 MINUTES AHEAD   4 SERVINGS

8   ounces thin spaghetti
2   tablespoons olive oil
1   tablespoon butter or margarine
6   slices bacon or ¼ pound salt pork, diced
3   eggs, at room temperature
¾   cup grated Parmesan cheese
¼   cup chopped parsley

1. Cook spaghetti as label directs; drain in colan-der and keep hot.

2. Meanwhile, in 10-inch skillet over medium heat, in hot oil and butter, fry bacon until crisp.

3. In large bowl with wire whisk, beat eggs; beat in cheese and parsley. Add hot spaghetti; toss with egg mixture to coat well.

4. Add bacon and 2 tablespoons drippings; toss to mix well. Serve immediately. Yields 3½ cups.

❋ Linguini with Pesto Sauce

Pesto is made in Northern Italy by pulverizing fresh basil and other ingredients with a mortar and pestle. Pesto has become extremely popular in American homes and restaurants, where it is quickly made in an electric blender or food processor. Serve it with pasta, as in this recipe, or stir a spoonful into your favorite vegetable soup.

BEGIN: 30 MINUTES AHEAD   6 SERVINGS

3   cups fresh basil leaves, stems removed
½   cup pine nuts
½   cup grated fresh Parmesan cheese
½   cup grated fresh Romano cheese
¾   cup olive oil
¼   cup hot water
¼   teaspoon salt
3   large cloves garlic
     Dash pepper
12   ounces linguini, cooked and drained

1. In covered blender container, combine all ingredients except linguini. At high speed, blend until smooth. Refrigerate until serving time.

2. To serve: Toss pesto with linguini. Yields 1½ cups sauce.

PARSLEY PESTO: Prepare as above but substitute *3 cups fresh parsley, stems removed,* for basil.

TIP: Substitute ½ cup slivered almonds or shelled sunflower seeds for pine nuts.

❋ Tortellini with Ham and Vegetables

Tortellini (little twists) are said to resemble the navel of Venus, goddess of gardens and the spring. The small pasta shapes, stuffed with cheese, meat or vegetable fillings, are available frozen or dried in Italian specialty stores or in supermarkets. They make a wonderful cold supper dish when combined with vegetables, ham and seasonings.

BEGIN: EARLY IN DAY   8 SERVINGS

16   ounces cheese or meat tortellini, cooked, drained and cooled
2   cups shredded carrots
2   cups shredded zucchini
½   cup sliced pitted ripe olives
1   cup diced cooked ham
¼   cup sliced green onions
¼   cup Vinaigrette (see page 186) or bottled Italian salad dressing
⅛   teaspoon pepper
     Grated Parmesan cheese

In medium bowl, toss tortellini with remaining ingredients except cheese to mix well. Sprinkle with Parmesan cheese. Refrigerate until serving time, at least 4 hours. Yields 10 cups.

Linguini with Pesto Sauce

❋ Linguini with White Clam Sauce

A sauce of oil or butter, garlic and parsley is the basis for many pasta dishes. In this country, the best known is Linguini with White Clam Sauce. But Italian-Americans might add tuna, shrimp, beans or peas instead. Or they may add tomatoes to make a red sauce.

BEGIN: 30 MINUTES AHEAD   4 SERVINGS

8   ounces linguini
2   cans (6½ ounces each) minced clams
¼   cup butter or margarine
2   tablespoons olive or salad oil
4   cloves garlic, minced
3   tablespoons chopped parsley

1. Cook linguini as label directs; drain in colander and keep hot.

2. Meanwhile, drain clams, reserving liquid. In 1-quart saucepan over medium-high heat, in hot butter and oil, cook garlic and parsley until garlic is lightly browned. Add clam liquid to butter mixture. Heat to boiling. Reduce heat to low; simmer 5 minutes.

3. Stir in clams. Heat to boiling. Toss sauce with pasta until well coated. Yields 4½ cups.

LINGUINI WITH RED CLAM SAUCE: Prepare as above in step 2 using 2-quart saucepan. Stir in *1 can (16 ounces) tomatoes, coarsely chopped, ¼ cup dry red wine, 3 tablespoons tomato paste, 1½ teaspoons basil leaves, crushed,* and *½ teaspoon sugar.* Heat to boiling. Reduce heat to low. Simmer, uncovered, 30 minutes, stirring occasionally. Stir in clams. Heat through. Meanwhile, cook linguini as label directs; drain. Serve sauce over linguini.

❋ Armenian Noodle-Rice Pilaf

Armenians have made many contributions to American cuisine with their excellent horticultural methods, their shish kabobs and other lamb dishes, and this popular rice and noodle pilaf.

BEGIN: 45 MINUTES AHEAD   6 SERVINGS

¼   cup butter or margarine
½   cup broken vermicelli
1   cup raw regular rice
3   cups chicken broth

1. In 2-quart saucepan over medium-high heat, in hot butter, cook vermicelli until browned, stirring constantly. Stir in rice; toss with vermicelli to coat.

2. Stir in broth; heat to boiling. Reduce heat to low. Cover; simmer 20 minutes or until rice is tender and all broth is absorbed. Yields 4 cups.

❋ Angel Hair with Caviar

The American caviar industry has had its ups and downs: during the nineteenth century we exported the salty fish roe to Europe, but for most of this century nearly all our caviar has been imported from the Caspian Sea area. Now, American caviar is coming back. It is produced all over the country, from the Columbia River of Oregon to the Arkansas River of Oklahoma to the Hudson River of New York. One way to show off this salty, flavorful fish roe, a symbol of elegant dining, is to serve it on a bed of the fine pasta known as angel hair.

BEGIN: 1 HOUR AHEAD   6 SERVINGS

8   ounces angel hair pasta or very fine egg
     noodles
1   cup plain yogurt
¾   cup light cream
¼   cup butter or margarine
2   tablespoons chopped parsley
2   hard-cooked eggs, diced
½   cup golden caviar or black caviar,
     drained

1. Cook pasta as label directs; drain in colander and keep hot.

2. Meanwhile, in 1-quart saucepan over low heat, heat yogurt, cream, butter, parsley and eggs until hot, stirring occasionally. Pour into large bowl. Add hot pasta; toss with cream mixture to coat well.

3. To serve: Divide pasta onto individual plates; top each serving with heaping tablespoon caviar. Yields 5½ cups.

TIP: Rinse caviar under cold water for a less salty flavor and purer color.

✳ Two-Bean Macaroni

An adaptation of the Italian Pasta e Fagioli *(pasta and beans), Two-Bean Macaroni incorporates American pinto beans and Cheddar cheese with Italian cannellini and macaroni. This type of dish has always been popular with Italian-Americans for its quick preparation, its satisfying quality and inexpensive nutrition.*

BEGIN: 45 MINUTES AHEAD   6 SERVINGS

4   **slices bacon, diced**
1   **large onion, thinly sliced**
1   **carrot, chopped**
1   **green pepper, chopped**
¼   **cup chopped parsley**
2   **teaspoons basil leaves, crushed**
1   **teaspoon oregano leaves, crushed**
1   **can (16 ounces) tomatoes, chopped**
1   **can (20 ounces) cannellini (white kidney beans), drained**
1   **can (16 ounces) pinto beans, drained**
2   **cups cooked elbow macaroni**
1   **teaspoon salt**
¼   **teaspoon pepper**
½   **cup shredded Cheddar cheese**

1. In 10-inch skillet over medium heat, fry bacon until almost crisp.

2. Stir in onion, carrot, green pepper, parsley, basil and oregano. Cook until vegetables are tender-crisp. Stir in tomatoes. Heat to boiling. Reduce heat to low. Cover; simmer 10 minutes.

3. Stir in beans, macaroni, salt and pepper. Cover; simmer 5 minutes more. Sprinkle with cheese. Yields 7 cups.

✳ Hasty Pudding

Twentieth-century Americans know hasty pudding because of Harvard's Hasty Pudding Club, and not the humble cornmeal porridge that inspired the name of that prestigious group. Hasty pudding has been known as musk, samp, suppawn and loblolly. In Italy, it is called polenta *and served, unsweetened, with main dishes.*

BEGIN: 30 MINUTES AHEAD   4 SERVINGS

5   **cups water**
1   **teaspoon salt**
1   **cup yellow cornmeal**
    Milk
    Butter or margarine
    Molasses or maple syrup

1. In 3-quart saucepan over high heat, heat water and salt to boiling. With wire whisk, gradually stir in cornmeal. Reduce heat to low. Simmer 20 minutes or until very thick, stirring often.

2. To serve: Spoon into cereal bowls; serve with milk, butter and molasses. Yields 4 cups.

FRIED CORNMEAL MUSH: Prepare as above but pour hot cornmeal mixture into 8- by 4-inch loaf pan. Cool; cover and refrigerate overnight. Remove from pan. Cut into ½-inch-thick slices. In 10-inch skillet over medium-high heat, in *2 tablespoons hot butter or margarine,* cook mush slices, a few at a time, 10 minutes on each side or until crisp and browned. Serve with butter and maple syrup.

❋ Hominy in Cream

Indians used ashes and water to remove corn hulls, and called the skinless corn tackhummin, *later shortened to hominy. European colonists used lye to remove the hulls, but today they are mechanically removed. Heated with a little cream, hominy is a fine breakfast dish or a substitute for bread or potatoes at supper.*

BEGIN: 15 MINUTES AHEAD   6 SERVINGS

¼   cup butter or margarine
2   cans (15 ounces each) hominy, drained
        and rinsed
½   cup heavy cream
¼   teaspoon salt
⅛   teaspoon sugar
⅛   teaspoon pepper
2   teaspoons chopped parsley (optional)

1. In 10-inch skillet over medium-low heat, in hot butter, cook hominy until heated through, stirring occasionally. Stir in cream, salt, sugar and pepper; heat through.

2. To serve: Spoon into bowl; sprinkle with parsley. Yields 2½ cups.

TO MICROWAVE: Use ingredients as above but reduce cream to ¼ cup. In 1½-quart microwave-safe casserole, place butter. Microwave on HIGH 1½ to 2 minutes until melted. Stir in hominy, *only ¼ cup cream,* salt, sugar and pepper; cover. Microwave on HIGH 3 to 4 minutes until hot, stirring occasionally. Sprinkle with parsley.

❋ Dixie Cheese Grits

When hominy is ground to a coarse meal it is known simply as grits. In the South, grits are served with butter, sugar, honey, maple syrup or gravy for breakfast. But Southerners also mix the grits with cheese and eggs to make delicious baked squares that make a hit at any meal.

BEGIN: 1½ HOURS AHEAD   8 SERVINGS

4   cups water
1   teaspoon salt
1   cup quick-cooking grits
3   cups shredded sharp Cheddar cheese
¼   cup butter or margarine
⅛   teaspoon garlic powder
⅛   teaspoon cayenne pepper
2   eggs

1. In 3-quart saucepan over high heat, heat water and salt to boiling. Gradually stir in grits. Reduce heat to low. Simmer 3 to 5 minutes until grits are thickened, stirring often. Remove from heat.

2. Stir in cheese, butter, garlic powder and cayenne until cheese and butter are melted. In small bowl with fork, beat eggs. Stir in a small amount of grits mixture. Slowly pour egg mixture back into grits mixture, stirring constantly. Pour mixture into 12- by 8-inch baking dish.

3. Bake at 350°F. 1 hour or until golden. Let stand 10 minutes. Cut into squares.

❋ Granola

Granola is the name J. H. Kellogg gave to the first ready-to-eat cereal he produced at his Seventh-Day Adventist health sanitorium. The name returned to prominence with the renewed interest in health foods of the 1960s and 1970s, when mixtures of oats, grains, fruits and nuts became popular as a breakfast food and a snack. Granola provides plenty of vitamins, minerals and fiber, but its enduring popularity is also due to its wonderful flavor.

BEGIN: 2 HOURS AHEAD   20 SERVINGS

4   cups uncooked old-fashioned oats
1   cup shredded coconut
1   cup wheat germ
1   cup pecan halves or cashews
1   cup raisins
1   cup hulled sunflower seeds
¾   cup honey
½   cup salad oil
1   teaspoon vanilla extract
½   teaspoon salt

1. Preheat oven to 350°F. In large bowl, combine first 6 ingredients; mix well.

2. In small bowl, combine honey, oil, vanilla and salt; mix well. Drizzle over cereal mixture. Toss to coat.

3. Spread mixture in thin layers on baking sheets or jelly-roll pans.

4. Bake 15 to 20 minutes until crisp and browned, stirring occasionally. Cool completely; store in airtight containers. Yields 10 cups.

❋ Rice Pilaf

Pilaf, pilaff, pilafé, pilau, pilav and pilaw are all different words for the well-seasoned rice mixtures that are basic to the cuisine of the Middle East and the American South. The rice is cooked with broth and a combination of herbs, spices, meats, vegetables, nuts and even fruits.

BEGIN: 45 MINUTES AHEAD   6 SERVINGS

2   tablespoons salad oil
1   small onion, finely chopped
1   cup raw regular rice
1   can (10½ ounces) condensed beef broth
      or chicken broth
1½ cups water
¼   teaspoon salt
¼   teaspoon pepper

1. In 2-quart saucepan over medium-high heat, in hot oil, cook onion until tender. Stir in rice. Cook until rice is golden brown, stirring constantly.

2. Stir in remaining ingredients. Heat to boiling. Reduce heat to low. Cover; simmer 25 minutes or until rice is tender and all liquid is absorbed. Yields 3½ cups.

BROWN RICE PILAF: Prepare as above but substitute *1 cup raw brown rice* for regular rice. Increase simmering time to 50 minutes.

BARLEY PILAF: Prepare as above but substitute *1 cup pearled barley* for regular rice. Increase simmering time to 1 hour.

MUSHROOM-RICE PILAF: Prepare as above but add *1 cup sliced mushrooms* with onion in step 1. Proceed as above.

FRUITED PILAF: Prepare as above but add *1½ teaspoons curry powder* and *½ cup chopped green pepper* with onion in step 1 and add *½ cup raisins* with broth in step 2. Garnish with *¼ cup toasted sliced almonds or pine nuts.*

✳ Fried Rice

Rice is probably the most important single food in the world. In Asia, a meal is not considered complete without rice. One Chinese style of preparing rice that has caught on in this country is Fried Rice, a good way to use leftover rice and small amounts of leftover meat, shrimp or vegetables.

Begin: 30 minutes ahead   6 Servings

8	slices bacon
¼	cup diagonally sliced green onions
¼	cup green pepper cut into thin strips
2	tablespoons chopped parsley
3	cups cold, cooked rice
2	tablespoons soy sauce
⅛	teaspoon pepper
2	eggs, beaten

1. In 10-inch skillet over medium heat, fry bacon until crisp. Remove to paper towels to drain; crumble and set aside. Spoon off all but 2 tablespoons drippings.

2. In bacon drippings, cook onions, green pepper and parsley until tender-crisp. Stir in rice, soy and pepper. Heat through.

3. Make a well in center of rice mixture. Pour beaten eggs into well. As eggs begin to set, stir lightly with fork so uncooked egg flows to bottom. Cook until set but still moist. Gently stir to mix all ingredients in skillet. Stir in reserved bacon. Yields 4 cups.

✳ Spanish Rice

Spanish Rice is not so much Spanish as American, a favorite accompaniment for family meals. It has a quality that appeals to children and adults, and it can be ready in short order, so it is a natural for cooks looking for fast, nourishing meals. Add leftover beef, chicken or shrimp five minutes before the rice is done and you have a satisfying one-dish meal.

Begin: 45 minutes ahead   8 Servings

4	slices bacon
½	cup chopped green pepper
½	cup chopped onion
2	cloves garlic, minced
1	can (28 ounces) tomatoes, coarsely chopped
1	cup water
1	cup raw regular rice
1	tablespoon chopped parsley
1	teaspoon salt
⅛	teaspoon pepper

1. In 10-inch skillet over medium heat, fry bacon until crisp. Remove to paper towels to drain; crumble and set aside.

2. Over medium-high heat, in bacon drippings, cook green pepper, onion and garlic until vegetables are tender-crisp.

3. Stir in remaining ingredients except bacon. Heat to boiling. Reduce heat to low. Cover; simmer 25 minutes or until rice is tender and all liquid is absorbed.

4. To serve: Sprinkle with reserved bacon. Yields 6 cups.

❊ Green Rice

Rice cooked with herbs takes on the delicate color that gives it its name.

BEGIN: 45 MINUTES AHEAD   6 SERVINGS

¼   **cup butter or margarine**
½   **cup chopped chives or green onions**
½   **cup chopped parsley**
2   **cups chicken broth**
1   **cup raw regular rice**
     Generous dash cayenne pepper

1. In 3-quart saucepan over medium-high heat, in hot butter, cook chives until tender. Stir in remaining ingredients. Heat to boiling. Pour into 1½-quart casserole; cover.

2. Bake at 350°F. 20 to 25 minutes until rice is tender and all broth is absorbed. Toss lightly with fork before serving. Yields 4 cups.

❊ Rice Fritters

Fried rice cakes are thoroughly Southern, invented as a substitute for bread when rice was more plentiful than wheat flour. Rice fritters can be served with jelly as a breakfast food, or seasoned and served as a snack or side dish.

BEGIN: 45 MINUTES AHEAD   4 SERVINGS

2   **cups cold, cooked rice**
½   **cup dried bread crumbs**
½   **cup shredded Cheddar cheese**
2   **tablespoons all-purpose flour**
1   **tablespoon chopped parsley**
1   **teaspoon prepared mustard**
¼   **teaspoon salt**
3   **eggs, separated, at room temperature**
     Salad oil

1. In large bowl, combine first 7 ingredients and egg yolks; mix well.

2. In small bowl with mixer at medium speed, beat egg whites until soft peaks form. Fold into rice mixture.

3. In 4-quart saucepan, heat 2 inches oil to 375°F. Meanwhile, firmly shape rice mixture into twelve 3- by 1-inch logs. Roll logs in additional dried bread crumbs. Fry a few at a time in hot oil until golden. Drain on paper towels; serve warm. Yields 12 fritters.

❊ Minnesota Wild Rice

Wild rice is not a true rice, but a grass that grows as rice does, on flooded land. It was an important food for the Indians of the Great Lakes area. Although some is now picked with machinery, most wild rice is still gathered as the Indians did it: a person in a canoe beats the grain by hand so it falls into the boat.

BEGIN: 1 HOUR AHEAD   6 SERVINGS

1   **cup raw wild rice**
¼   **cup butter or margarine**
2   **green onions, thinly sliced**
1   **stalk celery, thinly sliced**
2   **cups sliced mushrooms**
¼   **teaspoon oregano leaves, crushed**
¼   **teaspoon thyme leaves, crushed**
⅛   **teaspoon pepper**
2   **cups chicken broth**
½   **cup sliced almonds**

1. Wash rice thoroughly in warm water; drain well.

2. In 3-quart saucepan over medium-high heat, in hot butter, cook green onions and celery until tender. Stir in mushrooms, oregano, thyme and pepper. Cook 1 minute more.

3. Add rice and broth. Heat to boiling. Reduce heat to low. Cover; simmer 45 minutes or until rice is tender and all liquid is absorbed. Stir in almonds. Yields 4 cups.

SAUSAGE WILD RICE: Prepare as above but stir in *½ pound fresh pork sausage, cooked and crumbled,* along with the almonds.

❋ Tabbouleh

This tangy cracked wheat dish comes from the Eastern Mediterranean countries, but it has become one of America's hottest food trends. It may be served as an appetizer, with romaine leaves for dipping, or spooned onto lettuce-lined plates as a salad. If you have trouble locating the bulgur in your supermarket, try a health food or natural food store.

BEGIN: EARLY IN DAY   6 SERVINGS

1	cup bulgur (cracked wheat)
2	large tomatoes, finely chopped
1	cup chopped parsley
½	cup chopped fresh mint
½	cup chopped green onions
½	cup olive or salad oil
½	cup lemon juice
½	teaspoon salt
¼	teaspoon pepper
	Romaine leaves

1. In large bowl, cover bulgur with cold water. Let stand at room temperature 1 hour. Pour into cheesecloth-lined colander; squeeze out excess water. Return bulgur to bowl.

2. Stir in tomatoes, parsley, mint, onions, oil, lemon juice, salt and pepper. Cover; refrigerate until serving time, at least 4 hours.

3. To serve: Spoon tabbouleh onto romaine-lined salad plates or serve from a bowl with romaine leaves for dipping. Yields 5 cups.

❋ Refried Beans

Pinto beans are native to the New World, but it was the Spanish contribution of pork (therefore lard) that made refried beans possible. Through the years these mashed beans have come to be known as a Mexican specialty. The term "refried" is misleading; it doesn't mean the beans are fried twice, but that they are very well done.

BEGIN: 3½ HOURS AHEAD   8 SERVINGS

1	pound dry pinto beans
1	medium onion, chopped
2	cloves garlic, minced
6	cups water
½	cup lard or bacon fat
2	teaspoons salt

1. In 4-quart saucepan over high heat, heat beans, onion, garlic and water to boiling. Reduce heat to low. Cover; simmer 2½ hours or until beans are very tender.

2. Stir in lard and salt. With potato masher, crush beans until almost smooth. Cook 20 minutes more or until beans are thickened, stirring often. Yields 5 cups.

❋ Hoppin' John

A host of traditions surround Hoppin' John. It is said in the South that eating this dish on New Year's Day assures wealth and good fortune during the coming year; some cooks add a coin to the mixture of beans and rice, granting its finder additional good luck. Some people say the dish was named after the children who hopped around the dinner table before the meal. Others suggest it is derived from the greeting, "Hop in, John."

BEGIN: 2 HOURS AHEAD   12 SERVINGS

1	pound dry black-eyed peas
8	cups water
½	pound bacon, diced
1	medium onion, chopped
1	clove garlic, minced
1	bay leaf
2	teaspoons salt
¼	teaspoon crushed red pepper
¼	teaspoon pepper
1	cup raw regular rice

1. In 5-quart Dutch oven over high heat, heat peas and water to boiling. Reduce heat to low; simmer 2 minutes. Remove from heat. Cover; let stand 1 hour. *Do not drain.*

2. Stir in bacon, onion, garlic, bay leaf, salt, red pepper and pepper. Over medium-high heat, heat to boiling. Reduce heat to low. Cover; simmer 20 minutes or until beans are tender.

3. Stir in rice. Cover; simmer 15 minutes more or until rice is done. Serve immediately. Yields 11 cups.

❋ Boston Baked Beans

It was American Indians who first made the dish we know as Boston Baked Beans. They dug a pit in the ground, lined it with stones, then built a fire in the hole to heat the stones. When the fire died down, the beans were placed in the hole, covered with more stones or earth, then left to cook slowly for many hours. The Indians seasoned their beans with bear fat and maple syrup, but colonists used salt pork and molasses. The Europeans fashioned pots shaped like the bean holes Indians used, and many cooks still insist that only these narrow-necked earthenware pots make authentic Boston Baked Beans.

BEGIN: DAY AHEAD   8 SERVINGS

1   **pound dry pea beans (navy beans)**
1   **large onion, chopped**
¼   **pound salt pork**

2   **tablespoons dark brown sugar**
¼   **cup dark molasses**
2   **teaspoons dry mustard**
1   **teaspoon salt**
½   **teaspoon pepper**

1. In large bowl, cover beans with water; let stand 12 hours or overnight. Drain.

2. In 2-quart bean pot or casserole, combine beans and onion. Slash salt pork deeply in several places, leaving it in one piece; place in center of beans. In medium bowl, combine 3 cups water, brown sugar, molasses, mustard, salt and pepper. Pour over beans; cover.

3. Bake at 300°F. 5½ to 6 hours until beans are tender, stirring occasionally and adding more water as needed to keep beans moist. Yields 5 cups.

Boston Baked Beans

Corn on the Cob, Parsley-Dill Butter, Stir-Fried Green Beans, Whole Baked Onions, Broiled Tomatoes, Artichokes, Summer Zucchini Medley

VEGETABLES

Each tribe of North American Indians had its own civilization, with its own religion, language and customs. But all across the continent they depended on the same three vegetable crops: corn, beans and squash. These three vegetables formed the basis of Indian cooking. Augmented by game, berries and other wild fruits, they provided a well-rounded diet.

But these were not the only vegetables in the New World. North and South America provided the world with its first tomatoes, peppers, potatoes, sweet potatoes and Jerusalem artichokes. Other vegetables, such as wild onions, greens and mushrooms, were native to America as well as other parts of the world.

Each group of European settlers brought over seeds for their favorite vegetables. Particularly important were cabbage and root vegetables such as parsnips, turnips and carrots that could be stored for part of the winter. Preservation techniques were limited for those vegetables that were not easily stored. Like the Indians, the colonists dried green beans, pumpkin slices and corn. They also pickled cucumbers, beans, cabbage, cauliflower and other vegetables, especially in regions where there was a strong German influence.

Thomas Jefferson, our third President, imported the seeds of many European plants for his garden and kept records of how each crop fared. He was one of the first Americans to raise the then-controversial potatoes and tomatoes. Other vegetables he helped promote in America were broccoli, eggplant, asparagus, cucumbers, Brussels sprouts, cauliflower and sugar beets.

Early in the nineteenth century, the discovery of canning revolutionized food preservation. Commercially canned peas, corn and potatoes helped provide food for Civil War soldiers and Western gold prospectors. Home canning followed quickly, and many farm wives and homemakers added jars of fruits and vegetables to the supplies in their root cellars.

Despite this abundance of vegetables, it is only recently that the public has realized just how important vegetables are to the diet. During the first half of this century vitamins were discovered to be a factor in the prevention of many diseases, and vegetables are a good source of vitamins.

This discovery has led to a change in cooking habits. Vegetables used to be cooked for hours, until they became very soft. But many vitamins are destroyed by long periods of cooking, so nutritionists recommend that most vegetables cook only until tender-crisp, in a minimum of water.

Americans today are experimenting with exotic vegetables and rediscovering old ones. Steaming and stir-frying encourage cooks to take a new look at some of the vegetables we have taken for granted. A greater variety of fresh vegetables is available in grocery stores and farmers' markets; the time is right to expand your vegetable-cooking repertoire.

❋ Corn on the Cob

In both North and South America, corn was a mainstay of Indian society. Legends and religious rituals surrounded the planting and harvesting of the crop, and the Indians practiced irrigation and fertilization to ensure the success of the planting. Europeans learned how to plant and use corn from Indian farmers. It became an important crop for them because it grew quickly in cleared forests, even before the stumps were removed. These Indians and pioneers dried most of the corn to grind for breads, but in the summer they enjoyed the fresh corn on the cob, just as we do today.

BEGIN: 15 MINUTES AHEAD   6 SERVINGS

**6   ears corn, husked and trimmed
       Butter, margarine or Parsley-Dill Butter*
       Salt
       Pepper**

1. In 5-quart Dutch oven over high heat, in 3 inches boiling water, heat corn to boiling. Reduce heat to low. Cover; simmer 5 minutes or until corn is tender-crisp. Drain.

2. To serve: Season with butter, salt and pepper.

TO MICROWAVE: Trim corn, but do not remove husks. Rinse in cold water.
For 2 ears: Microwave on HIGH 4 to 5 minutes until done, rearranging once.
For 4 ears: Microwave on HIGH 8 to 10 minutes until done, rearranging once.
For 6 ears: Microwave on HIGH 12 to 14 minutes until done, rearranging once.
Remove husks; with clean towel, pull off any remaining silks.

TO GRILL: Trim corn, but do not remove husks. Rinse in cold water. Grill over hot coals 15 minutes or until husks are lightly browned, turning often. Remove husks; with clean towel, pull off any remaining silks.

*Parsley-Dill Butter

The traditional way to eat corn on the cob is generously buttered and sprinkled with salt and pepper. For a special treat, herbs are sometimes added to the butter, giving the corn an even fresher flavor. Parsley-Dill Butter and the other herb butters listed here are delicious on fresh corn, on or off the cob, as well as on most other vegetables.

**½   cup butter or margarine, softened
1   tablespoon chopped parsley
1   tablespoon chopped fresh dill or 1
       teaspoon dill weed, crushed**

In small bowl with mixer at medium speed, beat butter with seasonings until light and fluffy. Let stand 1 hour to blend flavors. Yields ½ cup.

SWEET HERB BUTTER: Prepare as above but substitute *½ teaspoon thyme leaves, crushed; ¼ teaspoon rosemary leaves, crushed;* and *¼ teaspoon summer savory leaves, crushed,* for parsley and dill.

HERB BUTTER: Prepare as above but substitute *1 teaspoon marjoram leaves, crushed,* and *½ teaspoon summer savory leaves, crushed,* for parsley and dill.

TARRAGON BUTTER: Prepare as above but substitute *¾ teaspoon tarragon leaves, crushed,* for parsley and dill.

❋ Corn Oysters

These corn-filled fritters are known as Corn Oysters because they are said to resemble oysters in flavor and appearance. We pour maple syrup over the fritters, but pioneer women made a syrup from corn cobs, sugar and water, an example of the frugality with which they used every part of the important corn crop.

BEGIN: 30 MINUTES AHEAD   6 SERVINGS

**1½   cups corn kernels
2   eggs
¼   cup all-purpose flour
¼   teaspoon salt
⅛   teaspoon pepper
4   tablespoons butter or margarine**

1. In medium bowl, combine all ingredients except butter; mix well.

2. In 10-inch skillet over medium heat, heat 2 tablespoons butter. Drop ½ of the corn mixture by rounded tablespoonfuls into butter to make 6 "oysters;" cook until browned on both sides, turning once. Repeat with remaining butter and corn mixture. Serve at once. Yields 12.

❄ Corn Pudding

Corn Pudding, a common dish in Colonial America, is an example of how the English used New World foods in their favorite puddings. They prepared Hasty Pudding and Indian Pudding from cornmeal, but when they had fresh corn they made this delicate Corn Pudding. Colonists made a similar pudding from dried corn during the winter; it still is made by the Pennsylvania Dutch.

BEGIN: 1 HOUR AHEAD   6 SERVINGS

2   eggs
1   cup milk
2   cups corn kernels
¼   cup finely chopped onion
1   tablespoon butter or margarine, melted
¼   teaspoon salt
    Generous dash white pepper

1. Butter 1-quart casserole. In medium bowl with fork, beat eggs slightly. Stir in remaining ingredients. Pour mixture into prepared casserole.

2. Set casserole in baking pan; place on oven rack. Add boiling water to baking pan to reach halfway up side of casserole. Bake at 350°F. 35 to 40 minutes until knife inserted 1 inch from edge comes out clean. Let stand 10 minutes before serving.

TIP: Substitute 2 cups canned whole kernel golden corn, drained, for fresh.

❄ Succotash

One of the first lessons the pioneers learned from the Indians was to grow beans and corn in the same field to conserve space and benefit both crops. Besides growing together, the two crops frequently found themselves in the same pot, making a stew the Indians called Succotash. In summer the beans and corn would be fresh; in winter both were dried.

BEGIN: 1½ HOURS AHEAD   6 SERVINGS

1½ **pounds baby lima beans, shelled**
3   **ears corn**
1   **tablespoon butter or margarine**
¼   **cup heavy cream**
    Salt
    Pepper

1. In 3-quart saucepan over medium heat, in 1 inch boiling, salted water, heat beans to boiling. Reduce heat to low. Cover; simmer 20 minutes or until beans are tender. Drain; return beans to saucepan.

2. Meanwhile, with sharp knife, cut corn from cob; with dull edge of knife, scrape pulp from cob.

3. Stir corn and butter into beans. Over low heat, cook 5 minutes. Stir in cream; heat through. Season with salt and pepper. Yields 4 cups.

TIP: Substitute 2 packages (10 ounces each) frozen baby lima beans for fresh lima beans and 1 package (10 ounces) frozen corn kernels for fresh corn. Cook each as package directs; drain beans and corn. Proceed as in step 3.

❋ Southern Green Beans

Besides eating them fresh, colonists threaded green beans on strings to dry and called them "leather britches." Many generations of cultivation have improved the beans so the cook no longer has to remove a string from each bean (despite the name "string beans"), but merely needs to snap off the ends of the beans (hence the name "snap beans"). Southerners traditionally cook green beans with bacon or pork and onions, often for several hours. Today, most cooks opt for a shorter cooking time, but some Southerners still prefer their beans well done.

BEGIN: 45 MINUTES AHEAD   6 SERVINGS

1   **pound green beans, cut into 1-inch pieces**
6   **slices bacon**
1   **medium onion, chopped**
⅛   **teaspoon pepper**

1. In 2-quart saucepan over medium heat, in 1 inch boiling, salted water, heat beans to boiling. Reduce heat to low. Cover; simmer 10 minutes or until beans are tender-crisp. Drain.

2. Meanwhile, in 10-inch skillet over medium heat, fry bacon until crisp; remove and crumble. Pour off all but 2 tablespoons bacon drippings. In hot drippings, cook onion until tender. Add cooked beans, reserved bacon and pepper. Heat through. Yields 3½ cups.

TIP: Substitute 2 packages (9 ounces each) frozen cut green beans for fresh green beans. Cook as label directs; drain. Proceed as in step 2.

❋ Green Bean Bake

Since its creation in 1955 Green Bean Bake has been served on countless supper tables, at potluck suppers and dinner parties. The reasons for its popularity are many: it is easy to prepare, easy to remember and leaves room for creativity.

BEGIN: 45 MINUTES AHEAD   6 SERVINGS

1   **can (10¾ ounces) condensed cream of mushroom soup**
½   **cup milk**
1   **teaspoon soy sauce**
    Dash pepper
2   **packages (9 ounces each) frozen cut green beans, cooked and drained**
1   **can (2.8 ounces) French fried onions**

1. In 1½-quart casserole, combine soup, milk, soy and pepper. Stir in green beans and ½ can onions.

2. Bake at 350°F. 25 minutes or until hot; stir. Top with remaining onions. Bake 5 minutes more. Yields 4½ cups.

TIP: Substitute 3 cups fresh cut green beans, cooked, or 2 cans (16 ounces each) cut green beans, drained, for frozen green beans.

TO MICROWAVE: In 2-quart microwave-safe casserole, combine soup, milk, soy and pepper. Stir in green beans and ½ can onions; cover. Microwave on HIGH 4 to 6 minutes until hot, stirring once. Top with remaining onions.

❋ Stir-Fried Green Beans

Green beans were not as important in the colonies as dried beans, because they had to be eaten shortly after picking. But the colonists' cooking methods should be blamed for making the beans unpalatable. Like dry beans, they often were cooked several hours, then mashed. Today most Americans cook young beans just until tender-crisp to preserve their nutrients. With a few Oriental vegetables, Stir-Fried Green Beans are a delightful side dish for any meal.

BEGIN: 45 MINUTES AHEAD   8 SERVINGS

2 tablespoons salad oil
1 pound green beans, diagonally cut into
   1-inch pieces
1 medium onion, sliced
½ cup diagonally sliced celery
1 cup bean sprouts
½ cup sliced water chestnuts
¼ cup pimento strips
¼ teaspoon salt
¼ teaspoon sugar
   Soy sauce

1. In 10-inch skillet or wok over high heat, in hot oil, cook green beans, onion and celery, stirring quickly and frequently (stir-frying) 4 to 5 minutes until nearly tender-crisp.

2. Add bean sprouts, water chestnuts, pimento, salt and sugar. Stir-fry until vegetables are tender-crisp. Serve with soy sauce. Yields 5 cups.

❋ Peas and Onions in Cream Sauce

It is said that Christopher Columbus planted the first peas in the Western Hemisphere in 1493, introducing one of the few European vegetable crops the American Indians liked well enough to cultivate for themselves. By the seventeenth century peas grew over most of North America. It was in this same time period that a French woman wrote in a letter about three popular topics of conversation: the anticipation of eating peas, the pleasure of having eaten them, and the desire to eat them again.

BEGIN: 1 HOUR AHEAD   8 SERVINGS

½ pound small whole onions (about 30)
2 pounds peas, shelled
1 tablespoon butter or margarine
1 tablespoon all-purpose flour
⅛ teaspoon salt
   Generous dash pepper
   Generous dash ground nutmeg
1 cup milk
1 teaspoon lemon juice

1. In 3-quart saucepan over medium heat, in 1 inch boiling, salted water, heat onions to boiling. Reduce heat to low. Cover; simmer 10 minutes or until tender-crisp. Add peas. Cover; simmer 5 minutes or until peas are tender. Drain in colander; set aside.

2. In same 3-quart saucepan over medium heat, melt butter. Add flour, salt, pepper and nutmeg. Stir together until smooth.

3. Gradually stir in milk; cook until mixture boils, stirring constantly. Cook 2 minutes more. Stir in reserved onions, peas and lemon juice. Heat 1 minute. Yields 5 cups.

TIP: Substitute 2 packages (10 ounces each) frozen peas for fresh peas.

❋ Minted Peas

The histories of food and table manners often intertwine, with fashions in one dictating changes in the other. Forks were rare in the early Colonial period, so all food was eaten with spoons or knives. Later, two-pronged forks became common, but they were clumsy for foods such as peas, which were often eaten from a knife. The popularity of peas during the eighteenth century may have had a part in inspiring the creation of a three-tined fork that could handle peas. Soon after these forks gained acceptance, eating with a knife became bad manners.

BEGIN: 45 MINUTES AHEAD   6 SERVINGS

2   **pounds peas, shelled**
     Mint sprig
2   **tablespoons butter or margarine**
½   **teaspoon sugar**
¼   **teaspoon salt**
     Dash pepper

1. In 2-quart saucepan over medium heat, in 1 inch boiling, salted water, heat peas and mint to boiling. Reduce heat to low. Cover; simmer 5 minutes. Drain; discard mint sprig.

2. Stir in butter, sugar, salt and pepper; heat through. Yields 3 cups.

To MICROWAVE: In 1-quart microwave-safe casserole combine peas, 1 tablespoon water and mint; cover. Microwave on HIGH 4 minutes. Drain; discard mint sprig. Stir in remaining ingredients; cover. Microwave on HIGH 2 to 3 minutes until heated through.

TIP: Prepare as above but substitute 2 packages (10 ounces each) frozen peas for fresh peas; cook as label directs. Substitute ½ teaspoon dried mint leaves, crushed, for fresh mint.

❋ Squash Casserole

There are two types of squashes. Summer squashes grow quickly and are gathered before their skins become hard; they may be eaten raw or quickly cooked. Winter squashes grow more slowly and require long cooking to tenderize them; neither the skins nor the seeds are eaten with the vegetable. Of the summer variety, zucchini, pattypan and yellow squash are the most popular examples.

BEGIN: 1 HOUR AHEAD   6 SERVINGS

6   **cups cubed yellow squash or zucchini**
1   **can (10¾ ounces) condensed cream of**
     chicken soup
½   **cup water**
¼   **cup chopped toasted almonds**
2   **tablespoons chopped pimento**
¼   **cup dried bread crumbs**
2   **tablespoons butter or margarine, melted**

1. In 3-quart saucepan over medium heat, in 1 inch boiling, salted water, heat squash to boiling. Reduce heat to low. Cover; simmer 3 minutes or until squash is tender. Drain.

2. In 10- by 6-inch baking dish, combine squash, soup, ½ cup water, almonds and pimento. In cup, combine bread crumbs and butter. Sprinkle crumb mixture over squash.

3. Bake at 350°F. 30 minutes or until heated through.

To MICROWAVE: Use ingredients as above but reduce water to ¼ cup. In 1½-quart microwave-safe casserole, combine squash and *only ¼ cup water;* cover. Microwave on HIGH 10 to 12 minutes until squash is tender, stirring occasionally. Drain, reserving ¼ cup liquid. Stir in reserved ¼ cup liquid, soup, almonds and pimento. In cup, combine bread crumbs and butter. Sprinkle crumb mixture over squash. Microwave on HIGH 6 to 8 minutes until heated through, turning occasionally.

❊ Savory Pattypan Squash

The pretty scalloped squash you find at markets in the summer goes by many names—pattypan, scallop, cymling, white squash or custard squash. Some farmers now pick them very small, about 1 inch in diameter; these have a particularly fresh, delicate flavor and unusual appearance.

BEGIN: 30 MINUTES AHEAD   6 SERVINGS

1   **pound small pattypan squash, sliced**
1   **leek, cut into julienne strips**
1   **carrot, cut into julienne strips**
2   **tablespoons butter or margarine**
¼   **teaspoon thyme leaves, crushed**
     Dash salt
     Dash pepper
2   **tablespoons grated Parmesan cheese**

1. In 2-quart saucepan over medium heat, in 1 inch boiling, salted water, heat squash, leek and carrot to boiling. Reduce heat to low. Cover; simmer 5 minutes or until tender-crisp. Drain in colander.

2. In same pan over medium heat, melt butter with thyme, salt and pepper. Add reserved vegetables; toss to coat. Sprinkle with Parmesan cheese. Yields 4 cups.

TIP: Substitute 1 pound very small pattypan squash, halved, for the sliced squash.

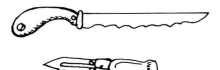

❊ Summer Zucchini Medley

Zucchini has become one of the most popular summer vegetables to grow and to eat. It is prepared in many ways, and in the Southwest, even the blossoms are eaten, usually deep-fried. One of the most delightful vegetable dishes of summer also is one of the easiest, Summer Zucchini Medley.

BEGIN: 45 MINUTES AHEAD   6 SERVINGS

2   **tablespoons butter or margarine**
1   **small onion, chopped**
1   **clove garlic, minced**
2   **medium zucchini or summer squash,**
     sliced
2   **cups sliced mushrooms**
½   **teaspoon salt**
½   **teaspoon dill weed, crushed**
     Dash pepper
1   **tomato, cut into thin wedges**
     Grated Parmesan cheese

1. In 10-inch skillet over medium-high heat, in hot butter, cook onion and garlic until tender.

2. Stir in zucchini, mushrooms, salt, dill and pepper. Cook 5 minutes or until vegetables are tender-crisp. Stir in tomato; cook 1 minute more.

3. To serve: Sprinkle with cheese. Yields 4 cups.

TO MICROWAVE: In 1½-quart microwave-safe casserole, combine butter, onion and garlic; cover. Microwave on HIGH 3 minutes or until tender, stirring once. Stir in zucchini, mushrooms, salt, dill and pepper; cover. Microwave on HIGH 3 to 4 minutes until vegetables are tender-crisp. Stir in tomato; cover. Microwave on HIGH 1 to 2 minutes until hot. Sprinkle with cheese.

Maple-Glazed Acorn Squash, Spaghetti Squash, Savory Pattypan Squash

❊ Maple-Glazed Acorn Squash

Winter squash are yellow- and orange-fleshed vegetables that include acorn, butternut and Hubbard squashes, as well as pumpkins. The first squashes to be cultivated by native Americans probably were raised for their seeds, which the Indians ate; today the seeds remain important in many South American cuisines. As centuries passed, the vegetables were bred for their nutritious, tasty flesh.

BEGIN: 1 HOUR AHEAD   4 SERVINGS

2	**small acorn squash**
	Salt
	Pepper
4	**tablespoons maple syrup**
4	**teaspoons butter or margarine**

1. Halve squash crosswise; remove seeds. Place squash, cut side up, in 13- by 9-inch baking pan.

2. Sprinkle halves with salt and pepper; divide syrup and butter equally among squash halves. Cover with foil.

3. Bake at 350°F. 45 minutes or until squash is fork-tender.

TO MICROWAVE: Prepare as above in steps 1 and 2 but use 12- by 8-inch microwave-safe baking dish and cover squash with plastic wrap. Microwave on HIGH 12 to 14 minutes until fork-tender, turning dish often. Let stand, covered, 2 to 3 minutes before serving.

TIP: Trim thin slice from bottoms so squash stand evenly in pan.

❋ Spaghetti Squash

The spaghetti squash is named for the way its flesh separates into spaghettilike strands. It probably originated in Japan, and only in the past few years has it been widely available in this country. The most popular way to use the squash is to serve it with a favorite pasta sauce. But its delicate flavor makes it good dressed simply with sautéed onion and red pepper.

BEGIN: 45 MINUTES AHEAD   6 SERVINGS

1	**medium spaghetti squash**
¼	**cup butter or margarine**
1	**medium onion, chopped**
1	**sweet red pepper, chopped**
¼	**teaspoon salt**
⅛	**teaspoon pepper**
	Grated Parmesan cheese

1. Halve squash lengthwise; remove seeds and stringy portions.

2. In 10-inch skillet over medium heat, in 1 inch boiling water, heat squash, cut side up, to boiling. Reduce heat to low. Cover; simmer 30 minutes or until fork-tender. Drain.

3. Meanwhile, in 2-quart saucepan over medium-high heat, in hot butter, cook onion and red pepper until vegetables are tender. Stir in salt and pepper; set aside.

4. With fork, lift spaghettilike strands to medium bowl; discard squash shells. Toss together squash and reserved onion mixture. Serve with Parmesan cheese. Yields 3 cups.

❋ Baked Potatoes

The potato is a relative newcomer to world cuisine. South American Indians were the first to discover the potato as a palatable food. When Europeans brought the plant back to Europe no one knew how to cook it. Queen Elizabeth's cook prepared the leaves of the plant for the court! Afterward the potato was grown only as an ornamental plant for many years. Even after they learned how to cook it, many Europeans simply refused to eat the potatoes, believing they caused health problems. But because the potato proved to have excellent qualities— nutritional value, short growing time, resistance to bad weather and adaptability to poor soil—it is now one of the world's five most important food crops.

BEGIN: 1 HOUR AHEAD   4 SERVINGS

4	**medium baking potatoes, unpeeled**
	Salad oil or shortening
	Butter, margarine or sour cream
	Chopped chives (optional)

1. Wash and dry potatoes; rub with oil. Place in shallow pan. Bake at 450°F. 45 minutes or until fork-tender.

2. To serve: Slash tops; garnish with butter or sour cream and chives.

TO MICROWAVE: Prepare as above but prick potatoes with fork and place on microwave-safe dish. Microwave on HIGH 12 to 14 minutes until tender, turning occasionally. Let stand 2 minutes before serving.

TO GRILL: Prepare as above but wrap potatoes individually in foil. Grill over hot coals 45 minutes or until fork-tender, turning often.

TWICE-BAKED POTATOES: Prepare as above in step 1. After baking, cut a thin slice horizontally from top of each potato. With spoon, carefully scoop cooked potato from shells; place pulp in medium bowl. Add *¼ cup milk, 2 tablespoons butter or margarine, ¼ teaspoon salt* and *dash pepper*. With mixer at low speed, beat until fluffy. Fill potato shells; sprinkle with *shredded Cheddar cheese* or *cooked crumbled bacon*. Arrange on baking pan. Bake at 450°F. 10 minutes or until hot.

❋ Scalloped Potatoes

Potatoes have been cooked in every way imaginable; some people even like them raw. The infamous bank robber, John Dillinger, used one to escape from prison—he carved it in the shape of a gun and dyed it with iodine. That is American ingenuity!

BEGIN: 2 HOURS AHEAD   6 SERVINGS

¼   cup butter or margarine
3   tablespoons all-purpose flour
½   teaspoon salt
    Dash pepper
2   cups milk
4   cups thinly sliced potatoes
1   small onion, thinly sliced and separated into rings
    Dash paprika
½   cup shredded Cheddar cheese

1. Butter 1½-quart casserole. For sauce, in heavy, 1-quart saucepan over medium heat, melt butter. Stir in flour, salt and pepper until smooth. Gradually stir in milk; cook until mixture boils, stirring constantly.

2. In prepared casserole, arrange ½ of the potatoes, ½ of the onion and ½ of the sauce. Repeat layers; sprinkle with paprika. Cover.

3. Bake at 350°F. 1 hour. Uncover; bake 15 minutes more or until potatoes are fork-tender. Sprinkle with cheese; bake 5 minutes more or until cheese is melted.

EASY SCALLOPED POTATOES: Use ingredients as above but omit flour and salt and use only 1 tablespoon butter and ½ cup milk. Butter 1½-quart casserole. For sauce, in medium bowl, combine *1 can (10¾ ounces) condensed cream of mushroom soup, only ½ cup milk* and pepper. Assemble as in step 2. Dot with *only 1 tablespoon* butter; proceed as in step 3.

SCALLOPED POTATOES WITH HAM: Prepare as above but use 2-quart casserole and add *1 cup diced cooked ham* to sauce before assembling dish.

❋ Hashed Brown Potatoes

Hashed Brown Potatoes, which originated as a way to reheat leftover boiled potatoes, are the breakfast cook's specialty from coast to coast. For the best Hashed Brown Potatoes, prepare your own or take a cue from American truckers and sample them at the diner where the most trucks are parked.

BEGIN: 1 HOUR AHEAD   6 SERVINGS

¼   cup bacon drippings or salad oil
8   medium potatoes, cooked, peeled and diced
1   onion, finely chopped
1   teaspoon salt
⅛   teaspoon pepper

1. In 10-inch skillet over medium-high heat, heat drippings. Add potatoes to skillet; press down firmly with spatula. Sprinkle with onion, salt and pepper. Reduce heat to medium. Cook until golden on bottom, pressing down potato mixture occasionally.

2. With spatula, turn potatoes about ¼ at a time; press down. Cook until golden, turning as necessary.

❋ Mashed Potatoes and Turnips

The turnip, often considered a humble vegetable, has played an important role in the history of the world's food. It fed the poor in times of famine; it has been an important source of animal feed; it also has been included in elegant dishes. In Colonial America, the turnip was grated to make a coleslawlike salad in German communities and baked into dessert pies in the South. Today it enjoys a certain vogue as one of the raw vegetables that are served as crudités with dips.

BEGIN: 45 MINUTES AHEAD   6 SERVINGS

3   medium potatoes, peeled and quartered
3   medium turnips, peeled and quartered
1½ teaspoons salt
¼   cup butter or margarine
¼   teaspoon white pepper

1. In 3-quart saucepan, combine potatoes, turnips and 1 teaspoon salt. Add water to cover. Over high heat, heat to boiling. Reduce heat to low. Cover; simmer 20 minutes or until vegetables are fork-tender. Drain.

2. In large bowl with mixer at low speed, beat vegetables, remaining ½ teaspoon salt, butter and pepper until fluffy. Yields 3 cups.

❋ Glazed Onions

For centuries the onion has been a respected home remedy and a legendary protection against evil. The onion is said to prevent or cure colds, earaches, burns and nervous disorders; onions growing in the garden have been credited with making roses sweeter and keeping insects away from other vegetables. Whatever the onion's nonfood attributes, it makes a delicious vegetable dish when served with a sweet, buttery glaze.

BEGIN: 45 MINUTES AHEAD   4 SERVINGS

1½ pounds small whole white onions, peeled
2   tablespoons butter or margarine
2   tablespoons sugar
¼   teaspoon salt

1. In 2-quart saucepan over medium heat, in 1 inch boiling water, heat onions to boiling. Reduce heat to low. Cover; simmer 10 to 15 minutes until onions are fork-tender. Drain well.

2. In 10-inch skillet over medium heat, stir butter, sugar and salt until mixed. Add onions; cook about 5 minutes or until onions are glazed, stirring constantly. Yields 3 cups.

TO MICROWAVE: In 2-quart microwave-safe casserole, combine onions and ½ cup water; cover. Microwave on HIGH 8 to 10 minutes until onions are fork-tender, stirring occasionally. Drain well. Add butter, sugar and salt. Toss until butter is melted; cover. Microwave on HIGH 1 minute or until onions are glazed. Let stand, covered, 2 minutes before serving.

❋ Whole Baked Onions

The onion probably is the most frequently used seasoning in American cooking. But onions also make a good vegetable side dish: baked, microwaved or grilled and seasoned with butter, salt and pepper.

BEGIN: 1¼ HOURS AHEAD   8 SERVINGS

8   medium onions, peeled
½   cup water
Butter or margarine, softened
Salt
Pepper

1. Trim thin slice from tops and bottoms of onions so the onions will stand evenly in pan. In 10- by 6-inch baking dish, arrange onions. Add water; cover with foil.

2. Bake at 400°F. 55 to 60 minutes until onions are fork-tender, turning once. Drain; season with butter, salt and pepper.

TO MICROWAVE: Trim slice from top and bottom of onions. In 3-quart microwave-safe casserole, arrange onions in circle. Add water; cover with lid or plastic wrap. Microwave on HIGH 15 to 17 minutes until fork-tender, rotating dish occasionally. Let stand, covered, 2 minutes. Drain; season with butter, salt and pepper.

TO GRILL: Place peeled onions on individual pieces of foil. Dot with butter; sprinkle with salt and pepper. Wrap foil around onion; seal tightly. Grill over hot coals 35 minutes or until fork-tender, turning often.

❋ Saratoga Chips

Potato chips can be found at every supermarket, convenience store and lunch counter in the United States, but the snack is said to have originated at a spa for the wealthy in Saratoga Springs, New York. The story goes that a diner at Moon's Lake House sent his French fries back to chef George Crum, complaining that they were not thin enough. To spite the patron, the chef sliced potatoes as thin as possible before frying them, and returned them to the customer. The new dish caught on with other guests at the spa, and has since become an enormous part of the snack food industry.

BEGIN: 30 MINUTES AHEAD   6 SERVINGS

4   **medium baking potatoes, unpeeled**
    Salad oil
    Salt

1. With sharp knife, cut potatoes into very thin slices. Rinse well in cold water; dry on paper towels.

2. In 4-quart saucepan, heat 2 inches oil to 375°F. Fry potato slices, a few at a time, until golden, turning occasionally. Drain on paper towels. Season to taste with salt. Yields 6 cups.

SWEET POTATO CHIPS: Prepare as above but substitute *4 small sweet potatoes, peeled,* for baking potatoes.

Saratoga Chips, Fried Onion Rings

❋ Fried Onion Rings

Suggestions for peeling and slicing onions without tears range from the practical to the ridiculous. You can peel onions under water, pour boiling water over them or chop them in a food processor (but watch out when you remove the cover). Other methods include holding an unlighted match or piece of bread in your teeth, wearing glasses, keeping your mouth tightly closed or leaving the onion's stem attached while cutting it up. Experiment with these while you prepare Fried Onion Rings.

BEGIN: 3 HOURS AHEAD   6 SERVINGS

1   **cup all-purpose flour**
½   **teaspoon baking powder**
¼   **teaspoon salt**
1   **egg**
⅔   **cup beer**
    Salad oil
1   **large onion, sliced and separated into**
      rings
    Salt

1. In medium bowl, combine first 5 ingredients and 1 teaspoon oil. With wire whisk, beat until smooth. Cover; chill at least 2 hours.

2. *About 30 minutes before serving:* In 4-quart saucepan, heat 2 inches oil to 375°F. Dip onion rings into batter. Fry a few at a time until golden. Drain on paper towels. Sprinkle with salt; serve immediately.

DEEP-FRIED VEGETABLES: Prepare as above but substitute *eggplant sticks, zucchini chunks* or *small whole mushrooms* for sliced onion.

TIP: Keep fried vegetables warm in 250°F. oven while frying remaining batches.

❋ Scalloped Tomatoes

With their high acidity and plentiful crops, tomatoes were naturally among the first vegetables to be canned. Tomatoes still are among the most frequently canned products in this country, and Scalloped Tomatoes is one of the most popular ways to use them. To the basic ingredients—tomatoes and buttered crumbs—Southern cooks add sugar; green peppers or chilies often are added in the Southwest.

BEGIN: 45 MINUTES AHEAD   6 SERVINGS

½   **cup butter or margarine**
1   **large onion, chopped**
4   **cups coarse soft bread crumbs**
2   **teaspoons sugar**
½   **teaspoon salt**
¼   **teaspoon pepper**
2   **cans (28 ounces each) tomatoes, drained**
      and cut up

1. In 2-quart saucepan over medium-high heat, in hot butter, cook onion until tender. Stir in bread crumbs, sugar, salt and pepper; set aside.

2. Arrange ½ of the tomatoes in 10- by 6-inch baking dish. Top with ½ of the crumb mixture. Repeat layers.

3. Bake at 350°F. 30 minutes or until hot.

TO MICROWAVE: Use ingredients as above, but reduce crumbs to 3 cups. In 2-quart microwave-safe casserole, combine butter and onion; cover. Microwave on HIGH 4 to 5 minutes until onion is tender, stirring once. Stir in *only 3 cups bread crumbs,* sugar, salt and pepper; set aside. Arrange ½ of the tomatoes in 10- by 6-inch microwave-safe baking dish. Top with ½ of the crumb mixture. Repeat layers. Microwave on HIGH 7 to 9 minutes until hot, turning dish occasionally.

❋ Broiled Tomatoes

Tomatoes originated in South America, probably in the area that is now Peru. Spanish explorers brought the fruit to the Old World, but it was many years before the general population felt safe eating them. Even in the 1800s, some cookbook authors recommended cooking tomatoes no less than three hours; until the middle of the nineteenth century the consumption of raw tomatoes was generally believed to cause death. Since that time the tomato has found its way into virtually every cuisine in the world.

BEGIN: 15 MINUTES AHEAD   8 SERVINGS

4   large ripe tomatoes
     Garlic salt
     Pepper
¼   cup Italian-seasoned dried bread crumbs
2   tablespoons grated Parmesan cheese
1   tablespoon chopped parsley
2   tablespoons butter or margarine, melted

1. Cut tomatoes in half crosswise; arrange cut side up on rack in broiler pan. Sprinkle with garlic salt and pepper. In cup, combine crumbs, Parmesan cheese, parsley and butter; mix well. Sprinkle over tomatoes.

2. Broil 6 inches from heat 3 minutes or until golden brown.

❋ Southern Greens

A great deal of Southern cooking originated with the African slaves who cooked for plantation owners and other Southern whites. For themselves they used foods out of their gardens and the leftovers from their owners' tables. Such dishes as Southern Greens grew out of that tradition, made from fresh greens and odd pieces of pork, such as bacon, hocks and jowls. The cooking liquid was never wasted; if it wasn't spooned over cornbread, it was added to soups or stews. Health-giving qualities have been ascribed to this "pot likker," which contains nutrients and flavor from the meat and vegetables cooked in it.

BEGIN: 1½ HOURS AHEAD   6 SERVINGS

½   pound country ham
3   cups water
1½   pounds turnip greens, kale, mustard
       greens or collard greens
¼   teaspoon salt
¼   teaspoon pepper
     Corn bread (optional)
     White vinegar (optional)

1. In 4-quart saucepan over medium-high heat, heat ham and water to boiling. Reduce heat to low. Cover; simmer 30 minutes.

2. Meanwhile, wash greens well under running cold water. Trim and discard ribs and stems; drain greens. Add greens, salt and pepper to saucepan.

3. Over medium-high heat, heat to boiling. Reduce heat to low. Cover; simmer 30 minutes or until greens are tender. Drain greens, reserving liquid. Cool greens and ham until easy to handle. Cut up greens and ham; stir together. Heat through. Serve liquid with corn bread; serve greens with vinegar. Yields 5 cups.

❋ Confetti Cabbage

Once known as a vegetable for the wealthy, cabbage also has been known as a food for the poor. A hardy vegetable, easy to grow and easy to store, it came to America with the earliest settlers. The settlers from Holland used it for coleslaw, Germans cured it to make sauerkraut and New Englanders included it in the traditional boiled dinner. In this recipe, the cabbage is stir-fried with carrots and zucchini just long enough to tenderize the leaves and bring out its fresh flavor.

BEGIN: 45 MINUTES AHEAD   6 SERVINGS

2   tablespoons salad oil
1   onion, sliced
2   cloves garlic, minced
6   cups thinly sliced cabbage
2   carrots, shredded
1   medium zucchini, cut into julienne strips
½   teaspoon salt
½   teaspoon caraway seed

1. In 5-quart Dutch oven over high heat, in hot oil, cook onion and garlic until onion is tender, stirring often.

2. Stir in remaining ingredients. Cook until cabbage is tender-crisp, about 10 minutes, stirring quickly and frequently (stir-frying). Yields 4 cups.

Confetti Cabbage

❋ Sweet and Sour Red Cabbage

Both green and red cabbage keep well into the winter months. German immigrants prepared cabbage with a sauce of vinegar and sugar for a tart, zesty flavor. Red cabbage adds color to cold-weather meals, and is a fine accompaniment to pot roast or wild game.

BEGIN: 2 HOURS AHEAD   6 SERVINGS

¼ **cup bacon drippings**
¼ **cup finely chopped onion**
1 **medium head red cabbage, shredded (about 8 cups)**
2 **medium cooking apples, peeled, cored and thinly sliced**
1 **cup water**
½ **cup wine vinegar**
¼ **cup packed brown sugar**
1 **teaspoon caraway seed**
½ **teaspoon salt**
⅛ **teaspoon pepper**

1. In 5-quart Dutch oven over medium-high heat, in hot bacon drippings, cook onion until tender.

2. Stir in remaining ingredients; heat to boiling. Reduce heat to low. Cover; simmer 1½ hours or until cabbage is very tender, stirring occasionally. Yields 5 cups.

TO MICROWAVE: Use ingredients as above but reduce water to ½ cup and vinegar to ¼ cup. In 3-quart microwave-safe casserole, combine bacon drippings and onion; cover. Microwave on HIGH 2 minutes. Stir in remaining ingredients, using *only ½ cup water* and *only ¼ cup vinegar;* cover. Microwave on HIGH 30 to 35 minutes until cabbage is very tender, stirring occasionally. Let stand, covered, 10 minutes before serving.

❋ Cauliflower with Cheese Sauce

Mark Twain called the cauliflower a cabbage with a college education. In a way, he was correct. Cauliflower is a member of the cabbage family that has been cultivated to form a head of undeveloped flowers. It may be white, green like cabbage or even purple. A creamy cheese sauce turns cauliflower into a dramatic vegetable dish.

BEGIN: 30 MINUTES AHEAD   8 SERVINGS

1   **medium head cauliflower**
     Cheese Sauce*
¼   **teaspoon ground nutmeg**

1. Remove any outer leaves from cauliflower. Core cauliflower and separate into flowerets.

2. In 3-quart saucepan over medium heat, in 1 inch boiling, salted water, heat cauliflower to boiling. Reduce heat to low. Cover; simmer 8 to 10 minutes until tender-crisp. Drain well.

3. Combine Cheese Sauce with nutmeg; pour over cauliflower. Yields 5 cups.

To MICROWAVE: Prepare cauliflower as in step 1. In 2-quart microwave-safe casserole, combine cauliflower and ¼ cup water; cover. Microwave on HIGH 10 to 12 minutes, stirring occasionally. Let stand, covered, 2 minutes before serving. Drain well. Proceed as in step 3.

*Cheese Sauce

The richness of a cheese sauce sets off the fresh flavor of vegetables. Serve it with cauliflower, as in the previous recipe, or on broccoli, green beans, potatoes or asparagus.

BEGIN: 15 MINUTES AHEAD   8 SERVINGS

2   **tablespoons butter or margarine**
2   **tablespoons all-purpose flour**
¼   **teaspoon salt**
¼   **teaspoon dry mustard**
     Dash pepper
1½   **cups milk**
1   **cup shredded Cheddar cheese**

1. In heavy, 1-quart saucepan over medium heat, melt butter. Stir in flour, salt, mustard and pepper until smooth.

2. Gradually stir in milk; cook until mixture boils, stirring constantly. Cook 2 minutes more. Add cheese; stir until melted. Yields 2 cups.

To MICROWAVE: Use ingredients as above but reduce milk to 1 cup. Place butter in 4-cup microwave-safe measure. Microwave on HIGH 30 seconds or until melted. Stir in flour, salt, mustard and pepper until smooth. Microwave on HIGH 1 to 1½ minutes, stirring twice. Gradually stir in *only 1 cup milk*. Microwave on HIGH 3½ to 5½ minutes until mixture boils, stirring occasionally. Add cheese; stir until melted and smooth.

❋ Vegetable Combo

To add a variety of colors and flavors to a menu, many cooks combine two or three different vegetables in a single side dish. The vegetables may vary with the season and personal preference, but this winter broccoli, cauliflower and carrot mixture is one of the best. The key is to start with the freshest vegetables, cooking them only until they are tender-crisp, then tossing them with a delicately flavored butter that lets the taste of the vegetables shine through.

BEGIN: 45 MINUTES AHEAD   8 SERVINGS

½   **pound carrots, sliced**
½   **pound broccoli, cut into 1-inch pieces**
1   **small head cauliflower, broken into**
     flowerets
¼   **cup butter or margarine**
1   **clove garlic, minced**
1   **tablespoon chopped parsley**
½   **teaspoon basil leaves, crushed**

1. In 5-quart Dutch oven over medium heat, in 1 inch boiling, salted water, heat carrots to boiling. Reduce heat to low. Cover; simmer 10 minutes. Add broccoli and cauliflower. Cover; simmer 10 minutes more or until vegetables are tender-crisp. Drain in colander.

2. In same pan over medium-high heat, in hot butter, cook garlic, parsley and basil 1 minute. Add vegetables; toss to coat. Heat through. Yields 5 cups.

❋ Casserole of Broccoli with Almonds

Besides green and red cabbage, the cabbage family includes cauliflower, collards, kale, Brussels sprouts, kohl-rabi and broccoli. Although broccoli has been a popular vegetable in America only since the 1920s, it has been used as a food since the times of the ancient Romans.

BEGIN: 1¼ HOURS AHEAD   6 SERVINGS

1   **pound broccoli, cut into 1-inch pieces**
6   **tablespoons butter or margarine**
2   **tablespoons all-purpose flour**
½   **teaspoon basil leaves, crushed**
1   **cup milk**
¼   **cup mayonnaise**
1   **can (8 ounces) sliced water chestnuts,**
     drained
¼   **cup chopped pimentos**
¼   **teaspoon salt**
⅛   **teaspoon pepper**
¼   **cup dried bread crumbs**
¼   **cup sliced almonds**

1. Butter 1½-quart casserole. In 3-quart saucepan over medium heat, in 1 inch boiling, salted water, heat broccoli to boiling. Reduce heat to low. Cover; simmer 10 minutes or until broccoli is tender-crisp. Drain in colander.

2. In same saucepan over medium heat, melt 4 tablespoons butter; stir in flour and basil until smooth. Gradually stir in milk. Cook until mixture boils, stirring constantly. Stir in mayonnaise, water chestnuts, pimentos, salt, pepper and drained broccoli. Spoon into prepared casserole.

3. In small saucepan over medium heat, melt remaining 2 tablespoons butter; stir in bread crumbs and almonds. Sprinkle crumb mixture over broccoli.

4. Bake at 350°F. 30 minutes or until hot.

TIP: Substitute 1 bag (20 ounces) frozen broccoli cuts for fresh broccoli. Cook as label directs. Proceed as in step 2.

❄ Broccoli Stir-Fry

Because good, fresh broccoli is now so easy to find, many ways of preparing it have been developed to take advantage of its freshness. One of these is this Broccoli Stir-Fry. For even more of an Oriental flavor, use the Japanese enoki *mushrooms when you can find them.*

BEGIN: 30 MINUTES AHEAD   6 SERVINGS

1   pound broccoli
2   tablespoons salad oil
1   clove garlic, halved
1   thin slice fresh ginger root
1   cup sliced mushrooms
¼   cup water or chicken broth
1   tablespoon soy sauce

1. Remove broccoli flowerets from stems. Peel tough outer portions of broccoli stems; cut stems into julienne strips. Separate flowerets into bite-sized pieces.

2. In wok or 10-inch skillet over high heat, heat oil. Add garlic and ginger; cook, stirring quickly and frequently (stir-frying) 30 seconds. Discard garlic and ginger.

3. Add broccoli and mushrooms; stir-fry 2 minutes. Add water and soy sauce. Cover; cook 1 minute. Uncover; stir-fry 1 minute more or until broccoli is tender-crisp. Yields 4 cups.

TIP: Substitute 1 can (10 ounces) *enoki* or golden mushrooms, drained, for sliced mushrooms.

❄ Brussels Sprouts and Walnuts

The British are the most enthusiastic consumers of the Brussels sprout today, and probably were responsible for its introduction to America. The vegetable has a fairly late season, producing even after frost; therefore, it has become traditional in many families as a Thanksgiving vegetable, particularly when combined with chestnuts.

BEGIN: 30 MINUTES AHEAD   4 SERVINGS

1   pound Brussels sprouts
2   tablespoons butter or margarine
½   cup broken walnuts

1. With sharp knife, trim stems from Brussels sprouts. Cut an X into stem end of sprouts to speed cooking time. Rinse sprouts.

2. In 2-quart saucepan over medium heat, in 1 inch boiling, salted water, heat sprouts to boiling. Reduce heat to low. Cover; simmer 10 to 15 minutes or until sprouts are tender-crisp. Drain.

3. Add butter and walnuts; toss to combine. Heat through. Yields 3 cups.

BRUSSELS SPROUTS AND CHESTNUTS: Prepare as above but substitute *1 cup cooked chestnuts* for walnuts. (See recipe for Chestnut Soup, page 18, to cook chestnuts.)

TO MICROWAVE: Prepare as above in step 1. In 2-quart microwave-safe casserole combine Brussels sprouts, ¼ cup water and ¼ teaspoon salt; cover. Microwave on HIGH 7 to 9 minutes until sprouts are tender-crisp, stirring occasionally. Drain. Add butter and walnuts; toss to coat sprouts. Let stand, covered, 2 minutes; stir again before serving.

❉ Mustard-Sauced Kohlrabi

Kohlrabi, another member of the cabbage family, is unlike any other vegetable. The leaves are sometimes used in mixtures of greens or soups, but the most commonly eaten part is an enlarged portion of the stem. It may be cooked, as in this recipe, or simply shredded or cubed for eating raw.

BEGIN: 1 HOUR AHEAD   6 SERVINGS

6	medium kohlrabi, peeled and cubed
2	tablespoons butter or margarine
¼	cup sliced green onions
2	tablespoons all-purpose flour
1	tablespoon prepared mustard
½	teaspoon dill weed, crushed
1	cup milk

1. In 3-quart saucepan over high heat, heat 1 inch water to boiling. Add kohlrabi. Cover; simmer 30 minutes or until tender; drain.

2. Meanwhile, in heavy, 1-quart saucepan over medium heat, in hot butter, cook green onions until tender. Add flour, mustard and dill weed; stir together until smooth.

3. Gradually stir in milk; cook until mixture boils, stirring constantly. Cook 2 minutes more. Pour sauce over kohlrabi. Yields 4 cups.

❉ Ambushed Asparagus

Although it is practically forgotten today, this presentation for asparagus was all the rage 100 years ago. Creamy asparagus was served in a dinner roll as a side dish or knife-and-fork appetizer. Use square or rectangular dinner rolls, 3 to 4 inches across.

BEGIN: 45 MINUTES AHEAD   6 SERVINGS

1	pound asparagus
6	hard dinner rolls
2	tablespoons butter or margarine
2	tablespoons all-purpose flour
½	teaspoon salt
¼	teaspoon pepper
	Dash nutmeg
1¼	cups milk
1	teaspoon lemon juice

1. Discard tough ends of asparagus and trim scales. Cut asparagus into 1-inch pieces; set aside. With bread knife, cut thin slice from top of each roll. Hollow out rolls, leaving ¼-inch shells. On baking sheet, arrange shells and covers. Bake at 250°F. 15 minutes or until hot and crisp.

2. Meanwhile, in 10-inch skillet over medium heat, in ½ inch boiling, salted water, heat asparagus to boiling. Reduce heat to low. Cover; simmer 5 minutes or until asparagus are tender-crisp. Drain.

3. In heavy, 1-quart saucepan over medium heat, melt butter. Add flour, salt, pepper and nutmeg; stir together until smooth. Gradually stir in milk. Cook until mixture boils, stirring constantly. Cook 2 minutes more. Stir in lemon juice and cooked asparagus; heat through.

4. To serve: Spoon asparagus mixture into hot rolls. Cover with tops or place tops alongside rolls.

To Microwave: Prepare as above in step 1. Meanwhile, in 1-quart microwave-safe casserole, combine asparagus and ¼ cup water; cover. Microwave on HIGH 4 to 6 minutes until asparagus are tender-crisp, stirring once. Drain. In 4-cup microwave-safe measure, place butter. Microwave on HIGH 30 seconds or until melted. Add flour, salt, pepper and nutmeg; stir together until smooth. Gradually stir in milk. Microwave on HIGH 3½ to 5 minutes until mixture boils, stirring occasionally. Stir in lemon juice and cooked asparagus. Serve as in step 4.

❊ Asparagus Quiche

For centuries, tender shoots of fresh asparagus have been a welcome sign of spring. The ancient Greeks and Romans enjoyed the vegetable as a food, and also considered it a remedy for ills such as toothache. Although asparagus is found throughout the world, it has always remained a delicacy. To achieve the pale color of white asparagus, the stalks are grown underground, away from the light. One fine way to serve asparagus is in a quiche, where the delicate flavor of the asparagus is enhanced by cheese and seasonings.

BEGIN: 1½ HOURS AHEAD   6 SERVINGS

1   **9-inch Unbaked Piecrust (see page 256)**
1½ **cups asparagus cut into 1-inch pieces,
        cooked and drained**
2   **cups shredded natural Swiss cheese**
2   **green onions, sliced**
1   **tablespoon all-purpose flour**
3   **eggs**
1   **cup milk**
¼   **teaspoon salt**
¼   **teaspoon pepper**
⅛   **teaspoon garlic powder
       Cooked asparagus spears**

1. Preheat oven to 425°F. Prepare Unbaked Piecrust. Bake 7 minutes or until crust is set; remove from oven. Reduce heat to 350°F.

2. In medium bowl, toss cut asparagus, cheese, green onions and flour. Spread into piecrust.

3. In same bowl with wire whisk, beat eggs, milk, salt, pepper and garlic powder. Pour over cheese mixture.

4. Bake 25 minutes. Arrange asparagus spears over quiche. Bake 5 to 10 minutes more until knife inserted about 1 inch from edge comes out clean. Let pie stand 10 minutes. Cut into wedges.

GREEN BEAN QUICHE: Prepare as above but substitute *1½ cups cooked, drained cut green beans* for asparagus.

❊ Mushrooms in Cream

Although mushrooms have been eaten for centuries, until recently they were used by the wealthy or by those who gathered them wild. Because they were difficult to cultivate, they were expensive. In the United States, mushrooms first were commercially grown late in the nineteenth century, when growers were not able to control temperature and humidity and the crop was limited. Cultivation techniques have improved so that production has more than doubled in the past 15 years.

BEGIN: 30 MINUTES AHEAD   4 SERVINGS

2   **tablespoons butter or margarine**
1   **green onion, finely chopped**
1   **pound mushrooms, sliced**
1   **teaspoon chopped fresh dill weed or ¼
        teaspoon dill weed, crushed**
½   **cup heavy cream**
¼   **teaspoon salt**
⅛   **teaspoon pepper**

1. In 10-inch skillet over medium-high heat, in hot butter, cook green onion until tender.

2. Stir in mushrooms and dill. Reduce heat to medium; cook until mushroom liquid evaporates, stirring constantly.

3. Stir in cream, salt and pepper; heat through. Yields 2 cups.

TO MICROWAVE: Use ingredients as above but reduce cream to ¼ cup. In 2-quart microwave-safe casserole, combine butter and green onion; cover. Microwave on HIGH 1½ minutes or until onion is tender. Stir in mushrooms and dill; cover. Microwave on HIGH 2 to 4 minutes until mushrooms are tender, stirring once. Drain well. Stir in *only ¼ cup heavy cream,* salt and pepper; cover. Microwave on HIGH 1 to 2 minutes until hot.

❊ Blushing Carrots

Blushing Carrots, also known as Copper Pennies, make a welcome change from ordinary vegetables. The cooked carrots are marinated with onion and green pepper, then served cold as a colorful side dish.

BEGIN: DAY AHEAD   8 SERVINGS

2   **pounds carrots, sliced**
1   **can (10¾ ounces) condensed tomato
      soup**
1   **cup sugar**
¾   **cup cider vinegar**
½   **cup salad oil**
1   **teaspoon dry mustard**
1   **teaspoon Worcestershire**
1   **large onion, sliced and separated into
      rings**
1   **green pepper, cut into strips**

1. In 3-quart saucepan over medium heat, in 1 inch boiling, salted water, heat carrots to boiling. Reduce heat to low. Cover; simmer 10 to 15 minutes until tender-crisp; drain.

2. Meanwhile, in 4-cup measure, combine soup, sugar, vinegar, oil, mustard and Worcestershire; mix well.

3. In medium bowl, arrange alternate layers of carrots, onion and green pepper. Pour tomato mixture over all. Refrigerate until serving time, at least 6 hours. Yields 6 cups.

Blushing Carrots

❊ Orange-Glazed Carrots

The carrot is a vegetable with a high sugar content that adds a certain sweetness to soups, salads, stews and even desserts. It is used in tortes from Austria, puddings from England, tsimmes from the Jews, and in American carrot cake. Bring out the sweetness of carrots with a slightly sweet sauce, as in this recipe for Orange-Glazed Carrots.

BEGIN: 45 MINUTES AHEAD   4 SERVINGS

1   **pound carrots, cut into julienne strips**
⅔   **cup water**
¼   **cup sugar**
3   **tablespoons butter or margarine**
1   **tablespoon grated orange peel**
1   **tablespoon chopped parsley**

1. In 10-inch skillet over medium heat, heat all ingredients except parsley to boiling. Reduce heat to low. Cover; simmer 10 to 12 minutes until carrots are tender-crisp.

2. Uncover; over medium-high heat, cook until liquid is reduced and carrots are glazed, stirring constantly. Sprinkle with parsley. Yields 2½ cups.

❋ Braised Celery and Leeks

The Welsh take the leek as a symbol of their nation, the Irish cite it in their religious tradition, Nero ate leek soup to improve his voice and the ancient Greeks considered it an aphrodisiac. But despite the magical qualities that recommend both celery and leeks, in America they most often are used as seasonings in soups, stews and sauces, often in combination. Prepare Braised Celery and Leeks to discover how the two vegetables enhance one another to make an elegant vegetable dish.

BEGIN: 45 MINUTES AHEAD   6 SERVINGS

2   celery hearts, cut into 3-inch-long strips
4   medium leeks, cut into 1-inch pieces
1¾ cups chicken broth
¼   cup butter or margarine
½   teaspoon basil leaves, crushed

1. In 3-quart saucepan over medium heat, heat celery, leeks and broth to boiling. Reduce heat to low. Cover; simmer 15 minutes or until tender. Drain; reserve broth for another use.

2. In same saucepan over medium heat, melt butter with basil. Add celery and leeks; toss to combine. Heat through. Yields 4 cups.

TIP: Clean the sand out of leeks by halving them lengthwise, then rinsing under running water.

❋ Celery Victor

Celery Victor is a San Francisco creation, made up by chef Victor Hirtzler of the St. Francis Hotel in the early part of this century. Of the many dishes he created, Celery Victor is the most enduring.

BEGIN: EARLY IN DAY   6 SERVINGS

2   celery hearts
1¾ cups chicken broth
4   parsley sprigs
1   bay leaf
⅛   teaspoon white pepper
½   cup olive or salad oil
¼   cup wine vinegar
1   teaspoon Dijon mustard
    Pimento strips
    Anchovy fillets

1. Trim celery; cut into 4-inch pieces. In 3-quart saucepan over medium heat, heat celery, chicken broth, parsley, bay leaf and pepper to boiling. Reduce heat to low. Cover; simmer 15 minutes or until tender. Discard parsley and bay leaf. Place celery and broth in medium bowl.

2. Stir in oil, vinegar and mustard. Cover; refrigerate overnight, turning celery occasionally.

3. To serve: With slotted spoon, remove celery from broth; arrange celery on platter. Garnish with pimento strips and anchovies. Yields 4 cups.

❋ Herbed Jerusalem Artichokes

The Jerusalem artichoke, native to America, is the root of a type of sunflower plant. First eaten by American Indians, its English name came from Italy. Italians call the sunflower girasole, *which sounded like Jerusalem to the British who imported the plant from Italy. A flavor reminiscent of artichokes gives the vegetable the second part of its name. "Sunchokes" is another name for this interesting vegetable.*

BEGIN: 45 MINUTES AHEAD   12 SERVINGS

1½ pounds Jerusalem artichokes
2   tablespoons butter or margarine
¼   teaspoon salt
¼   teaspoon basil leaves, crushed
⅛   teaspoon pepper
1   tablespoon chopped parsley

1. Scrub Jerusalem artichokes; cut into ¼-inch slices.

2. In 2-quart saucepan over medium heat, in 1 inch boiling, salted water, heat Jerusalem artichokes to boiling. Reduce heat to low. Cover; simmer 20 minutes or until Jerusalem artichokes are tender-crisp. Drain.

3. Add remaining ingredients; toss to combine. Heat through. Yields 7 cups.

Herbed Jerusalem Artichokes

❋ Sautéed Parsnips

Parsnips were among the first vegetables brought to the New World by colonists and were once far more common than they are today. Parsnips have a late season compared to most vegetables. Many growers leave the roots in the ground until after the first frost because the cold temperatures improve the flavor by converting some of the starch to sugar. Home gardeners sometimes leave the parsnips in the ground all winter, digging them up only when they are needed.

BEGIN: 30 MINUTES AHEAD   4 SERVINGS

1	**pound parsnips, cut into 1-inch pieces**
¼	**cup all-purpose flour**
½	**teaspoon salt**
⅛	**teaspoon ground cinnamon**
	Dash pepper
¼	**cup salad oil**
	Chopped parsley

1. In 3-quart saucepan over medium heat, in 1 inch boiling, salted water, heat parsnips to boiling. Reduce heat to low. Cover; simmer 8 to 10 minutes until tender-crisp. Drain well.

2. In pie plate, combine flour, salt, cinnamon and pepper. Coat parsnips with flour mixture.

3. In 10-inch skillet over medium-high heat, in hot oil, cook parsnips until golden brown. Drain on paper towels. Sprinkle with parsley. Yields 2½ cups.

❋ Marinated Roast Peppers

Green and red peppers appear as an ingredient in many recipes, but they also make a fine dish on their own. These roast peppers, with their Italian-style marinade, can be included in salads and sandwiches or served just as they are.

BEGIN: EARLY IN DAY   4 SERVINGS

2	**green peppers**
2	**sweet red peppers**
¼	**cup olive or salad oil**
1	**tablespoon vinegar**
2	**cloves garlic, halved**
¼	**teaspoon oregano leaves, crushed**
¼	**teaspoon salt**
⅛	**teaspoon pepper**

1. Place peppers on baking sheet; bake at 450°F. 25 minutes or until skin blisters and chars. Place peppers in paper bag. Close bag; cool until cool enough to handle. Remove thin skin from peppers. Discard skin, seeds and stems. Cut peppers into 1-inch-wide strips.

2. In medium bowl, stir together remaining ingredients. Add peppers; toss to coat. Cover; refrigerate until serving time, at least 4 hours. Remove garlic before serving. Yields 1½ cups.

ANCHOVIES AND PEPPERS: Prepare as above, but add *1 can (2 ounces) anchovy fillets, drained,* to oil mixture along with peppers.

❈ Candied Yams

Why yams and sweet potatoes are traditional at Thanksgiving is a mystery, since neither vegetable was native to North America. Yams originated in Africa, sweet potatoes in South America, and neither was served at the first Thanksgiving. Although the two vegetables are botanically very different, the world's cooks have found them similar in flavor, appearance and use. Candied yams probably originated in the South, but today they are served throughout the nation.

BEGIN: 1 HOUR AHEAD   6 SERVINGS

4   yams or sweet potatoes, unpeeled
1   teaspoon salt
½   cup butter or margarine
½   cup packed brown sugar
1   tablespoon grated orange peel
¼   cup orange juice or water
⅛   teaspoon ground cinnamon
     Generous dash pepper
½   cup coarsely chopped walnuts (optional)

1. In 4-quart saucepan, place yams and salt. Add water to cover. Over high heat, heat to boiling. Reduce heat to low. Cover; simmer 30 to 40 minutes until yams are fork-tender. Drain; cool slightly. Peel and quarter yams.

2. In same saucepan, combine butter, brown sugar, orange peel, orange juice, cinnamon and pepper. Heat to boiling. Add yams and nuts; heat until yams are glazed, spooning sauce over to coat.

SWEET POTATO CASSEROLE: Use ingredients as above but omit walnuts. Prepare as above in step 1. Butter 2-quart casserole. In large bowl with mixer at low speed, beat potatoes and remaining ingredients until light and fluffy. Spread potato mixture into prepared casserole. Top with *2 cups miniature marshmallows*. Bake at 375°F. 15 minutes or until topping is golden.

❈ Eggplant Parmesan

The eggplant was an Oriental vegetable, which made its way to Europe during the Middle Ages. At first the vegetable was known as a "mad" or "raging apple," and was believed to cause insanity or epilepsy. But later it became an integral part of European cuisine, particularly around the Mediterranean. The Italians originated the recipe for Eggplant Parmesan that later traveled to the New World.

BEGIN: 1½ HOURS AHEAD   8 SERVINGS

     Olive oil or salad oil
1   onion, finely chopped
1   clove garlic, minced
1   can (28 ounces) tomatoes, cut up
1   can (6 ounces) tomato paste
¼   teaspoon basil leaves, crushed
¼   teaspoon oregano leaves, crushed
1   cup Italian-seasoned dried bread crumbs
¼   cup all-purpose flour
⅛   teaspoon pepper
3   eggs
3   tablespoons milk
1   medium eggplant, cut into ½-inch slices
1   cup grated Parmesan cheese
1   package (6 ounces) sliced mozzarella cheese

1. In 3-quart saucepan over medium-high heat, in 2 tablespoons hot oil, cook onion and garlic until tender. Stir in tomatoes, tomato paste, basil and oregano. Reduce heat to low. Simmer, uncovered, 30 minutes, stirring occasionally.

2. Meanwhile, combine bread crumbs, flour and pepper on waxed paper; beat eggs and milk in pie plate. Dip eggplant slices in egg, then in crumbs. Repeat to coat slices twice.

3. In 10-inch skillet over medium heat, in 2 tablespoons hot oil, cook eggplant slices, a few at a time, until well browned; add more oil as needed.

4. Grease 12- by 8-inch baking dish. Preheat oven to 350°F. Arrange ½ of the eggplant slices in prepared dish; cover with ½ of the tomato sauce; sprinkle with ½ of the Parmesan. Repeat layers; top with mozzarella slices. Bake 30 to 35 minutes until hot and bubbly.

❋ Artichokes

Artichokes have been present in America for about 200 years. Brought from Europe and cultivated in California by Italians, the vegetable has always been regarded as a delicacy in this country; the average American eats only a small fraction of the amount consumed by a European. Perhaps this can be explained by the more casual dining habits in America; eating an artichoke requires attention, and it is usually served as a separate course. Artichokes are served whole, one to a person, with Hollandaise or melted butter. To eat one, pull off a leaf, dip it into the sauce and scrape off the thick smooth part of each leaf with your teeth.

BEGIN: 45 MINUTES AHEAD   4 SERVINGS

4   artichokes
1   lemon, quartered
    Hollandaise Sauce* or melted butter

1. With sharp knife, cut off stems and tops of artichokes. With scissors, trim thorny tips of leaves and pull loose leaves from around bottom of each artichoke.

2. In 6-quart Dutch oven over medium heat, in 1 inch boiling, salted water, place artichokes stem side down. Add lemon; heat to boiling.

3. Reduce heat to low. Cover; simmer 30 minutes or until leaf can be pulled away easily. Drain; serve with Hollandaise Sauce or melted butter.

*Hollandaise Sauce

Most experts attribute this classic sauce to France, although its name suggests a Dutch origin. Whatever the case, Hollandaise Sauce has been thoroughly integrated into the American cuisine. Serve it with artichokes or spoon it over asparagus, broccoli, cauliflower, eggs, fish, poultry and other foods. With whipped cream added, Hollandaise Sauce becomes Mousseline Sauce; with orange rind, it is Maltaise Sauce.

3   egg yolks
2   tablespoons lemon juice
½   cup butter or margarine, softened and
      cut into pieces
    Dash salt

1. In double-boiler top with wire whisk, beat egg yolks and lemon juice until well mixed. Place over double-boiler bottom containing hot, not boiling, water.

2. Stir ½ of the butter into yolk mixture, beating *constantly* until butter is completely melted.

3. Stir in remaining butter, a few pieces at a time, beating *constantly* until mixture is thickened and heated through. Remove from heat; stir in salt. Keep warm. Yields ¾ cup.

❋ Fried Okra

Okra probably grew first in Africa and was brought to America by slaves. In the Southern part of the United States it became a standard vegetable, particularly important in Creole dishes. Okra may be stewed, baked or coated with cornmeal and fried, as in this recipe.

BEGIN: 30 MINUTES AHEAD   4 SERVINGS

½   cup white cornmeal
½   teaspoon salt
⅛   teaspoon pepper
1   egg
2   tablespoons milk
1   pound okra, cut into ½-inch slices
¼   cup bacon drippings or salad oil

1. Combine cornmeal, salt and pepper on waxed paper; beat egg and milk in pie plate. Toss okra in egg mixture. With slotted spoon, remove okra to cornmeal mixture; coat well with cornmeal mixture.

2. In heavy, 10-inch skillet over medium heat, in hot bacon drippings, cook okra 3 to 4 minutes until tender and golden, stirring often and adding more drippings if necessary. Drain on paper towels. Yields 2 cups.

✳ Pickled Beets

The beet has evolved into four types of plants, each cultivated for a different purpose. The most readily recognized is the beet raised for its sweet, red root, which is served as a vegetable. Chard is a member of the beet family that has been bred for its tender leaves and stalks. The sugar beet, a commercially important source of sugar, and the mangel-wurzel, a beet raised for livestock feed, are two varieties you are not likely to see in your supermarket. The Pennsylvania Dutch are famous for pickled beets. Once the beets are eaten, the liquid is used to pickle hard-cooked eggs, which take on a beautiful color and zesty flavor.

BEGIN: 2 DAYS AHEAD

12 **small beets with tops (about 2 pounds)**
4   **small onions, sliced and separated into rings**
1½ **cups wine vinegar**
2   **tablespoons sugar**
2   **teaspoons whole cloves**
1   **teaspoon salt**

1. Trim beets, leaving 2 inches of tops and roots attached. Rinse beets under cold running water being careful not to damage skins.

2. In 4-quart saucepan over medium heat, in 1 inch boiling, salted water, heat whole beets to boiling. Reduce heat to low. Cover; simmer 30 to 60 minutes until beets are fork-tender (depending on maturity and size of beets). Drain beets; cool. With sharp knife, remove skins and stems. Cut beets into ¼-inch slices.

3. In medium bowl, combine beets with remaining ingredients. Cover; refrigerate until serving time, at least 2 days. Yields 5 cups.

RED PICKLED EGGS: Prepare as above. Drain beets, reserving marinade. In jar or casserole, combine reserved marinade and *6 hard-cooked eggs.* Refrigerate until serving time, at least 1 week.

✳ Harvard Beets

Beets are used in such diverse foods as Borscht, Red Flannel Hash and Chiffonade Dressing, but they also star in their own preparations such as New England's Harvard Beets and Yale Beets. To retain the rich red color that is said to have inspired the Harvard name (the university's school color), they must be cooked without peeling, or the color and flavor will leach into the cooking liquid, leaving a pale, unappealing vegetable.

BEGIN: 2 HOURS AHEAD   6 SERVINGS

12 **small beets with tops (about 2 pounds)**
¼   **cup sugar**
2   **teaspoons cornstarch**
¼   **teaspoon salt**
¼   **cup white vinegar**
1   **tablespoon butter or margarine**

1. Trim beets, leaving 2 inches of tops and roots attached. Rinse beets under cold running water, being careful not to damage skins.

2. In 4-quart saucepan over medium heat, in 1 inch boiling, salted water, heat whole beets to boiling. Reduce heat to low. Cover; simmer 30 to 60 minutes until beets are fork-tender. Drain beets; cool. With sharp knife, remove skins and stems; slice or dice beets.

3. In same saucepan, combine sugar, cornstarch and salt; slowly stir in vinegar. Add butter. Over medium heat, cook until mixture boils, stirring constantly.

4. Reduce heat to low. Stir in beets; cook just until heated through, stirring occasionally. Yields 3 cups.

YALE BEETS: Prepare as above but substitute *¼ cup orange juice* and *1 tablespoon lemon juice* for vinegar. Add *1 tablespoon grated orange peel* in step 3. Proceed as above.

TIP: Cooking time for beets varies, depending on maturity and size of beets. Add more boiling water during cooking if necessary.

Pickled Beets, Red Pickled Eggs

Carrot-Raisin Salad, Three-Bean Salad, Wilted Spinach Salad

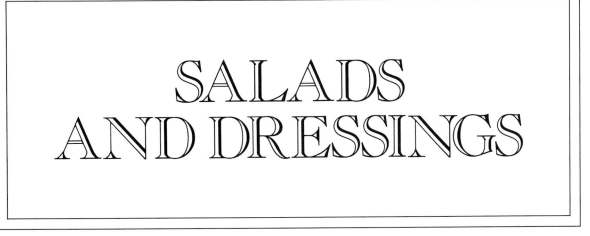

SALADS AND DRESSINGS

A salad is a dish of fruits or vegetables —usually raw and usually cold— served with a dressing. Salads are so popular in America, especially in California, that we forget that the first ones were the raw vegetables and herbs that the Greeks and Romans dressed with salt. In fact, it is the Latin word *sal,* meaning salt, that gives salad its name.

The first colonists in America planted gardens of lettuce and other greens, and also gathered wild greens, particularly dandelion and wild onions, to use in salads. Cabbage was a popular salad vegetable because it kept well and was available during much of the year.

American salads traditionally have centered on greens. Thomas Jefferson is known to have cultivated as many as twenty different varieties of lettuce. Another American, John Bibb, developed the popular Bibb lettuce during the nineteenth century.

The first dressings were mixtures of vinegar, salt and either oil or the fat left over from cooking meat. At the beginning of the nineteenth century, French vinaigrette and mayonnaise became more common.

Salads came into their own in the early 1900s. Restaurant chefs developed new salads and dressings, and the 1920s brought the first commercial dressings. Commercial gelatins, both unflavored and fruit-flavored, began America's fondness for sweet molded salads or "congealed salads," and the even-sweeter frozen salads.

Americans serve salads at different courses, as appetizers, main dishes, after the main dish or for dessert. When the salad is served as a separate course, it generally precedes the main dish, rather than following it, as is the European custom.

This custom of serving a salad before the main course may have been borrowed from the Italian *antipasto,* a selection of raw vegetables, cheese and meats served at the beginning of a meal. Or it may have been a way to keep restaurant diners busy while they waited for their meals.

The salad bar is a recent innovation in restaurants and cafeterias, where a selection of fresh salad ingredients is set out, and the diner is invited to assemble his own. The offerings may include lettuce and other greens, plus fruits and vegetables, meat, fish and egg salads, chilled shrimp and crabmeat, and a wide assortment of cheeses, garnishes and dressings. You can set up a salad bar at home with fresh greens and some of the prepared salads in this chapter.

✳ Tossed Green Salad

A tossed green salad, made with familiar iceberg, Boston or romaine lettuce, or with less-common chicory, watercress, spinach, radicchio or arugula, is unquestionably the most popular salad in the country. The greens must be fresh, clean and well-dried so that the dressing will cling to them. A vinaigrette dressing is classic, but you can use any other flavorful dressing.

BEGIN: 30 MINUTES AHEAD   6 SERVINGS

6   **cups mixed salad greens torn into
      bite-sized pieces
      Vinaigrette (see page 186)**

In salad bowl, place greens. Pour dressing over salad; toss gently to mix well. Yields 6 cups.

✳ Chef's Salad

The Chef's Salad is the main-dish version of the tossed salad. A familiar entry on restaurant menus from Alaska to Florida, it consists of ham, turkey, cheese and hard-cooked eggs laid over a tossed salad to provide a refreshing, protein-rich meal.

BEGIN: 45 MINUTES AHEAD   8 SERVINGS

6   **cups mixed salad greens torn into
      bite-sized pieces**
1   **cucumber, thinly sliced**
1   **carrot, thinly sliced**
3   **green onions, chopped**
6   **radishes, thinly sliced**
¼   **pound cooked chicken or turkey meat,
      cut into julienne strips**
¼   **pound cooked ham, cut into julienne
      strips**
½   **pound Swiss or Cheddar cheese, cut into
      julienne strips**
2   **hard-cooked eggs, sliced**
2   **tomatoes, cut into wedges
      Thousand Island Dressing (see page 184)**

1. In large salad bowl, combine greens, cucumber, carrot, onions and radishes; toss gently to mix well. Arrange chicken, ham, cheese, eggs and tomatoes on greens.

2. To serve: Pour dressing over salad; toss gently to mix well. Yields 12 cups.

✳ Multi-Layer Salad

A make-ahead version of a tossed salad, the Multi-Layer Salad is a great help to the busy host. It makes a beautiful presentation, yet can be made a day in advance. You can construct one from your favorite salad makings: try carrot slices, cherry tomatoes, cauliflowerets, sliced celery and other kinds of cheese. But avoid such ingredients as green peppers and onions that could overpower the salad during the holding time.

BEGIN: EARLY IN DAY   12 SERVINGS

6   **cups lettuce torn into bite-sized pieces
      Salt
      Pepper**
1   **package (10 ounces) frozen peas, thawed**
1   **cup sliced mushrooms**
1   **cup pitted ripe olives**
2   **cups sliced zucchini**
4   **hard-cooked eggs, sliced**
½   **pound bacon, cooked and crumbled**
1   **cup shredded Cheddar cheese**
1½   **cups mayonnaise**
1   **tablespoon lemon juice**
2   **green onions, diagonally sliced
      Paprika**

1. In 4-quart clear salad bowl, arrange lettuce; sprinkle with salt and pepper.

2. Spoon peas, mushrooms, olives and zucchini in layers evenly over lettuce. Arrange egg slices and bacon over vegetables. Sprinkle with cheese.

3. In small bowl, combine mayonnaise and lemon juice; spread mixture evenly over top. Cover; refrigerate until serving time, at least 6 hours.

4. To serve: Garnish with green onions; sprinkle with paprika. Spoon onto salad plates, reaching to the bottom of the bowl for each serving. Yields 15 cups.

TIP: If you don't have a bowl large enough for the salad, assemble it in two 2-quart bowls.

✳ Caesar Salad

The story goes that the Caesar Salad was created in California in the 1920s by Caesar Cardini, an Italian chef. It is made with ingredients we associate with Italy and the Mediterranean: romaine lettuce, olive oil, garlic, Parmesan cheese and anchovies. Because of its popularity in California, Caesar Salad is often called California Salad. Many versions have been developed through the years, most of them tossed together at the table with a showy flourish.

BEGIN: 30 MINUTES AHEAD   6 SERVINGS

2   cups water
1   egg, at room temperature
½   cup olive or salad oil
1   clove garlic, halved
2   slices bread, cubed
2   heads romaine lettuce, torn into
       bite-sized pieces
½   cup grated Parmesan cheese

2   tablespoons lemon juice
1   can (2 ounces) anchovy fillets, drained
       and chopped
¼   teaspoon cracked pepper

1. In small saucepan over high heat, heat water to boiling. Add egg in shell; cover and remove from heat. Let stand 1 minute. Remove egg from water; cool.

2. In 10-inch skillet over medium heat, in ¼ cup hot oil, cook garlic until golden. Discard garlic. Add bread cubes to hot oil. Cook until cubes are crisp and golden, stirring often. Drain on paper towels; set aside.

3. *Just before serving:* In large salad bowl, combine romaine and remaining ¼ cup oil; toss gently to coat. Add cheese, lemon juice, anchovies and pepper; toss gently. Break egg over salad; toss gently until all traces of egg disappear. Garnish salad with bread cubes; serve immediately. Yields 9 cups.

Caesar Salad

❋ Wilted Spinach Salad

Americans used to make wilted salads by pouring a dressing made with hot bacon drippings, vinegar and sugar over greens. Recently, interest in this type of salad has been rekindled. We now use spinach, fresh mushrooms and, often, Oriental accents such as water chestnuts, bean sprouts, sesame seed and soy sauce.

BEGIN: 45 MINUTES AHEAD   6 SERVINGS

10 ounces spinach
¼ pound mushrooms, sliced
1 can (8 ounces) water chestnuts, drained and sliced
2 hard-cooked eggs, sliced
4 slices bacon, cut into ½-inch pieces
¼ cup finely chopped onion
1 clove garlic, minced
¼ cup salad oil
¼ cup vinegar
1 tablespoon sugar
1 tablespoon Worcestershire

1. Into salad bowl, tear spinach. Add mushrooms, water chestnuts and eggs.

2. In 10-inch skillet over medium heat, fry bacon until crisp. Remove to paper towels to drain; set aside.

3. In bacon drippings, cook onion and garlic until tender. Stir in oil, vinegar, sugar and Worcestershire. Heat to boiling, stirring constantly.

4. To serve: Pour hot dressing over salad; toss gently to mix well. Sprinkle bacon over salad. Serve immediately. Yields 9 cups.

TO MICROWAVE: Prepare as above in step 1. In 4-cup microwave-safe measure, place bacon. Microwave on HIGH 4 to 5 minutes until crisp. With slotted spoon, remove to paper towels to drain; set aside. To bacon drippings, add onion and garlic. Microwave on HIGH 1 minute. Stir in oil, vinegar, sugar and Worcestershire. Microwave on HIGH 1 minute or until boiling. Proceed as in step 4.

❋ Taco Salad

Spanish explorers had a greater influence on the development of Mexican cuisine than they did on the food of the United States. Their contribution mingled with native foods to help shape today's Mexican cooking. This taco salad is an adaptation of the Mexican taco.

BEGIN: 45 MINUTES AHEAD   6 SERVINGS

1 medium head lettuce, torn into bite-sized pieces
¼ cup sliced radishes
½ pound ground beef
1 small onion, finely chopped
½ teaspoon chili powder
1 clove garlic, minced
2 medium tomatoes, diced
¼ cup chopped, seeded green chilies
¼ teaspoon salt
1 avocado, peeled and sliced
1 cup shredded Cheddar or Monterey Jack cheese
1 cup coarsely crushed corn chips
½ cup sliced pitted ripe olives

1. In salad bowl, arrange lettuce and radishes. Cover; refrigerate until serving time.

2. Meanwhile, in 10-inch skillet over medium-high heat, cook ground beef, onion, chili powder and garlic until onion is tender, stirring to break up meat. Pour off fat. Stir in tomatoes, chilies and salt; heat to boiling. Reduce heat to low; cook 5 minutes or until tomatoes are soft.

3. To serve: Pour hot beef mixture over lettuce and radishes. Top with avocado, cheese, corn chips and olives. Serve immediately.

TO MICROWAVE: Prepare as above in step 1. In 1-quart microwave-safe casserole, crumble ground beef. Stir in onion, chili powder and garlic; cover. Microwave on HIGH 2 to 3 minutes until meat is no longer pink; pour off fat. Stir in tomatoes, chilies and salt; cover. Microwave on HIGH 2 to 3 minutes or until tomatoes are soft. Proceed as in step 3.

Taco Salad

❇ Creamy Coleslaw

Cabbage salads have been made in the New World for more than three hundred years. The word coleslaw comes from the Dutch words kool *(cabbage) and* sla *(salad), and seventeenth-century Dutch settlers made slaws as soon as their first cabbages came up. Since that time American slaws have taken many forms. Some are creamy and mild, others are peppy with vinegar and spices, still others are sweet with fruit. You'll find this creamy slaw, with its sweet and sour flavor, at picnics, barbecues and fish fries all across the nation.*

BEGIN: 30 MINUTES AHEAD   8 SERVINGS

1	cup mayonnaise
3	tablespoons milk
3	tablespoons vinegar
1	teaspoon sugar
½	teaspoon celery seed
½	teaspoon salt
⅛	teaspoon paprika
⅛	teaspoon pepper
1	medium head cabbage, finely shredded
1	medium carrot, shredded
1	small onion, finely chopped

1. In small bowl, combine first 8 ingredients; mix well.

2. In large bowl, place cabbage, carrot and onion. Add mayonnaise mixture; toss gently to mix well. Cover; refrigerate until serving time. Yields 6 cups.

TIP: Add color to slaw by using ½ head red cabbage and ½ head green cabbage.

❇ Potato Salad

Found on picnic tables and at informal parties throughout the country, no salad is more varied or more thoroughly American than Potato Salad. It may be hot or cold. The potatoes may be whole, sliced, cubed or even mashed. The dressing may be piquant with vinaigrette or creamy with mayonnaise, sour cream, whipped cream or yogurt. The salad might include celery, sweet peppers, hard-cooked eggs, pickles, olives, radishes, fruit, cheese and meats.

BEGIN: EARLY IN DAY   8 SERVINGS

6	medium potatoes
2	stalks celery, chopped
1	medium onion, chopped
1	green pepper, chopped
3	hard-cooked eggs, sliced
2	tablespoons chopped parsley
½	teaspoon salt
¼	teaspoon pepper
1	cup mayonnaise

1. In 4-quart saucepan, place potatoes; add water to cover. Over high heat, heat to boiling. Reduce heat to medium-low. Cover; simmer 20 to 30 minutes until fork-tender; drain.

2. Cool potatoes slightly. With sharp knife, peel potatoes; discard peels. Cut potatoes into ¼-inch slices.

3. In large bowl, combine potatoes and remaining ingredients; toss gently to mix well. Season to taste. Cover; refrigerate until serving time, at least 3 hours. Yields 8 cups.

WHIPPED CREAM POTATO SALAD: Prepare as above but substitute *½ cup heavy cream, whipped,* and *½ cup mayonnaise* for 1 cup mayonnaise.

DILLED POTATO SALAD: Prepare as above but add *1 cucumber, chopped,* and *1 teaspoon dill weed, crushed,* to the vegetables. Substitute *½ cup sour cream* and *½ cup mayonnaise* for 1 cup mayonnaise.

❋ German Potato Salad

German-Americans dress hot, cooked potatoes with a mixture of bacon, vinegar and sugar—the proportions vary with the cook's preference for a sweeter or tarter salad. This salad is especially appropriate for winter menus that call for something substantial.

BEGIN: 1½ HOURS AHEAD   6 SERVINGS

6	medium potatoes
6	slices bacon, cut into ½-inch pieces
1	medium onion, chopped
1	stalk celery, chopped
1	tablespoon all-purpose flour
½	cup water
⅓	cup vinegar
2	tablespoons sugar
1	tablespoon chopped parsley
1	teaspoon salt
⅛	teaspoon pepper

1. In 4-quart saucepan, place potatoes; add water to cover. Over high heat, heat to boiling. Reduce heat to medium-low. Cover; simmer 20 to 30 minutes until fork-tender; drain.

2. Cool potatoes slightly. With sharp knife, peel potatoes; discard peels. Cut potatoes into ¼-inch slices.

3. In 10-inch skillet over medium heat, cook bacon until crisp. Remove to paper towels to drain; set aside. Spoon off all but 2 tablespoons bacon drippings.

4. In bacon drippings, cook onion and celery until tender. Add flour; stir together until blended. Gradually stir in water, vinegar, sugar, parsley, salt and pepper; heat to boiling, stirring constantly. Add potatoes; toss gently to mix well. Heat through. Garnish with bacon; serve immediately. Yields 5 cups.

❋ Macaroni Salad

In recent years cold pasta salads have become the rage, but Americans have long served macaroni salads at summer barbecues and picnics. This popular version has cheese, green pepper and onions in a creamy dressing.

BEGIN: EARLY IN DAY   8 SERVINGS

8	ounces elbow macaroni
1	cup diced Cheddar or Swiss cheese
½	cup chopped green pepper
¼	cup chopped green onions
1	cup mayonnaise
½	cup sour cream
¼	cup Vinaigrette (see page 186) or bottled Italian salad dressing
¼	cup sweet pickle relish
1	teaspoon prepared mustard
⅛	teaspoon pepper

1. Cook macaroni in boiling salted water as label directs; drain and rinse with cold water.

2. In large bowl, combine macaroni with remaining ingredients; toss gently to mix well. Season to taste. Cover; refrigerate until serving time, at least 3 hours. Yields 6 cups.

❋ Lentil Salad

Lentils were among the first vegetables cultivated; they have been eaten for more than one hundred centuries! Most often, they were served in sustaining soups or porridges, and it is said that it was lentil soup for which Esau relinquished his birthright. Modern American vegetarians have made this refreshing but substantial salad popular.

BEGIN: EARLY IN DAY   6 SERVINGS

1   cup dry lentils
1   stalk celery, diced
1   carrot, diced
1   clove garlic, minced
3   cups water
1   teaspoon salt
1   small onion, finely chopped
¼   cup chopped parsley
¼   cup olive or salad oil
2   tablespoons vinegar
½   teaspoon grated lemon peel
1   tablespoon lemon juice
¼   teaspoon pepper

1. In 2-quart saucepan over high heat, heat lentils, celery, carrot, garlic, water and ½ teaspoon salt to boiling. Reduce heat to low. Cover; simmer 30 minutes or until lentils are tender. Drain lentils and vegetables.

2. In medium bowl, combine lentils and vegetables with onion, parsley, oil, vinegar, lemon peel, lemon juice, pepper and remaining ½ teaspoon salt. Toss together to mix well. Cover; refrigerate until serving time, at least 4 hours. Makes 4 cups.

❋ Three-Bean Salad

This salad of marinated beans has become an American standard served as an appetizer or a side dish. There are many variations—some sweet, some tart; some including meat or cheese; some highly seasoned, some mild. The variety of beans changes, too. Besides green beans, wax beans and kidney beans, the recipe may include garbanzo beans and limas.

BEGIN: EARLY IN DAY   12 SERVINGS

½   cup olive or salad oil
½   cup wine vinegar
1   tablespoon sugar
1   teaspoon salt
¼   teaspoon pepper
2   cups cooked green beans or 1 can (16 ounces) cut green beans, drained
2   cups cooked wax beans or 1 can (16 ounces) cut wax beans, drained
2   cups cooked red kidney beans or 1 can (16 ounces) red kidney beans, drained
1   red onion, sliced and separated into rings

In large bowl, combine oil, vinegar, sugar, salt and pepper; stir until blended. Add beans and onion; toss gently to mix well. Cover; refrigerate until serving time, at least 6 hours. Yields 6½ cups.

❋ Cucumbers in Sour Cream

Immigrants from Middle-European and Scandinavian countries made salads of sliced cucumbers smothered in seasoned sour cream. It remains a popular tradition wherever they settled, particularly in the Midwest and Plains states.

BEGIN: 1½ HOURS AHEAD   6 SERVINGS

½   cup sour cream
2   tablespoons sugar
2   tablespoons vinegar
½   teaspoon salt
1   teaspoon dill weed, crushed (optional)
⅛   teaspoon pepper
2   medium cucumbers, peeled and thinly sliced
1   small onion, thinly sliced

In large bowl, combine sour cream, sugar, vinegar, salt, dill weed and pepper; mix well. Add cucumbers and onion; toss gently to mix well. Cover; refrigerate until serving time, at least 1 hour. Yields 3½ cups.

❋ Carrot-Raisin Salad

Carrots were brought to America by European colonists, and were successfully grown almost immediately. They grew so well, in fact, that wild carrots quickly spread across the country in the form of a weed known as Queen Anne's lace. Today carrots are enjoyed in numerous ways; here, they are featured in a very popular salad that combines vegetables and fruit.

BEGIN: 30 MINUTES AHEAD   8 SERVINGS

6   **medium carrots, shredded**
1   **cup shredded coconut**
½   **cup finely chopped celery**
½   **cup raisins**
½   **cup mayonnaise**
½   **teaspoon salt**

In medium bowl, combine all ingredients; toss gently to mix well. Cover; refrigerate until serving time. Yields 4 cups.

❋ Easy Tomato Aspic

Tomato aspic is one of the most versatile of salads. It can be sliced and served as the base of a seafood or meat salad, cubed and used as a garnish for other salads, tossed with other ingredients or served as a salad on its own. Old recipes for tomato aspic begin with fresh tomatoes and other vegetables, and require lots of preparation time. This recipe uses vegetable juice instead, saving you time without sacrificing flavor.

BEGIN: 4 HOURS AHEAD   6 SERVINGS

2   **envelopes unflavored gelatin**
3½   **cups V-8 vegetable juice**
     Lettuce leaves

1. In 2-quart saucepan, sprinkle gelatin over 1 cup vegetable juice to soften. Over low heat, heat until gelatin is dissolved, stirring often. Remove from heat; stir in remaining 2½ cups juice. Pour into 1-quart mold. Cover; refrigerate at least 3 hours until firm.

2. To serve: Unmold onto lettuce-lined platter. Yields 3½ cups.

CRUNCHY ASPIC: Prepare recipe as above in step 1, but pour gelatin mixture into bowl; refrigerate about 2 hours until mixture mounds slightly when dropped from spoon. Fold in ½ cup chopped celery, ½ cup finely chopped onion and ¼ cup finely chopped green pepper. Pour into 1-quart mold. Cover; refrigerate until firm. Serve as above.

TIP: Heat gelatin mixture in microwave oven to dissolve. Use ingredients as listed; in 2-quart microwave-safe dish, microwave on HIGH 1 to 1½ minutes or until dissolved. Proceed as above.

❋ Perfection Salad

Essentially a molded coleslaw, Perfection Salad was a prizewinner in a contest sponsored by a gelatin company at the turn of the century. Later recipes make it with sweetened lemon-flavored gelatin, but the original Perfection Salad was made with unflavored gelatin, vinegar, lemon juice and sugar, as this one is.

BEGIN: EARLY IN DAY   10 SERVINGS

½   **cup sugar**
2   **envelopes unflavored gelatin**
1   **teaspoon salt**
1   **cup boiling water**
1½   **cups cold water**
⅓   **cup vinegar**
2   **tablespoons lemon juice**
2   **cups finely shredded cabbage**
1½   **cups finely chopped celery**
½   **cup chopped pimentos**
     Lettuce leaves

1. In medium bowl, combine sugar, gelatin and salt. Add boiling water; stir until gelatin is dissolved. Stir in cold water, vinegar and lemon juice. Refrigerate about 2 hours or until mixture mounds slightly when dropped from spoon.

2. Fold in cabbage, celery and pimentos. Pour into 6-cup bowl or ring mold. Cover; refrigerate about 3 hours until firm.

3. To serve: Unmold onto lettuce-lined platter. Yields 5½ cups.

❋ Pineapple-Cheese Salad

Unflavored gelatin first appeared in granulated form near the beginning of this century. When sweetened fruit-flavored gelatin came onto the market it revolutionized the way Americans looked at salads. Fruit-flavored gelatin salads have included such varied ingredients as cheese, marshmallows, whipped cream, sour cream, nuts, wine, eggs, poultry and seafood.

BEGIN: EARLY IN DAY   6 SERVINGS

1   cup boiling water
1   package (3 ounces) lime-flavored gelatin
1   package (3 ounces) cream cheese, diced and softened
1   can (8 ounces) crushed pineapple
½   cup chopped pecans or walnuts
    Lettuce leaves

1. In medium bowl, pour boiling water over gelatin; stir until gelatin is dissolved. Stir in cream cheese until melted and well mixed. Stir in pineapple with juice; refrigerate about 2 hours or until mixture mounds slightly when dropped from spoon.

2. Fold in nuts. Pour into 3-cup ring mold. Cover; refrigerate at least 3 hours until firm.

3. To serve: Unmold onto lettuce-lined platter. Yields 3 cups.

❋ 24-Hour Fruit Salad

American cooks created an array of salads for picnics and potluck suppers that not only hold well, but actually improve with a day's aging. Potato salads, pasta salads and coleslaw are good examples; so is this rich and creamy fruit salad. In the past it would have been prepared with canned fruit, but with so many fresh fruits available all year long, you may prefer it as a fresh fruit salad.

BEGIN: DAY AHEAD   12 SERVINGS

1   can (20 ounces) pineapple chunks in juice
2   eggs
2   tablespoons sugar
2   tablespoons lemon juice
1   tablespoon butter or margarine
⅛   teaspoon salt
1   jar (17 ounces) Royal Anne cherries, drained and pitted
1   can (11 ounces) mandarin oranges, drained
1   cup seedless grapes, halved
2   cups miniature marshmallows
1   cup heavy cream, chilled

1. Drain pineapple, reserving 2 tablespoons juice. In heavy, small saucepan with wire whisk, beat eggs until foamy. Stir in reserved pineapple juice, sugar, lemon juice, butter and salt. Over medium heat, cook about 3 minutes until mixture coats back of spoon, stirring constantly. Cool to room temperature.

2. In large bowl, combine pineapple chunks, cherries, oranges, grapes and marshmallows. Add reserved egg mixture; toss gently to coat.

3. In small bowl with mixer at medium speed, beat cream until soft peaks form. Fold into fruit mixture. Cover; refrigerate until serving time, at least 24 hours. Yields 8 cups.

24-HOUR FRESH FRUIT SALAD: Prepare as above but substitute *2 cups cubed fresh pineapple, 2 cups pitted sweet cherries* and *2 oranges, peeled and sectioned,* for canned fruits. Substitute *2 tablespoons water* for 2 tablespoons pineapple juice.

FIVE-CUP SALAD: In large bowl, combine *1 can (8 ounces) crushed pineapple, drained; 1 can (11 ounces) mandarin oranges, drained; 1 cup flaked coconut; 1 cup miniature marshmallows* and *1 cup sour cream.* Toss gently to mix well. Cover; refrigerate until serving time.

❊ Waldorf Salad

This salad was created by maître d' Oscar Tschirky for the Waldorf-Astoria Hotel's opening in 1893. He combined apples, celery and mayonnaise on a bed of lettuce leaves; most Waldorf Salads today also include walnuts.

BEGIN: 30 MINUTES AHEAD   8 SERVINGS

4	large apples, cored and diced
2	stalks celery, diced
½	cup coarsely chopped walnuts
1	cup mayonnaise

In medium bowl, combine apples, celery and walnuts. Add mayonnaise; toss gently to mix well. Cover; refrigerate until serving time. Yields 5 cups.

❊ Three-Fruit Salad

The kiwi, sometimes called a Chinese gooseberry, is native to China, but most commercially grown kiwi comes from New Zealand in the summer and California in the winter. American cooks enjoy its attractive sunburst appearance and juicy, sweet flavor. Here it teams with two other fruits and a tangy sesame seed dressing in an arranged salad.

BEGIN: 1½ HOURS AHEAD   6 SERVINGS

½	cup salad oil
¼	cup sesame seed
¼	cup lime juice
¼	cup honey
	Dash salt
	Lettuce leaves
2	avocados, peeled and sliced
2	grapefruit, peeled and sectioned
2	kiwi fruit, peeled and sliced

Three-Fruit Salad

1. In small bowl or covered jar, combine oil, sesame seed, lime juice, honey and salt; stir with fork or cover and shake until thoroughly mixed. Cover; refrigerate until serving time, at least 1 hour.

2. *Just before serving:* Line platter with lettuce leaves; arrange avocados, grapefruit and kiwi fruit on lettuce. Stir or shake dressing; pour over fruit. Yields 1 cup salad dressing.

❋ Frozen Fruit Salad

Frozen fruit salads are popular party offerings for summer meals in the Midwest. They usually are sweet and rich with whipped cream, sour cream or cream cheese. Although canned fruits are the rule in these salads, some fresh fruits can also be used.

BEGIN: EARLY IN DAY   12 SERVINGS

1	package (8 ounces) cream cheese, softened
1	cup sour cream
2	tablespoons sugar
1	tablespoon grated lemon peel
2	cups sweet cherries, pitted, or 1 can (16 ounces) pitted dark sweet cherries, drained
2	cups chopped, peeled peaches or 1 can (16 ounces) peach halves, drained and chopped
1	can (8 ounces) crushed pineapple, drained
1	cup miniature marshmallows
1	cup chopped pecans
	Lettuce leaves

1. In medium bowl with mixer at high speed, beat cream cheese until fluffy. Beat in sour cream, sugar and lemon peel until well combined.

2. Fold in cherries, peaches, pineapple, marshmallows and pecans. Spread mixture in 8- by 8-inch baking pan. Cover; freeze until firm, at least 5 hours.

3. To serve: Remove salad from freezer; let stand 10 minutes. Cut into squares and serve on lettuce-lined plates.

TIP: For easy cutting, remove salad from pan to cutting board after standing time.

❋ Egg Salad in Tomato Cups

There are two ways to fill a tomato. First, you may slice off the tomato's top, then scoop out the seeds and pulp. The second method is easier and more attractive: simply cut the tomato into wedges almost to the base, then spread the wedges apart.

BEGIN: 1 HOUR AHEAD   4 SERVINGS

6	hard-cooked eggs, chopped
¼	cup mayonnaise
2	tablespoons chopped celery
2	tablespoons chopped green pepper
1	tablespoon prepared mustard
¼	teaspoon salt
⅛	teaspoon pepper
4	medium tomatoes

1. In medium bowl, combine all ingredients except tomatoes; toss gently to mix well. Cover; refrigerate until serving time.

2. Place tomatoes stem side down on cutting board. Cut each tomato into 8 wedges, being careful not to cut all the way through. Pull wedges apart to make tomato cup; spoon egg salad into center of each. Yields 1¾ cups salad.

❋ Seafood Salad

Seafood Salad is a regional dish, its flavor defined by the local catch. Whether you use West Coast Dungeness or King crab, East Coast blue crab or Gulf Coast stone crab, you will have an elegant, refreshing salad. If you cannot obtain fresh seafood, use frozen or canned.

BEGIN: 1 HOUR AHEAD   4 SERVINGS

2	cups cooked, shelled and deveined medium shrimp and/or cooked crabmeat, picked over
1	cup diced celery
2	tablespoons sliced green onion
½	cup mayonnaise
1	tablespoon lemon juice
½	teaspoon dry mustard
¼	teaspoon salt
⅛	teaspoon cayenne pepper
	Lettuce leaves or avocado halves

1. Cut shrimp in half lengthwise or break crab into chunks.

2. In medium bowl, combine seafood, celery, onion, mayonnaise, lemon juice, mustard, salt and cayenne; toss gently to mix well. Cover; refrigerate until serving time.

3. To serve: Spoon onto lettuce-lined salad plates or into avocado halves. Yields 3 cups.

TIP: Substitute small shrimp for medium and do not cut in half.

Seafood Salad

❋ Crab Louis

The superlative produce and abundant seafood of the West Coast have inspired many salads and seafood dishes. Not the least of these is Crab Louis, created either in Portland, Oregon, or San Francisco. There are many versions of the salad, all of them calling for a generous amount of crab with a dressing of mayonnaise, cream and chili sauce on a bed of shredded lettuce.

BEGIN: 1 HOUR AHEAD   6 SERVINGS

⅓   **cup heavy cream, chilled**
1   **cup mayonnaise**
¼   **cup chili sauce**
1   **tablespoon lemon juice**
½   **teaspoon salt**
⅛   **teaspoon cayenne pepper**
1   **small head lettuce, shredded**
1   **pound cooked crabmeat, picked over, or**
     3 packages (6 ounces each) frozen
     Alaska King crab, thawed and drained
2   **hard-cooked eggs, sliced**
1   **tomato, cut into wedges**
¼   **cup sliced green onions**

1. In small bowl with mixer at medium speed, beat cream until soft peaks form. With spatula, fold in mayonnaise, chili sauce, lemon juice, salt and cayenne. Cover; refrigerate until serving time, at least 30 minutes.

2. To serve: Arrange lettuce on large platter. Heap crab in center of lettuce; top with mayonnaise mixture. Garnish with sliced eggs, tomato wedges and green onions. Yields 1¾ cups salad dressing.

❋ Mayonnaise

Mayonnaise, a fine dressing for salads just as it is, is also incorporated into hundreds of salad dressings, sauces and dips. It has a long tradition in America, where homemakers were making the classic French mayonnaise early in the 1800s. At that time the only way to make mayonnaise was to beat it by hand with a whisk. Today you can make it in an electric mixer, blender or food processor as well.

BEGIN: 30 MINUTES AHEAD

3   egg yolks
¼   cup vinegar or lemon juice
1   teaspoon salt
¼   teaspoon dry mustard
2   cups salad oil

1. In small bowl with mixer at medium speed, beat egg yolks, vinegar, salt and mustard 2 minutes.

2. Continue beating, gradually adding ½ cup oil, about ½ teaspoon at a time, until thick and smooth.

3. Continue beating; add remaining 1½ cups oil, 1 tablespoon at a time, until mixture is thick and creamy. Cover; refrigerate until serving time. Serve on tossed greens, in sandwiches or recipes. Yields 2½ cups.

BLENDER MAYONNAISE: In covered blender container at low speed, blend first 4 ingredients 1 to 2 seconds until thoroughly mixed. Remove center of cover (or cover) and, at low speed, very slowly pour oil in steady stream into blender; continue blending until well mixed.

❋ Green Goddess Dressing

California's outstanding produce has inspired more salads and dressings than any other area in the country. Caesar Salad, Crab Louis and Green Goddess Dressing are three notable examples. Green Goddess Dressing was created at the Palace Hotel in San Francisco during the 1920s. It was named after a popular play of the time, as well as for its lovely green color and heavenly flavor.

BEGIN: 10 MINUTES AHEAD

1   cup mayonnaise
½   cup sour cream
¼   cup chopped parsley
2   tablespoons finely chopped green onion
2   tablespoons tarragon vinegar or lemon juice
1   teaspoon tarragon leaves, crushed
3   anchovy fillets, minced
1   clove garlic, minced
    Milk

In small bowl, combine all ingredients except milk; mix well. Thin with milk to desired consistency. Cover; refrigerate until serving time. Serve on tossed greens, chilled vegetables or cold seafood and poultry. Yields 1½ cups.

TIP: To use as a dip, omit milk.

❋ Thousand Island Dressing

Thousand Island Dressing is said to have been created for the opening of Chicago's Blackstone Hotel in 1910. Its name comes from the "islands" of green pepper, pickle relish and hard-cooked egg that stud the mixture of mayonnaise and chili sauce. It is a traditional favorite on wedges of lettuce; it's also good as a sandwich dressing.

BEGIN: 10 MINUTES AHEAD

1   cup mayonnaise
¼   cup chili sauce
2   tablespoons chopped green pepper
2   tablespoons sweet pickle relish
1   tablespoon chopped parsley
1   tablespoon grated onion
1   hard-cooked egg, chopped

In small bowl, combine all ingredients; mix well. Cover; refrigerate until serving time. Serve on tossed greens or Chef's Salad. Yields 1½ cups.

DRESSING LAMAZE: Prepare as above but omit chili sauce, green pepper and parsley. Stir in *1 can (10¾ ounces) condensed tomato soup, 1 tablespoon lemon juice* and *½ teaspoon prepared mustard.* Serve over greens or seafood. Yields 2 cups.

✳ Blue Cheese Dressing

Roquefort, the original blue cheese, was discovered by accident when a French shepherd left some cheese made from sheep's milk in a limestone cave. When he returned after several weeks, the cheese had developed a blue mold and an intriguing flavor. Since that time the cheese has inspired British Stilton, Italian Gorgonzola, Danish Blue and American blues made in Oregon and the Midwest. There are many salad dressings flavored with blue cheese. Some are based on oil and vinegar, some on cottage or cream cheese, but the most popular is a creamy mixture of mayonnaise, sour cream and blue cheese.

BEGIN: 10 MINUTES AHEAD

1 **cup mayonnaise**
½ **cup crumbled Roquefort or blue cheese**
½ **cup sour cream**
1 **small clove garlic, minced**
1 **teaspoon Worcestershire**
¼ **teaspoon salt**
⅛ **teaspoon pepper**
   Dash hot pepper sauce
   Milk

In small bowl, combine all ingredients except milk; mix well. Thin with milk to desired consistency. Cover; refrigerate until serving time. Serve on tossed greens. Yields 2 cups.

Blue Cheese Dressing, Green Goddess Dressing, Chiffonade Dressing, Poppy Seed Dressing

❋ Buttermilk Dressing

An old-fashioned dressing that has regained popularity recently is this well-seasoned buttermilk and mayonnaise mixture. It is delicious with a tossed salad, but it is also fine on baked potatoes, cooked vegetables and as a dip for crudités.

BEGIN: 10 MINUTES AHEAD

1	cup mayonnaise
⅔	cup buttermilk
¼	cup chopped parsley
1	tablespoon grated onion
1	tablespoon chopped chives
1	clove garlic, minced
¼	teaspoon salt
¼	teaspoon pepper

In small bowl, combine all ingredients; mix well. Cover; refrigerate until serving time. Serve on tossed greens or vegetables. Yields 1¾ cups.

❋ Vinaigrette

There is an old Spanish proverb that says it takes four people to make the perfect vinaigrette: a spendthrift with oil, a miser with vinegar, a wise man with salt and a madman to mix it. In this country, vinaigrette sometimes goes by other names; in many cookbooks it is listed as French dressing, while bottled vinaigrette is often called "oil and vinegar." The Chiffonade Dressing variation is a California creation that was popular in the first half of this century.

BEGIN: 10 MINUTES AHEAD

1	cup olive or salad oil
⅓	cup vinegar or lemon juice
¾	teaspoon salt
¼	teaspoon dry mustard (optional)
⅛	teaspoon pepper

In small bowl or covered jar, combine all ingredients. Stir with fork, or cover and shake until well mixed. Cover; refrigerate until serving time. Stir or shake just before serving. Serve on tossed greens or over fruit. Yields 1¼ cups.

CHIFFONADE DRESSING: Prepare as above but add *2 hard-cooked eggs, chopped; ¼ cup finely chopped green pepper; ¼ cup chopped cooked beets; 1 tablespoon finely chopped onion and 1 teaspoon chopped chives. Yields 2 cups.*

❋ Tomato French Dressing

Although the French dress their salads with oil, vinegar and seasonings, Americans added tomato and called the result "French dressing." The tomato may be added as ketchup, chili sauce, tomato juice, tomato paste or, as in this version, tomato soup.

BEGIN: 1 HOUR AHEAD

1	can (10¾ ounces) condensed tomato soup
½	cup salad oil
¼	cup vinegar
2	tablespoons sugar
1	tablespoon finely chopped onion
2	teaspoons dry mustard
1	teaspoon salt
¼	teaspoon pepper

In small bowl or covered jar, combine all ingredients. Stir with fork, or cover and shake until well mixed. Cover; refrigerate until serving time, at least 30 minutes. Stir or shake just before serving. Serve on tossed greens. Yields 2 cups.

BACON DRESSING: Prepare as above but add *4 slices bacon, cooked and crumbled.*

CELERY DRESSING: Prepare as above but add *1 tablespoon celery seed.*

GARLIC DRESSING: Prepare as above but add *1 large clove garlic, minced.*

HERB DRESSING: Prepare as above but add *1/2 teaspoon ground herb (rosemary, sage, savory, marjoram or thyme).*

❋ Poppy Seed Dressing

Early German immigrants to this country made sweetened oil and vinegar salad dressings. The sweetness varied according to the cook, with the sweeter dressings being used on fruit salads. Helen Corbitt, cookbook author and former manager of restaurants at Neiman-Marcus department stores, has been credited with popularizing this dressing as well as the mixing method, which makes a thick, smooth dressing.

BEGIN: 1½ HOURS AHEAD

½   cup sugar
⅓   cup vinegar or lemon juice
1   tablespoon grated onion
1   teaspoon salt
1   teaspoon dry mustard
1   cup salad oil
1   tablespoon poppy seed

1. In small bowl with mixer at medium speed, beat sugar, vinegar, onion, salt and mustard until well mixed.

2. Continue beating, gradually adding oil in thin stream. Beat until thick and smooth. Stir in poppy seed.

3. Cover; refrigerate until serving time, at least 1 hour. Stir well before using. Serve over fruit or tossed greens. Yields 1½ cups.

CELERY SEED DRESSING: Prepare as above but substitute *1 tablespoon celery seed* for the poppy seed.

❋ Avocado Salad Dressing

Europeans first met the avocado early in the sixteenth century when they were exploring Mexico and Central America, but natives of the area had known the fruit for centuries. Since the beginning of commercial avocado cultivation in 1900, the avocado has become readily available and well-liked all over the country.

BEGIN: 10 MINUTES AHEAD

1   egg yolk
2   tablespoons lemon juice
1   tablespoon grated onion
1   clove garlic, minced
½   teaspoon salt
    Dash hot pepper sauce
½   cup salad oil
1   avocado, peeled and cut up

1. In covered blender container at low speed, blend first 6 ingredients 1 to 2 seconds until thoroughly mixed. Remove center of cover (or cover) and, at low speed, very slowly pour oil in steady stream into blender; continue blending until well mixed.

2. Add avocado to blender; continue blending just until smooth. Serve immediately. Yields 1¾ cups.

White Bread, Whole Wheat Bread, Harvest Moon Doughnuts, Angel Biscuits, Cranberry-Nut Bread

BREADS

Every cuisine has its basic grains, and most of the grains are made into bread. The American Indians made bread from corn, which they ground into meal, then mixed with water and baked on coals or rocks near a fire. Some of the breads were leavened with a homemade yeast, but more often they were simply flat cakes of cornmeal and water, the forerunners of the jonnycake.

The European settlers had never seen corn before they came to this continent. But when their first attempts at growing wheat, barley, oats and rye failed because of the unfamiliar soil, climate and precipitation levels, they found ways to make the corn taste good. Many years of plantings and harvests came and went before their Old World crops began to thrive. In the meantime the Indians taught them to make corn cakes and bake them in the ashes of fires (ashcakes) or on the blade of a hoe (hoecakes).

When European grains finally took hold in the eighteenth century, American breads became more varied. Colonists combined corn with European grains to make Boston Brown Bread, Anadama Bread and Rye 'n' Injun Bread.

Although Europeans were accustomed to buying their bread, bread baking in America began in the home. It was a tedious process. First the grain was ground. Then homemade yeast was added. Kneading required strong arms, and timing the baking took a keen judge of oven temperature.

Besides homemade yeast breads, Americans made breads without yeast. Salt-rising bread depended on bacteria to make it rise: an unreliable procedure.

A popular alternative to yeast was sourdough. Part of the dough from a previous day's baking would be stirred into a new batch of dough to leaven it. Although this method had been used all over the world, it came to be identified with pioneers and prospectors in Alaska and the West. Tales were told of cooks who guarded their sourdough starter with their lives. They were said to wear bags of the starter around their necks, and to sleep with the starter on nights when it was in danger of freezing.

As the American population grew, mills were built and flour no longer had to be ground at home. Improved leavenings and thermostatically controlled ovens made home baking easier and more predictable while, at the same time, commercial bakers took over most bread production.

The introduction of baking powder and baking soda has made possible some of the quick breads Americans enjoy today, including biscuits, muffins, tea breads and doughnuts. These are popular because they are easy to prepare in a hurry, yet have a homemade taste.

Although the days when all bread was made at home have disappeared forever, there has been a new interest in bread making in the last decade. Both men and women are rediscovering the satisfaction that comes from making and eating a wholesome loaf of homemade bread.

❄ White Bread

Throughout history light-colored loaves of bread were admired because only the rich could afford the highly processed flours that produced them. Today the trend seems to be reversed, and the darker breads command higher prices. Cost aside, the unparalleled flavor and aroma of this white bread reminds us of the American farm wife baking loaves to be spread with butter made from fresh, sweet cream.

BEGIN: EARLY IN DAY   2 LOAVES

5¾ to 6¼ cups all-purpose flour
3   tablespoons sugar
2   teaspoons salt
1   package active dry yeast
1½ cups water
½   cup milk
3   tablespoons butter or margarine

1. In large bowl, combine 2 cups flour, sugar, salt and yeast. In 2-quart saucepan over low heat, heat water, milk and butter until mixture is very warm but you can still hold your finger in it (120° to 130°F.). Butter does not need to melt completely. With mixer at low speed, gradually pour liquid into dry ingredients; beat until just mixed. At medium speed, beat 2 minutes, scraping bowl with rubber spatula. Beat in ¾ cup flour or enough to make a thick batter; continue beating 2 minutes, scraping bowl occasionally. With spoon, stir in enough additional flour (about 3 cups) to make a soft dough.

2. Turn dough onto lightly floured surface and knead until smooth and elastic, about 10 minutes, adding more flour while kneading. Shape dough into ball; place in greased large bowl, turning dough over to grease top. Cover with towel; let rise in warm place (80° to 85°F.), free from draft, until doubled in bulk, about 1 hour.

3. Punch dough down by pushing center of dough with fist, then pushing edges of dough into center. Turn dough onto lightly floured surface; cut in half. Cover; let rest 15 minutes.

4. Grease two 9- by 5-inch loaf pans. With lightly floured rolling pin, roll one dough half into 12- by 8-inch rectangle. Starting at narrow end, roll tightly, jelly-roll fashion; pinch seam to seal. Press ends to seal and tuck under. Place seam side down in prepared loaf pan. Repeat with remaining dough. Cover with towel; let rise in warm place until doubled, about 1 hour.

5. Preheat oven to 400°F. If soft crust is desired, brush loaves with additional melted butter. Bake 30 minutes or until tops are golden and loaves sound hollow when tapped with finger. Remove from pans immediately; cool on wire racks.

WHOLE WHEAT BREAD: Prepare as above but omit sugar and increase yeast to *2 packages.* Substitute *6 cups whole wheat flour* for all-purpose flour. Add *¼ cup molasses* along with milk.

❄ Raisin Swirl Bread

A favorite breakfast bread is cinnamon bread with raisins. It is slightly sweet, has a beautifully swirled interior and makes delicious toast.

BEGIN: EARLY IN DAY   2 LOAVES

6½ to 7½ cups all-purpose flour
¾   cup sugar
1½ teaspoons salt
2   packages active dry yeast
1   cup milk
1   cup water
¼   cup butter or margarine
3   eggs, at room temperature
1   tablespoon ground cinnamon
2   tablespoons butter or margarine, melted
1   cup raisins
    Confectioners' Sugar Glaze*

1. In large bowl, combine 2 cups flour, ¼ cup sugar, salt and yeast. In 2-quart saucepan over low heat, heat milk, water and ¼ cup butter until mixture is very warm but you can still hold your finger in it (120° to 130°F.). Butter does not need to melt completely. With mixer at low speed, gradually pour liquid into dry ingredients; beat until just mixed. At medium speed, beat 2 minutes, scraping bowl with rubber spatula. Beat in eggs and 1½ cups flour or enough to make a thick batter; continue beating 2 minutes, scraping bowl occasionally. With spoon, stir in enough additional flour (about 3 cups) to make a soft dough.

2. Turn dough onto lightly floured surface and knead until smooth and elastic, about 10 minutes, adding more flour while kneading. Shape dough into ball and place in greased large bowl, turning dough over to grease top. Cover with towel; let rise in warm place (80° to 85°F.), free from draft, until doubled in bulk, about 1 hour.

3. Punch dough down by pushing center of dough with fist, then pushing edges of dough into center. Turn dough onto lightly floured surface; cut in half. Cover; let rest 15 minutes.

4. Grease two 9- by 5-inch loaf pans. In small bowl, combine remaining ½ cup sugar and cinnamon. Roll one dough half into 14- by 9-inch rectangle. Brush with 1 tablespoon melted butter. Sprinkle with ½ of the sugar mixture and ½ of the raisins. Starting at narrow end, roll tightly, jelly-roll fashion; pinch seam to seal. Press ends to seal and tuck under. Place seam side down in prepared pan. Repeat with remaining dough. Cover with towel; let rise in warm place until doubled, about 1 hour.

5. Preheat oven to 375°F. Bake 45 minutes or until tops are golden and loaves sound hollow when tapped with finger. Remove from pans immediately; cool on wire racks. Drizzle with Confectioners' Sugar Glaze.

Raisin Swirl Bread

*Confectioners' Sugar Glaze

BEGIN: 5 MINUTES AHEAD

1 cup confectioners' sugar
2 tablespoons milk

In small bowl, stir sugar and milk until smooth. Yields ½ cup.

❋ French Bread

To reproduce the delicious crusty breads that are made in France, the home baker has to simulate a French baker's oven. Some add a pan of water to the oven; others spray the bread with water, bake the bread on preheated tiles or in cylindrical pans, or allow the dough a long rising in a cool room. This recipe makes a wonderful loaf with a crisp, golden crust to make any baker proud.

BEGIN: EARLY IN DAY   2 LOAVES

5 to 6 cups all-purpose flour
1 tablespoon sugar
1 teaspoon salt
1 package active dry yeast
2 cups very warm water (120° to 130°F.)
  Cornmeal
1 egg white
1 tablespoon cold water
1 tablespoon sesame seed

1. In large bowl, combine 1½ cups flour, sugar, salt and yeast. With mixer at low speed, gradually pour warm water into dry ingredients; beat until just mixed. At medium speed, beat 2 minutes, scraping bowl with rubber spatula. Beat in 1 cup flour or enough to make a thick batter; continue beating 2 minutes, scraping bowl occasionally. With spoon, stir in enough additional flour (about 2½ cups) to make a soft dough.

2. Turn dough onto lightly floured surface and knead until smooth and elastic, about 10 minutes, adding more flour while kneading. Shape dough into ball; place in greased large bowl, turning dough over to grease top. Cover with towel; let rise in warm place (80° to 85°F.), free from draft, until doubled in bulk, about 1 hour.

3. Punch dough down by pushing center of dough with fist, then pushing edges of dough into center. Turn dough onto lightly floured surface; cut in half.

4. Grease 2 large baking sheets; sprinkle with cornmeal. Shape one dough half into 15-inch-long roll with tapered ends; place on prepared baking sheet. Repeat with remaining dough. Cover with towel; let rise in warm place until doubled, about 1 hour.

5. Preheat oven to 400°F. Place pan of hot water on bottom shelf of oven. With sharp knife, slash top of each loaf in 2 or 3 places. In cup, beat egg white and cold water; brush over loaves. Sprinkle with sesame seed. Bake 30 minutes or until tops are golden and loaves sound hollow when tapped with finger. Remove from baking sheets immediately; cool on wire racks.

❋ Challah

Baking Challah for Friday evening's Sabbath meal is a long tradition in Jewish families. Because of the Sabbath ban on work, the bread must be baked before the sun goes down. The eldest male of the family cuts the bread, saying a blessing, then gives everyone some of the rich, eggy loaf.

BEGIN: EARLY IN DAY   2 LOAVES

6½ to 7½ cups all-purpose flour
2 tablespoons sugar
2 teaspoons salt
2 packages active dry yeast
2 cups water
¼ cup butter or margarine
3 eggs, at room temperature
1 egg yolk
1 tablespoon cold water
1 teaspoon poppy seed

1. In large bowl, combine 2 cups flour, sugar, salt and yeast. In 2-quart saucepan over low heat, heat 2 cups water and butter until mixture is very warm but you can still hold your finger in it (120° to 130°F.). Butter does not need to melt completely. With mixer at low speed, gradually pour liquid into dry ingredients; beat until just mixed. At medium speed, beat 2 minutes, scraping bowl with rubber spatula. Beat in 3 eggs and 1½ cups

flour or enough to make a thick batter; continue beating 2 minutes, scraping bowl occasionally. With spoon, stir in enough additional flour (about 3 cups) to make a soft dough.

2. Turn dough onto lightly floured surface and knead until smooth and elastic, about 10 minutes, adding more flour while kneading. Shape dough into ball; place in greased large bowl, turning dough over to grease top. Cover with towel; let rise in warm place (80° to 85°F.), free from draft, until doubled in bulk, about 1 hour.

3. Punch dough down by pushing center of dough with fist, then pushing edges of dough into center. Turn dough onto lightly floured surface; cut in half. Cover; let rest 15 minutes. Grease 2 large baking sheets.

4. Set aside one dough half to use in step 5. Divide remaining dough half into 2 pieces, one about ⅓ of dough and the other ⅔ of dough. Divide larger piece into 3 equal pieces; roll each into 12-inch-long rope. On baking sheet, lay ropes of dough side by side. Braid; pinch ends to seal. Divide smaller piece into 3 equal pieces; roll each into 10-inch-long rope. Lay ropes of dough on large braid. Braid; pinch ends to seal.

5. Repeat rolling and braiding with remaining dough to form second loaf. Cover with towel; let rise in warm place until doubled, about 1 hour.

6. Preheat oven to 400°F. In cup, beat egg yolk and cold water; brush over loaves. Sprinkle with poppy seed. Bake 25 minutes or until tops are golden and loaves sound hollow when tapped with finger. Remove from baking sheets immediately; cool on wire racks.

❋ Sourdough Bread

Sourdough is unpredictable, varying with the temperature, the humidity, the geographic location, the recipe and the cook. San Franciscans claim that their sourdough is the best in the world, but it is Alaskans who are called sourdoughs. In any case, sourdough was important to the pioneers and to the prospectors who traveled West looking for gold in the nineteenth century. In those days a sourdough starter was something to be guarded, nursed and bequeathed in one's will.

BEGIN: DAY AHEAD   2 LOAVES

1   cup Sourdough Starter*
1   tablespoon sugar
2   teaspoons salt
5½ to 6½ cups all-purpose flour
1½ cups very warm water (105° to 115°F.)
1   package active dry yeast
    Cornmeal

1. *Day ahead, make sponge:* In large bowl, stir together starter, sugar, salt, 2 cups flour and 1 cup warm water until well mixed. Cover with towel; let rise at room temperature, free from draft, 18 to 24 hours.

2. *Early in day:* In cup, sprinkle yeast over remaining ½ cup warm water; stir to dissolve. Stir into sponge. Stir in 3 to 4 cups flour to make a soft dough.

3. Turn dough onto lightly floured surface and knead until smooth and elastic, 8 to 10 minutes, adding more flour while kneading. Shape dough into ball; place in greased large bowl, turning dough over to grease top. Cover with towel; let rise in warm place (80° to 85°F.), free from draft, until doubled in bulk, about 1½ hours.

4. Punch dough down by pushing center of dough with fist, then pushing edges of dough into center. Turn dough onto lightly floured surface; cut in half.

5. Sprinkle large baking sheet with cornmeal. Shape one dough half into a round loaf, about 6 inches in diameter. Place on prepared baking sheet. Repeat with remaining dough. Cover with towel; let rise in warm place until doubled, about 1 hour.

6. Preheat oven to 400°F. Place pan of hot water on bottom shelf of oven. Brush loaves with cold water. With sharp knife, cut a few crisscross slashes across top of each loaf. Bake 35 to 40 minutes until tops are golden and loaves sound hollow when tapped with finger. Remove from baking sheets; cool on wire racks.

*Sourdough Starter

BEGIN: 3 DAYS AHEAD

2   cups all-purpose flour
1   package active dry yeast
2   cups very warm water (120° to 130°F.)
1   tablespoon sugar or honey

1. In large glass bowl, stir together flour and yeast. Add water and sugar; mix well.

2. Cover with towel; let stand in warm place 3 days, stirring occasionally. Stir well before using. Use to make Sourdough Bread or cover and refrigerate until ready to use, up to 1 week.

TIP: To keep starter more than one week, add *1 cup all-purpose flour* and *1 cup warm water* to starter; stir to combine. Cover with towel and refrigerate; let stand at room temperature 24 hours before using. Repeat each time starter is used, at least once a week.

❋ Sally Lunn

This rich yellow bread is a descendant of little tea buns made in England in Colonial times. It was adopted in the South as an integral part of Southern cuisine, but the small buns became a large loaf, usually made in a tube pan or Turk's-head mold. The origin of the name is a mystery. Some say that Sally Lunn was the name of a girl who sold buns in England; others suggest that the name is a confused version of soleil et lune *(sun and moon), which described the contrast of the golden tops and white bottoms of the English buns.*

BEGIN: EARLY IN DAY   1 LOAF

3¾ to 4 cups all-purpose flour
¼   cup sugar
1   teaspoon salt
1   package active dry yeast
1   cup milk
½   cup butter or margarine
3   eggs, at room temperature

1. In large bowl, combine 1¼ cups flour, sugar, salt and yeast. In 2-quart saucepan over low heat, heat milk and butter until mixture is very warm but you can still hold your finger in it (120° to 130°F.). Butter does not need to melt completely. With mixer at low speed, gradually pour liquid into dry ingredients; beat until just mixed. At medium speed, beat 2 minutes, scraping bowl with rubber spatula. Beat in eggs and 1 cup flour or enough to make a thick batter; continue beating 2 minutes, scraping bowl occasionally. With spoon, stir in enough additional flour (about 1½ cups) to make a stiff batter.

2. Cover with towel; let rise in warm place (80° to 85°F.), free from draft, until doubled, about 1 hour.

3. Grease 10-inch tube pan. Stir batter down; beat well with wooden spoon about 30 seconds. Spread into prepared pan. Cover with towel; let rise in warm place until doubled, about 1 hour.

4. Preheat oven to 350°F. Bake 35 minutes or until top is golden and loaf sounds hollow when lightly tapped with finger. Remove from pan immediately; cool on wire rack.

❋ Anadama Bread

There are two versions of the naming of this corn and wheat bread. One is that a fisherman, tired of waiting for his lazy wife, baked his own bread, muttering, "Anna, damn her!" The other version claims that a man used the same words to boast that his wife was a wonderful cook.

BEGIN: EARLY IN DAY   2 LOAVES

7   to 8 cups all-purpose flour
1   cup yellow cornmeal
2⅛ teaspoons salt
2   packages active dry yeast
¼   cup butter or margarine, softened
2½ cups very warm water (120° to 130°F.)
½   cup molasses
2   teaspoons yellow cornmeal

1. In large bowl, combine 2½ cups flour, 1 cup cornmeal, 2 teaspoons salt and yeast; add butter. With mixer at low speed, gradually pour water and molasses into flour mixture; beat until just mixed. At medium speed, beat 2 minutes, scraping bowl with rubber spatula. Beat in 1½ cups flour or enough to make a thick batter; continue beating 2 minutes, scraping bowl occasionally. With spoon, stir in enough additional flour (about 3 cups) to make a soft dough.

2. Turn dough onto lightly floured surface and knead until smooth and elastic, about 10 minutes, adding more flour while kneading. Shape dough into ball; place in greased large bowl, turning dough over to grease top. Cover with towel; let rise in warm place (80° to 85°F.), free from draft, until doubled in bulk, about 1 hour.

3. Punch dough down by pushing center of dough with fist, then pushing edges of dough into center. Turn dough onto lightly floured surface; cut in half. Cover; let rest 15 minutes.

4. Grease two 9- by 5-inch loaf pans. Roll one dough half into 14- by 9-inch rectangle. Starting at narrow end, roll tightly, jelly-roll fashion; pinch seam to seal. Press ends to seal and tuck under. Place seam side down in prepared pan. Repeat with remaining dough. Cover with towel; let rise in warm place until doubled, about 1 hour.

5. Preheat oven to 400°F. Combine 2 teaspoons cornmeal and remaining ⅛ teaspoon salt. Sprinkle over loaves. Bake 15 minutes. Reduce heat to 350°F. and bake 25 minutes more or until tops are browned and loaves sound hollow when tapped with finger. Remove from pans immediately; cool on wire racks.

❋ Oatmeal Bread

Wheat flour has been favored for bread making because it rises well when mixed with leavening. But in cooler climates, wild oats sometimes took over wheat fields. The hardy grain withstood harsh growing conditions better than wheat and helped weather world famines. Because oats grew so readily, they became a favorite grain for cooking as well as for animal food.

BEGIN: EARLY IN DAY   2 LOAVES

2   cups water
¼   cup honey
¼   cup butter or margarine
1¾ cups uncooked quick-cooking oats
4   to 4½ cups all-purpose flour
2   teaspoons salt
2   packages active dry yeast
1   egg, beaten

1. In 2-quart saucepan over low heat, heat water, honey and butter until mixture is very warm but you can still hold your finger in it (120° to 130°F.). Butter does not need to melt completely. Stir in 1½ cups oats; set aside.

2. In large bowl, combine 1½ cups flour, salt and yeast. With mixer at low speed, gradually add oat mixture to dry ingredients; beat until just mixed. At medium speed, beat 2 minutes, scraping bowl with rubber spatula. Beat in ½ cup flour or enough to make a thick batter; continue beating 2 minutes, scraping bowl occasionally. With spoon, stir in enough additional flour (about 2 cups) to make a soft dough.

3. Turn dough onto lightly floured surface and knead until smooth and elastic, about 10 minutes, adding more flour while kneading. Shape dough into ball; place in greased large bowl, turning dough over to grease top. Cover with towel; let rise in warm place (80° to 85°F.), free from draft, until doubled in bulk, about 1 hour.

4. Punch dough down by pushing center of dough with fist, then pushing edges of dough into center. Turn dough onto lightly floured surface; cut in half. Cover; let rest 15 minutes.

5. Grease two 9- by 5-inch loaf pans. Roll one dough half into 12- by 8-inch rectangle. Starting at narrow end, roll tightly, jelly-roll fashion; pinch seam to seal. Press ends to seal and tuck under. Place seam side down in prepared pan. Repeat with remaining dough. Cover with towel; let rise in warm place until doubled, about 1 hour. Brush dough with beaten egg; sprinkle with remaining ¼ cup oats.

6. Preheat oven to 375°F. Bake 35 minutes or until tops are golden and loaves sound hollow when tapped with finger. Remove from pans immediately; cool on wire racks.

❊ Honey-Wheat Batter Bread

Honey was the only sweetener most people knew until sugar became readily available in the seventeenth century. Native Americans gathered honey and used it in cooking. The colonists also used honey, and some settlers even brought special bees from the Old World to increase the honey supplies in America. When cane sugar became cheap and abundant, honey lost its popularity, but today's proponents of natural foods have revived our interest in it.

BEGIN: EARLY IN DAY   2 LOAVES

2½ **cups whole wheat flour**
1   **teaspoon salt**
2   **packages active dry yeast**
2   **cups buttermilk**
½   **cup honey**
½   **cup butter or margarine**
1   **egg, at room temperature**
2   **cups all-purpose flour**

1. In large bowl, combine whole wheat flour, salt and yeast. In small saucepan over medium-high heat, heat buttermilk, honey and butter until mixture is very warm but you can still hold your finger in it (120° to 130°F.). With mixer at low speed, gradually pour liquid into dry ingredients; beat until just blended. At medium speed, beat 2 minutes, scraping bowl with rubber spatula. Add egg and 1 cup all-purpose flour or enough to make a thick batter; beat 2 minutes more, scraping bowl occasionally. With spoon, stir in remaining 1 cup flour to make a stiff batter. Cover with towel; let rise in warm place (80° to 85°F.), free from draft, until doubled in bulk, about 1 hour.

2. Grease two 9- by 5-inch loaf pans. Stir down batter; spread evenly into pans. Cover with towel; let rise in warm place until doubled in bulk, about 45 minutes.

3. Preheat oven to 350°F. Bake 35 minutes or until tops are golden and loaves sound hollow when tapped with finger. Cool in pans on wire racks 10 minutes. Remove from pans; cool on wire racks.

❊ Parker House Rolls

The Parker House was the best-known dining establishment in Boston during the restaurant boom of the mid-1800s. It was known for its wonderful food as well as for the famous people who met there, literary figures such as Emerson, Holmes, Whittier and Longfellow. One recipe that has impressed the name of the restaurant on the American public is that for light, delicate Parker House Rolls with their special pocketbook shape.

BEGIN: 3 HOURS AHEAD   24 ROLLS

3   **to 4 cups all-purpose flour**
2   **tablespoons sugar**
1   **teaspoon salt**
1   **package active dry yeast**
½   **cup water**
½   **cup milk**
½   **cup butter or margarine**
1   **egg, at room temperature**

1. In large bowl, combine 1 cup flour, sugar, salt and yeast. In 2-quart saucepan over low heat, heat water, milk and ¼ cup butter until mixture is very warm but you can still hold your finger in it (120° to 130°F.). Butter does not need to melt completely. With mixer at low speed, gradually pour liquid into dry ingredients; beat until just mixed. At medium speed, beat 2 minutes, scraping bowl with rubber spatula. Beat in egg and ½ cup flour or enough to make a thick batter; continue beating 2 minutes, scraping bowl occasionally. With spoon, stir in enough additional flour (about 1½ cups) to make a soft dough.

2. Turn dough onto lightly floured surface and knead until smooth and elastic, about 8 minutes, adding more flour while kneading. Shape dough into ball and place in greased large bowl, turning dough over to grease top. Cover with towel; let rise in warm place (80° to 85°F.), free from draft, until doubled, about 1 hour.

3. Grease 2 baking sheets. In small saucepan, melt remaining ¼ cup butter. Punch dough down by pushing center of dough with fist, then pushing edges of dough into center. Turn dough onto lightly floured surface; cut in half.

4. Roll one dough half to ½-inch thickness. Cut into 2½-inch rounds. Reroll and cut trimmings into rounds. With dull edge of knife, crease each round to one side of center. Brush each round with melted butter to within ¼ inch of edge. Fold larger side over smaller so edges just meet. Pinch well with fingers to seal. Place about 1 inch apart on prepared baking sheet. Repeat with remaining dough. Cover with towel; let rise in warm place until doubled, about 1 hour.

5. Preheat oven to 400°F. Brush rolls with remaining melted butter. Bake 8 to 10 minutes until they are golden and sound hollow when tapped with finger. Remove from baking sheets; serve warm.

❋ Pumpernickel Bread

This chewy rye bread is an import from Europe and is flavored with caraway seed, a favorite seasoning in Germany. But it also contains two elements closely associated with the Colonial period of America—cornmeal and molasses—and two other New World ingredients—chocolate and potatoes. Pumpernickel resembles Rye 'n' Injun bread, the heavy, coarse loaves made with rye and cornmeal that were a staple in the Colonial period.

BEGIN: EARLY IN DAY   2 LOAVES

3   cups all-purpose flour
1½   cups rye flour
½   cup cornmeal
2   teaspoons salt
2   packages active dry yeast
1½   cups water
2   tablespoons molasses
1   square (1 ounce) semisweet chocolate
1   tablespoon butter or margarine
1   cup mashed potatoes (at room
       temperature)
1   egg white
1   tablespoon cold water
2   teaspoons caraway seed

1. In medium bowl, combine all-purpose flour and rye flour. In large bowl, combine 2 cups flour mixture, cornmeal, salt and yeast. In 2-quart saucepan over low heat, heat water, molasses, chocolate and butter until chocolate is melted. Cool until mixture is very warm but you can still hold your finger in it (120° to 130°F.). With mixer at low speed, gradually pour liquid into dry ingredients; beat until just mixed. At medium speed, beat 2 minutes, scraping bowl with rubber spatula. With spoon, stir in mashed potatoes and ½ cup flour mixture or enough to make a thick batter; continue beating 2 minutes, scraping bowl occasionally. Stir in enough additional flour mixture (about 1 cup) to make a soft dough.

2. Turn dough onto lightly floured surface and knead until smooth and elastic, about 10 minutes, adding more flour mixture while kneading. Shape dough into ball; place in greased large bowl, turning dough over to grease top. Cover with towel; let rise in warm place (80° to 85°F.), free from draft, until doubled, about 1 hour.

3. Punch dough down by pushing center of dough with fist, then pushing edges of dough into center. Let rise again until doubled, about 30 minutes. Punch dough down again. Turn onto lightly floured surface; cut in half. Cover; let rest 15 minutes.

4. Grease two 8-inch round cake pans. Shape each dough half into a ball; place in prepared pans. Cover with towel; let rise in warm place until doubled, about 1 hour.

5. Preheat oven to 375°F. In cup, beat together egg white and cold water; brush over loaves. Sprinkle with caraway seed. Bake 40 minutes until tops are browned and loaves sound hollow when tapped with finger. Remove from pans immediately; cool on wire racks.

TIP: Break chocolate into small pieces to melt faster.

❋ Dill Casserole Bread

In this country, dill seeds once were known as "meetin' seeds" because parents gave them to their offspring to chew to keep them awake in church. Although it is best known for flavoring pickles, dill makes a surprisingly delicious contribution to this bread. A recipe similar to this one was a prize-winner in the Pillsbury Bake-Off of 1960. That recipe was developed by Leona Schnuelle of Crab Orchard, Nebraska, who won the $25,000 Grand Prize. It became so popular that it has been printed in many cookbooks since then.

BEGIN: EARLY IN DAY   1 LOAF

2½ **cups all-purpose flour**
2   **tablespoons sugar**
2   **teaspoons dill seed**
1   **teaspoon salt**
¼   **teaspoon baking soda**
1   **package active dry yeast**
2   **tablespoons butter or margarine**
1   **medium onion, finely chopped**
1   **cup creamed cottage cheese**
¼   **cup water**
1   **egg, at room temperature**

1. In large bowl, combine 1 cup flour, sugar, dill, salt, soda and yeast. In small saucepan over medium-high heat, in hot butter, cook onion until tender. Stir in cottage cheese and water. Heat until mixture is very warm but you can still hold your finger in it (120° to 130°F.). With mixer at low speed, gradually pour liquid into dry ingredients; beat until just blended. At medium speed, beat 2 minutes, scraping bowl with rubber spatula. Add egg and ½ cup flour or enough to make a thick batter; beat 2 minutes more, scraping bowl occasionally. With spoon, stir in remaining 1 cup flour to make a stiff batter. Cover with towel; let rise in warm place (80° to 85°F.), free from draft, until doubled, about 1 hour.

2. Grease 1½-quart casserole. Stir down batter; spread evenly into prepared casserole. Cover with towel; let rise in warm place until doubled, about 45 minutes.

3. Preheat oven to 350°F. Bake 35 minutes or until golden. Cool in pan on wire rack 10 minutes. Remove from pan; cool on wire rack.

Dill Casserole Bread

❋ Herbed Potato Rolls

Before yeast or baking powder was commercially available, potatoes were used to make homemade yeast and to start the bacterial growth for salt-rising bread. Although we rarely use potatoes for leavening today, we use them to add flavor and texture to loaves, rolls and doughnuts. This recipe starts with condensed potato soup so you don't have to cook potatoes. The herbs add freshness to the hearty potato flavor.

BEGIN: 3 HOURS AHEAD   32 ROLLS

6   to 6½ cups all-purpose flour
2   tablespoons sugar
1   teaspoon salt
1   package active dry yeast
1   can (10¾ ounces) condensed cream of
      potato soup
1½   cups water
¼   cup butter or margarine
¼   cup chopped fresh chives
¼   cup chopped parsley
1   egg
1   teaspoon water
      Poppy seed

1. In large bowl, combine 3 cups flour, sugar, salt and yeast. In 2-quart saucepan over low heat, heat soup, 1½ cups water and butter until mixture is very warm but you can still hold your finger in it (120° to 130°F.). Butter does not need to melt completely. With mixer at low speed, gradually pour liquid into dry ingredients.

2. Add chives and parsley; beat until just mixed. At medium speed, beat 2 minutes, scraping bowl with rubber spatula. Beat in ½ cup flour or enough to make a thick batter; continue beating 2 minutes, scraping bowl occasionally. With spoon, stir in enough additional flour (about 3 cups) to make a soft dough.

3. Turn dough onto lightly floured surface and knead until smooth and elastic, about 10 minutes. Shape dough into ball; place in greased large bowl, turning dough over to grease top. Cover with towel; let rise in warm place (80° to 85°F.), free from draft, until doubled in bulk, about 45 minutes.

4. Punch dough down by pushing center of dough with fist, then pushing edges of dough into center.

5. Grease two 9- by 9-inch baking pans. Shape dough into 32 balls; arrange 16 in each pan. In cup, beat egg and 1 teaspoon water; brush over rolls. Sprinkle with poppy seed. Cover with towel; let rise in warm place until doubled, 30 to 45 minutes.

6. Preheat oven to 375°F. Bake 20 minutes or until tops are golden and rolls sound hollow when tapped with finger. Remove from pans; serve warm.

❋ Angel Biscuits

These Southern-style biscuits are very light because they are made with three leavening agents: yeast, baking powder and baking soda. Southern cooks make a large batch of biscuit dough, then bake part of it each day in order to enjoy oven-fresh bread at every meal.

BEGIN: 2 HOURS OR FEW   36 BISCUITS
         DAYS AHEAD

1   package active dry yeast
2   tablespoons warm water (105° to 115°F.)
5   cups all-purpose flour
¼   cup sugar
1   tablespoon baking powder
1   teaspoon baking soda
1   teaspoon salt
1   cup shortening
2   cups buttermilk

1. In small bowl, sprinkle yeast over warm water; stir to dissolve.

2. In large bowl, combine flour, sugar, baking powder, baking soda and salt. With pastry blender or two knives, cut in shortening until mixture resembles coarse meal. Add reserved yeast mixture and buttermilk; mix with fork. Cover; chill dough at least 1 hour.

3. Remove enough dough to make desired number of biscuits. Turn dough onto lightly floured surface; knead 10 times. Roll dough to ½-inch thickness. Cut into 2½-inch rounds. Reroll and cut trimmings into rounds. With dull edge of knife, crease each round to one side of center. Fold larger side over smaller so edges just meet. Pinch well with fingers to seal. Place about 1 inch apart on baking sheet.

4. Preheat oven to 400°F. Bake 15 minutes or until golden. Remove from baking sheet; serve warm.

TIP: Dough may be kept 3 to 4 days in refrigerator.

❋ Philadelphia Sticky Buns

In the 1800s Philadelphians could purchase sweet, glazed rolls from street vendors and enjoy them at every meal. They came from Pennsylvania Dutch schnecken, or snails. What makes Philadelphia Sticky Buns different from those in other parts of the country? Residents claim they are stickier and better.

BEGIN: 4 HOURS AHEAD · · · · · 18 ROLLS

5½ to 6 cups all-purpose flour
½ cup sugar
1 teaspoon salt
1 teaspoon grated lemon peel
2 packages active dry yeast
1 cup water
½ cup milk
1 cup butter or margarine
2 eggs, at room temperature
1½ cups packed dark brown sugar
½ cup dark corn syrup
1 cup coarsely chopped pecans
2 teaspoons ground cinnamon
2 tablespoons butter or margarine, melted
1 cup raisins

1. In large bowl, combine 2 cups flour, sugar, salt, lemon peel and yeast. In 2-quart saucepan over low heat, heat water, milk and ½ cup butter until mixture is very warm but you can still hold your finger in it (120° to 130°F.). Butter does not need to melt completely. With mixer at low speed, gradually pour liquid into dry ingredients; beat until just mixed. At medium speed, beat 2 minutes, scraping bowl with rubber spatula. Beat in eggs and 1½ cups flour or enough to make a thick batter; continue beating 2 minutes, scraping bowl occasionally. With spoon, stir in enough additional flour (about 2 cups) to make a stiff batter.

2. Cover with towel; let rise in warm place (80° to 85°F.), free from draft, until doubled, about 1 hour. In 2-quart saucepan, melt remaining ½ cup butter. Add 1 cup brown sugar and corn syrup. Heat, stirring until sugar is dissolved. Pour into two 9- by 9-inch baking pans. Sprinkle with nuts. In small bowl, combine remaining ½ cup brown sugar and cinnamon; set aside.

3. Punch dough down by pushing center of dough with fist, then pushing edges of dough into center. Turn dough onto lightly floured surface; cut in half. Roll one dough half into 14- by 9-inch rectangle. Brush with 1 tablespoon melted butter. Sprinkle with ½ of the reserved cinnamon-sugar mixture and ½ cup raisins. Starting at narrow end, roll tightly, jelly-roll fashion; pinch seam to seal. Cut into nine 1-inch slices. Place cut side down in prepared pan. Repeat with remaining dough. Cover with towel; let rise in warm place until doubled, about 1 hour.

4. Preheat oven to 375°F. Bake 25 minutes or until tops are golden and rolls sound hollow when tapped with finger. Immediately invert onto serving platters to cool.

REFRIGERATOR STICKY BUNS: Prepare dough and shape buns as above. After shaping buns, cover with towel and refrigerate up to 24 hours. When ready to bake, remove from refrigerator and let stand in warm place about 1 hour. Bake as above.

❋ French Market Beignets

People who enjoy food like to vacation in New Orleans, a city of tempting flavors and aromas. One of the most exciting places to visit is the French Market, where fresh fruit and vegetable vendors sell their produce in the early morning. A trip to the market is not complete without a cup of chicory coffee and a French Market Beignet.

BEGIN: 3 HOURS AHEAD · · · · · 25 BEIGNETS

2¾ to 3 cups all-purpose flour
¼ cup sugar
½ teaspoon salt
1 teaspoon ground nutmeg
1 package active dry yeast
1 cup milk
2 tablespoons butter or margarine
1 egg, at room temperature
Salad oil
Confectioners' sugar

1. In large bowl, combine 2 cups flour, ¼ cup sugar, salt, nutmeg and yeast. In 1-quart saucepan over low heat, heat milk and butter until mixture is very warm but you can still hold your finger in it (120° to 130°F.). Butter does not need to melt completely. With mixer at low speed, gradually pour liquid into dry ingredients; beat until just mixed. At medium speed, beat 2 minutes, scraping bowl with rubber spatula. Beat in egg and ½ cup flour or enough to make a thick batter; continue beating 2 minutes, scraping bowl occasionally. With spoon, stir in enough additional flour (about ¼ cup) to make a stiff batter.

2. Cover with towel; let rise in warm place (80° to 85°F.), free from draft, until doubled, about 1 hour.

3. Turn dough onto lightly floured surface and knead until smooth and elastic, about 8 minutes. Cover; let rest 10 minutes.

4. Grease a baking sheet. Roll dough into 12- by 12-inch square. Cut into 25 squares. Place squares on prepared baking sheet. Cover with towel; let rise in warm place until doubled, about 1 hour.

5. In 4-quart saucepan, heat 2 inches oil to 375°F. Fry 2 to 3 beignets at a time 30 to 45 seconds on each side until golden, turning once with slotted spoon. Drain on paper towels. While warm, roll in confectioners' sugar.

❄ Apple Crumb Cake

German settlers introduced an array of sweet breads and the coffee klatch—a time for drinking coffee and eating cakes while exchanging news. This delightful custom fostered two distinctly American traditions, the coffee break and the coffeecake. The term coffeecake confuses people learning the language, who expect to find it a cake made with coffee. But to Americans, it is any type of sweet bread, often flavored with spices, nuts or fruit, that goes well with a cup of coffee.

BEGIN: 2½ HOURS AHEAD   8 SERVINGS

2¼ cups all-purpose flour
1   cup sugar
½   teaspoon salt
1   package active dry yeast
½   cup milk
½   cup butter or margarine
2   eggs, at room temperature
2   large apples, cored and sliced
2   teaspoons ground cinnamon

1. In small bowl, combine 1 cup flour, ½ cup sugar, salt and yeast. In small saucepan over low heat, heat milk and ¼ cup butter until mixture is very warm but you can still hold your finger in it (120° to 130°F.). Butter does not need to melt completely. With mixer at low speed, gradually pour liquid into dry ingredients; beat until just blended. At medium speed, beat 2 minutes, scraping bowl with rubber spatula. Add eggs and ½ cup flour or enough to make a thick batter; continue beating 2 minutes, scraping bowl occasionally. With spoon, stir in ½ cup flour to make a stiff batter.

2. Grease 9- by 9-inch baking pan. Spread batter evenly into pan; arrange apple slices over batter. In small bowl, combine remaining ½ cup sugar, remaining ¼ cup flour and cinnamon. With pastry blender or two knives, cut in remaining ¼ cup butter until mixture is crumbly. Sprinkle over apples. Cover with towel; let rise in warm place (80° to 85°F.), free from draft, until doubled, about 1 hour.

3. Preheat oven to 375°F. Bake 35 minutes or until golden. Cool in pan on wire rack 10 minutes. Remove from pan; serve warm.

❋ Popovers

English colonists baked beef-flavored Yorkshire Pudding with roasts, but it was Americans who created Popovers. Using the same batter, they left out the drippings and made high, crisp puffs to serve with butter and jam. Cast-iron popover pans are said to make the best Popovers, but you can use custard cups as well.

BEGIN: 1¼ HOURS AHEAD   6 POPOVERS

3   eggs
1   cup milk
3   tablespoons butter or margarine, melted
1   cup all-purpose flour
¼   teaspoon salt

1. Preheat oven to 375°F. Grease six 5-ounce custard cups or 6 sections of a popover pan.

2. In small bowl with mixer at low speed, beat eggs until frothy. Beat in milk and butter. Beat in flour and salt. Pour into prepared cups.

3. Bake 50 minutes. With sharp knife, make slit in each popover to let out steam; bake 10 minutes longer. Remove from custard cups; serve immediately with butter and jelly.

TIP: For easier handling, set custard cups in jelly-roll pan before baking.

YORKSHIRE PUDDING: Prepare batter as above in step 2 but double all ingredients and omit butter; mix in large bowl. Chill until needed. Preheat oven to 500°F. Pour ½ cup roast beef drippings into 13- by 9-inch baking or roasting pan (do not use glass dish). Heat in oven 5 minutes. Pour batter into drippings. Bake 15 minutes. Reduce heat to 350°F.; bake 15 minutes more or until crisp. Cut into squares; serve immediately.

TIP: Bacon drippings can be substituted for roast beef drippings in Yorkshire Pudding.

❋ Basic Muffins

American muffins are sweet and cakelike, an ideal bread for showing off fresh blueberries or cranberries or for flavoring with bacon, corn or cheese. Inventive cooks have made muffins with wheat flour, cornmeal, oatmeal and bran.

BEGIN: 30 MINUTES AHEAD   12 MUFFINS

1¾   cups all-purpose flour
¼   cup sugar
1   tablespoon baking powder
½   teaspoon salt
¾   cup milk
¼   cup salad oil
1   egg

1. Preheat oven to 400°F. Grease twelve 2½-inch muffin cups.

2. In large bowl, combine first 4 ingredients. In small bowl with fork, beat together milk, oil and egg. Pour all at once into dry ingredients. Stir just until flour is moistened. Spoon into prepared muffin cups.

3. Bake 20 minutes or until golden. Remove from pans immediately.

BLUEBERRY MUFFINS: Prepare Basic Muffins but add *1 cup fresh or frozen unsweetened blueberries* and *½ teaspoon grated orange peel* to egg mixture.

BACON MUFFINS: Fry *2 slices bacon* until crisp; crumble bacon and reserve drippings. Prepare Basic Muffins but reduce oil to 2 tablespoons and add *2 tablespoons reserved bacon drippings.* Add crumbled bacon to egg mixture.

CRANBERRY MUFFINS: Prepare Basic Muffins but add *1 cup cranberries, halved,* and *¼ teaspoon ground cinnamon* to egg mixture.

WHOLE WHEAT MUFFINS: Prepare Basic Muffins but reduce flour to 1 cup and add *¾ cup whole wheat flour.*

❄ Date-Bran Muffins

Bran muffins are a favorite breakfast food for people on the run because they are easy to eat and provide the good nutrition of bran cereal. The addition of dates or raisins makes them even more delicious.

BEGIN: 45 MINUTES AHEAD   12 MUFFINS

1½ **cups all-purpose flour**
2   **teaspoons baking powder**
½   **teaspoon baking soda**
¼   **teaspoon salt**
1½ **cups whole bran cereal**
1   **cup buttermilk**
1   **egg, beaten**
¼   **cup salad oil**
¼   **cup molasses**
¾   **cup chopped pitted dates**

1. Preheat oven to 400°F. Grease twelve 2½-inch muffin cups.

2. In large bowl, combine first 4 ingredients. In medium bowl with fork, mix together bran, buttermilk, egg, oil and molasses. Pour all at once into dry ingredients; stir just until flour is moistened. Fold in dates. Spoon into prepared muffin cups.

3. Bake 15 minutes or until toothpick inserted in center comes out clean. Remove from pans immediately.

TIP: Chop dates with floured scissors or knife to prevent dates from sticking.

Popovers, Basic Muffins, Blueberry Muffins, Date-Bran Muffins

❄ Corn Bread

Corn is a native American crop, and corn breads predate the coming of the colonists. When they found wheat flour hard to grow, the colonists invented hundreds of ways to use the Indian corn. Corn Bread was on tables all over the country by necessity then; now it is on the table because it is so good. Southerners enjoy a flat, white corn bread made without flour or sugar, while Northerners prefer a lighter, sweeter bread made with yellow cornmeal and additional wheat flour. Other corn breads include jonnycakes, spoon bread, tortillas, muffins, corn sticks and hush puppies, and cornmeal is included in Boston Brown Bread, Anadama Bread and even Pumpernickel Bread.

BEGIN: 45 MINUTES AHEAD   9 SERVINGS

1   cup cornmeal
1   cup all-purpose flour
1   tablespoon sugar
1   tablespoon baking powder
½   teaspoon salt
1   cup milk
2   eggs, beaten
¼   cup shortening, melted

1. Preheat oven to 425°F. Grease 8- by 8-inch baking pan.

2. In large bowl, combine first 5 ingredients. In small bowl with fork, beat together milk, eggs and shortening. Pour all at once into dry ingredients; stir just until flour is moistened. Pour into prepared pan.

3. Bake 25 minutes or until golden. Cut into squares; serve warm.

CORN STICKS: Preheat oven to 425°F. Grease 12 corn stick pans; preheat pans in oven. Meanwhile, prepare batter as above. Spoon batter into hot prepared pans. Bake 15 minutes or until golden.

CORN MUFFINS: Preheat oven to 425°F. Grease twelve 2½-inch muffin cups. Prepare batter as above. Spoon batter into prepared pans. Bake 15 minutes or until golden.

BACON CORN BREAD: Prepare Corn Bread as above but substitute *3 tablespoons bacon drippings* for shortening and add *4 slices bacon, crisply cooked and crumbled,* to egg mixture.

❄ Jalapeño Corn Bread

Jalapeño Corn Bread is popular throughout Texas, Colorado and the West, where chilies are easy to find. It is heartier and coarser than Eastern corn bread, with hotness from the chilies and substance from the corn and cheese. If you can't get fresh jalapeño peppers, canned or pickled ones will do. Be sure to remove the seeds and rinse the peppers thoroughly. Always avoid touching your eyes when handling fresh or canned chilies, because the oils in the peppers can be extremely irritating.

BEGIN: 1 HOUR AHEAD   9 SERVINGS

1   cup yellow cornmeal
½   teaspoon salt
2   teaspoons baking powder
2   eggs, beaten
1   can (8½ ounces) cream-style golden corn
¾   cup buttermilk
¼   cup salad oil or bacon drippings
1½   cups shredded Cheddar cheese
¼   cup finely chopped, seeded jalapeño
         peppers

1. Preheat oven to 375°F. Grease 9- by 9-inch baking pan.

2. In large bowl, combine cornmeal, salt and baking powder. In medium bowl with fork, beat together eggs, corn, buttermilk and oil. Pour all at once into dry ingredients; stir just until moistened.

3. Pour ½ of the batter into prepared pan. Sprinkle with cheese and peppers; top with remaining batter.

4. Bake 35 to 40 minutes until golden. Cut into squares; serve warm.

❋ Buttermilk Biscuits

Biscuits, known as often for being hard and tough as for being light and flaky, owe their popularity to their quick baking. In the times before baking powder, bakers used homemade yeast or pearl ash to raise their biscuits. On the Western ranges, biscuits usually were made with sourdough. In the kitchens of the South, cooks pounded the dough with mallets or hatchets for half an hour to make beaten biscuits. When baking powder became commercially available in the nineteenth century, biscuits became lighter and more dependable.

BEGIN: 30 MINUTES AHEAD   12 BISCUITS

2   cups all-purpose flour
1   tablespoon baking powder
1   teaspoon sugar
½   teaspoon salt
¼   teaspoon baking soda
½   cup shortening
¾   cup buttermilk or sour milk

1. Preheat oven to 450°F. In large bowl, combine flour, baking powder, sugar, salt and baking soda. With pastry blender or two knives, cut in shortening until mixture resembles coarse meal. Add milk; with fork, stir just until dough clings together.

2. Turn onto lightly floured surface; knead gently 10 to 12 strokes. Roll to ½-inch thickness. Cut into 2½-inch rounds. Reroll and cut trimmings into rounds. Place on ungreased baking sheet.

3. Bake 12 minutes or until golden.

TIP: To sour milk, place 1 tablespoon white vinegar in measuring cup; fill with fresh milk to ¾ cup mark.

BAKING POWDER BISCUITS: Prepare as above but substitute fresh milk for buttermilk and omit baking soda.

❋ Pioneer Pancakes

We call them griddlecakes, flap jacks, slap jacks, flannel cakes, hot cakes and pancakes, and serve them with toppings from maple syrup to creamed chicken. Pancakes also figure into our culture. Every year on Shrove Tuesday the women of Liberal, Kansas, run a race while flipping a pancake three times, then compare their winners via transatlantic telephone with the women of Olney, England.

BEGIN: 30 MINUTES AHEAD   4 SERVINGS

1   cup all-purpose flour
1   tablespoon sugar
2   teaspoons baking powder
½   teaspoon salt
1   egg
1   cup milk
2   tablespoons salad oil
     Butter
     Maple syrup

1. In medium bowl, combine first 4 ingredients. In small bowl, beat egg slightly; stir in milk and oil. Add to flour mixture and stir just until flour is moistened (batter will be lumpy).

2. Over medium-high heat, heat 10-inch skillet or griddle. Brush lightly with additional oil.

3. Using scant ¼ cup batter for each pancake, pour batter onto hot skillet, making a few pancakes at a time.

4. Cook until surface bubbles burst; edges will look slightly dry. With pancake turner, turn and cook until underside is golden. Repeat with remaining batter, brushing skillet with more oil as needed. Serve with butter and syrup. Yields 12 pancakes.

WAFFLES: Prepare as above in step 1. Preheat waffle baker as manufacturer directs. Pour batter into center of lower half of baker until it spreads to about 1 inch from edges. Cover and bake as manufacturer directs; do not lift the cover during baking time. Loosen baked waffle carefully with fork. Reheat baker before cooking next waffle.

❈ Spoon Bread

Spoon Bread is a fluffy bread that is served with a spoon. This version is made by the soufflé method, but some are simply stirred together and leavened with baking powder. Both methods produce a delicious hot bread that is creamy inside, crusty outside.

BEGIN: 1¾ HOURS AHEAD   6 SERVINGS

2   **cups boiling water**
1   **cup cornmeal**
2   **tablespoons butter or margarine,**
        softened
1   **teaspoon salt**
1   **cup milk**
4   **eggs, separated, at room temperature**

1. Preheat oven to 350°F. Butter 2-quart casserole.

2. In medium bowl, pour boiling water over cornmeal. With wire whisk, beat until smooth. Stir in butter, salt and milk; cool to lukewarm.

3. Add egg yolks, one at a time, beating well after each addition. In small bowl with mixer at high speed, beat egg whites until stiff peaks form. Gently fold into cornmeal mixture. Pour batter into prepared casserole.

4. Bake 70 to 75 minutes until knife inserted in center comes out clean. Spoon out immediately; serve with additional butter.

Jonnycakes, Jalapeño Corn Bread, Spoon Bread

❈ Jonnycakes

Jonnycakes were invented by native Americans, who taught the colonists how to make ground corn and water into a long-keeping flat bread. This bread was called Jonnycake (from journey cake or Shawnee cake). Colonists added salt, sugar and sometimes eggs to the basic bread, which was a staple food of pioneers and travelers. Rhode Islanders have organized a Society for the Propagation of the Jonnycake Tradition in Rhode Island, which encourages farmers to grow the particular corn that is best for the cakes, and teaches their history and how to prepare them.

BEGIN: 30 MINUTES AHEAD   12 CAKES

1   **cup stone-ground cornmeal**
1   **teaspoon sugar**
¼   **teaspoon salt**
1¼   **cups boiling water**
1   **tablespoon butter or margarine, melted**
        Bacon drippings
        Maple syrup

1. In medium bowl, combine cornmeal, sugar and salt. Add water and butter to cornmeal mixture; stir until smooth.

2. Over medium-high heat, heat 10-inch skillet. Brush lightly with bacon drippings. Drop batter by tablespoonfuls onto hot skillet, making a few cakes at a time.

3. Cook until crisp and browned on one side. With pancake turner, turn and cook until underside is golden. Repeat with remaining batter, brushing skillet with more bacon drippings as required. Serve with additional butter and syrup.

TIP: Stir in about ½ cup milk for thinner Jonnycakes.

❄ Hush Puppies

Besides oven-baked corn breads and those baked on skillets or griddles, Southerners made deep-fried Hush Puppies when fried fish (especially catfish) was on the menu. According to legend, the crisp, fried nuggets were named when they were fed to barking dogs to quiet them.

BEGIN: 45 MINUTES AHEAD   6 SERVINGS

1½ **cups white cornmeal**
¼ **cup all-purpose flour**
1   **teaspoon baking powder**
½   **teaspoon baking soda**
½   **teaspoon salt**
1   **cup buttermilk**
1   **egg, beaten**
¼   **cup grated onion**
    Salad oil

1. In medium bowl, combine cornmeal, flour, baking powder, soda and salt. In small bowl, beat together buttermilk, egg and onion. Pour all at once into dry ingredients; stir just until cornmeal is moistened.

2. In 4-quart saucepan, heat 2 inches oil to 375°F. Drop batter by tablespoonfuls into hot oil; fry a few at a time 1 to 2 minutes until golden. Drain on paper towels; serve hot. Yields 18.

❄ Harvest Moon Doughnuts

A piece of culinary trivia: The doughnut hole was invented by Captain Hanson Crockett Gregory of Rockport, Maine. While watching his mother fry cakes, he hit upon the idea of removing the centers before cooking to prevent them from becoming soggy. One hundred years later his discovery was commemorated with a plaque at his birthplace. This recipe, probably similar to the one Gregory's mother used, is also close to the croquignoles made just across the border from Maine in French Canada.

BEGIN: 2 HOURS AHEAD   20 DOUGHNUTS

4   **cups all-purpose flour**
¾   **cup sugar**
1   **cup buttermilk**
1   **egg**
2   **tablespoons shortening**
1   **teaspoon baking powder**
1   **teaspoon baking soda**
¼   **teaspoon salt**
¼   **teaspoon ground nutmeg**
    Salad oil
    Confectioners' sugar

1. In large bowl, combine 2 cups flour and remaining ingredients except salad oil and confectioners' sugar. With mixer at low speed, beat just until smooth, scraping bowl with rubber spatula. At medium speed, beat 1 minute, scraping bowl occasionally.

2. With spoon, stir in remaining flour to make a soft dough. Cover; chill 1 hour.

3. Turn dough onto lightly floured surface; roll dough to ½-inch thickness. With floured doughnut cutter, cut out doughnuts. Reroll and cut trimmings until all dough is used.

4. In 4-quart saucepan, heat 2 inches oil to 375°F. Fry 2 to 3 doughnuts at a time 45 seconds on each side until golden, turning once with slotted spoon. Drain on paper towels. Sprinkle with confectioners' sugar.

❄ Indian Fry Bread

The Indians of the Southwest make baking powder breads that they fry in hot fat, usually lard. The hole in the center, now traditional, was originally made by impaling the bread on a stick to lift it out of the hot fat.

BEGIN: 45 MINUTES AHEAD   16 SERVINGS

3   cups all-purpose flour
1   tablespoon baking powder
1   teaspoon salt
1   cup water
    Salad oil

1. In medium bowl, stir together flour, baking powder and salt. Add water; stir until well mixed, adding a little more water, if needed.

2. Divide dough into 16 equal parts; form each into a ball. On floured surface, roll each ball as thin as possible. Make hole in center of each with finger.

3. In 4-quart saucepan, heat 2 inches oil to 375°F. Fry 1 piece at a time about 30 seconds on each side until golden, turning once with slotted spoon. Drain on paper towels; serve warm. Yields 16.

Boston Brown Bread

❊ Boston Brown Bread

When New England colonists had difficulty growing wheat, they combined native corn and European rye, which adapted quickly to the new location, to stretch the supply of wheat flour they were able to grow or import. Boston cooks devised this steamed bread to accompany their famous baked beans.

BEGIN: 3 HOURS AHEAD   1 LOAF

½   cup whole wheat flour
½   cup rye flour
½   cup yellow cornmeal
1   teaspoon baking soda
½   teaspoon salt
1   cup sour milk or buttermilk
½   cup molasses
½   cup raisins

1. Grease 1-pound coffee can; line bottom with waxed paper. In large bowl, combine all ingredients; mix well.

2. Pour batter into prepared can; cover with foil and tie to can with string.

3. Place can on rack in deep saucepan; add boiling water to reach halfway up side of can. Cover pan.

4. Over low heat, simmer 1½ to 2 hours until toothpick inserted in center comes out clean. Remove from can immediately; cool on wire rack.

TIP: Release bread from can by opening bottom end of can with can opener.

TIP: Cut bread while warm with thread.

TIP: Substitute greased 1-quart casserole for coffee can. Cover with tight lid or foil.

❊ Sour Cream Coffeecake

This Sour Cream Coffeecake is prepared all across the United States, and recipes for it can be found in fund-raising cookbooks from every region.

BEGIN: 1½ HOURS AHEAD   16 SERVINGS

½   cup butter or margarine, softened
1   cup sugar
2   eggs
1   teaspoon vanilla extract
2   cups all-purpose flour
1   teaspoon baking powder
1   teaspoon baking soda
    Dash salt
1   cup sour cream
½   cup packed brown sugar
2   teaspoons ground cinnamon
2   tablespoons butter or margarine
1   cup chopped pecans or walnuts

1. Preheat oven to 350°F. Grease and flour 10-inch tube pan.

2. In large bowl with mixer at medium speed, cream ½ cup butter until light and fluffy. Gradually beat in sugar until well mixed, scraping bowl with rubber spatula. Beat in eggs, one at a time, beating well after each addition, scraping bowl occasionally. Add vanilla; mix well.

3. In medium bowl, combine flour, baking powder, soda and salt. Add dry ingredients alternately with sour cream to creamed mixture, mixing well after each addition, scraping bowl occasionally.

4. In small bowl, stir together brown sugar and cinnamon; cut in 2 tablespoons butter until mixture resembles coarse crumbs. Stir in nuts. Spoon ½ of the batter into prepared pan; top with ½ of the nut mixture. Repeat layers.

5. Bake 55 to 60 minutes until toothpick inserted in cake comes out clean. Cool in pan on wire rack 10 minutes. Remove from pan. Serve warm or cool.

TIP: Prepare cake in 13- by 9-inch baking pan. Bake 35 to 40 minutes until toothpick inserted in center comes out clean.

Funnel Cakes

✳ Funnel Cakes

These delicate fried breads come from Pennsylvania Dutch country, where they are made in a spiral pattern. Cooks often use a special pitcher with a spout like the end of a funnel, but a traditional funnel works just as well. Then dust the cakes with confectioners' sugar, or serve with molasses, maple syrup or jelly.

BEGIN: 1 HOUR AHEAD   10 SERVINGS

3   eggs
1   cup milk
2   cups all-purpose flour
1   tablespoon sugar
1   teaspoon baking powder
¼   teaspoon salt
     Salad oil
     Confectioners' sugar

1. In small bowl with wire whisk or mixer at medium speed, beat eggs and milk until frothy. Beat in flour, sugar, baking powder and salt until smooth.

2. In 10-inch skillet, heat 1 inch salad oil to 375°F. Holding finger over small opening in funnel, spoon batter into funnel. Using finger to control flow of batter, let batter fall into center of skillet, moving funnel in a spiral to make an 8-inch round. Cook 1 minute until golden. Drain on paper towels. Sprinkle with confectioners' sugar. Yields 10 funnel cakes.

✳ Banana-Nut Loaf

Breads made with baking powder or soda are called quick breads or tea breads, and often have a sweet flavor. This banana bread is a tribute to the role improved transportation has had in our diet. Bananas were scarce in the United States until the United Fruit Company was founded in the mid-1800s by an American sea captain and a railroad builder; since then, they have become a favorite year-round fruit, and banana breads are made in every state.

BEGIN: DAY AHEAD   1 LOAF

⅓   cup shortening
⅔   cup sugar
2   eggs
1   cup mashed ripe bananas (3 medium)
1   teaspoon grated orange peel
¼   cup orange juice
1¾   cups all-purpose flour
1   teaspoon baking powder
½   teaspoon baking soda
½   teaspoon salt
1   cup chopped walnuts

1. Preheat oven to 350°F. Grease 9- by 5-inch loaf pan.

2. In large bowl with mixer at medium speed, cream shortening and sugar. Add eggs, one at a time, beating well after each addition until light and fluffy. Beat in banana, orange peel and orange juice. Combine flour, baking powder, baking soda and salt. Beat into banana mixture for 1 minute, scraping bowl with rubber spatula. Stir in nuts. Spread into prepared pan.

3. Bake 60 minutes or until toothpick inserted in center comes out clean. Cool in pan on wire rack 10 minutes. Remove from pan; cool completely on wire rack. Wrap and store overnight.

❄ Zucchini Bread

During the gardening boom of the 1970s, home gardeners often found themselves with bumper crops of fast-growing zucchini. This abundance spawned more than one cookbook devoted entirely to using up the zucchini. Zucchini bread, with its moist texture and spicy flavor, became a popular treat during the zucchini harvest.

BEGIN: DAY AHEAD   1 LOAF

1¾ cups all-purpose flour
1   cup sugar
1   teaspoon ground cinnamon
½   teaspoon salt
¾   teaspoon baking soda
½   teaspoon baking powder
½   cup salad oil
2   eggs, beaten
1   teaspoon vanilla extract
2   cups shredded zucchini
1   cup chopped walnuts
½   cup raisins

1. Preheat oven to 350°F. Grease and flour 9- by 5-inch loaf pan.

2. In large bowl with mixer at medium speed, combine all ingredients except zucchini, nuts and raisins. Beat 1 minute, scraping bowl with rubber spatula. With spoon, stir in zucchini, nuts and raisins. Spread batter into prepared pan.

3. Bake 70 minutes or until toothpick inserted in center comes out clean. Cool in pan on wire rack 10 minutes. Remove from pan; cool completely on wire rack. Wrap and store overnight.

❄ Cranberry-Nut Bread

Only slightly less sweet and rich than a cake, a tea bread is usually baked in a loaf, thinly sliced, then spread with butter, cream cheese or jam. Cranberries add an appealing moistness, flavor and color to this tea bread.

BEGIN: DAY AHEAD   2 LOAVES

1½ cups chopped nuts
1½ cups halved cranberries
1   cup raisins
2½ cups all-purpose flour
1¼ cups sugar
½   cup butter or margarine, softened
2   eggs
2   tablespoons grated orange peel
1   teaspoon baking powder
1   teaspoon baking soda
¼   teaspoon salt
1   cup buttermilk or sour milk
½   cup orange juice
¼   teaspoon ground nutmeg

1. In medium bowl, combine nuts, cranberries, raisins and ½ cup flour; set aside. Preheat oven to 350°F. Grease and flour two 8- by 4-inch loaf pans.

2. In large bowl with mixer at medium speed, combine remaining 2 cups flour, ¾ cup sugar, butter, eggs, orange peel, baking powder, baking soda, salt and buttermilk. Beat 1 minute, scraping bowl with rubber spatula. With spoon, stir in cranberry mixture. Spread batter evenly into prepared pans.

3. Bake 50 minutes or until toothpick inserted in center comes out clean. Cool in pans on wire rack 10 minutes.

4. Meanwhile, in small saucepan over medium-high heat, heat remaining ½ cup sugar, orange juice and nutmeg to boiling; pour over warm breads. Cool completely in pans. Wrap and store overnight.

TIP: Most quick breads benefit from standing at least overnight. Tightly wrap cooled loaves; store at room temperature.

Pita Burgers, Club Sandwiches, Hero Sandwiches

SANDWICHES

From the beginning, Americans have been eating on the run. From the pioneers' jerky to modern American fast food, we like to take it with us.

The invention of the sandwich is attributed to John Montagu, the Earl of Sandwich, during the eighteenth century. Absorbed in a card game, he ordered meat to be placed between two bread slices so he could eat without interrupting his game or dirtying his hands.

But Lord Sandwich did not really invent the sandwich, he merely gave it a name. Bread has been wrapped around other foods as long as it has been made.

Every region of the world has its sandwiches, and we Americans have welcomed them all: Mexican tacos, Greek *gyros,* Chinese egg rolls, Swedish open-faced sandwiches, Italian pizza, French *croques-monsieur.* We not only took them in, but we mixed them all together. Who else would serve German frankfurters and Mexican chili on an all-American roll?

Delicatessens in the United States have done a great deal to promote the sandwich. Beginning as establishments in German neighborhoods of large cities, they soon incorporated the ethnic foods of other cuisines, especially those from Scandinavia, Italy and Eastern Europe. In the past decade or two, delicatessens have multiplied at an astonishing rate. Besides corner delis in cities, there are delicatessen departments in nearly every supermarket in the country. These dispense sandwiches of all kinds along with the sausages, meats, cheeses and breads for making them.

Today the American sandwich runs the gamut from plain to spectacular, mild to spicy, tiny to gargantuan. Nearly everything Americans eat has found its way into a sandwich, including New England baked beans, every kind of meat and cheese, all-American peanut butter, seafood, eggs, vegetables, fruits and all the trimmings.

Every day, children take peanut butter sandwiches to school in brown paper bags. Workers carry hero sandwiches in their lunch pails. Midwestern farmers eat leftover meat loaf and pickles on homemade rye bread. Office workers go out for a "BLT down" (toasted), a "cowboy" (Western omelet sandwich) or a "Coney Island chicken" (hot dog).

Is it any wonder that when the King and Queen of England visited the White House, President Franklin Roosevelt served them hot dogs on rolls?

❋ Hamburgers

Although no sandwich is more American than the hamburger, it carries the name of the German city of Hamburg (where, ironically, ground meat is sometimes called American steak). Cooked over charcoal, fried in a skillet or heated by microwave, the ground beef patty in a bun has become an American institution. As with most American foods, it changes character in different regions of the country. You may find it garnished with lettuce, tomato, chili, sauerkraut, coleslaw, bean sprouts, raw or cooked onion, bacon or cheese.

BEGIN: 30 MINUTES AHEAD   4 SERVINGS

1   **pound ground beef**
¼   **cup finely chopped onion**
½   **teaspoon salt**
⅛   **teaspoon pepper**
4   **sandwich buns, split and toasted**

1. In medium bowl, combine beef, onion, salt and pepper. With hands, shape mixture into 4 patties, each about 1 inch thick.

2. Over medium heat, heat 10-inch skillet until very hot. Cook patties 10 to 15 minutes until desired doneness, turning once.

3. Serve on buns with choice of garnishes: lettuce, tomato slices, cheese slices, pickle slices, onion slices, bacon slices, avocado slices, coleslaw, relish, mustard, mayonnaise or ketchup.

TO BROIL: Prepare patties as above; place on rack in broiler pan. Broil 4 inches from the heat 10 to 15 minutes until desired doneness, turning once.

TO GRILL: Prepare patties as above; grill over medium coals 10 to 15 minutes until desired doneness, turning once.

TERIYAKI BURGERS: Prepare as above but omit salt and add *1 tablespoon soy sauce, ½ teaspoon ground ginger* and *¼ teaspoon garlic powder* to meat mixture. Form into patties; pan-fry, broil or grill as above. Add *4 slices fresh or canned pineapple* to pan or grill during last minute of cooking. Top each burger with 1 pineapple slice.

PITA BURGERS: Prepare as above but add *¼ teaspoon garlic powder* and *½ teaspoon oregano leaves, crushed,* to meat mixture. Pan-fry, broil or grill as above. Cut *4 pita bread rounds* in half vertically; halve burgers. Place 1 burger half in each bread half. Spoon *plain yogurt, chopped tomato* and *chopped cucumber* into bread with burger.

❋ Souperburgers

A popular variation of the hamburger is a cooked mixture of all the traditional ingredients, spooned onto a sandwich bun. Such seasoned ground beef mixtures became popular in the 1950s and 1960s, called Spoonburgers, Skilletburgers, Coney Burgers or Sloppy Joes (with tomato sauce); Creoleburgers or Sloppy Louies (with chicken gumbo soup); Souperburgers (with mushroom, tomato, gumbo or pepperpot soup); Spanish Hamburgers, Pizza Burgers or Barbecue Beefwiches (with seasoned sauces).

BEGIN: 30 MINUTES AHEAD   6 SERVINGS

1   **pound ground beef**
½   **cup finely chopped onion**
1   **can (10¾ ounces) condensed chicken gumbo soup**
1   **tablespoon prepared mustard**
     Dash pepper
6   **sandwich buns, split and toasted**

1. In 10-inch skillet over medium-high heat, cook beef and onion until beef is browned, stirring to separate meat. Pour off fat.

2. Stir in soup, mustard and pepper. Heat, stirring occasionally. Serve on buns. Yields 3½ cups.

TO MICROWAVE: Into microwave-safe 1½-quart casserole, crumble beef. Stir in onion; cover. Microwave on HIGH 5 minutes, stirring once. Pour off fat. Stir in soup, mustard and pepper; cover. Microwave on HIGH 2 to 3 minutes until hot. Serve on buns.

❊ Tacos

This is the taco that most Americans recognize, made with seasoned ground beef, shredded lettuce, tomatoes and cheese. But to Mexicans, a taco is a folded, crisp tortilla or a fresh, soft tortilla wrapped around a filling of beef, chicken, turkey, pork, beans, guacamole, sour cream or just about anything you might put in a sandwich.

BEGIN: 1 HOUR AHEAD   10 SERVINGS

1   pound ground beef
1   medium onion, chopped
1½ cups chopped tomatoes
1   teaspoon salt
1   teaspoon chili powder
     Dash hot pepper sauce
10 Taco Shells* or packaged taco shells
1   cup shredded lettuce
1   cup shredded Cheddar cheese
     Taco sauce or hot pepper sauce
       (optional)

1. In 10-inch skillet over medium-high heat, cook beef and onion until beef is browned, stirring to separate meat. Pour off fat.

2. Stir in 1 cup chopped tomatoes, salt, chili powder and hot pepper sauce. Heat, stirring occasionally.

3. To serve: Fill each shell with 2 to 3 tablespoons meat filling. Top with lettuce, cheese and remaining chopped tomato. Sprinkle with taco sauce or hot pepper sauce.

To Microwave: Into microwave-safe 2-quart casserole, crumble beef. Stir in onion; cover. Microwave on HIGH 5 minutes, stirring once. Pour off fat. Stir in 1 cup chopped tomatoes, salt, chili powder and hot pepper sauce; cover. Microwave on HIGH 2 to 3 minutes until hot. Proceed as in step 3.

*Taco Shells

¼ cup salad oil
10 6-inch tortillas

In 6-inch skillet over medium-high heat, in hot oil, cook 1 tortilla about 15 seconds until limp. With tongs, fold tortilla and continue cooking about 30 seconds on each side until crisp, holding edges apart. Drain on paper towels; repeat to make more taco shells.

❊ Coney Islands

The all-American hot dog actually is an import, named after the German city of Frankfurt. Americans first served the sausages on a bun. The frankfurter may have first appeared in America at the amusement park in Coney Island. Today, a frankfurter with chili is often called a Coney, Coney dog or Coney Island, but at one time, the frankfurter itself was known as Coney Island chicken.

BEGIN: 15 MINUTES AHEAD   8 TO 10 SERVINGS

1   pound frankfurters
1   can (11¼ ounces) condensed chili beef
       soup
¼   cup water
8   to 10 hot dog buns, split
1   medium onion, finely chopped

1. Cook frankfurters as label directs. Meanwhile, in 1-quart saucepan over medium heat, heat soup and water just to boiling.

2. Place frankfurters in buns; spoon chili over. Sprinkle with chopped onion.

To Microwave: In microwave-safe 1½-quart casserole, place frankfurters; cover. Microwave on HIGH 2 to 3 minutes until hot. Let stand covered. Meanwhile, in microwave-safe 1-quart casserole, combine soup and water; cover. Microwave on HIGH 1 to 2 minutes until hot. Proceed as in step 2.

✳ Philly Cheese Steak Sandwiches

The favorite fast foods of the Philadelphia area, steak sandwiches and cheese steak sandwiches, are so well known that restaurants advertising "steaks" don't have to mention that the steaks are thin sandwich steaks, grilled and served on a long roll.

BEGIN: 30 MINUTES AHEAD   4 SERVINGS

¼ **cup butter or margarine**
3   **medium onions, sliced**
1   **package (16 ounces) frozen chipped
      sandwich steaks**
8   **slices American or provolone cheese**
4   **7-inch-long bread rolls, split
      Salt
      Pepper
      Ketchup (optional)**

1. In 10-inch skillet over medium heat, in hot butter, cook onions until tender; remove to bowl.

2. In same skillet over high heat, cook frozen steaks as label directs. Top each steak portion with cheese slice; cook until cheese melts. Place 2 steak portions in each roll. Top with reserved onions. Sprinkle with salt and pepper; top with ketchup. Serve at once.

MUSHROOM CHEESE STEAK SANDWICHES: Prepare as above but cook *3 cups sliced mushrooms* with onions. Proceed as in step 2.

PIZZA STEAK SANDWICHES: Prepare as above but substitute *mozzarella cheese* for American cheese and top each sandwich with about *3 tablespoons spaghetti sauce.*

✳ Reuben Sandwiches

New Yorkers claim that the Reuben sandwich originated in the now-closed Reuben's delicatessen in that city. But Nebraskans say it was created by Reuben Kay of Omaha at a card game in the mid-1950s. Whatever the case, it's a hearty sandwich that is enjoyed all over America.

BEGIN: 30 MINUTES AHEAD   4 SERVINGS

8   **slices rye bread
      Thousand Island Dressing (see page 184)
      or mayonnaise**
4   **slices Swiss cheese, halved crosswise**
½ **pound sliced corned beef**
1   **cup rinsed, drained sauerkraut
      Butter or margarine, softened**

1. Spread bread slices with dressing. On each of 4 bread slices, place a half-slice cheese, ¼ of the corned beef, ¼ of the sauerkraut and another cheese slice. Top with remaining bread slices, dressing side down. Spread outsides of sandwiches with butter.

2. In 10-inch skillet over low heat, cook sandwiches until browned on bottoms. Turn; cook until browned on other side. Cut each sandwich in half. Serve at once.

✳ Tuna Melts

Tuna is often combined with mayonnaise and celery to make a flavorful cold salad to eat as is or to spread on bread. Imaginative cooks vary the basic salad with such additions as olives, cucumber, shredded carrot, cheese, sour cream, pineapple, grapes, apples, oranges, nuts or herbs. Another way to make tuna special is to pile the filling onto sandwich buns, top with cheese and heat under the broiler.

BEGIN: 15 MINUTES AHEAD   4 SERVINGS

1   **can (7 ounces) tuna, drained and flaked**
⅓ **cup finely chopped celery**
¼ **cup finely chopped onion**
3   **tablespoons chopped pimento-stuffed
      olives**
⅓ **cup mayonnaise**
4   **hot dog buns, split**
2   **slices American cheese, halved**

1. In bowl, combine tuna, celery, onion, olives and mayonnaise. Place open hot dog buns on baking sheet; spoon tuna mixture onto buns. Top with cheese.

2. Broil 4 inches from heat until cheese is melted. Serve at once.

❄ Hero Sandwiches

A hero is a submarine is a hoagie is a grinder is a po'boy is a torpedo: all are hearty sandwiches made from cold cuts and cheeses piled onto long bread loaves. In recent years sandwich shops have appeared that sell heros by the foot, with six-foot-long sandwiches that can be custom-made and delivered to your party. Your own heros won't be so long, but they can be just as tasty.

BEGIN: 15 MINUTES AHEAD   4 SERVINGS

4   **7-inch-long bread rolls, split lengthwise**
    Italian salad dressing
1   **pound assorted sliced cold cuts**
½   **pound assorted sliced cheeses**
1   **medium red onion, thinly sliced and**
    separated into rings
1   **large tomato, thinly sliced**
    Shredded lettuce
    Hot pickled peppers (optional)

Sprinkle cut sides of rolls with Italian dressing. Arrange cold cuts and cheeses on rolls. Top with remaining ingredients; sprinkle with more Italian dressing. Cut each sandwich in half.

TIP: Use your favorite cold cuts and cheeses to make these sandwiches. Include one or more of the following: ham, bologna and salami; American, provolone and Swiss cheese.

❄ Italian Sausage Heros

The word hero *has come to mean any sandwich made on a long bread loaf. Most often it is made with cold cuts and cheeses, but Italian delicatessens also make hot versions with meatballs, veal Parmesan and other specialties. One favorite is made with Italian sausage links topped with fried onions and sweet peppers.*

BEGIN: 45 MINUTES AHEAD   6 SERVINGS

1½ **pounds Italian link sausage, cut into 6**
    pieces
¼   **cup water**
2   **tablespoons olive or salad oil**
1   **large onion, sliced and separated into**
    rings
3   **green peppers, cut into ½-inch strips**
2   **sweet red peppers, cut into strips**
1   **teaspoon salt**
½   **teaspoon Italian seasoning**
2   **large tomatoes, chopped**
6   **5-inch-long bread rolls, split lengthwise**

1. In 10-inch skillet over medium-high heat, heat sausages and water to boiling. Reduce heat to low. Cover; simmer 5 minutes. Uncover; cook about 15 minutes more until water is evaporated and sausages are browned, turning occasionally. Remove and keep warm.

2. In same skillet over medium-high heat, in hot oil, cook onion until tender. Add green and red peppers, salt and Italian seasoning. Reduce heat to medium; cook until peppers are just tender, stirring occasionally. Add tomatoes and reserved sausages. Cook until tomatoes are tender, stirring often.

3. Place a sausage piece in each roll; spoon vegetable mixture into each. Cut each sandwich in half. Serve at once.

✳ Quick Pizzas

Given the American mania for pizza, it was to be expected that someone would devise a way to shortcut its preparation. Toasted English muffins make a crunchy crust to top with spaghetti sauce, cheeses and other favorite pizza toppings. These have become a favorite party sandwich for children and teenagers.

BEGIN: 30 MINUTES AHEAD   6 SERVINGS

2   **tablespoons olive oil**
1   **cup sliced mushrooms**
½   **cup chopped green pepper**
¼   **cup chopped onion**
1   **jar (15½ ounces) spaghetti sauce**
6   **English muffins, split and toasted**
2   **cups shredded mozzarella cheese**
⅓   **cup grated Parmesan cheese**

1. In 10-inch skillet over medium heat, in hot oil, cook mushrooms, green pepper and onion until tender, stirring occasionally.

2. Stir in spaghetti sauce. Reduce heat to low; simmer 5 minutes. Spoon onto muffin halves; top with cheeses. Place on baking sheet.

3. Broil 4 inches from heat until cheese is melted and bubbly. Serve at once.

Combination Pizza

❋ Cheese Pizza

It is easy to forget that pizza has only recently become popular in this country. Although there were pizzerias in Italian neighborhoods as early as the turn of the century, the boom did not occur until after World War II. Today, pizza can be found everywhere.

BEGIN: 1 HOUR AHEAD 8 SERVINGS

2 cups all-purpose flour
1 teaspoon sugar
¼ teaspoon salt
1 package active dry yeast
½ cup very warm water (120° to 130°F.)
1 egg
 Salad oil
1 jar (15½ ounces) spaghetti sauce
½ cup grated Parmesan cheese
4 cups shredded mozzarella cheese (1 pound)

1. In small bowl, combine ½ cup flour, sugar, salt and yeast. With mixer at low speed, gradually pour water into dry ingredients; beat until just mixed. Add egg. At medium speed, beat 2 minutes, occasionally scraping bowl with rubber spatula. With spoon, stir in enough additional flour (about 1 cup) to make a soft dough.

2. Turn dough onto lightly floured surface and knead until smooth and elastic, about 5 minutes, adding more flour while kneading. Shape dough into ball; place in greased bowl, turning dough over to grease top. Cover with towel; let rise in warm place (80° to 85°F.), free from draft, 30 minutes.

3. Punch dough down by pushing center of dough with fist, then pushing edges of dough into center. Divide dough in half.

4. Preheat oven to 450°F. Grease two 12-inch pizza pans or baking sheets. With greased fingers, press one dough half into each prepared pan, making a 12-inch round and building up rim. Brush with salad oil.

5. Bake 5 minutes or until crust is set. Spread each crust with ½ of the spaghetti sauce. Sprinkle with cheeses. Bake 6 to 8 minutes more until lightly browned. Cut into wedges.

COMBINATION PIZZA: Prepare as above but add your favorite garnishes such as *anchovies, pepperoni, sausage, ground beef, olives, onion, green pepper, pimentos, garlic* and *mushrooms* before final baking.

❋ BLT

BLT stands for that lunch-counter favorite, the bacon, lettuce and tomato sandwich. Just as popular is the club sandwich, a double-decker concoction of turkey, bacon, lettuce and tomato. It may have been called a club sandwich because it is a fashionable selection in country club dining rooms, or because it was often served in the club cars of railroads.

BEGIN: 30 MINUTES AHEAD 4 SERVINGS

8 slices white bread, toasted
 Mayonnaise
 Lettuce leaves
1 large tomato, sliced
 Salt
 Pepper
8 slices bacon, cooked and drained

1. Spread one side of each toast slice with mayonnaise. Arrange lettuce leaves on 4 slices. Top with tomato slices; sprinkle with salt and pepper. Top each with 2 slices cooked bacon. Top with remaining toast, mayonnaise side down.

2. To serve: Cut sandwiches into fourths; secure each quarter with a wooden pick.

CLUB SANDWICHES: Prepare as above but use a total of *12 slices toast* and add *8 slices cooked chicken or turkey.* To assemble the sandwiches, spread one side of each toast slice with mayonnaise. Arrange lettuce leaves on 4 slices. Top each with tomato slices, salt and pepper, 2 slices bacon, 1 slice toast, more lettuce, 2 slices chicken or turkey, more salt and pepper and 1 slice toast, mayonnaise side down.

❋ Fruity Peanut Butter Sandwiches

The peanut butter sandwich is a truly American taste; people of other cultures can't understand the American fascination with it. Most conventional is the peanut-butter-and-grape-jelly-on-white, but sandwich connoisseurs know that peanut butter is just as good (or better) with honey, marmalade, bacon, marshmallows, tomatoes, and particularly with fruit.

BEGIN: 15 MINUTES AHEAD   4 SERVINGS

8 slices oatmeal bread
1 cup crunchy peanut butter
4 well-drained pineapple slices
2 medium bananas, sliced

Spread each bread slice with peanut butter. Top 4 slices with pineapple and banana slices. Place remaining slices of bread, peanut butter side down, on fruit. Cut each sandwich in half. Serve at once.

Fruity Peanut Butter Sandwiches

❋ Chicken Salad Sandwiches

Cooks like to vary chicken salad sandwiches in much the same way as for tuna salad. This open-faced version, with the added interest of oranges and grapes, is excellent made with poached chicken, leftover roast chicken or turkey, or canned chicken.

BEGIN: 30 MINUTES AHEAD   6 SERVINGS

1½ **cups diced cooked chicken or turkey**
½   **cup thinly sliced celery**
¼   **cup sliced green onions**
½   **cup mayonnaise**
½   **cup halved seedless green grapes**
¼   **teaspoon grated orange peel**
¼   **cup cut-up orange sections**
     Lettuce leaves
6   **slices white bread, toasted**

1. In medium bowl, combine chicken, celery, onions and mayonnaise; mix well. Stir in grapes, orange peel and orange sections.

2. Arrange lettuce on 6 slices toast. Spoon chicken salad onto lettuce.

TIP: Substitute 3 cans (5 ounces each) chunk white chicken for the cubed cooked chicken.

❋ Hot Roast Beef Sandwiches

One of the best ways to use leftover roast beef or turkey is in hot sandwiches. Quickly made from leftovers, they are especially suited to the hectic holiday season. But they are also popular in cafeterias in schools and businesses.

BEGIN: 15 MINUTES AHEAD   6 SERVINGS

1   **can (10¼ ounces) beef gravy or au jus**
     gravy
1   **pound roast beef, sliced**
6   **slices white bread**
     Prepared horseradish (optional)

1. In 10-inch skillet over high heat, heat gravy until just boiling; add roast beef slices. Heat through.

2. Arrange beef on each bread slice; spoon gravy over meat. Serve with horseradish.

TO MICROWAVE: Into microwave-safe 1½-quart casserole, pour gravy; cover. Microwave on HIGH 1½ to 2 minutes until hot. Add roast beef slices; cover. Microwave on HIGH 1 minute or until hot. Proceed as in step 2.

HOT TURKEY SANDWICHES: Prepare as above but substitute *sliced cooked turkey* for roast beef and *1 can (10½ ounces) turkey gravy* for beef gravy or au jus gravy. Omit horseradish.

Ambrosia, Peach Melba, Melon Cup

FRUITS

Wild fruits grew abundantly in America before the Europeans arrived. Strawberries, blackberries, raspberries, blueberries, elderberries and cherries were available to the Indians; so were the exclusively American cranberries, persimmons and native grapes.

European colonists planted their favorite fruits to add to this bounty. We all know the legend of Johnny Appleseed, who planted apple trees across the nation, but many others established apples, pears, plums, gooseberries and oranges in the soil of the new continent.

Improvements in preservation methods have made fruits available far from where they are grown. Native Americans and colonists dried fruits to preserve them. Colonial cooks also preserved fruits in liquor-syrup mixtures and in sweet spreads such as jams, jellies and fruit butters.

These cooks placed the preserves in glasses, sealed them with brandy-soaked paper, and stored them in cool cellars. Sometimes the jellies kept well, and sometimes they didn't. Later, homemakers found that the products spoiled less readily if the jelly glasses were sterilized and sealed with paraffin. Today, experts recommend processing jams and jellies in a boiling water bath or freezing them for even-greater protection from spoilage.

Innovations in technology and ingredients have made fruit preserving easier. Colonial cooks depended on the pectin found naturally in fruit to set their jellies and preserves. When commercial pectin became available, the process of preserving became more predictable. Commercial canning and freezing now allow us to have such fruits as peaches and cherries year round without doing the work ourselves.

Another way to keep surplus fruits is to turn them into beverages. Both fresh and fermented juices were prepared by colonists and native Americans. Once apple orchards began producing in the New World, cider, both sweet and fermented, became the universal drink.

Colonists made wines from wild and cultivated fruits: currants, blackberries, elderberries, gooseberries, cherries and rhubarb. They planted European wine grapes, at first in the East with poor results and later in the West with spectacular success.

Some of today's most familiar fruits were unknown to the colonists. Grapefruit is younger than the Declaration of Independence; it was developed from the more-bitter pomelo. Modern transportation makes tropical pineapples, bananas and kiwi fruit available in every market. Distributors supply the snow-bound North with oranges from Florida and California, and the Southern states with apples that grow better in cooler climates.

❊ Fruit Cocktail

Whether you serve it to begin or end a meal, a fruit cocktail may be composed of any combination of fruit, cut into small pieces. This mixture of citrus with pineapple and strawberries is pleasant any time of year. In summer, substitute melon and fresh berries for the citrus fruits.

BEGIN: 1½ HOURS AHEAD   12 SERVINGS

½   cup sugar
½   cup water
2   cups grapefruit sections
2   cups orange sections
2   cups pineapple chunks
2   cups whole strawberries
2   tablespoons orange liqueur or lemon
      juice
    Fresh mint leaves

1. In small saucepan over high heat, heat sugar and water to boiling, stirring occasionally; cool.

2. Meanwhile, cut large pieces of fruit into bite-sized pieces. In large bowl, combine fruits and liqueur. Pour reserved sugar syrup over fruit mixture. Cover; refrigerate until serving time. Serve in cocktail glasses garnished with mint leaves. Yields 8 cups.

MELON CUP: Prepare as above but omit grapefruit and orange sections; add *2 cups small cantaloupe balls, 2 cups small honeydew melon balls* and *2 cups blueberries.*

❊ Dried Fruit Compote

Drying is the oldest form of preservation for fruits. For centuries dried fruit has helped extend the harvest, preserving the crop for times of the year when it was unavailable. American Indians and colonists dried fruit, and settlers carried the preserved fruit with them whenever they moved to new places. A compote of dried fruit is worth making even now that drying is no longer a necessity. It makes a lovely warming dessert in the winter, or a refreshing cold one during the summer.

BEGIN: 30 MINUTES AHEAD   12 SERVINGS

1   cup dried apricot halves
1   cup dried pitted prunes
1   cup raisins
1   can (20 ounces) pineapple chunks in
      juice
1   jar (6 ounces) maraschino cherries
1   jar (12 ounces) orange marmalade
2   cups water
¼   cup orange liqueur

In 3-quart saucepan over medium-high heat, heat all ingredients to boiling. Reduce heat to low. Cover; simmer 10 minutes or until fruits are soft, stirring occasionally. Serve warm or cold. Yields 7 cups.

❊ Ambrosia

Named after the fabled food of the Greek and Roman gods, Ambrosia is a Christmas tradition in the South. Originally a mixture of oranges and coconut, the recipe has been embellished with such additions as dates, nuts, raisins, grapes, strawberries and pineapple. Sometimes it is further enriched with orange liqueur, sherry or ginger ale. As in so many cases, a simple version like this one is the most enduring.

BEGIN: EARLY IN DAY   8 SERVINGS

6   oranges
2   bananas, sliced
1   cup shredded coconut
¼   cup maraschino cherries

1. With sharp knife, cut off peel and white portion of oranges, being sure to remove membrane that covers pulp. Thinly slice oranges crosswise, removing any seeds.

2. In 2-quart serving bowl arrange ½ of the orange slices. Top with ½ of the banana slices and ½ of the coconut. Repeat layers. Cover; refrigerate several hours or overnight. Garnish with cherries.

❄ Broiled Grapefruit

Broiled Grapefruit has become a standard first course all over the United States, so it is hard to believe that grapefruit has been cultivated commercially for less than a hundred years. Grapefruit is now the world's second most important citrus crop (next to the orange), much of it coming from Florida, Texas and California.

BEGIN: 30 MINUTES AHEAD   4 SERVINGS

4   **grapefruit halves**
2   **tablespoons dark brown sugar**
¼   **teaspoon ground cinnamon**
    Cream sherry (optional)
4   **strawberries or cherries**

1. With grapefruit knife, cut around sections of grapefruit, staying inside membrane. Place grapefruit halves cut side up on broiler pan.

2. In small bowl, combine brown sugar and cinnamon; mix well. Sprinkle over grapefruit halves. Drizzle with sherry.

3. Broil 4 inches from heat until sugar is melted and fruit is hot. Garnish each grapefruit half with strawberry or cherry.

TO MICROWAVE: Prepare as above in steps 1 and 2 but place each grapefruit half on individual microwave-safe plate or bowl. Microwave on HIGH 3 to 4 minutes or until hot, turning dishes once.

❄ Plugged Watermelon

A slice of icy cold watermelon on a hot summer day is hard to beat; no wonder it is a standard offering at picnics and barbecues. Plugged Watermelon, steeped in rum and cut into wedges, is served in all parts of the country, with the type of liquor varying from place to place. Our recipe features rum; other liquors you could use include vodka, brandy, champagne, bourbon and gin. Watermelon is considered an all-American fruit, but it originated in Africa, spreading from there to all parts of the world, and reaching America by way of Europe.

BEGIN: DAY AHEAD   12 SERVINGS

1   **large watermelon**
    Light rum

1. Cut a deep plug about 2 inches square in watermelon. Remove plug. With long knife, make several deep incisions through opening. Slowly fill with rum, using as much as melon will hold, about 2 cups. Replace plug. Refrigerate overnight, turning melon occasionally.

2. To serve: Cut melon into wedges.

❄ Baked Apples

A simple dessert that is always welcome is apples, cored, filled with cinnamon-sugar and baked until they are tender. There are dozens of variations on this basic theme —the cored apples may be stuffed with raisins, mincemeat, candied fruit, nuts, jelly, marmalade or cream cheese. Prepare this basic recipe first, then improvise the next time you bake apples.

BEGIN: 1½ HOURS AHEAD   6 SERVINGS

6   **medium cooking apples**
½   **cup packed brown sugar**
½   **teaspoon ground cinnamon or nutmeg**
3   **tablespoons butter or margarine**
½   **cup apple juice or water**
    Heavy cream or vanilla ice cream

1. Core apples; starting from stem end, peel one-third of each apple. Arrange in 10- by 6-inch baking dish. In small bowl, combine brown sugar and cinnamon. Fill centers of apples with brown sugar mixture. Dot with butter. Pour juice over apples.

2. Bake at 350°F. 50 to 60 minutes until apples are fork-tender, occasionally basting with juice from pan. Serve hot or cold with cream or ice cream.

❋ Spicy Applesauce

Besides its role as a side dish or dessert, applesauce is a familiar ingredient in cookies, cakes, breads and coffee-cakes. Long before it was available in cans and jars, applesauce was made in the home. The first fallen apples of the season went into the sauce, in order to salvage the undamaged parts of bruised fruit.

BEGIN: 45 MINUTES AHEAD   8 SERVINGS

8   cups sliced, peeled and cored cooking
       apples
½   cup water
½   cup sugar
¼   teaspoon ground cinnamon
¼   teaspoon ground nutmeg

1. In 3-quart saucepan over medium-high heat, heat apples and water to boiling. Reduce heat to low. Cover; simmer 10 to 15 minutes until very tender, stirring occasionally.

2. Stir in remaining ingredients; cook 1 minute more. Serve warm or cold. Yields 3½ cups.

TO MICROWAVE: In 3-quart microwave-safe casserole, combine apples and water; cover. Microwave on HIGH 10 to 12 minutes until very tender, stirring occasionally. Stir in remaining ingredients.

TIP: Stir in 1 tablespoon lemon juice and 1 tablespoon butter or margarine for tarter, richer applesauce.

TIP: Some good examples of cooking apples are Cortland, Golden Delicious, Granny Smith, Jonathan, McIntosh, Newtown Pippin, Rhode Island Greening, Rome Beauty, Stayman, Winesap and York Imperial.

❋ Apple Fritters

Apple Fritters are served along with sausage, scrapple or bacon at any meal. They also can be a dessert or a snack. Here, we slice the apples into rings to make fritters that look like doughnuts.

BEGIN: 45 MINUTES AHEAD   20 FRITTERS

2   cups all-purpose flour
¼   cup sugar
1   tablespoon baking powder
1   teaspoon salt
½   teaspoon ground nutmeg
2   eggs
1   cup milk
4   large cooking apples, peeled, cored and
       cut into ½-inch rings
    Salad oil
    Confectioners' sugar or maple syrup

1. In medium bowl, combine first 5 ingredients. In small bowl, beat eggs with milk; add to flour mixture and beat well.

2. In 4-quart saucepan, heat 2 inches oil to 375°F. Dip apple slices into batter. Fry a few at a time until golden, turning once. Drain on paper towels. Sprinkle with confectioners' sugar or serve with syrup.

PEACH FRITTERS: Prepare as above but substitute *6 peaches, peeled, pitted and cut into wedges,* for apple slices.

❃ Cranberry Sauce

Native Americans boiled wild cranberries with maple syrup or honey to make cranberry sauce. European settlers added the refined sugar they brought to the New World. The recipe has not changed since that time; it is simply cranberries, sugar and water briefly simmered together, a traditional Thanksgiving favorite.

BEGIN: EARLY IN DAY   12 SERVINGS

1½ **cups sugar**
1   **cup water**
1   **package (12 ounces) cranberries**

1. In 2-quart saucepan over medium-high heat, heat sugar and water to boiling.

2. Stir in cranberries; heat to boiling. Reduce heat to low. Cover; simmer 10 to 15 minutes until cranberries pop. Spoon into small bowl. Cover; refrigerate until serving time, at least 6 hours. Yields 3 cups.

TIP: For a special presentation, serve cranberry sauce in orange shells. Halve oranges crosswise; scoop out fruit. Cut a scalloped edge if desired.

❃ Cranberry-Orange Relish

Cranberries are raised and harvested differently from other berries. They grow on vines in bogs, and are often gathered by flooding the fields so that the berries float to the top. The berries are separated by a machine that capitalizes on the bouncing ability of cranberries, which have at times been known as bounceberries; the best fruit bounces well, while the damaged fruit does not.

BEGIN: DAY AHEAD   12 SERVINGS

1   **package (12 ounces) cranberries**
1   **orange, unpeeled, quartered and seeded**
1   **apple, cored and quartered**
2   **cups sugar**

1. Using coarse blade of food grinder or in food processor, chop cranberries; pour into medium bowl. With grinder or food processor, chop orange and apple; add to cranberries.

2. Combine fruits with sugar; mix well. Cover; refrigerate until serving time, at least 12 hours. Yields 3 cups.

❃ Rhubarb Sauce

A vegetable that is used as a fruit, rhubarb originally was raised for its roots, which were thought to have medicinal properties. By the early 1600s, some Englishmen tried cooking the leaves of the plant, but found them to be unpalatable; the leaves are now known to be poisonous and should never be eaten. Later, Englishmen and Americans learned to eat the flavorful stalk. In some parts of the world rhubarb is eaten raw, but in the United States it most often turns up in Rhubarb Pie, or in this piquant sauce, an excellent topping for ice cream or cake.

BEGIN: 30 MINUTES AHEAD   8 SERVINGS

4   **cups sliced rhubarb**
¼   **cup water**
½   **cup sugar**
½   **teaspoon ground cinnamon**

In 2-quart saucepan over medium-high heat, heat all ingredients to boiling. Reduce heat to low. Cover; simmer 10 minutes or until tender. Serve warm or cold. Yields 4 cups.

TIP: Substitute 1 package (20 ounces) frozen rhubarb for fresh rhubarb and increase water to 1 cup.

❋ Bananas Flambé

Flaming banana desserts are popular in the South. Bananas Foster, made with rum and banana liqueur and served over ice cream, is a New Orleans classic served at the famous Brennan's Restaurant. This version is made with orange juice, brandy and a hint of cinnamon.

BEGIN: 30 MINUTES AHEAD   8 SERVINGS

4   **bananas**
¼   **cup butter or margarine**
¼   **cup packed brown sugar**
¼   **cup orange juice**
¼   **teaspoon ground cinnamon**
¼   **cup brandy**
     Vanilla ice cream

1. Peel bananas. Halve bananas crosswise, then halve lengthwise.

2. In chafing dish or 10-inch skillet over medium-high heat, melt butter. Stir in brown sugar, orange juice and cinnamon. Cook 1 minute to blend, stirring constantly. Add bananas; cook until heated through, tossing gently to coat.

3. In small saucepan over low heat, heat brandy to lukewarm. Ignite and quickly pour over bananas. Serve over ice cream.

❋ Fresh Cherries Jubilee

Cherries Jubilee is a showy and popular dessert whose origin has been attributed to England, France and the American South. Wherever it began, it has become an American classic made with all-American ice cream and succulent American cherries. The trick to lighting the brandy is to warm it first.

BEGIN: 45 MINUTES AHEAD   8 SERVINGS

½   **cup red currant jelly**
¼   **cup apple juice or water**
2   **teaspoons cornstarch**
1   **pound sweet cherries, pitted**
¼   **cup brandy**
     Vanilla ice cream

1. In 2-quart saucepan or chafing dish over low heat, melt jelly. In cup, combine juice and cornstarch; stir into jelly. Cook until mixture boils, stirring constantly. Stir in cherries; heat through.

2. In small saucepan over low heat, heat brandy until lukewarm. Ignite and quickly pour over cherries. Serve over vanilla ice cream. Yields 2 cups.

CHERRIES JUBILEE: Prepare as above but substitute *1 can (16 ounces) pitted dark sweet cherries, drained,* for fresh sweet cherries. Substitute *¼ cup cherry liquid* for apple juice.

Fresh Cherries Jubilee

❈ Poached Pears with Fudge Sauce

Poached pears are often served simply chilled in their poaching syrup or topped with cream. An especially luscious presentation is to cloak the pears in a warm chocolate sauce to set off the fruity flavor of the pears.

BEGIN: EARLY IN DAY   6 SERVINGS

6   pears
1   cup sugar
1   cup water
1   cup dry white wine
2   cinnamon sticks
     Hot Fudge Sauce (see page 242)

1. Peel pears; core each pear from bottom (do not remove stems). In 3-quart saucepan, combine sugar, water, wine and cinnamon. Over medium-high heat, heat to boiling, stirring constantly. Add pears; heat to boiling.

2. Reduce heat to low. Cover; simmer 20 minutes or until fork-tender, basting often. Cool in syrup to room temperature. Cover; refrigerate in syrup until serving time, at least 4 hours.

3. *About 20 minutes before serving:* Prepare Hot Fudge Sauce. Place each pear in serving dish. Top each with about 2 tablespoons sauce.

TIP: Pears may require up to 45 minutes poaching if not fully ripened.

❈ Peach Melba

Peach Melba was created by Escoffier to honor the Australian songstress Dame Nellie Melba. It combines the summer flavors of peaches and raspberries in a sophisticated ice cream sundae.

BEGIN: EARLY IN DAY   8 SERVINGS

4   cups water
1   cup sugar
2   tablespoons vanilla extract
4   large peaches, peeled, halved and pitted
1   package (10 ounces) frozen raspberries, thawed
¼   cup red currant jelly
1   teaspoon cornstarch
1   tablespoon water
     Vanilla ice cream

1. In 3-quart saucepan over high heat, heat water and sugar to boiling. Boil 5 minutes or until consistency of thin syrup. Stir in vanilla; add peaches.

2. Reduce heat to low; simmer, uncovered, 10 minutes or until peaches are barely tender. Cool to room temperature. Cover; refrigerate in syrup until serving time, at least 6 hours.

3. Meanwhile, with wooden spoon, force raspberries through sieve to remove seeds. In small saucepan, combine raspberry purée and jelly. Over medium-high heat, heat until jelly is melted, stirring constantly.

4. In cup, combine cornstarch and water. Stir into raspberry mixture. Cook until mixture boils, stirring constantly. Remove from heat. Cover; refrigerate until serving time, at least 4 hours.

5. To serve: In each of 8 dessert dishes or stemmed glasses, place 1 scoop of ice cream. Drain peaches (reserve liquid for another use). Top each ice cream scoop with peach half, hollow side down. Spoon raspberry sauce over peach.

TIP: Substitute 1 can (28 ounces) peach halves, chilled, for fresh peaches. Omit first 4 ingredients and begin with step 3.

✳ Tutti-Frutti

Before the introduction of canning in the nineteenth century, one way fruits were preserved was by soaking them in an alcoholic liquid. Tutti-Frutti, also known as Rumtopf or Bachelor's Jam, is a good example of this type of preserve. A homemaker would begin the mixture with the earliest strawberries, sugar and brandy or rum, then add more sugar and fruits as they ripened. The old recipes called for equal parts of fruit and sugar, but today's tastes prefer a less-sweet mixture.

BEGIN: 2 TO 3 MONTHS AHEAD

1   **bottle (750 ml) brandy**
    Fresh fruit
    Sugar

1. Into 3-quart crock or glass jar, pour brandy. Add fruit and sugar using ½ cup sugar for each cup fruit; stir occasionally to dissolve sugar.

2. Cover; store in cool room several weeks, stirring occasionally. Add more fruit and sugar as you use fruit from crock. Serve over ice cream or cake.

TIP: Use fruits in season, such as strawberries, pitted cherries, sliced peeled peaches, sliced peeled plums, sliced peeled pineapple, blueberries, peeled seedless grapes, sliced peeled pears and sliced peeled kiwi fruit.

✳ Freezer Berry Jam

The methods for making jams and jellies have changed through the years. Two innovations in the process—commercial pectin and the home freezer—combine in this recipe to make a fresh-tasting jam that does not require cooking. The jam keeps well in the refrigerator for three weeks or in the freezer for a year.

BEGIN: DAY AHEAD   5 HALF-PINTS

4   **cups raspberries or strawberries**
4   **cups sugar**
1   **pouch (3 ounces) liquid pectin**
2   **tablespoons lemon juice**

1. In medium bowl with fork, mash berries. Measure 2 cups mashed berries (reserve any remaining berries for another use). Stir sugar into mashed berries. Let stand 10 minutes until sugar dissolves, stirring occasionally.

2. In bowl, combine pectin and lemon juice. Add to berry mixture; stir constantly 5 minutes.

3. Ladle at once into 5 sterilized half-pint jars, leaving ½-inch headspace; seal. Let stand at room temperature until set. Freeze. Thaw before serving. Yields 5 cups.

✳ 4-Fruit Marmalade

While most fruit preserving is done in the summer, marmalade is made in the winter, when citrus fruit is at its best. Any citrus fruit may be made into marmalade, or a combination may be used, as in this 4-Fruit Marmalade. Although we usually think of marmalade as a citrus preserve, the word can apply to any fruit preserve. In fact, it comes from the Portuguese word for quince (marmelo), a fruit that often was made into marmalade.

BEGIN: DAY AHEAD   5 PINTS

1   **lemon**
1   **lime**
1   **grapefruit**
1   **orange**
8   **cups sugar**

1. Peel fruit and cut the peel into *very thin* slices. Chop fruit; discard seeds and grapefruit core. Combine fruit, juice and peel; measure mixture.

2. In 6- or 8-quart Dutch oven, combine fruit mixture with three times as much water. Over medium-high heat, heat to boiling. Reduce heat to medium. Simmer 1½ hours or until mixture is reduced to 8 cups; stir occasionally. Stir in sugar.

3. Over medium heat, heat mixture to boiling, stirring often. Set candy thermometer in place and continue cooking until temperature reaches 220°F., the jelling point (mixture will be liquid). Skim off foam. Pour marmalade into 5 hot, sterilized pint jars, leaving ½-inch headspace; seal. Yields 10 cups.

4-Fruit Marmalade, Freezer Berry Jam, Apple Butter

❈ Apple Butter

The making of Apple Butter was a traditional autumn activity in America's rural days. Whole families would gather to peel bushels of apples, which they tossed into huge kettles of boiling cider over outdoor fires. This was a day-long event, a time for socializing as well as for peeling fruit and stirring the mixture. We give a recipe for a smaller quantity, more suited to today's smaller families and year-round apple supply.

BEGIN: 3 HOURS AHEAD   5 HALF-PINTS

4   **cups apple cider**
4   **pounds cooking apples, peeled, cored**
      and thinly sliced
2   **cups sugar**
1   **cup packed brown sugar**

1. In 5-quart Dutch oven over high heat, heat cider and apples to boiling. Reduce heat to medium-low. Cover; simmer 10 minutes or until very tender, stirring often. Force through sieve or food mill. Return to pan.

2. Stir in sugars. Simmer, uncovered, 2 hours or until spreading consistency, stirring often. Pour into 5 hot, sterilized half-pint jars, leaving ½-inch headspace; seal. Refrigerate or freeze until serving time. Yields 5 cups.

SPICY APPLE BUTTER: Prepare as above but add *⅛ teaspoon ground cinnamon* and *⅛ teaspoon ground cloves* to puréed apple mixture.

Gooseberry Fool, Tipsy Parson, Cheesecake, Syllabub

DESSERTS

The American sweet tooth is famous world-wide. An Italian may end his meal with fruit, and a Frenchman with cheese; in this country we don't feel satisfied until we've had something sweet.

When the colonists came to America many of the foods they knew were hard to find. Without wheat flour or white sugar they couldn't prepare their favorite desserts. But the Indians introduced them to new fruits, grains and sweeteners, and they soon created new American desserts.

Because ovens were scarce and poorly regulated, the colonists made steamed puddings, such as those they had enjoyed in England. Dense and moist, studded with fruit and nuts and crowned with sweet sauces, the puddings were steamed in pudding molds or boiled in muslin bags. Modern cooks, with their reliable ovens, find the steaming process a nuisance and have adapted many early-American pudding recipes to make cakes.

Fruit desserts were popular during the Colonial era, and were a good way to use up an abundant crop. Countless combinations of fruit and pastry were devised and given rustic local names. New England in particular is known for its cobblers, slumps, buckles, grunts and pandowdys.

As life became easier, American desserts became more elaborate and more refined. Ever since the eighteenth century ice cream has been an all-American way to end a meal. Although it began in the Old World, Americans took it to heart, creating such treats as the ice cream soda, the sundae, the cone, ice cream on a stick and Baked Alaska. Today's concern about high fat and cholesterol in the diet have made frozen yogurt and ices popular, but there is little chance they will ever replace ice cream.

There is not room in one chapter for the whole spectrum of American desserts, but you will find a good sampling of our favorite puddings, ice creams and fruit treats. From old-fashioned puddings such as Tipsy Parson to desserts made possible by new products such as gelatin, to those that America has perfected such as cheesecake, they show why Americans have a world-wide reputation as dessert lovers.

❈ Colonial Steamed Pudding

We usually think of steamed puddings as British desserts, but American colonists made them often, adding whatever ingredients were on hand to make such substantial desserts as this carrot-flecked pudding, which also includes potato, apple, raisins and nuts.

BEGIN: 3½ HOURS AHEAD   6 SERVINGS

½   **cup butter or margarine, softened**
½   **cup packed brown sugar**
1   **egg**
1   **cup all-purpose flour**
½   **teaspoon baking soda**
½   **teaspoon ground cinnamon**
½   **teaspoon ground nutmeg**
¼   **teaspoon salt**
¼   **teaspoon ground allspice**
½   **cup orange juice**
½   **cup shredded carrot**
½   **cup shredded potato**
½   **cup chopped, peeled and cored apple**
½   **cup raisins**
½   **cup chopped walnuts**
    Orange Hard Sauce*

1. Grease 1½-quart heatsafe bowl or pudding mold. In large bowl with mixer at medium speed, cream butter and brown sugar. Beat in egg until light and fluffy.

2. In medium bowl, combine flour, baking soda, cinnamon, nutmeg, salt and allspice. Add dry ingredients alternately with orange juice to creamed mixture, mixing well after each addition, occasionally scraping bowl with rubber spatula.

3. Stir in carrot, potato, apple, raisins and nuts. Turn mixture into prepared bowl. Cover with foil and tie with string.

4. Place on rack in 5-quart Dutch oven. Add boiling water to reach halfway up side of bowl. Cover; over low heat, simmer about 2½ hours until top of pudding appears dry. Remove from Dutch oven; cool on wire rack 10 minutes. Invert onto serving plate.

5. To serve: Cut pudding into wedges. Top each serving with Orange Hard Sauce.

*Orange Hard Sauce

Steamed puddings were often served with some kind of a sweet sauce: a warm, buttery syrup, a light custard sauce or a hard sauce. To the basic butter and sugar of a hard sauce, cooks added fruit peels, bourbon, rum, candied fruits and spices.

¼   **cup butter or margarine, softened**
1   **cup confectioners' sugar**
    Dash salt
½   **teaspoon grated orange peel**
1   **tablespoon orange juice**

In small bowl with mixer at medium speed, beat butter until light and fluffy. Beat in sugar and salt. Beat in orange peel and juice. Drop by tablespoonfuls onto waxed paper. Chill until firm; serve with warm pudding. Yields ¾ cup.

❈ Indian Pudding

Indian pudding was one of the earliest published American recipes, with three versions in the 1796 American Cookery *by Amelia Simmons. Originally a sweetened cornmeal mush made by the Indians, it was modified by the colonists, who added molasses, milk and spices to it. Later Indian puddings include eggs, sugar and raisins, but this simple version remains one of the best.*

BEGIN: 2 HOURS AHEAD   8 SERVINGS

4   **cups milk**
½   **cup yellow cornmeal**
½   **cup molasses**
2   **tablespoons butter or margarine**
½   **teaspoon salt**
½   **teaspoon ground cinnamon**
½   **teaspoon ground ginger**

1. Preheat oven to 325°F. In heavy, 2-quart saucepan, gradually stir milk into cornmeal. Over medium-high heat, heat mixture to boiling, stirring constantly. Reduce heat to medium-low; simmer about 15 minutes until thickened, stirring often.

2. Stir in molasses, butter, salt, cinnamon and ginger. Pour into 1½-quart casserole.

3. Bake 30 minutes; stir. Bake 30 minutes more. Cool on wire rack 15 minutes. Serve warm or cold.

❄ Custard Rice Pudding

Rice pudding is a wonderful dessert that belies its humble makings—ingredients that most cooks always have on hand. One interesting custom that was practiced in the Southwest earlier in this century was the rice pudding contest: blindfolded couples tried to feed each other the largest amount of creamy pudding in the least time, messy for the participants but amusing to the audience.

BEGIN: 1 HOUR AHEAD   6 SERVINGS

½ cup raw regular medium-grain rice
3 cups milk
¼ teaspoon salt
4 eggs
¾ cup sugar
2 teaspoons vanilla extract
½ teaspoon ground nutmeg

1. In 4-quart saucepan over medium heat, heat rice, milk and salt just to boiling. Reduce heat to low. Cover; simmer 30 minutes or until rice is tender, stirring occasionally.

2. Meanwhile, in medium bowl, beat together eggs, sugar and vanilla. With wooden spoon, gradually stir beaten egg mixture into rice. Heat just to boiling, stirring constantly. Serve warm or cold. Spoon into dessert dishes; sprinkle with nutmeg. Yields 3½ cups.

❄ Persimmon Pudding

The first European settlers found persimmons growing wild all over the southeastern part of America. Their reaction to the strange fruit varied considerably, depending on whether the persimmons were fully ripe; the fruit is very astringent before it matures. Today, the most commonly available persimmon in supermarkets is from Japan, a bright orange fruit about the size of a peach. Cherry-sized native persimmons are too fragile to be shipped, but local recipes for the fruit abound.

BEGIN: 2½ HOURS AHEAD   12 SERVINGS

1½ quarts small persimmons
1   cup sugar
½   cup butter or margarine, melted
3   eggs
2   cups all-purpose flour
1   teaspoon baking soda
1   teaspoon baking powder
½   teaspoon ground ginger
½   teaspoon ground cinnamon
½   teaspoon ground nutmeg
3   cups milk
    Whipped cream

1. Put persimmons through colander or food mill to make 2 cups pulp; discard skins and seeds. In medium bowl, combine pulp and sugar; set aside.

2. Butter 13- by 9-inch baking pan. Preheat oven to 350°F. In large bowl, combine remaining ingredients except cream. With mixer at medium speed, beat 1 minute or until well mixed. Beat in reserved persimmon mixture until well mixed. Pour into prepared pan.

3. Bake 70 to 75 minutes until set. Cool on wire rack 10 minutes. Serve warm or cold with whipped cream.

TIP: Substitute 4 large Japanese persimmons for domestic persimmons.

✳ Bread Pudding

Bread Pudding is a comforting, homey dessert of English ancestry that originated with the need to use up stale bread. Served with this Whiskey Sauce, it is an American specialty that is enjoying new popularity in restaurants and homes across the country.

BEGIN: 2½ HOURS AHEAD   8 SERVINGS

3	**eggs**
3	**cups milk**
½	**cup sugar**
1	**tablespoon vanilla extract**
¼	**teaspoon salt**
4	**cups soft white bread cubes**
½	**cup raisins or chopped, pitted dates**
	Whiskey Sauce*

1. Preheat oven to 325°F. Butter 1½-quart casserole. In large bowl with wire whisk, beat eggs until frothy. Beat in milk, sugar, vanilla and salt until combined. Stir in bread cubes and raisins; let stand 5 minutes. Stir again; pour mixture into prepared casserole.

2. Set casserole in baking pan; place on oven rack. Add boiling water to baking pan to reach halfway up side of casserole. Bake 1½ hours or until knife inserted near center comes out clean. Serve warm with Whiskey Sauce.

TIP: Soft bread makes a creamier pudding; firm-textured bread yields a firmer pudding.

Bread Pudding, Whiskey Sauce

*Whiskey Sauce

Bourbon is the most American of liquors, and this Whiskey Sauce makes ice cream, puddings and cakes into special treats.

½   cup butter or margarine
1   cup packed brown sugar
⅓   cup bourbon
¼   teaspoon ground nutmeg

In 1-quart saucepan over medium-high heat, heat all ingredients to boiling. Serve warm over Bread Pudding. Yields 1 cup.

❅ Baked Custard

Custards and custard sauces provide the starting point for many other foods: bread pudding, rice pudding, cake fillings, ice cream, corn pudding and cheese strata. But Baked Custard is a delicious dessert just as it is, or with the addition of coconut. Add a caramelized sugar coating, and it becomes elegant enough for any occasion.

BEGIN: 1 HOUR AHEAD   5 SERVINGS

3   eggs
2   cups milk
¼   cup sugar or honey
½   teaspoon vanilla extract
    Dash salt
    Ground nutmeg

1. In medium bowl with whisk, beat eggs, milk, sugar, vanilla and salt until smooth. Pour into five 5-ounce custard cups. Sprinkle with nutmeg.

2. Set custard cups in shallow baking pan; place on oven rack. Pour boiling water around cups to reach halfway up sides of cups. Bake at 350°F. 30 to 35 minutes until knife inserted in center comes out clean. Let stand 10 minutes before serving. Serve warm or cold.

COCONUT CUSTARD: Prepare as above but add ½ *cup flaked coconut* to milk mixture.

CARAMEL CUSTARD: In heavy skillet over medium heat, cook ¼ *cup sugar* until melted and lightly browned, stirring constantly. Quickly pour syrup into five 5-ounce custard cups. Prepare custard as above, pouring egg mixture into prepared cups. To serve: Invert cups onto dessert dishes.

❄ Tipsy Parson

Known also as Tipsy Squire or Tipsy Pudding, Tipsy Parson is an American adaptation of English trifle. It is a holiday tradition in the South at Christmas and New Year's, and Christmas visitors to Colonial Williamsburg enjoy this creamy dessert as much as they do the old-fashioned decorations.

BEGIN: EARLY IN DAY   12 SERVINGS

    Hot Milk Sponge Cake (see page 261)
⅓   cup cream sherry
⅓   cup sugar
2   tablespoons cornstarch
    Dash salt
2   cups light cream
3   eggs
2   teaspoons vanilla extract
1   cup sliced almonds, toasted

1. With sharp knife, cut cake horizontally in half; sprinkle sherry over both halves. Cover; chill.

2. In 2-quart saucepan, combine sugar, cornstarch and salt; stir in cream. Over medium heat, cook until mixture boils, stirring constantly. Remove from heat.

3. In small bowl with wire whisk, beat eggs. Stir in small amount of hot mixture. Slowly pour egg mixture into hot mixture, stirring rapidly. Over medium heat, cook until mixture just coats back of metal spoon, stirring constantly. Remove from heat; stir in vanilla. Place waxed paper on surface of pudding; chill.

4. Place one cake layer on serving plate; top with ½ of the pudding, then ½ of the almonds. Repeat layers. Refrigerate until serving time.

❄ Cheesecake

American cheesecake has very little in common with the first cheesecakes of the ancient Greeks and Romans. Indeed, it has little resemblance to early American cheesecakes, which were made from farmer cheese. Rich modern cheesecakes made from cream cheese and sour cream are New York specialties.

BEGIN: DAY AHEAD   12 SERVINGS

2   **cups graham cracker or zwieback crumbs**
½   **cup butter or margarine, melted**
3   **packages (8 ounces each) cream cheese, softened**
1¼ **cups sugar**
4   **eggs**
1   **teaspoon grated lemon peel**
1½ **teaspoons vanilla extract**
     Dash salt
1   **cup sour cream**

1. In small bowl, combine crumbs and melted butter. Press mixture firmly onto bottom and 1½ inches up side of 9-inch springform pan.

2. Preheat oven to 325°F. In large bowl with mixer at medium speed, beat cream cheese until light and fluffy. Beat in 1 cup sugar until well mixed. Beat in eggs, lemon peel, 1 teaspoon vanilla and salt until very smooth. Pour mixture into crumb crust.

3. Bake 1 hour or until center is just set. Cool on wire rack 20 minutes.

4. In small bowl, combine sour cream, remaining ¼ cup sugar and ½ teaspoon vanilla; mix well. Spread over cheesecake. Bake 10 minutes more. Cool on wire rack; refrigerate until serving time, at least 8 hours.

❄ Peach Cobbler

The name "cobbler" comes from the expression "cobble-up," meaning put together fast, and a cobbler is a quick version of a deep-dish pie. A shortcake-like dough is spooned over the fruit, so you save the time and inconvenience of rolling out a piecrust, yet preserve the wonderful flavor.

Peach Cobbler

BEGIN: 1 HOUR AHEAD   6 SERVINGS

4   cups thinly sliced, peeled peaches
½   cup sugar
1   tablespoon cornstarch
1   cup all-purpose flour
2   tablespoons sugar
1½ teaspoons baking powder
½   teaspoon salt
¼   cup butter or margarine
⅓   cup milk or light cream
1   egg, beaten

1. In 10- by 6-inch baking dish, combine peaches, ½ cup sugar and cornstarch. Let stand while preparing cobbler batter.

2. Preheat oven to 350°F. In medium bowl, combine flour, 2 tablespoons sugar, baking powder and salt. With pastry blender or 2 knives used scissor-fashion, cut in butter until mixture resembles coarse crumbs. Stir in milk and egg to form a soft dough. Drop dough in 6 equal portions atop peaches.

3. Bake 40 minutes or until topping is golden. Serve warm or cold.

❋ Blueberry Slump

Slump is probably one of the first uses the colonists made of blueberries, a native American fruit that helped sustain them during their first few years on this continent. Sometimes known as Blueberry Grunt, this dessert was sometimes baked and sometimes boiled.

BEGIN: 45 MINUTES AHEAD   6 SERVINGS

2   cups fresh or frozen blueberries
½   cup water
½   cup sugar
2   tablespoons lemon juice
½   teaspoon ground cinnamon
1   cup all-purpose flour
2   tablespoons sugar
1½ teaspoons baking powder
½   teaspoon salt
¼   cup shortening
½   cup milk

1. In 3-quart saucepan, combine berries, water, ½ cup sugar, lemon juice and cinnamon; over medium-high heat, heat to boiling. Reduce heat to low. Cover; simmer 5 minutes.

2. Meanwhile, in medium bowl, combine flour, 2 tablespoons sugar, baking powder and salt. With pastry blender or 2 knives used scissor-fashion, cut in shortening until mixture resembles coarse crumbs. Stir in milk to form a soft dough.

3. Drop by heaping tablespoonfuls onto bubbling berries. Cover; simmer 15 minutes without lifting lid. Serve immediately, spooning berries over dumplings.

❋ Apple Crisp

The crunchy topping of oats, cinnamon and sugar provides a flavorful contrast to tart, juicy apples. Pour dairy-fresh cream over each warm serving for a particularly satisfying end to any meal.

BEGIN: 1½ HOURS AHEAD   6 SERVINGS

6   cups sliced, peeled and cored cooking
      apples
¼   cup sugar
2   tablespons lemon juice
¾   cup packed brown sugar
½   cup all-purpose flour
½   cup uncooked quick-cooking oats
1   teaspoon ground cinnamon
¼   cup butter or margarine

1. Place apples in 9- by 9-inch baking pan. Sprinkle with sugar and lemon juice.

2. In small bowl, combine brown sugar, flour, oats and cinnamon; mix well. With pastry blender or 2 knives used scissor-fashion, cut in butter until mixture resembles coarse crumbs. Sprinkle over apples.

3. Bake at 350°F. 35 minutes or until golden.

RHUBARB CRISP: Prepare as above but substitute *6 cups diced rhubarb* for apples and omit lemon juice.

❊ Apple Brown Betty

Apple Brown Betty is a cross between a pie and bread pudding. Some betties are moist and solid; others are drier. Some call for dried bread crumbs, some for fresh, some for cubes. Cinnamon is always included, contributing to the flavor and appealing brown color.

BEGIN: 2 HOURS AHEAD   6 SERVINGS

4   cups soft bread cubes
⅓   cup butter or margarine, melted
4   cups thinly sliced, peeled and cored
        cooking apples
1   cup packed brown sugar
1   teaspoon ground cinnamon
2   tablespoons lemon juice
¼   cup water
     Heavy cream

1. Preheat oven to 350°F. Grease 2-quart casserole. In medium bowl, combine bread cubes and butter; mix well.

2. In another medium bowl, toss together apples, brown sugar and cinnamon. Sprinkle with lemon juice.

3. Layer ⅓ of the bread cubes in prepared casserole, then ½ of the apple mixture. Repeat layers, ending with bread cubes. Sprinkle with water.

4. Bake 1 hour or until golden. Serve warm with cream.

PEACH BROWN BETTY: Prepare as above but substitute *4 cups sliced, peeled peaches* for apples.

❊ Gooseberry Fool

English colonists liked Gooseberry Fool so much that they brought their treasured gooseberry bushes across the Atlantic. Today, you won't find gooseberries in your market unless they are grown locally, but you can re-create this simple dessert with canned gooseberries or with another berry.

BEGIN: 4 HOURS AHEAD   6 SERVINGS

1   can (16 ounces) gooseberries, blueberries
        or blackberries
¼   cup sugar
1   tablespoon cornstarch
1   cup heavy cream

1. Force berries and syrup through sieve to make purée; discard seeds. In 1-quart saucepan, combine sugar and cornstarch. Gradually stir in berry purée. Over medium-high heat, heat mixture to boiling. Reduce heat to low. Simmer, uncovered, 1 minute. Cover; chill at least 3 hours.

2. *Just before serving:* In large bowl with mixer at medium speed, beat cream until stiff peaks form. Fold in chilled berry mixture just until mixture is marbled. Serve immediately. Yields 3 cups.

TIP: For deeper color when using gooseberries, add a few drops green and yellow food coloring to berry mixture in step 1.

❊ Syllabub

Syllabub is a foamy dessert made with white wine, Madeira, brandy, sherry or cider. Some folks like to sip Syllabub, while others prefer to eat it with a spoon. Early recipes called for milking a cow directly into the liquor and sugar to make it frothy; today we beat the mixture instead.

BEGIN: 3 HOURS AHEAD   12 SERVINGS

1   lemon
1½   cups dry white wine
4   cups half-and-half
¾   cup sugar
⅓   cup brandy
     Ground nutmeg

1. Using vegetable peeler, thinly peel lemon; reserve peel. Squeeze juice from lemon; reserve 2 tablespoons juice. In small bowl, cover lemon peel with wine; chill 2 to 3 hours. Discard peel.

2. *15 minutes before serving:* In large bowl with mixer at low speed, beat half-and-half until frothy; gradually beat in chilled wine, sugar, brandy and reserved lemon juice until well mixed. Pour into stemmed glasses; sprinkle with nutmeg. Serve immediately. Yields 6½ cups.

❄ Wine Jelly

This gelatin dessert flavored with wine became popular after commercial unflavored gelatin was introduced in 1890. Before that, gelatin had been made at home by a time-consuming process of boiling parts of animals or fish. Naturally, the gelatin retained some of the flavor of the animal, and much seasoning was needed to cover it up. The new type of gelatin, without the objectionable flavor, allowed the delicate taste of the wine to dominate.

BEGIN: EARLY IN DAY   8 SERVINGS

⅔   cup sugar
2   envelopes unflavored gelatin
     Dash salt
2   cups cream sherry
1   cup water
½   cup orange juice
2   tablespoons lemon juice
     Whipped cream

1. In 2-quart saucepan, combine sugar, gelatin and salt. Stir in sherry, water, orange juice and lemon juice. Over low heat, cook gelatin mixture until sugar and gelatin are dissolved.

2. Pour mixture into 4-cup mold; cover and refrigerate at least 6 hours or until set. Unmold onto chilled serving plate. Serve with cream.

❄ Vanilla Ice Cream

Although ice cream originated in Europe and Asia long before it was brought to the New World, Americans are responsible for the home ice cream freezer, commercial ice cream makers, ice cream sodas, sundaes and cones, and for countless flavor innovations (although vanilla is still the most popular). Dolley Madison served strawberry ice cream during her time as the President's hostess, and it might have been made from a simple recipe like this.

BEGIN: 4 HOURS AHEAD   16 SERVINGS

3   eggs
1½ cups sugar
3   cups heavy cream
3   cups milk
3   tablespoons vanilla extract
20 pounds cracked ice
2   to 3 pounds rock salt

1. In small bowl with mixer at high speed, beat eggs until foamy. Gradually beat in sugar, 2 tablespoons at a time, until thick and lemon-colored.

2. In 4-quart ice cream can, combine egg mixture with cream, milk and vanilla. Place dasher in can; put lid on can and place can in bucket. Attach motor or hand crank.

3. Fill bucket half full with ice; sprinkle with ¼ cup rock salt. Add 1 inch ice and ¼ cup salt; repeat to 1 inch below can lid. Freeze according to manufacturer's directions, adding more ice and salt as needed. Freezing will take 30 to 40 minutes.

4. Remove motor or crank. Wipe can lid and remove; remove dasher. With spoon, pack down ice cream. Cover opening of freezer can with waxed paper and replace lid. Add more ice and salt to cover lid. Let stand to harden 2 to 3 hours, adding more ice and salt as needed. Yields about 4 quarts.

STRAWBERRY ICE CREAM: In medium bowl, combine *½ cup additional sugar* and *2 pints strawberries, crushed;* set aside. Prepare vanilla ice cream as above but reduce vanilla extract to 1 teaspoon. Stir in sweetened strawberries before freezing.

PEACH ICE CREAM: In medium bowl, combine *½ cup additional sugar* and *3 cups chopped peeled peaches;* set aside. Prepare vanilla ice cream as above but reduce vanilla extract to 1 teaspoon. Stir in sweetened peaches before freezing.

COFFEE ICE CREAM: Prepare as above but add *2 tablespoons instant coffee crystals* along with the sugar and reduce vanilla extract to 1 teaspoon.

❊ Chocolate Custard Ice Cream

Ice cream was fashionable in this country at the time of the Revolution, and such notable Americans as George Washington and Thomas Jefferson are known to have enjoyed it often. Jefferson even served guests a dessert of ice cream that was baked in pastry, no small feat in that time. One recipe that has survived from Monticello begins with a custard, as this recipe does.

BEGIN: EARLY IN DAY   8 SERVINGS

1	cup sugar
¼	cup all-purpose flour
¼	teaspoon salt
4	cups milk
6	egg yolks, at room temperature
1	package (12 ounces) semisweet-chocolate pieces
2	cups heavy cream
1	teaspoon vanilla extract
20	pounds cracked ice
2	to 3 pounds rock salt

1. In heavy, 3-quart saucepan, combine sugar, flour and salt. Stir in milk. Over medium heat, heat mixture to boiling, stirring constantly; remove from heat.

2. In medium bowl with wire whisk, beat egg yolks. Stir in small amount of hot mixture. Slowly pour egg mixture into hot mixture, stirring rapidly. Over medium heat, cook until mixture just coats back of spoon, stirring constantly. Remove from heat.

3. Immediately stir in chocolate pieces until melted. Cover surface with waxed paper; refrigerate until completely cool, at least 2 hours.

4. Pour chocolate mixture into 4-quart ice cream can. Add cream and vanilla. Place dasher in can; put lid on can and place can in bucket. Attach motor or hand crank.

5. Fill bucket half full with ice; sprinkle with ¼ cup rock salt. Add 1 inch ice and ¼ cup salt; repeat to 1 inch below can lid. Freeze according to manufacturer's directions, adding more ice and salt as needed. Freezing will take 30 to 40 minutes.

6. Remove motor or crank. Wipe can lid and remove; remove dasher. With spoon, pack down ice cream. Cover opening of freezer can with waxed paper and replace lid. Add more ice and salt to cover lid. Let stand to harden 2 to 3 hours, adding more ice and salt as needed. Yields about 2 quarts.

❊ Hot Fudge Sauce

The ice cream sundae was invented to get around a Sunday ban in Virginia on drinking ice cream sodas at the turn of this century. Clever ice cream purveyors simply dispensed with the soda water to create the sundae. Try this rich, chocolate sauce on Strawberry Ice Cream and Raspberry Frozen Yogurt; the traditional favorite, of course, is fudge served over Vanilla Ice Cream with nuts, whipped cream and a cherry.

BEGIN: 15 MINUTES AHEAD

¼	cup butter or margarine
3	squares (1 ounce each) unsweetened chocolate
1	cup sugar
½	cup light cream or milk
	Dash salt
1	teaspoon vanilla extract

In heavy, 1½-quart saucepan over very low heat, melt butter and chocolate, stirring constantly. Stir in sugar, cream and salt. Over medium heat, cook until sugar dissolves, stirring constantly. Remove from heat; stir in vanilla. Yields 1½ cups.

❄ Baked Alaska

This elegant dessert was created not by a chef, but by an American scientist. Benjamin Thompson was experimenting with beaten egg whites as insulation against heat when he first made the dish he called Omelette Surprise. Thompson's other contributions to the art of cooking include designs for stoves, coffee percolators, and a nourishing soup to feed the poor.

BEGIN: EARLY IN DAY   12 SERVINGS

   **Hot Milk Sponge Cake (see page 261) or
      1 9-inch round cake layer**
1 **quart chocolate or strawberry ice cream**
4 **egg whites, at room temperature
      Generous dash salt**
¼ **teaspoon cream of tartar**
½ **cup sugar**

1. Prepare cake; cool to room temperature. Remove ice cream from freezer; let stand in refrigerator about 30 minutes until softened. Pack ice cream firmly into a bowl 7 inches in diameter. Cover; freeze 2 hours or until ice cream is firm.

2. *About 20 minutes before serving:* Preheat oven to 450°F. In large bowl with mixer at high speed, beat egg whites, salt and cream of tartar until soft peaks form. At high speed, gradually sprinkle in sugar, 2 tablespoons at a time, beating until stiff peaks form.

3. Center cake on a heatsafe plate or baking sheet. Dip bowl of ice cream into warm water to loosen ice cream; invert ice cream onto cake. Quickly spread meringue over ice cream and cake, covering ice cream completely and sealing meringue to plate.

4. Bake 5 minutes or until meringue is golden. Serve immediately.

TIP: Soften ice cream in the microwave oven: Microwave on HIGH 30 seconds at a time until ice cream is desired consistency.

❄ Raspberry Frozen Yogurt

Frozen yogurt has only recently gained popularity in this country, but that popularity has been overwhelming. One of the most popular flavors is raspberry. Because they are so perishable, fresh raspberries are hard to find in the supermarket, even in season. Luckily, the freezer can keep them for months, so you can enjoy this treat any time of the year.

BEGIN: DAY AHEAD   6 SERVINGS

1 **package (10 ounces) frozen raspberries,
      thawed**
3 **cups plain yogurt**
1 **cup sugar**
1 **teaspoon vanilla extract**

1. Force raspberries through sieve to remove seeds. In medium bowl, combine yogurt, sugar and vanilla; stir in raspberry purée. Pour mixture into 9- by 9-inch baking pan; cover with foil.

2. Freeze 3 hours or until partially frozen. Spoon raspberry mixture into large chilled bowl. With mixer at medium speed, beat until smooth but still frozen. Return mixture to pan; cover.

3. Freeze 2 hours or until partially frozen. Beat again as in step 2. Freeze mixture until firm.

4. To serve: Let frozen yogurt stand at room temperature 5 minutes; spoon into dessert dishes.

Vanilla Ice Cream, Hot Fudge Sauce, Cranberry-Orange Ice, Deep-Fried Ice Cream

❋ Cranberry-Orange Ice

Cranberries are among the foods that originated in America, and although we associate them with Thanksgiving, they are used year-round to make breads, cakes, cookies, punches, salads, preserves and ices.

BEGIN: EARLY IN DAY   8 SERVINGS

½ cup sugar
1   envelope unflavored gelatin
3   cups cranberry juice cocktail
1   teaspoon grated orange peel
1   cup orange juice

1. In 2-quart saucepan, combine sugar and gelatin. Stir in cranberry juice. Over low heat, heat until gelatin and sugar are dissolved, stirring constantly. Remove from heat; stir in orange peel and orange juice. Pour mixture into 9- by 9-inch baking pan; cover with foil.

2. Freeze 3 hours or until partially frozen. Spoon cranberry mixture into large chilled bowl. With mixer at medium speed, beat until smooth but still frozen. Return mixture to pan; cover.

3. Freeze 2 hours or until partially frozen. Beat again as in step 2. Freeze mixture until firm.

4. To serve: Let ice stand at room temperature 5 minutes; spoon into dessert dishes.

❋ Deep-Fried Ice Cream

This fun-to-prepare dessert is also a bit tricky, so be sure to practice once or twice before you perform for guests. Its crunchy coating is reminiscent of the coconut-pecan frosting traditionally spread between layers of German chocolate cake. Serve it with Hot Fudge Sauce for an even-richer dessert.

BEGIN: EARLY IN DAY   6 SERVINGS

1   quart vanilla ice cream
1   cup vanilla wafer crumbs (30 cookies)
½ cup finely chopped pecans or walnuts
½ cup flaked coconut
2   eggs
    Salad oil

1. With ice cream scoop, form 6 ice cream balls. Place on baking sheet; freeze several hours until very firm.

2. In pie plate, combine cookie crumbs, nuts and coconut; in another pie plate, beat eggs. Coat ice cream balls with crumb mixture, pressing crumbs firmly into ice cream. Dip ice cream in eggs; coat again with crumbs. Place on waxed-paper-lined baking sheet; freeze at least 2 hours.

3. *Just before serving:* In 4-quart saucepan, heat 2 inches oil to 385°F. Fry 2 ice cream balls at a time 20 to 25 seconds or until browned (keep remaining ice cream in freezer while frying). Drain on paper towels; serve immediately.

Lattice-Top Cherry Pie, Strawberry Chiffon Pie, Apple Pie, Pumpkin Pie

PIES

Although pies are not native to this continent, they have become identified with American cooking and are considered to be as American as, well, as apple pie.

The first pies on the continent were made by English colonists, who brought with them the tradition of meat pies, as well as some fruit pies. Early American farmers often ate pie for breakfast before a day in the fields. Even today, in Northern New England, a hearty breakfast might consist of a fruit pie accompanied by ham or fried steak and eggs.

Pie fillings varied with the season, from the earliest spring rhubarb to the latest autumn apples. When fresh fruits were gone, cooks used dried fruit, nuts and easily stored pumpkins and sweet potatoes. When even these supplies were depleted, an imaginative cook could still whip up a vinegar pie or one made from preserves or marmalade.

In the first American cookbook, Amelia Simmons' *American Cookery,* there are nine different recipes for "paste" or pastry dough; another early cookbook, Eliza Leslie's *Pastry, Cakes and Sweetmeats,* gave pastry a spot in the title. These early recipes are charming but vague, with their listings of a lump of butter the size of an egg or a handful of flour. Many early authors just listed the ingredients, assuming the cook would know how to combine them.

We know how popular pies were in nineteenth-century America by the numbers of pie safes found in pantries and kitchens. These were cabinets with several cooling shelves and a screen or perforated tin door protecting their contents from insects. Autumn fruit pies were often stockpiled in outdoor sheds, where they froze solid until the cook brought them indoors to serve in midwinter.

With the introduction of the refrigerator, many new kinds of pies were developed: chiffon pies with gelatin, whipped cream and egg whites; frozen pies made with ice cream; and custard pies. With chilled pies came cookie-crumb crusts, which hold up well under refrigeration.

Today, pie baking is easier than ever. American cooks can assemble their pies from piecrust mixes, frozen pastry, refrigerated dough, ready-made crumb crusts and canned pie fillings and custard mixes. But by rolling out pastry and filling a crust with fresh fruit, we can feel a kinship with Colonial and pioneer women who did just the same things two hundred years ago.

❋ Apple Pie

We say, "as American as apple pie." Yet in Vermont, the apples are sweetened with maple sugar; in Wisconsin, the pie is topped with savory Cheddar cheese; the Pennsylvania Dutch version is made from dried apples; and in the Northwest, where most American apples are grown, apple pie is simply the freshest apples baked in a flaky crust.

BEGIN: 2 HOURS AHEAD   8 SERVINGS

    Pastry for 2-Crust Pie (see page 256)
1   **cup sugar**
2   **tablespoons all-purpose flour**
1   **teaspoon ground cinnamon**
¼   **teaspoon salt**
6   **cups thinly sliced, peeled and cored cooking apples**
2   **tablespoons butter or margarine**
1   **tablespoon lemon juice**

1. Prepare pastry. Roll out half of pastry and line 9-inch pie plate. Preheat oven to 425°F.

2. In large bowl, combine sugar, flour, cinnamon and salt. Add apples; toss to mix well. Spoon mixture into piecrust. Dot with butter; sprinkle with lemon juice.

3. Roll out remaining pastry for top crust; cut a few slashes and cover apple mixture with slashed top crust. Flute edge.

4. Bake 35 to 40 minutes until crust is golden brown.

TIP: If piecrust edges begin to brown too much during baking, cover them with strips of foil to prevent overbrowning.

❋ Apple Dumplings

Still another Colonial dish of fruit and pastry is Apple Dumplings. Individual apples are wrapped in pastry and baked with a sweet sauce. Sometimes the colonists sweetened them with maple syrup, making the dumplings an American dish, different from German apple strudel, French open-faced tarts and British apple pie.

BEGIN: 2 HOURS AHEAD   6 SERVINGS

    Pastry for 2-Crust Pie (see page 256)
6   **small apples, peeled and cored**
½   **cup packed brown sugar**
1   **teaspoon ground cinnamon**
2   **tablespoons butter or margarine**
1½   **cups water**
½   **cup sugar**
1   **cinnamon stick**

1. Prepare pastry. On floured surface, roll pastry to 18- by 12-inch rectangle. Cut into 6 squares. Place 1 apple on each square.

2. In small bowl, combine brown sugar and ground cinnamon. Spoon some of cinnamon mixture into cavity of each apple; dot each with 1 teaspoon butter. With a few drops of water, moisten points of pastry square and bring them up and over apple, overlapping and sealing well. Repeat with remaining apples. Place dumplings in 13- by 9-inch baking pan.

3. Preheat oven to 425°F. In 1-quart saucepan over medium-high heat, heat water, sugar and cinnamon stick to boiling. Boil 5 minutes. Discard cinnamon stick. Pour syrup around dumplings in pan.

4. Bake 40 to 45 minutes until golden brown. Cool 10 minutes.

5. To serve: Place dumplings in dessert dishes; spoon syrup over dumplings.

❄ Lattice-Top Cherry Pie

Whether there is any truth to the legend of George Washington's chopping down the cherry tree, it has become part of the American tradition, and we celebrate Washington's birthday with cherry pies and cherry tarts. The United States leads the world in cherry production, both sweet and sour, but the sour variety is preferred for pastry.

BEGIN: 2 HOURS AHEAD   8 SERVINGS

Pastry for 2-Crust Pie (see page 256)
2   **cans (16 ounces each) pitted tart cherries**
1   **cup sugar**
6   **tablespoons cornstarch**
    Dash salt
2   **tablespoons butter or margarine**
    Few drops almond extract

1. Prepare pastry. Roll out half of pastry and line 9-inch pie plate. Preheat oven to 425°F.

2. Drain cherries, reserving 1 cup liquid; set aside. In 2-quart saucepan, combine sugar, cornstarch and salt. Stir in cherry liquid. Over medium heat, cook until mixture boils, stirring constantly. Remove from heat; stir in butter and almond extract until butter is melted. Stir in cherries. Pour cherry mixture into piecrust.

3. Roll remaining pastry to 11-inch circle and cut into strips of equal width. Crisscross pastry strips over filling to form a lattice top. Fasten ends to edge of bottom crust. Flute edge.

4. Bake 25 to 30 minutes until crust is golden.

CHERRY TARTS: Prepare cherry filling as above but *double pastry recipe.* Roll out pastry, half at a time, to ⅛-inch thickness. Cut each half into ten 4-inch rounds. Fit rounds into twenty 3-inch muffin cups to make tart shells. Reroll trimmings to ⅛-inch thickness. Cut twenty 2-inch circles; set aside. Divide cherry mixture among tart shells. Top each with 2-inch pastry circle. Bake at 400°F. 25 minutes or until pastry is golden.

❄ Rhubarb Pie

After a long winter of cooking with stored foods, American cooks welcomed rhubarb, the first of the fresh pie makings. Because it was so easy to grow, it found its way into many gardens. Also known as "pieplant," rhubarb was featured in pie recipes in the earliest American cookbooks.

BEGIN: 2 HOURS AHEAD   8 SERVINGS

Pastry for 2-Crust Pie (see page 256)
1¼ **cups sugar**
⅓   **cup all-purpose flour**
⅛   **teaspoon salt**
4   **cups cut-up rhubarb**
2   **tablespoons butter or margarine**

1. Prepare pastry. Roll out half of pastry and line 9-inch pie plate. Preheat oven to 425°F.

2. In medium bowl, combine sugar, flour and salt. Add rhubarb; toss to mix well. Spoon rhubarb mixture into piecrust. Dot with butter.

3. Roll out remaining pastry for top crust; cut a few slashes and cover rhubarb mixture with slashed top crust. Flute edge.

4. Bake 35 to 40 minutes until crust is golden brown.

STRAWBERRY-RHUBARB PIE: Prepare as above but substitute *2 cups quartered strawberries* and 2 cups cut-up rhubarb for 4 cups cut-up rhubarb. Reduce sugar to 1 cup.

TIP: Substitute 2 packages (16 ounces each) frozen rhubarb, thawed, for fresh rhubarb.

❇ Spicy Raisin Pie

Raisins have been important in pies since the coloniza-tion of America, when dried fruit was the only pie fruit available year round. They were used in mincemeat and mock-lemon pies, and were the main ingredient in Penn-sylvania Dutch "funeral pie," a lattice-topped raisin pie favored for its transportability, which was traditionally served at post-funeral meals. This recipe has a similar richness and spiciness, enhanced by the addition of to-mato soup.

BEGIN: 2 HOURS AHEAD   8 SERVINGS

    Pastry for 2-Crust Pie (see page 256)
2   tablespoons cornstarch
½   teaspoon grated orange peel
1¼ cups orange juice
1   can (10¾ ounces) condensed tomato
      soup
2   cups raisins
⅔   cup sugar
⅓   cup chopped walnuts
½   teaspoon ground cinnamon
⅛   teaspoon ground cloves
2   tablespoons butter or margarine

1. Prepare pastry. Roll out half of pastry and line 9-inch pie plate. Preheat oven to 425°F.

2. In small bowl, combine cornstarch, orange peel and ¼ cup juice until smooth; set aside. In 2-quart saucepan over low heat, cook soup, rais-ins and remaining 1 cup juice 10 minutes, stir-ring occasionally.

3. Stir in cornstarch mixture and remaining in-gredients. Cook over medium heat until mixture boils, stirring constantly. Remove from heat; pour into crust.

4. Roll remaining pastry to 11-inch circle and cut into strips of equal width. Crisscross pastry strips over filling to form a lattice top. Fasten ends to edge of bottom crust. Flute edge.

5. Bake 25 to 30 minutes until crust is golden.

❇ Streusel Peach Pie

The first two-crust fruit pie was probably developed by a baker with too little fruit who needed a second crust to help fill the pie plate. Sometimes creative cooks would replace the upper crust with a streusel mixture of sugar, butter and flour. Other times, a crumbly mixture of oat-meal and nuts was added.

BEGIN: 2 HOURS AHEAD   8 SERVINGS

1   9-inch Unbaked Piecrust (see page 256)
½   cup sugar
¾   cup all-purpose flour
½   teaspoon ground cinnamon
4   cups peeled, sliced peaches
¼   cup packed brown sugar
¼   cup butter or margarine

1. Prepare Unbaked Piecrust. Preheat oven to 425°F.

2. In large bowl, combine sugar, ¼ cup flour and cinnamon. Add peaches; toss to mix well. Spoon mixture into piecrust.

3. In small bowl, combine remaining ½ cup flour and brown sugar. With pastry blender or 2 knives used scissor-fashion, cut in butter until mixture resembles coarse crumbs. Sprinkle over peaches.

4. Bake 35 to 40 minutes until golden.

STREUSEL APPLE PIE: Prepare as above but sub-stitute *4 cups sliced, peeled and cored cooking apples.* for peaches. Increase sugar to ¾ cup.

❄ Blueberry Pie

A summer favorite, blueberry pie is one of the pies New Englanders have always enjoyed for breakfast. This modern blueberry pie is made with an unusual technique that combines the best of raw and cooked berries to make a fresh-tasting pie.

BEGIN: EARLY IN DAY   8 SERVINGS

1   **9-inch Baked Piecrust (see page 256)**
5   **cups fresh blueberries**
¾   **cup sugar**
2   **tablespoons cornstarch**
¼   **teaspoon ground cinnamon**
    Dash salt
½   **cup water**
1   **tablespoon butter or margarine**
    Whipped cream

1. Prepare piecrust; cool. In large bowl, toss 2 cups blueberries and ¼ cup sugar; set aside.

2. In 2-quart saucepan, combine remaining ½ cup sugar, cornstarch, cinnamon, salt and water. Stir in remaining 3 cups blueberries and butter. Over medium heat, heat to boiling, stirring constantly; cook 2 minutes more or until thickened and clear.

3. Pour hot mixture over reserved berries and sugar mixture in bowl; stir just to combine. Pour blueberry mixture into piecrust. Cover; refrigerate until serving time, at least 6 hours. Serve with whipped cream.

❄ Pumpkin Pie

The early colonists might have starved had not the Indians showed them how to use pumpkins. At first, the settlers simply roasted and boiled the pumpkins, but they soon adapted them to make puddings and pies. A poem that has come to us from seventeenth-century New England stresses the importance of pumpkins to the settlers:

For pottage, and puddings, and custards, and pies,
Our pumpkins and parsnips are common supplies.
We have pumpkins at morning and pumpkins at noon.
If it were not for pumpkins we should be undoon.

BEGIN: 4 HOURS AHEAD   8 SERVINGS

1   **9-inch Unbaked Piecrust (see page 256)**
2   **eggs**
2   **cups mashed cooked pumpkin**
¾   **cup packed light brown sugar**
1   **teaspoon ground cinnamon**
½   **teaspoon ground ginger**
½   **teaspoon ground allspice**
¼   **teaspoon salt**
1   **can (13 ounces) evaporated milk**

1. Prepare Unbaked Piecrust. Preheat oven to 375°F.

2. In medium bowl with wire whisk, beat eggs well. Stir in remaining ingredients. Pour filling into crust.

3. Bake 55 to 60 minutes until knife inserted about 1 inch from edge comes out clean. Cool before serving.

TIP: Substitute 1 can (16 ounces) pumpkin for 2 cups cooked pumpkin.

SWEET POTATO PIE: Prepare as above but substitute *2 cups mashed cooked sweet potato* for pumpkin and *½ cup sugar* for ¾ cup brown sugar. Omit ginger and allspice.

❋ Pecan Pie

Just mention Southern cooking and pecan pie is bound to come up. You can find this specialty in all the Southern states, and many claims are made as to who prepared the first pie. Because pecans are grown almost exclusively in North America (and mostly in the South), this sinfully rich pie remains an all-American and very Southern dish. George Washington planted pecan trees in 1775 that are still growing at Mount Vernon today; perhaps he loved pecan pie as much as the rest of us do.

BEGIN: 4 HOURS AHEAD   8 SERVINGS

1   **9-inch Unbaked Piecrust (see page 256)**
3   **eggs**
1   **cup dark corn syrup**
⅔   **cup sugar**
¼   **cup butter or margarine, melted**
1½ **teaspoons vanilla extract**
¼   **teaspoon salt**
1½ **cups pecan halves**

1. Prepare Unbaked Piecrust. Preheat oven to 375°F.

2. In medium bowl with wire whisk, beat eggs well. Beat in corn syrup, sugar, butter, vanilla and salt until well blended; pour into piecrust, reserving ¼ cup syrup mixture.

3. Arrange pecan halves in single layer over filling; drizzle reserved syrup over nuts.

4. Bake 45 to 50 minutes until knife inserted about 1 inch from edge comes out clean. Cool before serving.

Pecan Pie

❋ Key Lime Pie

This lime pie is a relatively new dessert developed when sweetened condensed milk was first produced after the Civil War. The lime juice reacts with the milk and egg yolks to produce a tasty, thick filling that does not need cooking. Key limes, yellow-skinned fruit from the Florida Keys, are reputed to be tarter and juicier than regular limes and to make an especially fine pie.

BEGIN: EARLY IN DAY   8 SERVINGS

1   **9-inch Baked Piecrust (see page 256)**
6   **egg yolks**
2   **cans (14 ounces each) sweetened condensed milk**
1   **teaspoon grated lime peel**
1   **cup lime juice**
1   **cup heavy cream, whipped**

1. Prepare Baked Piecrust; cool. In medium bowl with wire whisk, beat egg yolks. Stir in condensed milk, lime peel and lime juice; mix well until slightly thickened.

2. Pour mixture into piecrust. Cover; refrigerate until serving time, at least 6 hours.

3. To serve: Spread whipped cream over pie.

❊ Lemon Meringue Pie

Lemon pies in this country have taken many forms. One recipe that found popularity in years past is associated with the Shakers of Ohio; it combines thinly sliced lemons with sugar and eggs between two layers of pastry. Lemon custard pies have been made in every state of the Union, and different variations of these custard pies have been said to be the favorites of Presidents Grant, Coolidge and Lincoln. And there have been lemon chiffon pies, lemon sponge pies, frozen lemon pies and lemon chess pies, but the lemon pie most often served today is Lemon Meringue Pie.

BEGIN: EARLY IN DAY   8 SERVINGS

1   9-inch Baked Piecrust (see page 256) or
       Baked Graham-Cracker Crumb Crust
       (see page 256)
1¾   cups sugar
⅓   cup cornstarch
¼   teaspoon salt
½   cup cold water
1   teaspoon grated lemon peel
½   cup lemon juice
4   eggs, separated, at room temperature
1½   cups boiling water
2   tablespoons butter or margarine

1. Prepare piecrust; cool. In 2-quart saucepan, combine 1¼ cups sugar, cornstarch and ⅛ teaspoon salt. Stir in ½ cup water, lemon peel, lemon juice and egg yolks; mix well. Stir in boiling water. Over medium heat, cook until mixture boils, stirring constantly. Remove from heat.

2. Stir in butter until thoroughly blended. Pour mixture into piecrust.

3. Preheat oven to 350°F. In small bowl with mixer at high speed, beat egg whites and remaining ⅛ teaspoon salt until soft peaks form. At high speed, sprinkle in remaining ½ cup sugar, 2 tablespoons at a time, beating after each addition until sugar is dissolved and stiff peaks form.

4. With back of spoon, spread meringue over filling; seal to piecrust all around edge. Swirl up points to make attractive top.

5. Bake 10 minutes or until golden. Cool on wire rack.

❊ Strawberry Chiffon Pie

Chiffon pies are popular summer desserts, when their light, cool texture makes them refreshing in the heat. They are especially welcome made with the fresh fruits of summer—strawberries, raspberries or peaches. Other favorite chiffon pies include lemon, eggnog, pumpkin and coffee, and rum-flavored Black Bottom Pie.

BEGIN: EARLY IN DAY   8 SERVINGS

     **Baked Graham-Cracker Crumb Crust (see
       page 256)**
1   **pint strawberries**
½   **cup sugar**
1   **envelope unflavored gelatin**
¼   **cup water**
3   **egg whites**
¼   **teaspoon cream of tartar**
½   **cup heavy cream**

1. Prepare Baked Graham-Cracker Crumb Crust; cool.

2. In large bowl, crush enough berries to make 1 cup; reserve remaining berries for garnish. Stir ¼ cup sugar into crushed berries; let stand 20 minutes.

3. In 1-quart saucepan, sprinkle gelatin over water to soften. Let stand 1 minute. Over low heat, heat until gelatin is dissolved, stirring constantly. Stir into crushed berries. Chill about 10 minutes until mixture mounds when dropped from spoon, stirring occasionally.

4. In small bowl with mixer at high speed, beat egg whites and cream of tartar until soft peaks form; gradually sprinkle in remaining ¼ cup sugar, 2 tablespoons at a time, beating until sugar is dissolved and stiff peaks form. Gently fold egg whites into chilled berry mixture.

5. In small bowl with mixer at high speed, beat cream until soft peaks form; gently fold into berry mixture. Pour into piecrust. Refrigerate until serving time, about 2 hours. Garnish with reserved berries.

RASPBERRY CHIFFON PIE: Prepare as above but substitute *1 pint raspberries* for the strawberries.

PEACH CHIFFON PIE: Prepare as above but substitute *1¾ cups chopped, peeled peaches* for the strawberries.

❋ Coconut Cream Pie

Before the late nineteenth century, cream pies were really layer cakes with custard fillings, like Boston Cream Pie. Now we make true cream pies, filling flaky crusts with custard or pudding, then topping them with meringue or whipped cream.

BEGIN: EARLY IN DAY   8 SERVINGS

1   9-inch Baked Piecrust (see page 256) or
      Baked Graham-Cracker Crumb Crust
      (see page 256)
⅔   cup sugar
½   cup cornstarch
½   teaspoon salt
4   cups milk
1   cup flaked coconut
6   egg yolks
¼   cup butter or margarine
2   teaspoons vanilla extract
¼   teaspoon almond extract
1   cup heavy cream
      Toasted coconut

1. Prepare piecrust; cool. In 3-quart saucepan, combine sugar, cornstarch and salt; stir in milk and 1 cup coconut. Over medium heat, cook until mixture boils, stirring constantly. Remove from heat.

2. In small bowl with wire whisk, beat egg yolks. Stir in small amount of hot mixture. Slowly pour egg mixture into hot mixture, stirring rapidly to prevent lumping. Over medium heat, cook until mixture is very thick, stirring constantly (do not boil). Remove from heat.

3. Stir in butter, vanilla and almond extract. Cool slightly. Pour into piecrust; cover surface with waxed paper. Chill.

4. In medium bowl with mixer at medium speed, beat cream until stiff peaks form. With pastry tube, pipe whipped cream in lattice pattern over top or spread over pie in decorative swirls. Garnish with toasted coconut. Refrigerate until serving time.

CHOCOLATE CREAM PIE: Prepare as above but omit coconut and almond extract and increase sugar to 1¼ cups. Melt *4 squares (1 ounce each) unsweetened chocolate* in milk during cooking time; proceed as above.

BANANA CREAM PIE: Prepare as above but omit coconut and almond extract. Reduce all ingredients except piecrust and cream by half. Spread ⅓ of the custard mixture into piecrust. Slice *2 bananas.* Arrange ½ of the banana slices over custard. Repeat layers, ending with custard. Cover; chill. *Just before serving:* Slice *1 additional banana;* arrange slices over pie. Whip cream and top pie as in step 4. Serve at once.

TIP: Prepare fillings as above for puddings to enjoy without the crust. Pour filling into dessert dishes; garnish with whipped cream.

❋ Black Bottom Pie

This light, luscious dessert of rum and chocolate has a black bottom of chocolate under a white top of rum custard and whipped cream. A Southern dish, it was traditionally made with a gingersnap crumb crust. You might prefer to use a graham-cracker crust; chocolate fanatics might even use chocolate wafers.

BEGIN: EARLY IN DAY   8 SERVINGS

      Gingersnap Crumb Crust (see page 256)
1   envelope unflavored gelatin
¼   cup cold water
½   cup sugar
2   tablespoons cornstarch
      Dash salt
2   cups milk
3   eggs, separated
2   squares (1 ounce each) unsweetened
      chocolate, melted
1   teaspoon vanilla extract
2   tablespoons light rum
¼   teaspoon cream of tartar
⅓   cup sugar
1   cup heavy cream, whipped
      Chocolate curls

1. Prepare Gingersnap Crumb Crust; cool.

2. In 1-quart saucepan, sprinkle gelatin over cold water to soften. Stir in ½ cup sugar, cornstarch and salt. Stir in milk and egg yolks. Over medium heat, cook until mixture boils and coats back of spoon, stirring constantly. Remove from heat. Measure 1 cup of mixture into small bowl.

3. Into 1 cup custard mixture, stir chocolate and vanilla. Pour into crust; refrigerate.

4. Add rum to remaining custard mixture; chill until mixture mounds when dropped from a spoon.

5. In small bowl with mixer at high speed, beat egg whites and cream of tartar until soft peaks form; gradually sprinkle in ⅓ cup sugar, 2 tablespoons at a time, beating until sugar is dissolved and stiff peaks form. Gently fold egg whites into chilled rum mixture. Spread over chocolate layer. Refrigerate until serving time, at least 6 hours.

6. To serve: Spread whipped cream over pie; garnish with chocolate curls.

❋ Shoofly Pie

A classic of Pennsylvania Dutch cuisine, shoofly pie can be moist like a pudding or dry like a cake; either way it has a cinnamon-molasses flavor. The name may be derived from the French chou-fleur, or cauliflower, in reference to the pie's crumbly appearance. But folks who have tasted it like the idea of a woman shooing flies away from the sweet, warm pies cooling on a windowsill.

BEGIN: 2 HOURS AHEAD   8 SERVINGS

1	9-inch Unbaked Piecrust (see page 256)
2	cups all-purpose flour
¾	cup packed brown sugar
½	teaspoon ground cinnamon
¼	teaspoon salt
½	cup butter or margarine
¾	cup boiling water
½	cup molasses
¾	teaspoon baking soda

1. Prepare Unbaked Piecrust. Preheat oven to 375°F.

2. In large bowl, combine flour, brown sugar, cinnamon and salt. With pastry blender or 2 knives used scissor-fashion, cut in butter until mixture resembles coarse crumbs.

3. In medium bowl, combine boiling water and molasses; stir in soda.

4. Spread ¼ of the crumb mixture in piecrust; pour ⅓ of the molasses mixture over crumbs. Repeat layers, ending with crumb mixture.

5. Bake 35 to 40 minutes until pie is set. Serve warm or cool.

❋ Pastry for 2-Crust Pie

Although the basic components of pastry are always flour, fat and liquid, the variations in ingredients and techniques are infinite. Cooks argue tirelessly about the comparative merits of shortening, lard, oil or butter, of water or milk, and whether to add sugar, eggs, vinegar or lemon juice. This recipe combines the superior qualities of lard with a simple mixing procedure that produces a crisp, flaky crust.

BEGIN: 1 HOUR AHEAD   PASTRY FOR ONE 9-INCH 2-CRUST PIE OR TWO 9-INCH PIECRUSTS

2   cups all-purpose flour
1   teaspoon salt
½   cup lard
¼   cup shortening
5   to 6 tablespoons cold water

1. In medium bowl with fork, combine flour and salt. With pastry blender or 2 knives used scissor-fashion, cut in lard and shortening until mixture resembles coarse crumbs.

2. Sprinkle in cold water, a tablespoon at a time, mixing lightly with fork after each addition until pastry just holds together. With hands, shape pastry into a ball. Wrap in waxed paper and refrigerate about 30 minutes while making pie filling, if desired.

3. *For 2-crust pie:* Divide pastry into 2 parts, one slightly larger. Gently shape each piece into a ball. On lightly floured surface, roll larger ball to a 13-inch circle. Transfer to pie plate, easing into plate. Fill as recipe directs.

4. For top crust, roll smaller ball to 11-inch circle. With sharp knife, cut a few slashes in center; place over filling in bottom crust.

5. Trim top crust ½ inch beyond edge of pie plate. Fold overhang under bottom crust; pinch a high edge. Flute pastry around edge. Bake pie as directed in recipe.

TIP: Omit lard and increase shortening to ¾ cup.

PASTRY FOR 1-CRUST PIE: Prepare as above in steps 1 and 2 but reduce all ingredients by half.

UNBAKED PIECRUST: Prepare as above but reduce all ingredients by half. Roll out as in step 3. Trim pastry edges, leaving ½ inch beyond edge of pie plate. Fold overhang under crust; pinch a high edge. Flute pastry around edge.

BAKED PIECRUST: Preheat oven to 425°F. Prepare as above for Unbaked Piecrust. With fork, prick bottom and side of crust to prevent puffing during baking. Bake 12 to 15 minutes until golden. Cool.

❋ Baked Graham-Cracker Crumb Crust

When refrigeration became commonplace in American homes, cold pies became popular and clever cooks discovered that piecrusts made from cookie crumbs remained crisp and appetizing during chilling. Such cookies as gingersnaps, chocolate wafers, vanilla wafers and zwieback have been used to make wonderful bases for pies.

BEGIN: 1 HOUR AHEAD   ONE 9-INCH PIECRUST

18   graham crackers (1¼ cups crumbs)
¼   cup sugar
¼   cup butter or margarine, melted

1. In covered blender container, blend crackers, ¼ at a time, until finely crumbed; or place crackers in strong plastic bag and roll fine with rolling pin.

2. Preheat oven to 375°F. In medium bowl, combine crumbs, sugar and melted butter; mix well. With back of spoon, press mixture on bottom and side of 9-inch pie plate, making a small rim.

3. Bake 8 minutes or until set. Cool in pan on wire rack.

GINGERSNAP CRUMB CRUST: Prepare as above but substitute *21 gingersnaps* for graham crackers. Reduce sugar to 2 tablespoons.

Black Bottom Pie, Coconut Cream Pie

Lane Cake, Lane Cake Filling, Gingerbread, Lemon Sauce, Devil's Food Cake, Chocolate Butter Frosting

CAKES

Today's cook can make a cake from any period in our nation's history: one day, a pound cake from the 1700s and the next, a chiffon cake less than a century old. But it was not always so easy for the American baker.

Since all cooking was done in fireplaces in Colonial times, cooks had to use community ovens or improvise spaces in their kitchens. The Dutch oven, a large iron pot, was used as a baking cavity. In it, a cake could be cooked on a trivet, away from the direct heat of the fire.

Fireplaces often had brick cavities hollowed out of their side walls. These were heated by placing coals inside until the cavity was warm enough for baking. The cook tested the heat by throwing a handful of flour onto the bottom to see if it scorched or by placing a hand in the oven and counting off the seconds she could bear to leave it there. Then ashes were swept from the oven, the cake pans were put inside and the door was closed. Heat held in the bricks did the job, but timing was largely guesswork.

The cook had to contend with a lack of reliable leavenings, too. Cakes rose if enough air was beaten into the batter; some recipes from Colonial times tell the cook to beat for five hours—without an electric mixer! Homemade yeast, adequate for bread dough, was too uncertain for delicate cake batters.

In the late eighteenth century, pearl ash, a forerunner of baking soda, was discovered. Made from burned wood, it reacted with the acid ingredients to produce carbon dioxide, which leavened the cake. But pearl ash had an unpleasant, bitter flavor and often left green streaks in a cake. Later came saleratus, or baking soda, which gave better results.

In the 1850s a much more acceptable leavener, baking powder, was produced. It found gradual acceptance among people who first thought it to be poisonous.

The nineteenth century also brought the first practical freestanding ranges with ovens that were quickly heated with wood and controlled with dampers. Gas and electric ranges followed in the twentieth century, along with electric mixers to make beating the batter an easy affair. Cake mixes simplified baking even more.

Now, Americans enjoy all kinds of homemade cakes, from the steamed puddings of Colonial times to the canned-soup cakes of the 1940s and the lofty layer cakes we serve on special occasions.

❋ Kentucky Bourbon Cake

This fruity cake is fragrant with bourbon and crunchy with pecans—two foods that delight Southerners. Even a Yankee will understand, once he tastes this luscious cake.

BEGIN: EARLY IN DAY   16 SERVINGS

1 **cup butter or margarine, softened**
2 **cups sugar**
6 **eggs**
3 **cups all-purpose flour**
2 **teaspoons ground nutmeg**
2 **teaspoons baking powder**
⅛ **teaspoon salt**
1 **cup bourbon**
3 **cups chopped pecans**
2 **cups raisins**
    Confectioners' sugar

1. Preheat oven to 325°F. Grease 10-inch tube pan.

2. In large bowl with mixer at medium speed, cream butter until light and fluffy. Gradually beat in sugar until well mixed, constantly scraping bowl. At low speed, beat in eggs, one at a time, beating well after each addition, occasionally scraping bowl.

3. In medium bowl, combine flour, nutmeg, baking powder and salt. Add dry ingredients alternately with bourbon to creamed mixture, mixing well after each addition, occasionally scraping bowl with rubber spatula. Stir in pecans and raisins. Pour batter into prepared pan.

4. Bake 1¼ to 1½ hours until toothpick inserted in cake comes out clean. Cool in pan on wire rack 10 minutes. Remove from pan; cool completely. Sprinkle with confectioners' sugar.

❋ Pound Cake

Pound cake was originally made with a pound each of butter, sugar, eggs and flour. It required a strong arm to beat air into the batter, since no leavening was added. The cook could flavor the cake with rum, brandy, vanilla, lemon or orange peel, or nutmeg. This version of pound cake is not in the traditional proportions, but is designed to work with the electric mixer, while representing the flavor and texture of the original.

BEGIN: EARLY IN DAY   16 SERVINGS

1 **cup butter or margarine, softened**
1⅔ **cups sugar**
1 **teaspoon vanilla extract**
½ **teaspoon ground mace or nutmeg**
6 **eggs, at room temperature**
2 **cups all-purpose flour**

1. Preheat oven to 300°F. Grease and flour two 8- by 4-inch loaf pans.

2. In large bowl with mixer at medium speed, cream butter until light and fluffy. Gradually beat in sugar, vanilla and mace until well mixed, constantly scraping bowl. At low speed, beat in eggs, one at a time, beating well after each addition, occasionally scraping bowl.

3. Gradually beat in flour, constantly scraping bowl with rubber spatula (do not overbeat). Turn into prepared pans.

4. Bake 55 to 60 minutes until toothpick inserted in center comes out clean. Cool in pans on wire rack 10 minutes. Remove from pans to wire rack; cool completely.

LEMON POUND CAKE: Prepare as above but add *1 tablespoon grated lemon peel* with mace in step 2. Proceed as above.

TIP: Pound Cake can be baked in greased and floured 10-inch tube pan. Bake at 300°F. 1½ hours or until toothpick inserted in cake comes out clean.

✳ Hot Milk Sponge Cake

Before baking powder made its debut in the marketplace, cakes baked with chemical leavenings and homemade yeast produced variable results. One week, a cake might be light and airy; the next week, it could be flat and dense. Sponge cakes were developed to avoid these unreliable leavenings: they depended on the air beaten into eggs to raise the cake. Hot Milk Sponge Cake has the aid of modern baking powder to insure success. It is a quick cake that makes a perfect base for other desserts such as Baked Alaska and Tipsy Parson.

BEGIN: 3 HOURS AHEAD   ONE 9-INCH LAYER

2   eggs, at room temperature
²⁄₃ cup sugar
²⁄₃ cup all-purpose flour
½   teaspoon baking powder
⅛   teaspoon salt
¼   cup milk
1   tablespoon butter or margarine

1. Preheat oven to 350°F. Grease and flour 9-inch round cake pan.

2. In large bowl with mixer at high speed, beat eggs until thick and lemon-colored. Gradually beat in sugar until dissolved. Stir in flour, baking powder and salt.

3. In small saucepan over medium heat, heat milk and butter until butter is melted; stir into egg mixture. Pour into prepared pan.

4. Bake 20 minutes or until top springs back when lightly touched with finger. Cool in pan on wire rack 10 minutes. Remove from pan to wire rack; cool completely.

✳ Jelly Roll

A showy relative of the sponge cake is the jelly roll. Rolled up around preserves or jellies, then sliced to show the spiral, it appears harder to make than it is. Americans of French and French-Canadian ancestry frost a similar cake with chocolate and make Bûche de Noël, *or Yule Log, at Christmastime.*

BEGIN: EARLY IN DAY   12 SERVINGS

¾   cup all-purpose flour
1   teaspoon baking powder
¼   teaspoon salt
4   eggs, separated, at room temperature
1   cup sugar
⅓   cup water
½   teaspoon vanilla extract
    Confectioners' sugar
1   jar (10 ounces) currant jelly or strawberry preserves

1. Preheat oven to 375°F. Grease 15½- by 10½-inch jelly-roll pan; line with waxed paper.

2. In small bowl, combine flour, baking powder and salt; set aside. In medium bowl with mixer at high speed, beat egg whites until soft peaks form; gradually sprinkle in ½ cup sugar, 2 tablespoons at a time, beating until stiff peaks form; set aside.

3. In large bowl with mixer at high speed, beat egg yolks until thick and lemon-colored; gradually sprinkle in remaining ½ cup sugar. At low speed, beat in water and vanilla. Sprinkle flour mixture over yolks. With rubber spatula, gently fold to blend thoroughly. Fold in egg whites. Spread batter in prepared pan.

4. Bake 20 minutes or until top springs back when lightly touched with finger.

5. Meanwhile, sprinkle towel with confectioners' sugar. Immediately invert hot cake onto towel; gently remove waxed paper. While warm, carefully roll up cake and towel from narrow end. Cool cake completely on rack.

6. Unroll cake and spread with jelly. Reroll without towel; sprinkle with confectioners' sugar.

YULE LOG: Prepare as above in steps 1 through 5; omit jelly. Unroll cake and spread with ½ recipe *Chocolate Whipped Cream* (see page 273); reroll without towel. Frost sides of roll with ½ recipe *Chocolate Butter Frosting* (see page 272), leaving ends unfrosted. Draw tines of fork along roll to resemble bark of tree. Slice about 2 inches from one end of frosted roll. Attach cut piece to side of roll to resemble branch.

❋ Angel Food Cake

This wonderfully light cake is made from ingredients that were available in Colonial times, but it could not have been made during that period. The reason? Ovens built into the sides of fireplaces could not provide the even heat needed for sensitive egg whites. It was the advent of the regulated oven that made the angel food cake possible. An American original, the cake's creation has been attributed to a thrifty Pennsylvania Dutch woman with a bright idea for using the whites left after making egg noodles.

BEGIN: EARLY IN DAY   12 SERVINGS

1   cup confectioners' sugar
1   cup cake flour
1½ cups egg whites (12 to 14), at room
     temperature
1½ teaspoons cream of tartar
1   teaspoon vanilla extract
½ teaspoon almond extract
¼ teaspoon salt
¾ cup sugar
    Sweetened Whipped Cream (see page
     273) (optional)
    Strawberries (optional)

1. Preheat oven to 375°F. In small bowl, combine confectioners' sugar and flour; set aside.

2. In large bowl with mixer at high speed, beat egg whites, cream of tartar, vanilla, almond extract and salt until soft peaks form; gradually sprinkle in sugar, 2 tablespoons at a time, beating just until sugar is dissolved and stiff peaks form.

3. With rubber spatula, fold in flour mixture, about ¼ at a time, just until flour disappears. Pour batter into ungreased two-piece 10-inch tube pan. With spatula, cut through batter to break any large air bubbles.

4. Bake 35 minutes or until top springs back when lightly touched with finger. Invert cake in pan onto funnel; cool completely. With spatula, loosen cake from pan and remove to plate. Frost with Sweetened Whipped Cream; garnish with strawberries.

❋ Yellow Cake

When cake mixes appeared in grocery stores during the 1940s, a revolution began in the American kitchen, and mix cakes became commonplace. But as good as cake mixes are, a homemade layer cake such as this one gives you the satisfaction of knowing you made it yourself. This is a scaled-down version of the popular "1-2-3-4 Cake," which is named for its original proportions of 1 cup butter, 2 cups sugar, 3 cups flour and 4 eggs.

BEGIN: EARLY IN DAY   12 SERVINGS

¾ cup butter or margarine, softened
1½ cups sugar
3   eggs
1   teaspoon vanilla extract
2¼ cups all-purpose flour
2   teaspoons baking powder
½ teaspoon salt
1   cup milk
    Chocolate Butter Frosting (see page 272)

1. Preheat oven to 350°F. Grease and flour two 8-inch round cake pans or one 13- by 9-inch baking pan.

2. In large bowl with mixer at medium speed, cream butter until light and fluffy. Gradually beat in sugar until well mixed, constantly scraping bowl. Beat in eggs, one at a time, beating well after each addition, occasionally scraping bowl. Add vanilla; mix well.

3. In medium bowl, combine flour, baking powder and salt. Add dry ingredients alternately with milk to creamed mixture, mixing well after each addition, occasionally scraping bowl with rubber spatula. Pour batter into prepared pans.

4. Bake 35 to 40 minutes or until toothpick inserted in center comes out clean. Cool in pans on wire racks 10 minutes. Remove from pans; cool completely. Frost with Chocolate Butter Frosting; decorate if desired.

CUPCAKES: Prepare batter as above. Place liners in twenty-four 3-inch muffin cups or grease and flour cups. Spoon batter into cups, filling each half full. Bake 30 minutes; cool. Dip tops of cupcakes into frosting, turning slightly to coat.

MARBLE CAKE: In small saucepan over very low heat, melt *2 squares (1 ounce each) unsweetened chocolate;* set aside to cool. Prepare batter as above. Stir 1 cup batter into melted chocolate. Alternately spoon plain and chocolate batters into pans. With knife, cut through batter a few times to marble. Bake, cool and frost as above.

Yellow Cake, Chocolate Butter Frosting, Cupcakes, Creamy Butter Frosting

✳ Devil's Food Cake

Devil's food is the favorite American chocolate cake. When it became popular at the turn of this century, the large amount of baking soda in the batter made the chocolate appear red; thus, it became known as red devil's food. Later recipes reduced the soda and added red food coloring. Today's recipe reflects the trend toward more natural cooking, with neither an excess of soda nor the addition of color. Instead, it has a deep-brown hue and a rich, dark flavor.

BEGIN: EARLY IN DAY   12 SERVINGS

¾   cup butter or margarine, softened
1½   cups sugar
3   eggs, separated, at room temperature
1½   teaspoons vanilla extract
2¼   cups all-purpose flour
½   cup cocoa
1½   teaspoons baking soda
½   teaspoon salt
1   cup water
2   tablespoons vinegar
     Chocolate Butter Frosting (see page 272)

1. Preheat oven to 350°F. Grease two 8-inch round cake pans and line bottoms with waxed paper.

2. In large bowl with mixer at medium speed, cream butter until light and fluffy. Gradually beat in sugar until well mixed, constantly scraping bowl. Beat in egg yolks, one at a time, beating well after each addition, occasionally scraping bowl. Add vanilla; mix well.

3. In medium bowl, combine flour, cocoa, baking soda and salt. In 2-cup measure, combine water and vinegar; set aside. Add dry ingredients alternately with water to creamed mixture, mixing well after each addition, occasionally scraping bowl with rubber spatula.

4. In small bowl with mixer at high speed, using clean beaters, beat egg whites until soft peaks form. Fold into batter; pour into prepared pans.

5. Bake 35 to 40 minutes until toothpick inserted in center comes out clean. Cool in pans on wire racks 10 minutes. Remove from pans; cool completely. Frost with Chocolate Butter Frosting.

✳ Lane Cake

This sweet, fruity cake was named for Emma Rylander Lane, in whose cookbook it first appeared in the late nineteenth century. Layers of white cake sandwich a rich filling liberally dosed with bourbon or brandy.

BEGIN: EARLY IN DAY   16 SERVINGS

8   egg whites, at room temperature
2   cups sugar
1   cup butter or margarine, softened
2¾   cups all-purpose flour
1   cup milk
1   tablespoon baking powder
½   teaspoon salt
1   teaspoon vanilla extract
     Lane Cake Filling*
     Candied red cherries

1. Preheat oven to 350°F. Grease and flour three 9-inch round cake pans.

2. In large bowl with mixer at high speed, beat egg whites until soft peaks form; gradually sprinkle in 1 cup sugar, 2 tablespoons at a time, beating until stiff peaks form. Set aside.

3. In another large bowl with mixer at low speed, beat remaining 1 cup sugar, butter, flour, milk, baking powder, salt and vanilla until mixed, constantly scraping bowl. At medium speed, beat 4 minutes more. Fold in reserved egg whites. Pour into prepared pans.

4. Bake 30 minutes or until toothpick inserted in center comes out clean. Cool in pans on wire racks 10 minutes. Remove from pans; cool completely. Prepare Lane Cake Filling. Assemble with filling between layers and on top. Garnish with cherries.

*Lane Cake Filling

8   egg yolks
1   cup sugar
½   cup butter or margarine, softened
⅓   cup bourbon or brandy
1   cup chopped pecans
1   cup shredded coconut
1   cup raisins
¾   cup chopped candied red cherries
1   teaspoon vanilla extract

In 2-quart saucepan with wire whisk, beat egg yolks and sugar until smooth. Stir in butter. Over low heat, cook until sugar is dissolved and mixture is thickened. Remove from heat. Stir in remaining ingredients. Cool to room temperature. Use to fill and top Lane Cake. Yields 4 cups.

✳ Jam Cake

This spice cake owes its special color and flavor to the jam in the batter. Jam cake is found in many regions of the country—Northeast, South, Midwest and West—where settlers found it appealing because it kept well and improved with age.

BEGIN: EARLY IN DAY   16 SERVINGS

6 eggs, separated, at room temperature
2 cups sugar
1 cup blackberry jam or preserves
1 cup butter or margarine, softened
2½ cups all-purpose flour
1 teaspoon baking soda
1 teaspoon ground cinnamon
1 teaspoon ground cloves
¾ teaspoon ground allspice
¾ cup buttermilk or sour milk
1 cup chopped walnuts
   Cream Cheese Frosting (see page 272)

1. Preheat oven to 350°F. Grease and flour three 9-inch round cake pans.

2. In medium bowl with mixer at high speed, beat egg whites until soft peaks form; gradually sprinkle in ½ cup sugar, 2 tablespoons at a time, beating until stiff peaks form. Set aside.

3. In large bowl with mixer at low speed, beat egg yolks, remaining 1½ cups sugar, jam, butter, flour, baking soda, cinnamon, cloves, allspice, buttermilk and walnuts until mixed, constantly scraping bowl. At medium speed, beat 3 minutes more. Fold in reserved egg whites. Pour into prepared pans.

4. Bake 35 minutes or until toothpick inserted in center comes out clean. Cool in pans on wire racks 10 minutes. Remove from pans; cool completely. Frost with Cream Cheese Frosting.

✳ Scripture Cake

Versions of this cake appeared in all regions of the United States during Colonial and pioneer times. What they all have in common is a recipe that refers to the Bible for the ingredients of a spicy cake studded with figs, raisins and almonds. Because the Bible mentions these foods more than once, each new version might send the cook back to the Bible for references. A typical recipe might call for Judges 5:25, Jeremiah 6:20, Exodus 16:31, Isaiah 10: 14, I Kings 4:22, Luke 14:34, Amos 4:5, I Kings 10:2, Judges 4:19, II Samuel 16:1, Nahum 3:12, and Numbers 17:8.

BEGIN: EARLY IN DAY   12 SERVINGS

½ cup butter or margarine, softened
¾ cup sugar
¼ cup honey
3 eggs
2 cups all-purpose flour
2 teaspoons baking powder
½ teaspoon ground cinnamon
¼ teaspoon ground cloves
⅛ teaspoon ground ginger
⅛ teaspoon salt
½ cup milk
1 cup raisins
1 cup chopped dried figs
1 cup chopped almonds

1. Preheat oven to 300°F. Grease and flour 9- by 5-inch loaf pan.

2. In large bowl with mixer at medium speed, cream butter until light and fluffy. Gradually beat in sugar and honey until well mixed, constantly scraping bowl. At low speed, beat in eggs until light and fluffy.

3. In medium bowl, combine flour, baking powder, cinnamon, cloves, ginger and salt. Add dry ingredients alternately with milk to creamed mixture, mixing well after each addition, occasionally scraping bowl with rubber spatula. Stir in raisins, figs and almonds. Pour batter into prepared pan.

4. Bake 2 hours or until toothpick inserted in center comes out clean. Cool in pan on wire rack 10 minutes. Remove from pan; cool completely.

❋ Boston Cream Pie

Not a pie at all, but a two-layer cake with a creamy filling, Boston Cream Pie is a classic New England dessert. There have been several spin-offs of this recipe, including George Washington Pie, filled with raspberry jam, and Martha Washington Pie, filled with both jelly and custard. The traditional dusting of confectioners' sugar is often replaced by a chocolate glaze like the one in this recipe.

BEGIN: EARLY IN DAY   12 SERVINGS

	Vanilla Cream Filling*
⅓	cup butter or margarine, softened
1	cup sugar
2	eggs, separated, at room temperature
½	teaspoon vanilla extract
1½	cups all-purpose flour
2	teaspoons baking powder
½	teaspoon salt
1	cup milk
	Chocolate Glaze*

1. Prepare Vanilla Cream Filling; chill. Preheat oven to 350°F. Grease and flour two 9-inch round cake pans.

2. In large bowl with mixer at medium speed, cream butter until light and fluffy. Gradually beat in sugar until well mixed, constantly scraping bowl. Beat in egg yolks, one at a time, beating well after each addition, occasionally scraping bowl. Add vanilla; mix well.

3. In small bowl, combine flour, baking powder and salt. Add dry ingredients alternately with milk to creamed mixture, mixing well after each addition, occasionally scraping bowl.

4. In small bowl with mixer at high speed, using clean beaters, beat egg whites until soft peaks form. Fold into batter; pour into prepared pans.

5. Bake 25 to 30 minutes until toothpick inserted in center comes out clean. Cool in pans on wire racks 10 minutes. Remove from pans; cool completely.

6. Spread Vanilla Cream Filling between cake layers. Spread top with warm Chocolate Glaze. Refrigerate until serving time.

*Vanilla Cream Filling

BEGIN: EARLY IN DAY

1	cup milk
⅓	cup sugar
2	tablespoons cornstarch
	Dash salt
2	egg yolks, beaten
1	teaspoon vanilla extract

1. In heavy, 2-quart saucepan with wire whisk or electric mixer, beat all ingredients except vanilla. Over medium heat, cook until mixture just boils, stirring constantly.

2. Remove from heat; stir in vanilla. Cover; chill. Yields 1¼ cups.

*Chocolate Glaze

BEGIN: 15 MINUTES AHEAD

2	tablespoons butter or margarine
1	square (1 ounce) unsweetened chocolate
1	cup confectioners' sugar
½	teaspoon vanilla extract
2	tablespoons hot water

In heavy, 1-quart saucepan over very low heat, melt butter and chocolate, stirring constantly. Stir in sugar, vanilla and enough hot water to make of spreading consistency. Remove from heat; beat well. Immediately spread on cake.

❄ Gingerbread

Dark with molasses, gingerbread was a favorite cake in Colonial times when white sugar was scarce and keeping quality was important. It was known as the prime refreshment during New England's Muster Day drills, annual day-long military training sessions for all able-bodied men. And it has been made by many ethnic groups, such as the Moravians and Germans. Serve it plain, with whipped cream or Lemon Sauce.

BEGIN: 1½ HOURS AHEAD   9 SERVINGS

¼ cup butter or margarine, softened
½ cup packed dark brown sugar
½ cup dark molasses
1 egg
2 cups all-purpose flour
½ teaspoon salt
1½ teaspoons baking powder
½ teaspoon baking soda
2 teaspoons ground ginger
1 teaspoon ground cinnamon
1 cup sour milk
   Lemon slices
   Lemon Sauce*

1. Preheat oven to 350°F. Grease 9- by 9-inch baking pan.

2. In large bowl with mixer at medium speed, cream butter until light and fluffy. Gradually beat in brown sugar and molasses until well mixed, constantly scraping bowl. At low speed, beat in egg until well mixed.

3. In medium bowl, combine flour, salt, baking powder, baking soda, ginger and cinnamon. Add dry ingredients alternately with milk to creamed mixture, mixing well after each addition, occasionally scraping bowl with rubber spatula. Turn into prepared pan.

4. Bake 35 to 40 minutes until toothpick inserted in center comes out clean. Cool in pan on wire rack 30 minutes. Cut into squares; garnish with lemon slices. Serve with Lemon Sauce.

TIP: To make 1 cup sour milk, measure 1 tablespoon vinegar into 1-cup measure. Fill measure to 1-cup mark with milk.

*Lemon Sauce

The smooth, tangy flavor of this sauce is a perfect contrast to sweet gingerbread, but it is also good spooned over fruit-flavored cakes.

BEGIN: 15 MINUTES AHEAD

½ cup sugar
2 tablespoons cornstarch
   Dash salt
1 cup water
2 tablespoons butter or margarine
1 teaspoon grated lemon peel
¼ cup lemon juice
   Dash ground nutmeg
   Slivered lemon peel

1. In small saucepan, combine sugar, cornstarch and salt; stir in water. Over medium-high heat, heat mixture just until boiling, stirring constantly.

2. Stir in butter, grated lemon peel, lemon juice and nutmeg. Remove from heat. Pour into serving bowl; garnish with slivered lemon peel. Serve at once over Gingerbread. Yields 1½ cups.

TO MICROWAVE: In 4-cup microwave-safe measure, combine all ingredients except butter. Beat with rotary beater until smooth. Microwave on HIGH 2 minutes. Beat well; stir in butter. Microwave on HIGH 2 to 2½ minutes until sauce is thickened.

❊ Lady Baltimore Cake

Another rich cake from the South, Lady Baltimore Cake earned its reputation in Charleston, South Carolina, rather than Baltimore. Owen Wister's 1906 novel Lady Baltimore, *set in Charleston, described this tempting cake in a way that immortalized it. Because the recipe uses half a dozen egg whites between the cake and frosting, someone created a yellow cake using the same number of yolks, mischievously dubbing it Lord Baltimore Cake.*

BEGIN: EARLY IN DAY   16 SERVINGS

4   egg whites, at room temperature
1½   cups sugar
2¼   cups all-purpose flour
¾   cup milk
½   cup shortening
1   tablespoon baking powder
½   teaspoon salt
½   teaspoon almond extract
⅓   cup chopped pecans
⅓   cup raisins, chopped
¼   cup dried figs, finely chopped
     Seven-Minute Frosting (see page 273)

1. Preheat oven to 375°F. Grease and flour two 9-inch round cake pans.

2. In small bowl with mixer at high speed, beat egg whites until soft peaks form; gradually sprinkle in ½ cup sugar, 2 tablespoons at a time, beating until stiff peaks form. Set aside.

3. In large bowl at low speed, beat remaining 1 cup sugar, flour, milk, shortening, baking powder, salt and almond extract until mixed, constantly scraping bowl. At medium speed, beat 3 minutes more. Fold in reserved egg whites. Pour into prepared pans.

4. Bake 25 minutes or until toothpick inserted in center comes out clean. Cool in pans on wire racks 10 minutes. Remove from pans; cool completely.

5. In small bowl, combine pecans, raisins and figs; set aside. Prepare Seven-Minute Frosting. Stir 1 cup frosting into reserved nut-fruit mixture; spread between cake layers. Spread remaining frosting on top and sides of cake.

❊ Tomato Soup Cake

Resourceful Americans have always made the most of every food available to them. This moist spice cake was first made with canned tomatoes, but the tomatoes were replaced by soup in the 1920s, not long after condensed tomato soup was introduced into the marketplace. Since that time, this basic recipe has changed very little, but it has been transformed into a fruitcake, pineapple upside-down cake and a microwave cake.

BEGIN: EARLY IN DAY   16 SERVINGS

2   cups all-purpose flour
1⅓   cups sugar
4   teaspoons baking powder
1   teaspoon baking soda
1½   teaspoons ground allspice
1   teaspoon ground cinnamon
½   teaspoon ground cloves
1   can (10¾ ounces) condensed tomato
     soup
½   cup shortening
2   eggs
¼   cup water
     Confectioners' sugar

1. Preheat oven to 350°F. Grease and flour 10-inch bundt pan.

2. Into large bowl, measure all ingredients except confectioners' sugar. With mixer at low speed, beat until well mixed, constantly scraping bowl with rubber spatula. At high speed, beat 4 minutes, occasionally scraping bowl. Pour into prepared pan.

3. Bake 1 hour or until toothpick inserted in cake comes out clean. Cool in pan on wire rack 10 minutes. Remove from pan; cool completely. Sprinkle with confectioners' sugar.

TOMATO SOUP LAYER CAKE: Preheat oven to 350°F. Grease and flour two 8-inch round cake pans. Prepare batter as above; pour into prepared pans. Bake 35 to 40 minutes. Cool in pans on wire racks 10 minutes. Remove from pans; cool completely. Frost with *Cream Cheese Frosting* (see page 272).

❋ Apple-Nut Cake

Pioneers planted apple orchards across the continent. John Chapman (Johnny Appleseed) established apple-tree nurseries from Pennsylvania to Indiana in the early 1800s. The apples in this cake contribute flavor and moistness; the buttery glaze adds sweetness and richness.

BEGIN: 2 HOURS AHEAD   12 SERVINGS

3   cups all-purpose flour
2   cups sugar
1   teaspoon baking powder
1   teaspoon baking soda
½   teaspoon salt
1½   cups salad oil
3   eggs
2   teaspoons vanilla extract
3   cups chopped, peeled and cored apples
1   cup chopped walnuts or pecans
½   cup packed brown sugar
¼   cup butter or margarine
2   tablespoons water
⅛   teaspoon ground nutmeg

1. Preheat oven to 350°F. Grease and flour 13-by 9-inch baking pan.

2. Into large bowl, measure first 8 ingredients. With mixer at low speed, beat until well mixed, constantly scraping bowl. With rubber spatula, fold in apples and nuts. Spread batter in prepared pan.

3. Bake 60 to 65 minutes until toothpick inserted in center comes out clean. Cool in pan on wire rack 10 minutes.

4. Meanwhile, in small saucepan over medium heat, heat brown sugar, butter, water and nutmeg to boiling; boil 1 minute. Spoon over warm cake in pan. Serve warm or cool.

❋ Pineapple Upside-Down Cake

A cast-iron skillet, or spider, was indispensable to the Colonial cook and to the pioneers who carried their skillets west for cooking over open fires. It is the traditional utensil for making upside-down cake. Most often made with pineapple, a Caribbean discovery, the cake grew in popularity in the 1940s when canned pineapple became readily available.

BEGIN: 1½ HOURS AHEAD   6 SERVINGS

¼   cup butter or margarine
½   cup packed brown sugar
1   can (8¼ ounces) pineapple slices
     Candied cherries
     Pecan or walnut halves
1   cup all-purpose flour
¾   cup sugar
1½   teaspoons baking powder
¼   teaspoon salt
¼   cup shortening
1   teaspoon vanilla extract
1   egg

1. Preheat oven to 350°F. In 8- by 8-inch baking pan or 9-inch ovensafe skillet, place butter; heat in oven until butter is melted. Sprinkle brown sugar over butter.

2. Meanwhile, drain pineapple slices, reserving juice. Add water to juice to make ½ cup liquid; set aside. Arrange fruit and nuts in decorative pattern in bottom of pan.

3. In small bowl, combine juice mixture and remaining ingredients. With mixer at low speed, beat until well mixed, constantly scraping bowl with rubber spatula. At high speed, beat 2 minutes, occasionally scraping bowl. Carefully spoon batter over fruit in prepared pan.

4. Bake 40 to 45 minutes until toothpick inserted in center comes out clean. Cool in pan on wire rack 10 minutes. Invert pan onto serving plate. Serve warm or cool.

APPLE UPSIDE-DOWN CAKE: Prepare as above but substitute *2 medium apples, peeled, cored and sliced,* for pineapple slices and *½ cup orange juice* for pineapple juice mixture. Omit candied cherries and nuts.

❋ Carrot Cake

A hearty full-flavored dessert, carrot cake has found a new generation of admirers in the past twenty years. Perhaps this phenomenon is due to the health food movement, but carrot cake interests more than just healthy eaters! Loosely based on traditional carrot tortes and breads from Europe, carrot cake has become thoroughly Americanized and can be found at fast-food outlets as well as bakeries and supermarkets.

BEGIN: 2½ HOURS AHEAD   16 SERVINGS

2   **cups all-purpose flour**
1⅓ **cups packed brown sugar**
4   **teaspoons baking powder**
1   **teaspoon baking soda**
½   **teaspoon ground allspice**
½   **teaspoon ground cinnamon**
½   **teaspoon ground nutmeg**
1   **can (10¾ ounces) condensed tomato soup**
½   **cup shortening**
2   **eggs**
¼   **cup honey**
1   **cup shredded carrots**
    Orange Glaze*

1. Preheat oven to 350°F. Grease and flour 10-inch bundt pan.

2. Into large bowl, measure all ingredients except carrots and Orange Glaze. With mixer at low speed, beat until well mixed, constantly scraping bowl with rubber spatula. At high speed, beat 4 minutes, occasionally scraping bowl. With rubber spatula, fold in carrots. Pour batter into prepared pan.

3. Bake 1 hour or until toothpick inserted in cake comes out clean. Cool in pan on wire rack 10 minutes. Remove from pan. Spoon Orange Glaze over warm cake. Serve warm or cool.

TIP: Place cake on wire rack in jelly-roll pan to catch excess glaze.

*Orange Glaze

½   **cup packed brown sugar**
¼   **cup orange juice**
1   **tablespoon butter or margarine**
2   **teaspoons light corn syrup**
¼   **cup sour cream**

1. In small saucepan over medium-high heat, heat sugar, orange juice, butter and corn syrup to boiling. Reduce heat to low; simmer 5 minutes. With wire whisk, blend in sour cream.

2. Spoon over warm cake; allow cake to absorb glaze. Repeat until all glaze has been used.

Carrot Cake, Orange Glaze

❋ Orange Chiffon Cake

The chiffon cake is a twentieth-century invention that substitutes oil for shortening in cake batter. The result is a light, moist cake that lends itself to many variations. This orange cake is especially popular in California and Florida. Notice the mixing method, which is peculiar to chiffon cakes.

BEGIN: EARLY IN DAY 16 SERVINGS

1 cup egg whites (7 to 8), at room
 temperature
½ teaspoon cream of tartar
1½ cups sugar
2½ cups cake flour
1 tablespoon grated orange peel
1 cup orange juice
½ cup salad oil
6 egg yolks
1 tablespoon baking powder
½ teaspoon salt
 Sunshine Glaze*

1. Preheat oven to 325°F. In large bowl with mixer at high speed, beat egg whites and cream of tartar until soft peaks form; gradually sprinkle in ½ cup sugar, 2 tablespoons at a time, beating just until sugar is dissolved and stiff peaks form; set aside.

2. In another large bowl with mixer at low speed, beat remaining 1 cup sugar, flour, orange peel, orange juice, oil, egg yolks, baking powder and salt until well mixed.

3. With rubber spatula, gently fold egg whites into orange mixture. Pour batter into ungreased 10-inch tube pan.

4. Bake 1¼ hours or until top springs back when lightly touched. Invert in pan on funnel; cool completely. With spatula, loosen cake from pan and remove to plate. Drizzle cake with Sunshine Glaze.

*Sunshine Glaze

1 cup confectioners' sugar
2 tablespoons orange juice

In small bowl, stir sugar and orange juice until smooth. Yields ½ cup.

❋ Election Cake

In eighteenth-century New England, cooks used bread dough to leaven cakes made with fruit, spice and liquor, then served the Election Cakes at town meetings. One of the first versions began with 30 quarts of flour; it must have been a crowd pleaser. Later, Election Cake came to be associated with election-day celebrations.

BEGIN: EARLY IN DAY 16 SERVINGS

1½ cups raisins
½ cup brandy
1 package active dry yeast
1 cup warm water (105° to 115°F.)
1 tablespoon sugar
4 cups all-purpose flour
¾ cup butter or margarine, softened
1 cup packed dark brown sugar
1 tablespoon grated lemon peel
1 teaspoon ground cinnamon
1 teaspoon ground nutmeg
½ teaspoon salt
¼ teaspoon ground cloves
2 eggs

1. In small bowl, cover raisins with brandy; set aside.

2. In medium bowl, sprinkle yeast over warm water; stir to dissolve. Stir in 1 tablespoon sugar and 1 cup flour until smooth. Cover with towel; let rise in warm place (80° to 85°F.), free from draft, until doubled, about 1 hour.

3. Grease 10-inch tube pan. In large bowl with mixer at medium speed, cream butter until fluffy. Beat in brown sugar, lemon peel, cinnamon, nutmeg, salt and cloves until well combined. Beat in eggs until mixture is light and fluffy.

4. Stir in raisin mixture, yeast mixture and remaining 3 cups flour; mix well. Turn dough into prepared pan. Cover with towel; let rise in warm place until doubled, about 1½ hours.

5. Bake at 350°F. about 45 minutes or until golden. Cool in pan on wire rack 20 minutes. Remove from pan; cool completely.

❋ Strawberry Shortcake

English settlers were amazed at the huge strawberries they found growing wild in the New World. The Indians were already cultivating them and mixing them with meal to make a strawberry bread. Traditional strawberry shortcake is a split biscuit filled and topped with sweetened strawberries. Use the same cake for other seasonal fruits such as peaches, blueberries and raspberries.

BEGIN: 45 MINUTES AHEAD   6 SERVINGS

2   pints strawberries
½   cup sugar
2   cups all-purpose flour
1   tablespoon sugar
1   tablespoon baking powder
½   teaspoon salt
½   cup shortening
½   cup milk
     Butter or margarine, softened
1   cup heavy cream, whipped

1. Preheat oven to 400°F. Grease 8-inch round cake pan.

2. Wash and hull strawberries; reserve 6 berries for garnish. With potato masher or fork, mash remaining berries lightly; sprinkle with ½ cup sugar. Let stand while preparing shortcake.

3. In large bowl, combine flour, remaining 1 tablespoon sugar, baking powder and salt. With pastry blender, cut in shortening until mixture resembles coarse crumbs. Add milk; with fork, mix just until mixture forms soft dough. Turn onto lightly floured surface; knead 8 to 10 times. Pat dough evenly into prepared pan.

3. Bake 15 to 20 minutes until golden. Invert shortcake onto platter; with long, sharp knife, carefully split hot shortcake horizontally. Spread both cut surfaces evenly with softened butter.

4. Onto bottom half, spoon half of sweetened strawberries; top with other cake half. Spoon remaining strawberries over top. Mound whipped cream over strawberries; garnish with reserved whole strawberries.

❋ Creamy Butter Frosting

Butter frosting is the favorite homemade frosting because it is quickly prepared and spreads easily. It can be flavored with everyday vanilla, chocolate and mocha and/or with lemon, orange and other fruit flavors. Add food coloring to correspond with the flavor or to decorate a cake.

BEGIN: 15 MINUTES AHEAD

½   cup butter or margarine, softened
1   package (16 ounces) confectioners' sugar
4   to 5 tablespoons milk
1   teaspoon vanilla extract
     Dash salt

In large bowl with mixer at medium speed, beat all ingredients until very smooth, adding more milk if necessary to make frosting of spreading consistency. Yields 2½ cups.

CHOCOLATE BUTTER FROSTING: Prepare as above but add *½ cup cocoa* and increase milk to 6 tablespoons.

MOCHA BUTTER FROSTING: Prepare as above but dissolve *2 tablespoons instant coffee crystals* in milk. Add *½ cup cocoa* and reduce vanilla to ½ teaspoon.

❋ Cream Cheese Frosting

Cream Cheese Frosting is for those who prefer a frosting with a tangy accent. Once rarely found in cookbooks, it is now preferred for spice cakes, particularly tomato soup cake and carrot cake.

BEGIN: 15 MINUTES AHEAD

1   package (8 ounces) cream cheese, softened
2   tablespoons milk
1   teaspoon vanilla extract
4   cups confectioners' sugar

In medium bowl with mixer at medium speed, beat cream cheese, milk and vanilla until fluffy. Gradually beat in sugar until frosting is smooth and of spreading consistency. Yields 3 cups.

❊ Seven-Minute Frosting

This sweet white frosting is wonderfully adaptable. With fruit and nuts added, it is the filling for Lady Baltimore Cake. Sprinkled with coconut, it is the traditional favorite for coconut cakes. Made with brown sugar instead of granulated sugar, it goes well with spice cakes. And just as it is, it makes a good complement for chocolate, cherry, white and angel food cakes.

BEGIN: 30 MINUTES AHEAD

1½ **cups sugar**
¼ **teaspoon cream of tartar**
⅛ **teaspoon salt**
¼ **cup water**
2 **egg whites, at room temperature**
1 **teaspoon vanilla extract**

1. In double-boiler top over simmering water, with mixer at high speed, beat sugar, cream of tartar, salt, water and egg whites until frosting forms soft peaks, about 7 minutes.

2. Remove from heat. Add vanilla; continue beating until mixture forms stiff peaks, scraping bowl occasionally. Yields 3½ cups.

❊ Coconut-Pecan Topping

Broiled toppings are perfect for cakes still warm from the oven. Because you do not have to wait for the cake to cool, you can begin baking the cake as little as an hour before you serve it. Coconut-Pecan Topping and its variations make a cake special without making it overly sweet. Try this topping on Hot Milk Sponge Cake (see page 261).

BEGIN: 15 MINUTES AHEAD

2 **tablespoons butter or margarine, softened**
⅓ **cup packed brown sugar**
½ **teaspoon vanilla extract**
 Dash salt
½ **cup flaked coconut**
½ **cup chopped pecans**
1 **8- or 9-inch cake layer**

1. In small bowl, stir together butter and sugar until well combined. Stir in vanilla, salt, coconut and pecans until well mixed.

2. Spread mixture onto warm cake in pan. Broil 4 inches from heat 2 to 3 minutes until topping is lightly toasted. Serve warm or cool.

CHERRY-PECAN TOPPING: Prepare as above but substitute *½ cup chopped candied cherries* for coconut.

BUTTER-RUM TOPPING: Prepare as above but substitute *½ teaspoon rum flavoring* for vanilla.

❊ Sweetened Whipped Cream

Sweetened Whipped Cream is an all-purpose garnish for fancy cakes or homespun desserts. Try the coconut and chocolate variations for a change of pace on angel food or yellow cake.

BEGIN: 15 MINUTES AHEAD

2 **cups heavy cream, chilled**
½ **cup confectioners' sugar**
1 **teaspoon vanilla extract**

In small bowl with mixer at medium speed, beat cream until soft peaks form; gradually sprinkle in sugar, 2 tablespoons at a time, until stiff peaks form. Fold in vanilla. Refrigerate until serving time. Yields 4 cups.

COCONUT WHIPPED CREAM: Prepare as above but substitute *½ teaspoon almond extract* for vanilla; fold in *1 cup flaked coconut*.

CHOCOLATE WHIPPED CREAM: Prepare as above but mix confectioners' sugar with *½ cup cocoa* before adding to cream.

TIP: To stabilize Whipped Cream Frosting, in cup, sprinkle *1 teaspoon unflavored gelatin* over *2 tablespoons cold water.* Place cup over simmering water until gelatin is dissolved, stirring occasionally; cool to lukewarm. Gradually beat into cream before adding sugar.

Chocolate Chip Cookies, Lemon Bars, Pinwheel Cookies, Peanut Butter Cookies

COOKIES

Although Americans make English tea cakes, Scottish shortbread and Scandinavian spritz, we call them all cookies, after the Dutch *koetje,* or little cake. Like many other immigrant groups, the Dutch brought their cookie recipes with them when they settled in what is now New York.

Early settlers often had to improvise on their traditional cookie recipes when familiar ingredients could not be found. Housewives, forced to cook without butter, used cinnamon and ginger to cover the strong flavors of animal fats. The scarcity of sugar made molasses and honey popular sweeteners. When Old World nuts were not available, bakers turned to American hickories, walnuts and pecans.

As new foods came along, cookie makers included them in their favorite recipes. That's how peanut butter and chocolate came to be used in cookie making. American cookbooks over the years have included such unlikely cookie ingredients as potato chips, breakfast cereals, carrots, hard-cooked eggs, pepper, ketchup and tomato soup.

At Christmas, American cookie baking reaches its peak. Then, cooks pull out recipes and cookie molds that have been in their families for generations, and prepare their grandmothers' and great-grandmothers' traditional Christmas cookies. Bakers start months ahead making varieties of long-keeping little sweets. Often, the whole family takes part, with children cutting out star and bell shapes, then helping with the decorations.

But Christmas has no monopoly on cookies. Valentine's Day has its heart-shaped sugar cookies; Halloween has its pumpkin-shaped ones. And, every day, cookies are packed in lunch boxes, sold at bake sales, taken along on hikes and picnics. We buy cookies at supermarkets, at bakeries and now in specialty shops that produce nothing but cookies. But no matter how trendy cookies may become, none can equal the flavor and emotional satisfaction of those made at home.

❋ Sugar Cookies

When the rolling pin and cookie cutters emerge from storage, it is a good bet that a festive occasion is approaching. Rolled sugar cookies have always been a favorite for celebrating Christmas and other holidays. Children love the special shapes and enjoy cutting out little Christmas trees and stars. If you prefer soft cookies, roll the dough out to the thicker measurement; for crisper cookies, make them thin.

BEGIN: EARLY IN DAY   36 COOKIES

¾ cup butter or margarine, softened
1   cup confectioners' sugar
1   egg
2   tablespoons milk
1   teaspoon vanilla extract
½   teaspoon almond extract
2   cups all-purpose flour
1½ teaspoons baking powder
½   teaspoon salt
     Sugar

1. In large bowl with mixer at medium speed, cream butter and confectioners' sugar. Beat in egg, milk, vanilla and almond extract until well mixed, occasionally scraping bowl. Stir in flour, baking powder and salt until well mixed. Cover with plastic wrap; chill several hours or overnight.

2. Preheat oven to 375°F. On lightly floured surface, with floured rolling pin, roll chilled dough ⅛ inch to ¼ inch thick. With floured 2½-inch cookie cutters, cut dough into desired shapes. Sprinkle with sugar. Reroll trimmings and cut more cookies. Place cookies 1 inch apart on cookie sheets.

3. Bake 8 to 10 minutes until cookies are lightly browned. Immediately remove cookies to wire racks; cool.

TIP: Shape dough into 1½-inch balls instead of rolling it out. Using a flat-bottomed glass dipped in sugar, flatten balls on cookie sheets.

❋ Shortbread

Made from only three ingredients, Shortbread is one of the simplest cookies you can bake, with a buttery flavor that makes it a favorite among adults as well as children. The recipe came to America with the first settlers from Scotland. American cooks added native American hickory nuts or pecans for additional flavor.

BEGIN: 2 HOURS AHEAD   24 COOKIES

2   cups all-purpose flour
½   cup confectioners' sugar
1   cup butter or margarine, cut into pieces
2   tablespoons sugar

1. Preheat oven to 325°F. In medium bowl, stir together flour and confectioners' sugar. With fingers, rub butter into flour mixture until well combined. Knead until dough holds together. Form into a ball. Divide dough in half.

2. On each of 2 cookie sheets, pat half of dough to 9-inch round. Prick all over with fork.

3. Bake 20 to 25 minutes until no imprint remains when shortbread is lightly touched with finger. Sprinkle with sugar; cut each into 12 wedges while warm. Cool completely on pan on wire rack.

NUT SHORTBREAD: Prepare as above but add *1 cup finely chopped hickory nuts or pecans* along with flour.

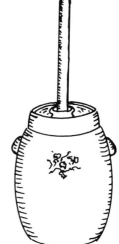

❋ Oatmeal-Raisin Cookies

Oats are a popular food in England and Scotland, but it took New World ingenuity to use them in cookies. Oatmeal cookies seem especially wholesome—appealing to the soul as well as to the appetite. Embellished with spices, nuts, coconut, dried fruit, candied fruit or chocolate chips, they remain an American classic.

BEGIN: 1 HOUR AHEAD   36 COOKIES

¾ cup shortening
1½ cups packed brown sugar
2 eggs
¼ cup milk
1 teaspoon vanilla extract
2 cups uncooked quick-cooking oats
1 cup all-purpose flour
½ teaspoon salt
½ teaspoon baking soda
½ cup raisins
½ cup chopped walnuts

1. Preheat oven to 375°F. In large bowl with mixer at medium speed, beat shortening, brown sugar, eggs, milk and vanilla until well mixed, occasionally scraping bowl. Stir in oats, flour, salt and baking soda until well mixed. Stir in raisins and nuts. Drop by rounded tablespoonfuls 2 inches apart onto cookie sheets.

2. Bake 10 to 12 minutes until cookies are lightly browned. Immediately remove cookies to wire racks; cool.

OATMEAL-CINNAMON COOKIES: Prepare as above but add *1 teaspoon ground cinnamon* with dry ingredients in step 1.

OATMEAL-COCONUT COOKIES: Prepare as above but substitute *¾ cup flaked coconut* for ½ cup raisins and ½ cup chopped nuts in step 1.

OATMEAL-FRUIT COOKIES: Prepare as above but substitute *½ cup chopped mixed candied fruit* for ½ cup raisins in step 1.

OATMEAL-CHOCOLATE CHIP COOKIES: Prepare as above but substitute *1 package (6 ounces) semisweet chocolate pieces* for ½ cup raisins in step 1.

❋ Hermits

Recipes for Hermits abound in old cookbooks. Some are bars; some are soft drop cookies. Some are frosted, some are glazed, and others are sprinkled with confectioners' sugar. They can be made with milk, sour cream, coffee, fruit juice or molasses. What they all have in common is some sort of dried fruit, usually raisins, and a light, spicy flavor.

BEGIN: EARLY IN DAY   48 COOKIES

½ cup shortening
¾ cup packed dark brown sugar
1 egg
⅓ cup milk
2 cups all-purpose flour
2 teaspoons baking powder
½ teaspoon salt
½ teaspoon ground cinnamon
½ teaspoon ground nutmeg
¼ teaspoon ground cloves
1½ cups raisins
1 cup confectioners' sugar
2 tablespoons milk
½ teaspoon vanilla extract

1. Preheat oven to 375°F. In large bowl with mixer at medium speed, cream shortening and brown sugar. Beat in egg and ⅓ cup milk until well mixed, occasionally scraping bowl. Stir in flour, baking powder, salt, cinnamon, nutmeg and cloves until well mixed. Stir in raisins. Drop by rounded teaspoonfuls 1 inch apart onto cookie sheets.

2. Bake 10 to 12 minutes until cookies are lightly browned. Immediately remove cookies to wire racks; cool slightly.

3. In small bowl, stir together confectioners' sugar, 2 tablespoons milk and vanilla; spoon over warm cookies to glaze.

TIP: Place cooling rack in jelly-roll pan to catch excess glaze.

✳ Joe Froggers

Molasses cookies have always been popular in the United States, because molasses was a less expensive, less scarce alternative to sugar in Colonial times. Joe Froggers is the name given to these huge molasses cookies, attributed to a possibly mythical Massachusetts man called Uncle Joe. He made cookies as large as lily pads and the large frogs that perched on them. Form the dough into smaller rounds to make gingersnaps, another American favorite.

BEGIN: EARLY IN DAY   24 COOKIES

¾ cup shortening
½ cup sugar
1 cup molasses
¼ cup milk
4 cups all-purpose flour
1 teaspoon salt
1 teaspoon baking soda
2 teaspoons ground ginger
½ teaspoon ground cinnamon
½ teaspoon ground cloves

1. In large bowl with mixer at medium speed, beat shortening, sugar, molasses and milk until well mixed, occasionally scraping bowl. Stir in flour, salt, soda and spices until well mixed. Cover with plastic wrap; chill several hours or overnight.

2. Preheat oven to 375°F. On lightly floured surface, with floured rolling pin, roll chilled dough ¼ inch thick. With floured 3-inch round cookie cutter, cut dough into large rounds. Reroll trimmings and cut more cookies. Place cookies 2 inches apart on cookie sheets.

3. Bake 10 to 12 minutes until cookies are set. Immediately remove cookies to wire racks; cool.

GINGERSNAPS: Prepare as above in step 1. Preheat oven to 375°F. Lightly grease cookie sheets. With hands, shape dough into ¾-inch balls; roll each in *sugar* to coat. Place 2 inches apart on prepared cookie sheets. With flat-bottomed glass, flatten each ball of dough to ⅛-inch thickness, dipping glass in sugar as necessary to prevent sticking. Bake 8 minutes or until cookies are set. Immediately remove cookies to wire racks; cool. Yields 120.

✳ Snickerdoodles

Although Snickerdoodles probably originated with the Pennsylvania Dutch, recipes for these crisp, cinnamon cookies were found in many regional cookbooks by the mid-1800s. Historians believe that the whimsical name was used simply because it was fun to say.

BEGIN: 2 HOURS AHEAD   60 COOKIES

¾ cup shortening
1 cup sugar
2 eggs
1 teaspoon vanilla extract
2¼ cups all-purpose flour
1½ teaspoons cream of tartar
¾ teaspoon baking soda
¼ teaspoon salt
¼ cup finely chopped pecans or walnuts
2 tablespoons sugar
1 teaspoon ground cinnamon

1. Preheat oven to 375°F. In large bowl with mixer at medium speed, beat shortening, 1 cup sugar, eggs and vanilla until well mixed, occasionally scraping bowl. Stir in flour, cream of tartar, baking soda and salt until well mixed. In small bowl, combine nuts, 2 tablespoons sugar and cinnamon.

2. With hands, shape dough into 1-inch balls. Roll each in nut mixture to coat. Place cookies 2 inches apart on cookie sheets.

3. Bake 8 to 10 minutes until cookies are flattened and lightly browned. Immediately remove cookies to wire racks; cool.

✳ Chocolate Chip Cookies

If there is one most favored cookie in this country, it must be this one. Ruth Wakefield of the Toll House Restaurant in Massachusetts chopped up a bar of semisweet chocolate and added it to a batch of cookie dough. She was surprised that the chocolate did not melt into the dough, but she was delighted by the results. That "mistake" led to commercial production of the chips now used to make chocolate chip cookies.

BEGIN: 2 HOURS AHEAD   96 COOKIES

1 cup butter or margarine, softened
¾ cup sugar
¾ cup packed brown sugar
2 eggs
1 teaspoon vanilla extract
2¼ cups all-purpose flour
1 teaspoon salt
1 teaspoon baking soda
1 package (12 ounces) semisweet-chocolate
   pieces
2 cups chopped walnuts or pecans

1. Preheat oven to 375°F. In large bowl with mixer at medium speed, cream butter with sugars. Beat in eggs and vanilla until well mixed, occasionally scraping bowl. Stir in flour, salt and baking soda until well mixed. Stir in chocolate pieces and nuts. Drop by rounded teaspoonfuls 2 inches apart onto cookie sheets.

2. Bake 10 to 12 minutes until cookies are lightly browned. Immediately remove cookies to wire racks; cool.

✳ Rosy Rocks

The name of these spicy cookies refers not to their texture, but to their lumpy, rocklike appearance. Very popular around the turn of the century, there are countless variations of rocks. This unusual recipe includes tomato soup, which gives the cookies a rosy color. They keep well, so recipes for them nearly always yield at least 100 cookies.

BEGIN: 3 HOURS AHEAD   108 COOKIES

¾ cup butter or margarine, softened
1 cup sugar
2 eggs
1 cup all-purpose flour
1 teaspoon baking powder
½ teaspoon baking soda
½ teaspoon salt
2 teaspoons ground cinnamon
1 teaspoon ground nutmeg
1 can (10¾ ounces) condensed tomato
   soup
3 cups uncooked quick-cooking oats
2 cups raisins, chopped
1 cup chopped walnuts

1. Preheat oven to 350°F. In large bowl with mixer at medium speed, cream butter and sugar. Beat in eggs until well mixed, occasionally scraping bowl.

2. In medium bowl, combine flour, baking powder, soda, salt, cinnamon and nutmeg. Add dry ingredients alternately with soup to creamed mixture, mixing well after each addition. Stir in oats, raisins and nuts. Drop by rounded teaspoonfuls 1 inch apart onto cookie sheets.

3. Bake 15 minutes or until lightly browned. Immediately remove cookies to wire racks; cool.

✳ Benne Seed Wafers

Slaves from Africa carried with them some of the foods of their native land, such as sesame seed. Called benne by the Africans, the seeds were thought to bring good luck and good health, and slaves scattered them among the other crops for good fortune. These delicate cookies have become a Southern classic.

BEGIN: 2 HOURS AHEAD   48 COOKIES

¾ cup sesame seed
½ cup butter or margarine, softened
1 cup packed light brown sugar
1 egg
1 teaspoon vanilla extract
1 cup all-purpose flour
¼ teaspoon baking powder
¼ teaspoon salt

1. Preheat oven to 325°F. On jelly-roll pan, spread out sesame seed. Toast in oven 15 minutes until lightly browned. Cool.

2. Meanwhile, in large bowl with mixer at medium speed, cream butter and sugar. Beat in egg and vanilla until well mixed, occasionally scraping bowl. Stir in toasted sesame seed, flour, baking powder and salt until well mixed. Drop by teaspoonfuls 2 inches apart onto cookie sheets.

3. Bake 10 to 12 minutes until lightly browned. Cool on cookie sheets 1 minute; remove cookies to wire racks to cool completely.

LACE BENNE SEED WAFERS: Prepare as above but increase butter or margarine to 1 cup. Cookies will spread and become thin and lacy.

❄ Meringue Cookies

These cookies are descended from sixteenth-century Italian confections made of egg whites, sugar and almonds; the recipe was brought to America by French settlers in Louisiana. Adapt this recipe to suit your taste by substituting chocolate, nuts or fruit for the coconut. Or make it an all-American treat by using two native ingredients: chocolate chips and peanuts.

BEGIN: 2 HOURS AHEAD   24 COOKIES

2   egg whites, at room temperature
     Dash salt
²/₃ cup sugar
1   cup shredded coconut
1   teaspoon vanilla extract

1. Preheat oven to 250°F. Lightly grease large cookie sheet. In small bowl with mixer at high speed, beat egg whites and salt until soft peaks form. Beating at high speed, gradually sprinkle in sugar, 2 tablespoons at a time, beating until stiff peaks form.

2. With rubber spatula, fold in coconut and vanilla extract. Drop mixture by rounded teaspoonfuls about 1 inch apart onto prepared cookie sheet. Bake 45 to 55 minutes until dry. Remove cookies to wire racks; cool.

TIP: Substitute 1 cup semisweet-chocolate pieces, chopped nuts or candied fruit for coconut. Or, use a combination of any of these totaling 1 cup.

❄ Refrigerator Cookies

When refrigeration became common in American households, some clever cookie baker thought of chilling the dough in cylinder shapes, then slicing the cookie dough to make thin, round cookies. The convenience of this method quickly caught on, and today many cooks keep a roll of dough in their refrigerators or freezers so they can have warm, fresh cookies at a few minutes' notice.

BEGIN: EARLY IN DAY   96 COOKIES

1   cup butter or margarine, softened
1   cup sugar
½   cup packed light brown sugar
1   egg
1   teaspoon vanilla or almond extract
2   cups all-purpose flour
¼   teaspoon salt
1   cup finely chopped almonds or pecans

1. In large bowl with mixer at medium speed, cream butter and sugars until light and fluffy. Beat in egg and extract until well mixed, occasionally scraping bowl. Stir in flour, salt and nuts until well mixed.

2. Shape dough into rolls about 1½ inches in diameter. Wrap in waxed paper; refrigerate until firm, at least 4 hours.

3. Preheat oven to 375°F. Cut rolls into ¼-inch-thick slices. Place slices 1 inch apart on cookie sheets. Bake 8 to 10 minutes until lightly browned. Immediately remove cookies to wire racks; cool.

SPICE COOKIES: Prepare as above but add *1 teaspoon ground cinnamon, ½ teaspoon ground nutmeg and ¼ teaspoon ground allspice* along with sugar.

PINWHEEL COOKIES: Prepare dough as above; divide dough in half. Add *2 squares (1 ounce each) semisweet chocolate, melted and cooled,* to one half of the dough, mixing well. Divide each portion of the dough in half. On waxed paper covered with *confectioners' sugar,* with lightly sugared rolling pin, roll one portion of light dough to 12- by 6-inch rectangle. Repeat rolling with one portion of dark dough. Invert dark dough onto light; peel off top paper. Trim doughs to same size. Starting with long end, roll doughs jelly-roll fashion, peeling back waxed paper while rolling; wrap. Repeat rolling and wrapping with remaining dough; refrigerate until firm, about 4 hours. Slice and bake as directed above.

LEMON COOKIES: Prepare as above but add *2 teaspoons grated lemon peel* and omit vanilla or almond extract.

CHOCOLATE COOKIES: Prepare as above but add *4 squares (1 ounce each) semisweet chocolate, melted and cooled,* along with egg.

SPICY SPRITZ: Prepare as above but omit almond extract and stir in *1 teaspoon ground cinnamon* and *½ teaspoon ground nutmeg* along with flour.

LEMON SPRITZ: Prepare as above but omit almond extract and stir in *1 teaspoon grated lemon peel* along with eggs.

❈ Spritz

Swedish immigrants brought cookie presses for making buttery Spritz when they came to America. Now these cookies are popular all over, often with the addition of chocolate, spices or fruit peels.

BEGIN: 2 HOURS AHEAD — 60 COOKIES

Spritz

1 cup butter or margarine, softened
½ cup sugar
2 eggs
1 teaspoon vanilla extract
½ teaspoon almond extract
2½ cups all-purpose flour
Candied fruit (optional)
Colored sugars (optional)

1. Preheat oven to 375°F. In large bowl with mixer at medium speed, cream butter and sugar. Beat in eggs, vanilla and almond extract until well mixed, occasionally scraping bowl. Stir in flour until well mixed.

2. Using cookie press fitted with desired shape, press dough onto cookie sheets, about ½ inch apart. Decorate with candied fruit and colored sugars.

3. Bake 8 to 10 minutes until edges of cookies are lightly browned and cookies are set. Immediately remove cookies to wire racks; cool.

CHOCOLATE SPRITZ: Prepare as above but omit almond extract and stir in *3 squares (1 ounce each) semisweet chocolate, melted and cooled,* along with eggs.

❋ Peanut Butter Cookies

Of all the American innovations in cuisine, peanut butter is one of the most popular at home and the least understood abroad. Invented in 1890 by a Midwestern doctor, it was a health food: a high-protein spread that was easy to digest. Today, the peanut butter and jelly sandwich is in lunch boxes all over the country, and peanut butter cookies are among our favorite snacks. All told, Americans eat about 500 million pounds of peanut butter each year.

BEGIN: 2 HOURS AHEAD   48 COOKIES

¾ cup creamy or chunky peanut butter
½ cup butter or margarine, softened
½ cup sugar
½ cup packed brown sugar
2   eggs
1½ cups all-purpose flour
1   teaspoon baking powder

1. Preheat oven to 375°F. In large bowl with mixer at medium speed, cream peanut butter and butter. Beat in sugars and eggs until well mixed, occasionally scraping bowl. Stir in flour and baking powder until well mixed.

2. With hands, shape dough into 1½-inch balls. Place 1 inch apart on cookie sheets. Dip a fork into flour and press deeply across top of each cookie; repeat in opposite direction to make crisscross pattern.

3. Bake 8 to 10 minutes until cookies are lightly browned. Immediately remove cookies to wire racks; cool.

PEANUT BUTTER AND JELLY COOKIES: Prepare dough as above and form into 1½-inch balls. Place balls 1 inch apart on cookie sheets. Using a flat-bottomed glass dipped in sugar, flatten each ball. Top each cookie with ¼ *teaspoon jelly;* bake as directed.

❋ Thumbprint Cookies

These Scandinavian cookies are most popular in the Midwest, where many Scandinavians settled. Children love to help make them by pushing their thumbs into the balls of dough to make indentations for filling.

BEGIN: 2 HOURS AHEAD   48 COOKIES

1   cup butter or margarine, softened
½ cup packed brown sugar
1   egg
2   cups all-purpose flour
⅛ teaspoon salt
1   cup finely chopped almonds or pecans
½ cup jam or jelly

1. Preheat oven to 375°F. In medium bowl with mixer at medium speed, cream butter and sugar. Beat in egg until well mixed, occasionally scraping bowl. Stir in flour and salt until well mixed.

2. With hands, shape dough into 1-inch balls. Roll balls in nuts. Place 1 inch apart on cookie sheets. With thumb, make deep indentation in center of each ball.

3. Bake 8 to 10 minutes until cookies are lightly colored. Spoon about ½ teaspoon jam into center of each. Bake 2 minutes more. Immediately remove cookies to wire racks; cool.

❋ Fudgy Brownies

Brownies are as American as the chocolate that gives them their rich flavor. There are hundreds of recipes for these delectable bar cookies; they can be made with chocolate syrup, cocoa, chocolate chips, or even without chocolate at all. But the most ferocious debate is about their texture: should they be fudgy or cakelike?

Begin: 2 hours ahead   16 Brownies

1   cup butter or margarine
3   squares (1 ounce each) unsweetened
       chocolate
1½ cups sugar
3   eggs
1   cup all-purpose flour
1   teaspoon vanilla extract
¼   teaspoon salt
1   cup chopped walnuts or pecans

1. Preheat oven to 350°F. Grease 9- by 9-inch baking pan. In 3-quart saucepan over very low heat, melt butter and chocolate, stirring constantly; remove from heat.

2. With wooden spoon, stir in sugar. Add eggs, one at a time, beating until well blended after each addition. Stir in flour, vanilla and salt; mix well. Stir in nuts. Pour into prepared pan.

3. Bake 40 minutes or until toothpick inserted near center comes out clean. Cool in pan on wire rack; cut into squares.

Fudgy Brownies

❋ Cakelike Brownies

As you can see by comparing the two brownie recipes, the cakelike brownies are less chocolaty than the fudgy ones, and are made by a slightly different method. If you wish to gild the lily, ice them with a chocolate frosting.

Begin: 2 hours ahead   16 Brownies

½ cup butter or margarine
2 squares (1 ounce each) unsweetened chocolate
2 eggs
1 cup sugar
¾ cup all-purpose flour
½ teaspoon baking powder
¼ teaspoon salt
1 cup chopped walnuts or pecans

1. Preheat oven to 350°F. Grease 9- by 9-inch baking pan. In small saucepan over very low heat, melt butter and chocolate, stirring constantly; remove from heat.

2. Meanwhile, in small bowl with mixer at high speed, beat eggs and sugar until light and fluffy. Stir in chocolate mixture. With wooden spoon, stir in flour, baking powder and salt; mix well. Stir in nuts. Pour into prepared pan.

3. Bake 30 to 35 minutes until toothpick inserted near center comes out clean. Cool in pan on wire rack; cut into squares.

❋ Butterscotch Brownies

Butterscotch Brownies, chewy bar cookies with a butterscotch flavor, have the size, shape and texture of a chocolate brownie, without the chocolate. These chewy bar cookies satisfy nearly any sweet tooth.

Begin: 2 hours ahead   16 Brownies

½ cup butter or margarine
2 cups packed brown sugar
2 eggs, beaten
2 teaspoons vanilla extract
1 cup all-purpose flour
¼ teaspoon salt
1 cup chopped walnuts or pecans

1. Preheat oven to 350°F. Grease 9- by 9-inch baking pan. In 3-quart saucepan over low heat, melt butter. Stir in sugar; cook until mixture bubbles, stirring constantly. Remove from heat; cool to lukewarm.

2. Beat in eggs and vanilla until smooth. Stir in flour, salt and nuts; mix well. Pour into prepared pan.

3. Bake 35 to 40 minutes until toothpick inserted near center comes out clean. Cool in pan on wire rack; cut into squares.

❋ Lemon Bars

The recipe for fresh-tasting, lemony squares has been passed from cook to cook, becoming a kind of folk classic. You will find it in many of the cookbooks published by women's clubs and church groups as fund raisers. Perhaps the key to the cookies' success is the simplicity of the recipe.

Begin: early in day   36 Bars

1   **cup butter or margarine, softened**
½   **cup confectioners' sugar**
2¼   **cups all-purpose flour**
4   **eggs**
2   **cups sugar**
1   **teaspoon baking powder**
1   **tablespoon grated lemon peel**
¼   **cup lemon juice**
     Confectioners' sugar

1. Preheat oven to 350°F. In large bowl with mixer at medium speed, beat butter, ½ cup confectioners' sugar and 2 cups flour until well mixed. Press mixture into 13- by 9-inch baking pan. Bake 15 to 20 minutes until golden.

2. Meanwhile, in same bowl with mixer at medium speed, beat eggs with sugar until well mixed. Beat in remaining ¼ cup flour, baking powder, lemon peel and lemon juice until smooth; pour over baked layer.

3. Bake 25 to 30 minutes until lightly browned. Cool slightly in pan on wire rack; sprinkle with confectioners' sugar. Cool completely; cut into bars.

❋ Bourbon Balls

Not only is our native bourbon the indispensable ingredient in Mint Juleps, but its flavor is prized in cakes, pies and cookies. Southern pecans add crunch to these no-bake Bourbon Balls. Originally made from stale cake crumbs, Bourbon Balls can be made with vanilla wafers even when you do not have leftover cake. Because they keep well, they are popular at Christmas.

Begin: 3 days ahead   36 Balls

60   **vanilla wafers (2½ cups crumbs)**
1   **cup finely chopped pecans**
2   **tablespoons cocoa**
¼   **cup dark corn syrup**
¼   **cup bourbon, brandy or rum**
     Sugar or confectioners' sugar

1. In covered blender container at medium speed, blend cookies, ¼ at a time, until finely crumbed; or place cookies in strong plastic bag and roll fine with rolling pin.

2. In medium bowl, combine crumbs, nuts and cocoa. Stir in corn syrup and bourbon. With hands, shape dough into 1-inch balls; roll in sugar or confectioners' sugar to coat. Cover tightly; store 3 or 4 days before serving.

Tip: When ready to serve, roll cookies in additional sugar or confectioners' sugar.

❋ Seven-Layer Bars

Called Seven-Layer Bars or Hello Dollies, these are a cross between a cookie and a candy, easy to bake and sinfully rich. Be sure to cut the bars very small, because they are very sweet.

Begin: early in day   48 Bars

½   **cup butter or margarine**
1½   **cups graham cracker crumbs**
1   **cup shredded coconut**
1   **can (14 ounces) sweetened condensed milk**
1   **package (6 ounces) semisweet-chocolate pieces**
1   **package (6 ounces) butterscotch-flavored pieces**
1   **cup chopped pecans, walnuts or peanuts**

1. Preheat oven to 350°F. In 13- by 9-inch baking pan, place butter; heat in oven until butter is melted. Sprinkle with graham cracker crumbs; spread evenly in bottom of pan. Sprinkle with coconut. Pour sweetened condensed milk evenly over coconut. Sprinkle with chocolate pieces, butterscotch pieces and nuts. Press gently to compact mixture.

2. Bake 25 to 30 minutes until mixture is set. Cool in pan on wire rack; cut into small bars.

Lollipops, Maple Syrup Candy, Apricot Leather, Butter Mints, Pralines

CANDIES

Although candy was first made thousands of years ago, it was quite different from the sweets we know today. Based on honey, the most common sweetener of the time, it was flavored with spices and herbs, and only the very rich could afford it.

American colonists were fond of sweets, but candy was scarce. American Indians taught the Europeans to make maple candy by pouring hot syrup over clean snow. The Indians also had chewing gums of resin from the spruce and chicle from the sapodilla tree.

Through the centuries candy has changed as new foods were added to the world pantry. Most important to the candy of today was the discovery of sugar cane and how to refine it. Europeans had sugar more than a thousand years ago, but it was so scarce that it was considered a spice. Not until the seventeenth century was sugar available to people other than nobility or apothecaries.

Another ingredient that changed candymaking is chocolate. Brought to Europe from Central America in the sixteenth century, the Europeans sweetened it and flavored beverages with it, but it was not used in candy until the nineteenth century, when Daniel Peter of Switzerland introduced milk chocolate to the world.

Candies and chewing gum first were produced commercially about the same time; drugstores and general stores became the first retail outlets. Penny candy became a popular treat for children, including such confections as gumdrops, taffy, licorice and hard candies.

Many folks began making confections in the home, but it required a great deal of expertise: keen judgment of a syrup's consistency, a strong arm for beating fudge or divinity, and an ability to adapt to changing ingredients. Nonetheless, home candymaking flourished, and often became a family or social event; your grandmother may be able to tell you about a party where the entertainment was pulling taffy, then eating it.

Is it worth the bother to make candy at home? Yes, certainly, now that we have mechanical mixers and reliable thermometers. We are assured of having sweets made with the best butter, cream and chocolate, and it is fun to do. When we pull taffy or break peanut brittle into pieces, we feel a kinship with our American forefathers who had to work for their sweet treats.

❋ Apricot Leather

Fruit leathers are popular with hikers and backpackers, who appreciate their light weight and the concentrated energy they provide. Originally, fruit leathers were made by drying fruit butters on large trays in the sun in order to preserve the fruit through the winter. Today, we use the oven to reduce the drying time.

BEGIN: EARLY IN DAY

½   pound dried apricots
1   cup water
¼   cup sugar

1. In 1-quart saucepan over medium-high heat, heat apricots and water to boiling. Reduce heat to low. Cover; simmer 25 to 30 minutes until fruit is very soft, adding more water if needed.

2. In covered blender container or food processor, blend ½ of the mixture at a time until smooth. Return to saucepan; stir in sugar. Over low heat, cook 5 minutes or until sugar is dissolved and mixture is very thick, stirring constantly.

3. Preheat oven to 300°F. Line large baking sheet with foil. Spread apricot mixture onto foil on pan, making a thin, even layer.

4. Reduce oven heat to 200°F. Bake 1 to 1½ hours until fruit is no longer sticky, rotating pan every 20 minutes. Turn off oven; open oven door and allow to cool in oven.

5. When cool, invert apricot leather onto large sheet of waxed paper. Carefully peel off foil. Trim off ⅛ inch on each edge. Roll up leather and waxed paper together. To eat, unroll a portion of leather; cut or tear off a small amount, peeling paper away from candy.

TIP: You will have to use your judgment when making this candy. The amount of water needed will vary, depending on the dryness of the apricots, and the drying time will depend on the type of oven you use.

❋ Butter Mints

Mint is popular not only as a flavoring for food, but also for its ability to stimulate the appetite and improve the digestion. That is why mint candies are a traditional ending for a meal. These uncooked candies are popular with home cooks because they are so easy to make.

BEGIN: 1½ HOURS AHEAD   60 MINTS

¼   cup butter, softened
1   package (16 ounces) confectioners' sugar
3   tablespoons heavy cream
1   teaspoon peppermint or wintergreen extract
    Few drops red or green food coloring (optional)
    Sugar

1. In large bowl with mixer at medium speed, cream butter. Add ½ of the confectioners' sugar, cream, extract and food coloring; beat until smooth. With wooden spoon or hands, work in remaining confectioners' sugar until smooth.

2. Shape mixture into ½-inch balls; flatten with a fork dipped in granulated sugar (or shape with candy molds). Let dry on wire racks 1 hour. Yields 1 pound.

CREAM CHEESE MINTS: Prepare as above but substitute *1 package (3 ounces) cream cheese, softened,* for butter.

TIP: Keep mint mixture covered with damp cloth while shaping candy to prevent mixture from drying out. If mixture becomes dry, add a few drops of water.

❋ Fudge

Fudge has been a Christmas treat in America for generations, but it was not always so easy to make. Packaged marshmallows and chocolate have made the cooking of homemade fudge practically foolproof. And the occasional candymaker doesn't even have to invest in a candy thermometer; a timer or clock to measure boiling time will do. This fudge is easy to make, and just as delicious as the old-fashioned kind.

BEGIN: 2 HOURS AHEAD   80 PIECES

2½ **cups sugar**
½   **cup butter or margarine**
1   **can (5⅓ ounces) evaporated milk**
½   **teaspoon salt**
1   **package (12 ounces) semisweet-chocolate**
     pieces
1   **jar (7 ounces) marshmallow cream**
1   **cup chopped walnuts or pecans**
1   **tablespoon vanilla extract**
     Walnut or pecan halves (optional)

1. Butter 13- by 9-inch baking pan. In heavy, 3-quart saucepan, combine sugar, butter, evaporated milk and salt. Over medium heat, heat mixture to a rolling boil. Cook 5 minutes, stirring constantly.

2. Remove from heat; stir in chocolate pieces until melted. Stir in marshmallow cream, chopped nuts and vanilla; beat until well blended. Pour mixture into prepared pan. Press nut halves into fudge.

3. Cool in pan on wire rack; cut into squares with a sharp knife. Yields 2¾ pounds.

Fudge, Divinity

❋ Pralines

American pralines differ from the European ones because they are made from the ingredients available to settlers in this country: pecans and brown sugar rather than almonds and white sugar. Developed by French and Spanish colonials in the South and West of the United States, pralines also are popular in Mexican cuisine. They can be sugary, fudgelike or as chewy as caramels, depending on the preference of the region where you find them. This recipe leans toward the sugary variety.

BEGIN: 2 HOURS AHEAD   48 PIECES

3   cups packed light brown sugar
1   cup evaporated milk
¼   cup butter or margarine
¼   teaspoon salt
2   cups pecan halves
2   teaspoons vanilla extract

1. In heavy, 3-quart saucepan, combine brown sugar, evaporated milk, butter and salt. Over medium heat, heat to boiling, stirring until sugar is dissolved. Set candy thermometer in place; continue cooking, stirring occasionally, until temperature reaches 238°F. or until a small amount of mixture dropped into very cold water forms a soft ball that flattens on removal from water.

2. Remove from heat; stir in pecans and vanilla. With wooden spoon, beat until candy loses its gloss and thickens slightly.

3. Drop by teaspoonfuls onto waxed paper. If candy becomes too stiff, stir in a few drops of hot water. Cool until firm.

❋ Penuche

Penuche, also known as brown sugar fudge, resembles pralines in color and flavor. And like pralines, penuche is sometimes made from caramelized sugar instead of brown sugar. The creamy texture and caramel flavor of the candy has inspired a popular icing for spice cakes, penuche frosting.

BEGIN: 2 HOURS AHEAD   36 PIECES

2   cups packed dark brown sugar
¾   cup milk
⅛   teaspoon salt
¼   cup butter or margarine, softened
1   teaspoon vanilla extract
1   cup coarsely chopped pecans

1. Butter 8- by 8-inch baking pan. In heavy, 3-quart saucepan, combine sugar, milk and salt. Over medium heat, heat to boiling, stirring constantly. Set candy thermometer in place; continue cooking, without stirring, until temperature reaches 238°F. or until a small amount of mixture dropped into very cold water forms a soft ball that flattens on removal from water. Remove from heat; add butter and vanilla.

2. Cool mixture, without stirring, to 110°F. or until outside of saucepan feels lukewarm.

3. With wooden spoon, beat until mixture becomes thick and begins to lose its gloss; quickly stir in pecans. Pour into pan. Cool in pan on wire rack; cut into squares. Yields 1½ pounds.

❋ Caramels

Americans have a reputation as lovers of sweets, and one of our favorite candies is the caramel. We eat caramel as a coating on apples and popcorn and in candy bars, mixed with nuts and covered with chocolate. But one of the best ways to enjoy caramels' tooth-sticking sweetness is plain and homemade.

BEGIN: EARLY IN DAY   81 PIECES

2   cups sugar
2   cups light corn syrup
1   can (14 ounces) sweetened condensed milk
½   cup butter or margarine
2   tablespoons vanilla extract

1. Butter 9- by 9-inch baking pan. In heavy, 3-quart saucepan, combine sugar, corn syrup, milk and butter. Over medium heat, heat to boiling, stirring until sugar is dissolved. Set candy thermometer in place; continue cooking, stirring occasionally, until temperature reaches 248°F. or until a small amount of mixture dropped into very cold water forms a firm ball that does not flatten on removal from water.

2. Remove from heat; stir in vanilla. Pour into prepared pan.

3. Cool in pan on wire rack; cut into squares. Wrap each caramel in plastic wrap. Yields 3 pounds.

❉ Caramel Popcorn Balls

Legend has it that the Pilgrims first encountered popcorn at the end of the first Thanksgiving meal. The Indians certainly discovered the properties of this special corn: Christopher Columbus is said to have seen Indians wearing strings of it as ornaments. Even the pioneers, who carried only necessities with them, popped popcorn over their fires.

BEGIN: 2 HOURS AHEAD   20 POPCORN BALLS

12 cups popped corn
2   cups salted peanuts
1   cup sugar
1   cup molasses
¼   cup butter or margarine
1   tablespoon white vinegar
1   teaspoon vanilla extract

1. In large roasting pan, combine popped corn and peanuts.

2. In heavy, 2-quart saucepan, combine sugar, molasses, butter and vinegar. Over medium heat, heat mixture to boiling, stirring until sugar is dissolved. Set candy thermometer in place; continue cooking, without stirring, until temperature reaches 250°F. or until a small amount of mixture dropped into very cold water forms hard, yet pliable, ball.

3. Remove from heat; stir in vanilla. Slowly pour syrup over popped corn mixture, tossing to coat well. Cool slightly.

4. With buttered hands, shape mixture into 2½-inch balls.

❉ Divinity

The name of this confection describes it well. Divinity is an adaptation of fudge that has been made since the beginnings of this country, when it required a strong arm and plenty of endurance on the part of the cook. Now the electric mixer makes the recipe much easier. At Christmastime, add chopped candied cherries along with the nuts.

BEGIN: 1½ HOURS AHEAD   40 PIECES

2½ cups sugar
½   cup light corn syrup
½   cup water
2   egg whites, at room temperature
¼   teaspoon salt
1   teaspoon vanilla extract
½   cup chopped walnuts or pecans

1. In heavy, 2-quart saucepan, combine sugar, corn syrup and water. Over medium heat, heat to boiling, stirring until sugar is dissolved. Set candy thermometer in place; continue cooking, without stirring, until temperature reaches 260°F. or until a small amount of mixture dropped into very cold water forms a hard, yet pliable, ball.

2. Meanwhile, in large bowl with mixer at high speed, beat egg whites with salt until stiff peaks form. While beating at high speed, slowly pour hot syrup into egg whites. Add vanilla; continue beating until candy holds stiff, glossy peaks, about 5 minutes. Stir in nuts.

3. Working quickly, drop by heaping teaspoonfuls onto waxed paper. Cool completely before storing.

TIP: Avoid making Divinity on a humid day; candy will not set.

✿ Molasses Taffy

Taffy pulls were once a popular activity for gatherings of family and friends. Guests would pull the warm taffy into golden ropes, then cut the candy and eat it. Even today, the candymaker appreciates an extra pair of hands to pull the taffy while it is at the proper temperature. Be sure to wrap each piece individually so the pieces do not stick together.

BEGIN: 2 HOURS AHEAD   60 PIECES

2   cups sugar
1   cup light molasses
1   cup water
1   tablespoon vinegar
    Dash salt
¼   cup butter or margarine, softened

1. Butter large jelly-roll pan. In heavy, 4-quart saucepan, combine sugar, molasses, water, vinegar and salt. Over medium heat, heat mixture to boiling, stirring constantly. Set candy thermometer in place. Reduce heat to low; continue cooking, stirring often, until temperature reaches 262°F. or until small amount of mixture dropped into very cold water forms hard, yet pliable, ball.

2. Remove from heat; stir in butter. Pour onto prepared pan. Let cool 15 to 20 minutes until cool enough to handle.

3. Divide mixture in half. Pull and twist each half until candy is light in color and becomes hard to pull. Pull candy into long rope about ¾ inch in diameter.

4. With buttered kitchen shears or sharp knife, cut rope into 1-inch pieces. Wrap each piece in waxed paper. Store in airtight container in a cool, dry place. Yields 1½ pounds.

TIP: Temperature of molasses mixture will rise very slowly at first, but watch it carefully because it will rise more quickly later.

TIP: If candy becomes too cool to pull easily, warm it a few minutes in oven at 350°F.

✿ Salt Water Taffy

Atlantic City is famous for its salt water taffy, reputed to be made from sea water. Shops on the boardwalk sell the candy in all colors of the rainbow, with fruit, cinnamon, mint and chocolate flavors. Experiment until you have found your own favorite combinations: the taffy you make at home can be just as good or better than that produced beside the sea.

BEGIN: 2 HOURS AHEAD   50 PIECES

2   cups sugar
1   cup light corn syrup
1   cup water
1½   teaspoons salt
2   tablespoons butter or margarine, softened
2   teaspoons vanilla extract

1. Butter large jelly-roll pan. In heavy, 2-quart saucepan, combine sugar, corn syrup, water and salt. Over medium heat, heat mixture to boiling, stirring until sugar is dissolved. Set candy thermometer in place; continue cooking, without stirring, until temperature reaches 262°F. or until small amount of mixture dropped into very cold water forms hard, yet pliable, ball.

2. Remove from heat; stir in butter and vanilla. Pour onto prepared pan. Let cool 10 to 15 minutes until cool enough to handle.

3. Divide mixture in half. Pull and twist each half with buttered hands until candy holds its shape and is light in color. Pull mixture into long rope about ¾ inch in diameter.

4. With buttered kitchen shears or sharp knife, cut rope into 1- to 2-inch pieces. Wrap each piece in waxed paper. Store in airtight container in a cool, dry place. Yields 2½ pounds.

TIP: Add few drops flavoring oil and food coloring while pulling taffy, if desired.

❋ Butterscotch Candies

Like most hard candies, butterscotch was first produced commercially by local pharmacists. Butterscotch differs from other hard candies in that it is flavored with butter.

BEGIN: 3 HOURS AHEAD · 36 PIECES

1 cup packed light brown sugar
¼ cup water
¼ cup dark corn syrup
2 teaspoons white vinegar
Dash salt
¼ cup butter or margarine, softened
1 teaspoon vanilla extract

1. Butter 8- by 8-inch baking pan. In heavy, 2-quart saucepan, combine sugar, water, corn syrup, vinegar and salt. Over medium heat, heat to boiling, stirring until sugar is dissolved. Set candy thermometer in place; continue cooking, without stirring, until temperature reaches 290°F. or until a small amount of mixture dropped into very cold water separates into threads which are hard but not brittle.

2. Remove from heat; stir in butter and vanilla. Pour into prepared pan. Cool slightly.

3. While warm, with a buttered knife, mark candy into 36 squares. Cool in pan on wire rack; break into squares. Yields ¾ pound.

❋ Lollipops

Lollipops are most children's first candy. The name is said to come from the words "lolly" (slang for tongue) and "pop" for the sound children like to make when they pull them out of their mouths.

BEGIN: 1½ HOURS AHEAD · 32 LOLLIPOPS

32 lollipop sticks
2 cups sugar
¾ cup light corn syrup
¾ cup water
1 teaspoon oil of lemon or ¼ teaspoon oil of peppermint or cinnamon
Few drops food coloring
Candy decorations

1. Line 4 baking sheets with foil. Arrange lollipop sticks on foil.

2. In heavy, 2-quart saucepan, combine sugar, corn syrup and water. Over medium heat, heat to boiling, stirring until sugar is dissolved. With wet pastry brush, wipe side of pan to remove sugar crystals.

3. Set candy thermometer in place; cook, without stirring, until thermometer reaches 300°F. or until a small amount of mixture dropped into very cold water separates into hard, brittle threads. Remove from heat.

4. Stir in flavoring oil and food coloring, working quickly.

5. Drop mixture by tablespoonfuls over end of each lollipop stick. If desired, press candy decorations into hot candy. Cool thoroughly; remove from baking sheets.

TIP: Use bamboo meat skewers for lollipop sticks; cut off pointed ends before using.

TIP: To make perfectly round lollipops, pour mixture into greased lollipop molds on foil-lined baking sheets. Or make your own molds from paper hot-drink cups: cut off top 1½ inches of each cup to make a ring. Cut slit in side of ring from narrow end almost to rim; do not cut through rim. Grease insides of molds; place rim side down on foil-lined baking sheets. Place lollipop sticks in slit.

Peanut Brittle

Peanut Brittle

American botanist George Washington Carver promoted peanuts as a crop to renew the nutrients in soil worn out from overproduction of other cash crops. To convince farmers that there was a market for peanuts, he developed 300 uses for the "goobers," more than 100 for human nourishment. Americans should be grateful to Carver when they savor the tasty peanut brittle he originated.

BEGIN: 2 HOURS AHEAD

1 cup sugar
½ cup light corn syrup
½ cup water
½ teaspoon salt
1½ cups shelled raw peanuts
2 tablespoons butter or margarine, softened
1 teaspoon baking soda

1. Butter large cookie sheet. In heavy, 3-quart saucepan, combine sugar, corn syrup, water and salt. Over medium heat, heat to boiling, stirring until sugar is dissolved. Stir in peanuts. Set candy thermometer in place; continue cooking, stirring frequently, until temperature reaches 300°F. or until a small amount of mixture dropped into very cold water separates into hard, brittle threads.

2. Remove from heat; immediately stir in butter and baking soda. Pour at once onto cookie sheet.

3. With 2 forks, lift and pull peanut mixture into 14- by 12-inch rectangle. Cool in pan on wire rack; with hands, break candy into small pieces. Yields 1¼ pounds.

❊ Maple Syrup Candy

Northeastern American Indians used maple sugar and syrup long before the colonists arrived. The settlers took to the strange sweeteners because they were inexpensive and readily available. Pure maple syrup is no longer the cheap sweetener it once was, and in many parts of the country it is hard to find. This candy uses the more readily available maple-flavored syrup to bring the flavor and aroma of maple candy into your kitchen.

BEGIN: 2 HOURS AHEAD

1½ cups maple-flavored syrup
¾ cup sugar
1 tablespoon white vinegar
1 tablespoon baking soda

1. Butter 9- by 9-inch baking pan. In heavy, 3-quart saucepan, combine syrup, sugar and vinegar. Over medium heat, heat mixture to boiling, stirring until sugar is dissolved. Set candy thermometer in place; continue cooking, without stirring, until temperature reaches 300°F. or until a small amount of mixture dropped into very cold water separates into hard, brittle threads.

2. Remove from heat. Immediately sprinkle soda over candy; stir just to mix. Pour into prepared pan.

3. Cool in pan on wire rack; break into bite-sized pieces. Yields ¾ pound.

❊ Marshmallows

No camping trip is complete without fluffy white marshmallows to toast over the campfire. Campers with an extra-sweet tooth like to sandwich the melting marshmallows with a hunk of milk chocolate between two graham crackers to make S'Mores (from the comment "I want s'more"). Marshmallows were named for the marsh mallow, a plant that was used in making them. Today they are made with gelatin, egg whites or both.

BEGIN: EARLY IN DAY   72 MARSHMALLOWS

Confectioners' sugar
4 envelopes unflavored gelatin
1½ cups water
2 cups sugar
½ cup light corn syrup
2 egg whites, at room temperature
1 tablespoon vanilla extract
Dash salt

1. Butter 13- by 9-inch baking pan; sprinkle generously with confectioners' sugar. In small bowl, sprinkle gelatin over 1 cup water to soften; set aside.

2. In heavy, 2-quart saucepan, combine remaining ½ cup water, sugar and corn syrup. Over medium heat, heat to boiling, stirring until sugar is dissolved. Set candy thermometer in place; continue cooking, without stirring, until temperature reaches 240°F. or until small amount of mixture dropped into very cold water forms a soft ball that flattens on removal from water. Remove from heat; cool 5 minutes. Stir in softened gelatin.

3. In large bowl with mixer at high speed, beat egg whites with vanilla and salt until stiff peaks form. While beating at high speed, slowly pour hot syrup into egg whites. Continue beating until candy holds its shape, about 20 minutes. Pour into prepared pan.

4. Cool in pan on wire rack. Cut into 72 squares. Roll each square in confectioners' sugar to coat. Let dry on wire rack.

TIP: For easier cutting, dip knife into warm water when it begins to stick.

Holiday Eggnog, Mint Julep, Hot Buttered Rum

BEVERAGES

When the first Europeans arrived in North America they saw the Indians drinking teas brewed with herbs, barks and roots, as well as juices and fermented beverages made from grapes, berries and squash. But these Indians knew few of the beverages we enjoy today.

Naturally, the colonists brought some of their own favorite liquids with them. Imported tea, coffee and chocolate were expensive, and alcoholic beverages were the rule. Hard cider and beer were made at home, and gin, whiskey and rum were available at taverns and inns. But once orchards and dairy herds became established, apple cider and milk became more-available, less-costly alternatives.

The cocktail was an American invention, described by Dickens in his accounts of travels to this country. No one knows how it was named. Some say a Colonial barmaid stirred rum and fruit juice mixture with a feather, and called the drink a cock's tail. Others claim the drink was named for the French *coquetier,* a small egg cup used in New Orleans to serve mixed drinks of cognac and bitters.

Of all foods, alcoholic drinks have been the most tied to politics and legislation in our history. Tea was not the only beverage that was taxed before the Revolution: European wines had exorbitant duties placed on them, and rum was tied to the slave trade. Even after the Revolution freed Americans from foreign taxation, American levies on liquor were high, causing insurrections such as the Whiskey Rebellion of 1794, when Pennsylvania bootleggers rebelled against the government.

Hard-drinking Americans and temperance groups always have been at odds. Many individual states had already prohibited the sale of alcohol when, in 1919, an amendment to the Constitution was ratified, beginning fourteen years of national Prohibition.

The soft drink industry emerged during the furor over alcohol caused by Prohibition. Forerunners of the bottled soft drink were fruit juices and bark teas that were made at home. Carbonated water, first popularized in the early nineteenth century, was being mixed with fruit juices and herb syrups by the mid-1800s.

Cola drinks began as a syrupy headache cure. The next step happened by chance. A druggist spilled soda water into the syrup, creating a carbonated cola beverage, today's most popular soft drink. The soft drink industry is now enormous, producing more than thirty-five gallons of soda pop each year for every person in the nation!

The variety of beverages available today is enormous. Besides dozens of soft drinks and a wide assortment of alcoholic beverages, there are many kinds of teas and herbal teas, flavored coffees, fruit juices from all over the world, vegetable juices, milk and ice cream drinks. You can even choose among many types of bottled waters.

❋ Fresh Lemonade

Making and selling lemonade is often a child's first experience with the world of commerce. Makeshift lemonade stands operated by eager boys and girls are a familiar sight in many neighborhoods every summer. You can make lemonade with mixes and frozen concentrates or from frozen or bottled juice, but squeezing fresh lemons produces an aroma that makes the lemonade taste extra special.

BEGIN: EARLY IN DAY   12 SERVINGS

2   cups sugar
2   cups lemon juice
8   cups cold water
1   lemon, thinly sliced
    Ice cubes
    Mint sprigs

In 3-quart pitcher, combine sugar, lemon juice and water; stir until sugar is dissolved. Add lemon slices. Cover; chill. Pour over ice cubes in 10-ounce glasses; garnish each with mint sprig. Serve immediately. Yields 11 cups.

PINK LEMONADE: Prepare as above but stir in ¼ cup maraschino cherry juice.

❋ Ginger Ale

From the day when soda water and headache syrup first were mixed, millions upon millions of gallons of carbonated beverages have been consumed by eager Americans. You can prepare soft drinks at home by making a flavored syrup to mix with club soda. This ginger-flavored syrup makes an invigorating beverage that you may prefer to the bottled variety.

BEGIN: DAY AHEAD   6 SERVINGS

4   ounces fresh ginger root, finely chopped
1½ cups water
½   cup sugar
    Peel of ½ lemon
    Ice cubes
    Club soda, chilled

1. In 1-quart saucepan over medium-high heat, heat ginger and water to boiling. Reduce heat to low. Cover; simmer 5 minutes. Cool; refrigerate overnight.

2. Line sieve with cheesecloth; strain ginger mixture. Discard ginger. Return liquid to saucepan. Stir in sugar and lemon peel.

3. Over medium heat, heat to boiling. Boil 2 minutes, stirring occasionally. Cool slightly. Strain; refrigerate until serving time.

4. To serve: Over ice cubes in tall glass, spoon 3 tablespoons ginger syrup. Fill glass with 1 cup club soda. Yields 1¼ cups syrup.

❋ Root Beer

Based on a homemade brew of roots, barks, berries and wintergreen, root beer was initially marketed as a dry mixture to flavor a home-fermented drink. First bottled as a ready-to-drink beverage in 1893, it was one of the first soft drinks to reach the American public. Today, root beer is available in extract form; you can brew your own at home following the directions that come with the bottle. Or follow our recipe for a syrup you can mix with club soda to make a flavorful, nonalcoholic root beer.

BEGIN: EARLY IN DAY   4 SERVINGS

1   cup water
½   cup sugar
1   teaspoon root beer extract
1   bottle (28 ounces) club soda, chilled
    Ice cubes

1. In small saucepan over medium-high heat, heat water and sugar to boiling. Reduce heat to low; simmer 5 minutes. Stir in root beer extract. Cool completely. Cover; refrigerate until serving time.

2. *Just before serving:* In pitcher, stir together syrup mixture and club soda; add ice cubes. Yields 4½ cups.

TIP: To make individual servings: In 12-ounce glass, combine ¼ cup syrup and 1 cup club soda; add ice.

❄ Hot Cocoa

The Aztecs of Mexico were drinking cold unsweetened chocolate before the Spaniards arrived. The Spaniards are credited with adding sugar to the beverage and heating it to make Hot Cocoa as we know it today. A fad for hot chocolate quickly spread throughout Europe and the beverage came back to the Colonies with European settlers; at one time it was as popular as coffee and tea.

BEGIN: 15 MINUTES AHEAD   8 SERVINGS

½ **cup cocoa**
½ **cup sugar**
   Dash salt
½ **cup water**
6 **cups milk**
1 **teaspoon vanilla extract**
   Whipped cream or marshmallows

1. In 3-quart saucepan, stir together cocoa, sugar and salt until well mixed. Stir in water until smooth. Over medium heat, heat to boiling, stirring constantly. Cook 2 minutes more, stirring constantly.

2. Stir in milk; heat until tiny bubbles form around edge, stirring occasionally. Remove from heat.

3. Add vanilla; with hand beater, beat until smooth and foamy. Pour cocoa into 8-ounce mugs. Top each with whipped cream or marshmallows. Yields 7 cups.

TIP: Place a peppermint stick candy in each serving for a stirrer.

MEXICAN CHOCOLATE: Prepare as above but add *½ teaspoon ground cinnamon* to mixture. Garnish with *cinnamon sticks.*

❄ Iced Spiced Tea

According to legend, a tea vendor at the St. Louis International Exposition of 1904 decided the hot weather was hampering business. He added ice to his hot tea and discovered one of the most refreshing beverages of summer, iced tea. Another businessman created the tea bag that same year. This tea salesman had his tea samples sewed into little bags; his customers realized that these were a convenience for everyday tea brewing.

BEGIN: EARLY IN DAY   6 SERVINGS

3 **lemons**
3 **oranges**
6 **tea bags**
1 **teaspoon whole cloves**
2 **cinnamon sticks**
2 **cups boiling water**
1 **cup sugar**
2 **cups cold water**
   Ice cubes

1. With vegetable peeler, thinly peel lemons and oranges; reserve peels. Squeeze juice; set aside.

2. In 6-cup teapot, combine peels, tea bags, cloves and cinnamon sticks. Add boiling water; steep 5 minutes. Discard tea bags.

3. Stir in sugar until dissolved. Add reserved fruit juices and 2 cups cold water; chill.

4. To serve: Strain over ice cubes in 8-ounce glasses. Serve immediately. Yields 5 cups.

SPICED TEA PUNCH: Prepare as above. Stir in *1 bottle (28 ounces) club soda* just before serving. Yields 8½ cups.

RUSSIAN TEA: Prepare as above in steps 1 and 2, using 2-quart saucepan. Stir in sugar, fruit juices and remaining water; heat through. Pour into 8-ounce mugs; serve at once.

❋ Café Brûlot

We all know about England's exorbitant taxation on teas and about the Boston Tea Party, but other events in history helped make coffee America's most popular hot beverage. For example, the War of 1812 interfered with the shipping in the tea trade, but not with the South American coffee importation. Café Brûlot is a spectacular way to serve this beverage, particularly popular in the French-inspired cuisine of New Orleans.

BEGIN: 15 MINUTES AHEAD   10 SERVINGS

1   orange
1   cup brandy
6   whole cloves
3   small cinnamon sticks
10 sugar cubes
4   cups hot strong black coffee

1. With vegetable peeler, thinly peel orange (reserve orange for another use). In 1-quart saucepan over medium heat, heat orange peel, brandy, cloves, cinnamon and sugar until warm.

2. Pour into warmed heatsafe serving bowl. Carefully ignite brandy; slowly pour coffee into flaming brandy. Ladle into warmed demitasse cups. Yields 4½ cups.

Café Brûlot, Mexican Chocolate

❄ Mulled Cider

As soon as apples were harvested in the New World, cider became an important beverage. It was inexpensive, tasted good and it was far less likely to cause sickness than the milk or water of Colonial times. The natural fermentation of the cider also made a palatable alcoholic beverage that could be mild or potent. Cider is still a favorite drink, served cold in the early autumn or mulled with spices on a brisk fall evening.

BEGIN: 15 MINUTES AHEAD   8 SERVINGS

2   quarts apple cider
4   cinnamon sticks
1   teaspoon whole cloves
1   teaspoon whole allspice

In 3-quart saucepan over high heat, heat all ingredients to boiling. Reduce heat to low; simmer 5 minutes, stirring occasionally. Strain cider into 10-ounce mugs or heatsafe glasses. Yields 8 cups.

❄ Sunshine Punch

The word "punch" comes from a Hindi word meaning "five," the number of ingredients in the traditional mixture—water, sugar, spices, spirits and lime. It applies to a variety of beverages made from combinations of ingredients. Many of them have the alcoholic "punch," but others are refreshing, fruity and innocent like this one.

BEGIN: 15 MINUTES AHEAD   32 SERVINGS

1   can (46 ounces) pineapple juice, chilled
1   can (6 ounces) frozen lemonade
       concentrate, thawed
1   can (6 ounces) frozen orange juice
       concentrate, thawed
4   cups cold water
3   bottles (28 ounces each) ginger ale,
       chilled
     Orange slices
     Lemon slices
     Ice ring or cubes

In chilled punch bowl, combine all ingredients. Ladle into 6-ounce punch cups. Yields 5 quarts.

SUNSHINE CHAMPAGNE PUNCH: Prepare as above but substitute *3 bottles (750 ml each) champagne, chilled,* for ginger ale.

TIP: To make ice ring, pour water or fruit juice into ring mold or bundt pan. Add fruit slices if desired. Freeze. Dip mold into warm water to unmold.

Sunshine Punch, Fresh Lemonade, Spiced Tea Punch

❊ White Sangría

In Spain, Sangría usually consists of red wine with one or more fruits floating in it, and sometimes includes stronger spirits. Colonial Americans called their version of the drink Sangaree; the name could refer to almost any sweetened wine drink with added fruit. This White Sangría was popularized in California. Like Spanish Sangría, it includes wine and fruit; like Sangaree it is sweetened. But it is a light drink, based on white wine, extended with club soda and only slightly sweetened.

BEGIN: 2½ HOURS AHEAD   10 SERVINGS

1   **bottle (750 ml) dry white wine, chilled**
1   **cup orange juice**
¼   **cup lemon juice**
½   **cup sugar**
1   **orange, thinly sliced**
1   **lemon, thinly sliced**
1   **bottle (28 ounces) club soda, chilled**
      Ice cubes

1. In large pitcher, combine wine, orange juice, lemon juice and sugar; mix well to dissolve sugar. Add orange and lemon slices. Refrigerate until serving time, at least 2 hours.

2. *Just before serving:* Add club soda and ice cubes. Pour into 10-ounce glasses or wine glasses. Yields 10 cups.

SANGRÍA: Prepare as above but omit orange juice and substitute *1 bottle (750 ml) dry red wine, chilled,* for dry white wine. If desired, remove fruit slices just before serving; replace with fresh fruit.

❊ May Wine Bowl

May wine is a sweet white wine from Germany or Austria flavored with the spring flower known as sweet woodruff. In spring it is served well chilled with strawberries and spring flowers floating in it. Purchase May wine from an American vineyard, or sweeten a Moselle or Rhine wine to make a similar beverage.

BEGIN: EARLY IN DAY   10 SERVINGS

2   **bottles (750 ml each) Moselle or Rhine wine**
1   **cup sugar**
1   **cup whole small strawberries**
      Ice cubes
      Spring flowers (woodruff, violets)
      Mint sprigs

1. In punch bowl, stir together wine and sugar until sugar is dissolved. Cover; chill.

2. *Just before serving:* Add strawberries and ice cubes. Float spring flowers and mint sprigs on wine. Ladle into 6-ounce punch cups. Yields 7 cups.

❊ Daiquiris

Named for the Cuban city of Daiquiri, this exotic drink was invented by a pair of American mining engineers, supposedly for the purpose of preventing yellow fever. We do not know if it did the job, but it became a very popular cocktail.

BEGIN: JUST BEFORE SERVING   8 SERVINGS

3   **cups cracked ice**
1½   **cups light rum**
1   **can (6 ounces) frozen limeade concentrate, thawed**

Over cracked ice in 1½-quart pitcher, pour rum and limeade concentrate; stir to mix. Strain into cocktail glasses. Serve immediately.

FROZEN DAIQUIRIS: In covered blender container at high speed, blend *6 cups cracked ice,* rum and limeade concentrate until slushy. Pour into cocktail glasses.

FRUIT DAIQUIRIS: Prepare Frozen Daiquiris as above but add *1 cup peeled, sliced fruit* to mixture before blending. Choose from bananas, peaches, apricots, strawberries, pineapple and other fruits.

❈ Roman Punch

In the late 1800s Roman Punch was served as a cooler in the middle of a large meal. President Grant often served it during twenty- to thirty-course dinners at the White House. President Hayes, who succeeded Grant, preferred not to serve liquor. At one party, orange shells filled with what appeared to be Roman Punch were offered, and the guests thought they were imbibing spirits. But President Hayes confided in his diary that the punch was flavored to taste like rum, yet made without liquor, and he delighted in having fooled so many people.

BEGIN: EARLY IN DAY   8 SERVINGS

1   **quart lemon sherbet, softened**
1   **cup dark rum**

In medium bowl, combine sherbet and rum; cover and freeze. (Mixture does not freeze solid.) Scoop into chilled 5-ounce punch cups or dessert dishes. Yields 4 cups.

Roman Punch, Fruit Daiquiri, Root Beer

❋ Holiday Eggnog

Eggnog evolved from an English drink made with ale or wine. Early Americans fortified the drink with stronger American bourbon or rum and served it to strengthen invalids and travelers. Today, eggnog is most often served at Christmas, New Year's and Easter parties.

BEGIN: EARLY IN DAY   16 SERVINGS

6	eggs, separated, at room temperature
½	cup sugar
1	cup bourbon
1	cup light rum
3	cups milk
½	teaspoon ground nutmeg
1	cup heavy cream

1. In large bowl with mixer at high speed, beat egg yolks with sugar until thick and lemon-colored, frequently scraping bowl.

2. At medium speed, carefully beat in bourbon and rum, 1 tablespoon at a time, to prevent curdling mixture. Pour into punch bowl. Cover; chill.

3. *About 20 minutes before serving:* Stir milk and ground nutmeg into punch bowl.

4. In large bowl with mixer at high speed, using clean beaters, beat egg whites until soft peaks form.

5. In small bowl with mixer at medium speed, beat cream until stiff peaks form. With wire whisk, gently fold egg whites and cream into yolk mixture until just blended.

6. To serve: Sprinkle additional ground nutmeg over eggnog; ladle into 6-ounce punch cups. Yields 10 cups.

❋ Philadelphia Fish House Punch

Named after a private Philadelphia club, this punch has a reputation as an extremely potent beverage. As far back as the early 1700s, Fish House Punch was favored by hard-drinking Colonials and Revolutionary War soldiers; the punch is supposed to be responsible for several blank pages in one General's diary. It is traditionally served with a huge block of ice in the bowl, so the punch stays cold with little melting to dilute it.

BEGIN: EARLY IN DAY   18 SERVINGS

2	cups lemon juice
¾	cup sugar
½	cup water
1	bottle (750 ml) dark rum
½	bottle (750-ml size) cognac
¼	cup peach brandy
	Ice

In punch bowl, combine lemon juice, sugar and water. Stir until sugar is dissolved. Stir in rum, cognac and peach brandy. Cover; chill. Add large block of ice to punch; ladle mixture into 5-ounce punch cups. Yields 9 cups.

❋ Bloody Mary

Made from tomato or vegetable juice and vodka, then spiced to taste, the Bloody Mary is enjoyed for its hearty, peppy flavor. The Bloody Bull is a cross between a Bloody Mary and a Bullshot (consommé with vodka).

BEGIN: EARLY IN DAY   6 SERVINGS

3	cups tomato juice or V-8 vegetable juice
1	tablespoon lemon juice
1	teaspoon Worcestershire
	Dash celery salt
	Dash hot pepper sauce
6	ounces vodka (¾ cup)
	Crushed ice
	Lemon wedges
	Celery stalks

1. In large pitcher, combine tomato juice, lemon juice, Worcestershire, celery salt, hot pepper sauce and vodka. Cover; chill.

2. To serve: Stir mixture; pour over ice in 8-ounce highball glasses. Serve immediately. Garnish with lemon wedges and celery stalks. Yields 3½ cups.

BLOODY BULL: Prepare as above but stir in *1 can (10½ ounces) condensed beef broth.* Yields 5 cups.

✳ Mint Julep

Firmly associated with the South, the Mint Julep is a drink for hot summer afternoons. Julep fanciers agree that the drink must include fresh mint, liquor and crushed ice, but there is no agreement about how the drink is assembled. The mint may be crushed or not, the liquor may be bourbon, rye, rum or brandy, and each bartender has his own stirring technique.

BEGIN: JUST BEFORE SERVING   1 SERVING

5   **sprigs mint**
1   **teaspoon sugar**
1   **tablespoon water**
    Finely crushed ice
1½ **ounces bourbon**

1. Place 4 sprigs mint, sugar and water in a chilled 12-ounce highball glass or silver mint-julep mug. With handle of wooden spoon, crush mint leaves and sugar until sugar is dissolved.

2. Fill glass to brim with ice; add bourbon. Stir gently until outside of glass is frosted; add more ice to fill glass. Garnish with remaining mint sprig. Serve with straw.

✳ Mulled Wine

Early wines in America were made at home, from flowers, berries and other fruits as well as grapes. It was not until late in the nineteenth century that the first commercial domestic wines were produced. Throughout our history both homemade and commercial wines have been heated with spices and fruits to make Mulled Wine.

BEGIN: 15 MINUTES AHEAD   10 SERVINGS

1   **cup sugar**
3   **cinnamon sticks**
12 **whole cloves**
12 **whole allspice**
2   **oranges, sliced**
1   **lemon, sliced**
2   **bottles (750 ml each) dry red wine**

In 3-quart saucepan, combine all ingredients. Over high heat, heat to boiling. Reduce heat to low; simmer 5 minutes, stirring occasionally. Ladle into 6-ounce punch cups or heatsafe glasses. Yields 7 cups.

✳ Cranberry Punch

Besides making a fine tart sauce to accompany the Thanksgiving turkey, cranberries make a lovely punch. The Pilgrims probably used them to make beverages, too. Cranberries were named by the Pilgrims, who called them craneberries. But did they name the berries for the cranes who fed on them, or for their flowers, whose shape is said to resemble the silhouette of the crane?

BEGIN: 15 MINUTES AHEAD   16 SERVINGS

1   **bottle (32 ounces) cranberry juice**
    cocktail, chilled
2   **cups cold water**
½   **cup lemon juice**
½   **cup sugar**
1   **bottle (28 ounces) ginger ale, chilled**
    Lemon slices
    Ice cubes

In chilled punch bowl, combine all ingredients; stir to dissolve sugar. Ladle into 6-ounce punch cups. Yields 10 cups.

✳ Hot Buttered Rum

As early as the early 1600s, rum was important in the economy of the American Colonies. Molasses was imported from the West Indies to produce rum; when it was sold the profits were used to buy African slaves. As long as man has been drinking rum, he has enjoyed Hot Buttered Rum as a warming drink on cold winter nights.

BEGIN: 15 MINUTES AHEAD 1 SERVING

2	teaspoons confectioners' sugar
3	ounces light rum
1	tablespoon butter
	Dash ground cloves
	Dash ground nutmeg
	Cinnamon stick
	Boiling water

In 8-ounce mug, combine sugar and rum; stir until sugar is dissolved. Add butter, cloves, nutmeg and cinnamon stick. Fill mug with boiling water. Serve immediately.

TIP: Heat mug by rinsing with hot water.

TO MICROWAVE: In 8-ounce microwave-safe mug, combine all ingredients except water. Fill mug with tap water. Microwave on HIGH 2 to 3 minutes or until hot. Sprinkle with additional nutmeg. Serve immediately.

✳ Tom and Jerry

The Tom and Jerry has been a favorite hot drink in American bars and homes for over a century. It is supposed to have been created by Jerry Thomas, a San Francisco bartender and author of the Bon-Vivant's Companion. *A cross between a hot milk punch and eggnog, the Tom and Jerry is a terrific warming drink for winter parties.*

BEGIN: 30 MINUTES AHEAD 12 SERVINGS

6	eggs, separated, at room temperature
1	teaspoon vanilla extract
¼	cup sugar
12	ounces light rum (1½ cups)
12	ounces brandy (1½ cups)
4½	cups hot milk
	Ground nutmeg

1. In large bowl with mixer at high speed, beat egg whites and vanilla until soft peaks form. Gradually sprinkle in sugar, 2 tablespoons at a time, beating until stiff peaks form.

2. In small bowl with mixer at high speed, beat yolks until thick and lemon-colored. Fold into whites.

3. To serve: Spoon ½ cup egg mixture into each of twelve 10-ounce mugs. To each, add 1 ounce rum and 1 ounce brandy. Fill each mug with hot milk; stir. Sprinkle with nutmeg. Serve immediately. Yields 12 cups.

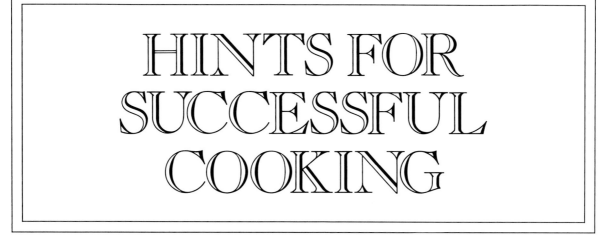

HINTS FOR SUCCESSFUL COOKING

There is no magic involved in preparing recipes successfully every time—just a little care. You can be a wonderful cook if you learn to follow recipes exactly. (After preparing a recipe once, you may then wish to modify it to your own tastes and habits.)

First, read the recipe from beginning to end, noting the ingredients and equipment you'll need. Also consider the amount of time required for each step, as well as chilling, cooling, etc.

The times given above our recipes tell you approximately how long you will need from the time you begin the recipe until it is ready to serve. The time includes chopping, resting, chilling, cooling and standing times.

The number of servings suggested in the recipe is an approximate indication of how many people each will satisfy. If you are serving people with extra-hearty or very small appetites, adjust the servings accordingly. Many recipes also include a yield that will give you an idea of the total quantity of food prepared.

Here are a few hints to help you use these recipes with complete confidence.

✳ Ingredient Pointers

When you assemble ingredients, it is important to make sure you are using the right food. For example, baking powder and baking soda sound alike and even look alike, but they do not have the same effect in a recipe. Below, some frequently used ingredients are clarified for you.

BREAD CRUMBS

Soft bread crumbs are made by crumbling day-old or fresh bread with the fingers or in a blender or food processor. Each slice of bread makes ½ to ¾ cup crumbs.

Dried bread crumbs are made from bread that has been thoroughly dried in the oven, then crushed in the blender or with a rolling pin. Each slice of bread makes about ¼ cup crumbs. Ready-made dried crumbs can be purchased in your supermarket.

HERBS

In these recipes, all herbs are dried unless fresh is specified. Parsley and chives are the only exceptions—they are fresh unless dried is specified.

Hard-Cooked Eggs

To hard-cook eggs: In saucepan, cover eggs with cold water by 1 inch. Over high heat, heat water and eggs just to boiling. Remove from heat; cover and let stand 20 minutes. Rinse eggs with cold water; peel.

Whipped Cream

To whip cream for use in recipe: With mixer at medium speed, beat well-chilled heavy cream just until soft peaks form; use at once.

For use as garnish: Whip cream until stiff peaks form; if desired, sweeten with 1 to 2 tablespoons sugar.

Canned Fruits and Vegetables

Use liquid in can unless recipe says to drain it.

Shortening

This term refers to the white vegetable shortening that you buy in a can. Do not substitute butter or oil; the results will be quite different.

❊ Cutting Terms

Using the right-sized pieces in a recipe can be important to its success. Pieces that are too large will need more cooking time; pieces that are too small may disintegrate in a long-cooking dish. Sometimes, even the shape of the pieces can be important. We will explain the terms so you'll know them when you see them.

Cube: Cut into ½-inch or larger, cube-shaped pieces.

Dice: Cut into ¼-inch, cube-shaped pieces.

Chop: Cut into irregular pieces, about ¼ inch across.

Mince: Cut into very tiny irregular pieces.

Julienne: Cut into long, thin pieces the size of matchsticks.

❊ Measuring Pointers

You cannot be assured of success if you don't measure carefully, so have accurate measuring cups and spoons available, and use them. Always level ingredient in measures; do not heap in cup or spoon.

- Measure each ingredient before you complete the preparation that follows a comma. For example, if the recipe reads "1 cup strawberries, sliced," measure the strawberries before you slice them; if it says "1 cup sliced strawberries," slice before measuring.

- Sifting flour is unnecessary. Simply stir the flour, then spoon lightly into measuring cup and level the top.

- Brown sugar is measured by packing the sugar firmly into a measuring cup.

- When measuring shortening, pack it firmly into cup, then slice through with spatula to break up air pockets. Another way to measure shortening is to fill a liquid measure with cold water to level of 2 cups minus the amount of shortening needed (for example, fill to 1¼ cups if you need ¾ cup shortening), then add shortening until water level reaches 2 cups. Drain off water.

- If you wish to double or halve a recipe, remember that not all the ingredients should be doubled or halved.

—For example, in a stew, do not use twice as much liquid, because less evaporation will occur. The seasonings might also be too strong if doubled.

—For cakes and other baked goods, it is wise to make the recipe twice rather than doubling the ingredients, because these products are sensitive to proper mixing methods and pan sizes.

—The cooking time may change when you alter the ingredient quantities, particularly for casseroles or other baked or roasted foods.

Emergency Substitutions

Whenever possible, use the exact ingredient specified in a recipe. But when you cannot, refer to this list to help you out of an emergency.

1 whole egg	—2 egg yolks (for most purposes)
1 cup milk	—½ cup evaporated milk plus ½ cup water
	—⅓ cup nonfat dry milk mixed with 1 cup water
1 cup buttermilk	—1 tablespoon vinegar with milk to fill cup; let stand 5 minutes
	—1 cup plain yogurt
1 cup cake flour	—1 cup less 2 tablespoons all-purpose flour
1 tablespoon cornstarch	—2 tablespoons all-purpose flour (for thickening)
1 teaspoon baking powder	—¼ teaspoon baking soda plus ½ teaspoon cream of tartar
1 ounce unsweetened chocolate	—3 tablespoons cocoa plus 1 tablespoon butter or margarine
1 clove garlic	—⅛ teaspoon garlic powder
1 teaspoon dried herb	—1 tablespoon fresh herb
1 tablespoon prepared mustard	—1 teaspoon dry mustard
3 tablespoons chopped parsley	—1 tablespoon dried parsley flakes
Juice of 1 lemon	—2 tablespoons bottled lemon juice
Juice of 1 orange	—¼ cup bottled orange juice or diluted orange juice concentrate

❋ Cooking Methods

Cooking on the Range-Top

Whether you are boiling water, melting butter or simmering a stew, match the size of the pan you use to the burner on your gas or electric range and learn to control the heat for your particular range.

Recipes often specify "low," "medium" or "high" heat. These terms may or may not correspond directly with the markings on your range, but they are intended as a guide to the amount of heat required. It is more important to keep liquid simmering or fat at the proper temperature than to set the indicator at "medium." Learn to recognize the following terms for successful results.

Boil: Large bubbles constantly rise to the surface and break.

Simmer: Small bubbles form slowly and break just below the liquid's surface.

Fry: Cook with fat.

- *Deep-fry:* Fat is deep enough for food to be completely covered. Use a thermometer to judge the fat's temperature and do not allow the temperature to vary. Vegetable oil is recommended for deep-frying.

- *Shallow-fry:* Fat does not cover food; it may be a thin coating on pan's bottom or up to 1 inch deep.

- *Stir-fry:* Using a small amount of oil in wok or skillet, keep stirring and turning food over very high heat.

Cooking in the Oven

The oven cooks by indirect heat; that is, the hot air heats the container and the food.

- Preheating the oven has been a standard practice for many years. The energy crisis, however, taught us that preheating sometimes is a waste of energy. We tell you when it is important to preheat.

  —For those foods that are delicate or require only a short baking time, preheating is essential for successful results.

  —But for foods that require long cooking times and are not fragile, preheating is not necessary.

  —To preheat, follow manufacturer's directions, or simply turn on oven to specified temperature 10 minutes before using oven.

- Use the middle oven rack for most baking and roasting, and leave space between pans to allow air circulation.

- In most baking and roasting, the food is not covered. This allows the hot air to cook the food and promotes surface browning. Some recipes specify that a food should be covered; in that case, cover a dish with its lid or foil.

- Sometimes a food will become brown before it is completely done. Covering the browned portions with small pieces of foil or a loose tent of foil will help prevent burning while the rest of the food cooks. This technique is particularly helpful for the edges of pies and the legs and wing tips of poultry.

- Always bake in a utensil of the proper size. The ingredients and cooking times are based on the size of dish listed in the recipe. When dimensions are listed (such as "10- by 6-inch baking dish"), the dish referred to is a rectangular one. You can use an oval dish if the dimensions are similar and the dish holds the same amount of food as the rectangular one.

- A casserole is deeper than a baking dish, but may be of any shape. To determine the capacity of a casserole, measure the amount of water needed to fill the dish to the top.

COOKING UNDER THE BROILER

The broiler cooks food from above with radiant heat. Gas and electric broilers work differently; the best way to understand yours is to read the manufacturer's use and care manual.

- Follow manufacturer's directions on preheating the broiler. Generally, electric broilers are preheated, gas ones are not.

- Most broiling is done 4 to 6 inches from the heating element. To determine this distance, measure from the top surface of the food to the heat source.

COOKING OUTDOORS

There's no question about it—Americans enjoy cooking outside. And their barbecues are made easy and fun by an industry that makes products just for them. It is said that Henry Ford produced the first charcoal briquettes for the market (a by-product of burning scrap wood in his automobile plants). These first briquettes were sold by the automobile dealers.

Today you can buy briquettes, along with lighter fluids and jellies, wood chips and other barbecue accessories in supermarkets, drugstores, department stores, even gas stations. And they are easy to use. Just follow these simple guidelines.

If your grill comes with instructions for building a fire, be sure to read them. For a gas or electric grill, always follow the manufacturer's directions for operating the grill and controlling the heat.

Always place grill away from areas with dry grass or other flammable objects that might catch live sparks. Grill should be in a level area where it will receive adequate air circulation, but not high winds.

BUILDING A CHARCOAL FIRE

- Line bottom of grill with heavy foil if desired, to keep grill clean and reflect heat. Make holes in foil at vents to keep air circulating.

- Stack charcoal briquettes in a pyramid in center of grill or follow special directions from manufacturer. Add lighter fluid or jelly according to label directions.

- Light charcoal with a long match. Wait 20 to 40 minutes or until all coals glow red and are evenly covered with gray ash.

- Using tongs, separate coals to make a single layer of coals in grill.

- Set grid into place and test for heat intensity: hold hand at grid level and count the number of seconds you can leave your hand in place comfortably. If you can leave it there for more than 5 seconds, the coals are at low heat; for 3 to 4 seconds, the coals are at medium heat; for less than 3 seconds, the coals are at high heat. Use medium heat for most grilling purposes.

- Increase heat by moving coals closer together or lowering grid. Reduce heat by moving coals farther apart or raising grid.

- For longer periods of cooking, add more coals to edges of fire to ignite, then push toward center as other coals die down.

TIPS FOR GRILLING

- Trim excess fat from meat to avoid flare-ups. Extinguish flare-ups with water from a spray bottle.

- Use hickory, mesquite or other green wood chips to impart a smoky flavor. Soak chips in water about 1 hour, then sprinkle over live coals while barbecuing.

- Turn meats with tongs to avoid piercing meat and losing flavorful juices.

- In a hurry? Partially cook chicken or other meats in the microwave oven; then finish on grill.

Special Helps from Your Microwave Oven

Food	Amount	Dish/Directions	Setting/Cook Time
Cook bacon	4 slices	Microwave-safe rack in dish	HIGH/ 3½ to 4½ minutes
	8 slices		HIGH/ 6 to 7 minutes
Melt butter or margarine	¼ cup	Custard cup	HIGH/ 1 minute
	½ cup		HIGH/ 2 minutes
Soften butter or margarine	½ cup	Small bowl	LOW/ 15 to 20 seconds
	1 cup		LOW/ 30 to 40 seconds
Melt semisweet-chocolate pieces	1 package (6 ounces)	Small bowl	HIGH/ 2½ minutes
Melt unsweetened chocolate	1 square (1 ounce)	Custard cup	HIGH/ 2 minutes
	2 squares (1 ounce each)		HIGH/ 2 minutes
	4 squares (1 ounce each)		HIGH/ 2½ minutes
Soften cream cheese	1 package (3 ounces)	Small bowl	HIGH/ 15 seconds
	1 package (8 ounces)		HIGH/ 30 seconds
Thaw frozen fish fillets	1 pound	Baking dish	DEFROST/ 8 to 10 minutes; let stand 5 minutes
Thaw frozen fruit	1 package (10 ounces)	Slit plastic pouch; place on dish	DEFROST/ 3 to 5 minutes (center will be icy)
Cook chopped onion in oil	½ cup onion in 1 tablespoon salad oil	Covered casserole	HIGH/ 2 to 3 minutes
Heat condensed soup	1 can (10¾ ounces) plus 1 can water	Casserole or 2 soup bowls	HIGH/ 3½ to 4½ minutes
Heat spaghetti sauce	1 jar (15½ ounces)	Covered dish; stir once	HIGH/ 3 to 4 minutes
	1 jar (32 ounces)		HIGH/ 6 minutes
Heat canned vegetables	1 can (15 ounces) undrained	Covered dish	HIGH/ 2½ to 4 minutes
Cook frozen vegetables	1 package (10 ounces)	Covered dish	HIGH/ 6 to 10 minutes

COOKING IN THE MICROWAVE OVEN

The microwave oven has found its way into about one out of every four American homes. And it has made a great impact on the way these Americans cook.

We have included microwave directions for many of our recipes, and you may wish to adapt others for microwave use. If you are not sure how to prepare certain foods in your microwave, always check the manufacturer's directions. Do not prepare any foods in your microwave oven that are not recommended by the manufacturer.

- All dishes used to microwave food should be microwave-safe. To test for suitability follow these simple steps:
  1. Fill 1-cup glass measure with water.
  2. Place empty dish in microwave oven next to measure of water.
  3. Microwave on HIGH 1 to 2 minutes.
  4. Feel the empty dish. If it is warm or hot in spots, it is not suitable for microwave use, because it absorbs the energy, rather than letting it pass through.

- Some foods cook more evenly when stirred during microwave cooking. Dense foods benefit from standing a few minutes before serving to allow temperature to even out.

- Our recipes were tested in countertop microwave ovens rated at 600 to 700 watts. If your oven has a lower wattage, you may need to increase the cooking time. If your oven has a higher wattage, watch carefully; you may need a shorter cooking time.

- Also keep in mind that our timings are based on ingredients that start at normal storage temperature. For example, milk is refrigerated, onions are at room temperature.

- At left is a chart that can help you take advantage of the smaller cooking tasks that the microwave does well. It can help you with many of the recipes you prepare every day.

✷ Wine

Americans have enjoyed wine for centuries. The colonists imported wines from Europe or made their own from other fruits and wild grapes; however, they were unsuccessful at growing European wine grapes in the New World. The climate and soil in the East were not suitable to those varieties, and American grapes made inferior wine.

But California later proved a perfect place for growing European wine grapes, and Western vineyards now produce some of the best wines in the world. The Eastern vineyards have developed new grape hybrids that also produce excellent wines.

TYPES OF WINES

Wines generally are classified by their place in a meal.

Table wines, including red, white and rosé, are wines that are most pleasing with a meal.

Appetizer wines include dry sherry, vermouth and other specially flavored wines that often are served as cocktails. Some table wines may also double as appetizer wines.

Dessert wines, such as cream sherry, port and muscatel, are sweeter wines with a slightly higher alcohol content than table wines, and usually are served after a meal.

Sparkling wines are effervescent, made bubbly by an additional fermentation process. Champagne, Cold Duck and sparkling Burgundy fall into this category. Sparkling wines may be served with any food, but they usually are reserved for special occasions.

SERVING WINE

People who are new to wine drinking often worry about which wine to serve with which food. A good rule of thumb is that the fuller flavor of a red wine goes well with the heartier taste of red meats, while the more delicate white wines go well with lighter chicken and fish. But the food and wine combinations you choose are purely a matter of personal taste.

Experts agree that wines must be served at the proper temperature for full enjoyment. Therefore, red wines should be at a cool room temperature (65° to 75°F.), white wines should be slightly chilled (55°F.), sparkling wines should be well chilled (45°F.). Most appetizer wines are also served chilled.

Serve dessert wines in 2- to 3-ounce portions, table wines in 4- to 6-ounce servings. In each case, choose a stemmed glass that will hold the desired portion when half-filled.

COOKING WITH WINE

When you cook with wine, the alcohol evaporates, leaving only a wonderful flavor and aroma in the food. Use a drinkable wine for cooking; a wine that has become sour won't do justice to the food.

When a recipe calls for a dry white wine, you may use a Chablis or Rhine wine with good results; if it calls for a dry red wine, try a Burgundy. If the recipe specifies a certain wine, it is always best to use that particular type.

It is interesting to drink the wine you have used in cooking along with the prepared dish, and compare the flavors.

Finishing Touches

Once you have prepared a meal, you are still not quite finished. A great deal of appetite appeal is in the way the dish is presented. Sometimes a simple garnish can make the difference between a good meal and an exceptional one. Here are several of our favorites.

GREENS:

· A parsley sprig is traditional for adding color to a plate; also use fresh herbs such as dill, thyme, mint or rosemary.

· Salad greens such as curly endive, romaine, celery leaves or broccoli rabe make attractive beds for all kinds of foods.

GREEN ONION OR CELERY BRUSHES: Slash 2 or 3 inches of tops lengthwise into very thin pieces. Cover with ice water; refrigerate until ends curl.

FLUTED MUSHROOMS: Carve curving grooves in mushroom caps from center to edge. In skillet over medium heat, in hot butter, cook mushrooms just until colored, if desired.

TOMATOES: Cut into wedges; dip center edge in chopped parsley or mint.

CHERRY TOMATO FLOWERS: For each, use 1 large and 1 small cherry tomato. With stem end down, cut each into 4 to 6 wedges, cutting to, but not through, bottom of tomato. Scoop out seeds from each; fit smaller tomato inside larger one. Cut a ¾-inch length of green onion; slash ½ inch of one end lengthwise as for green onion brush. Fit into center of smaller tomato.

GREEN AND RED PEPPERS: Slice peppers into rings. Make a chain of rings: cut slit on one side of each ring, slip rings together to form a chain.

CUCUMBERS: With fork, score unpeeled cucumber lengthwise; slice crosswise to make rounds.

CITRUS FRUITS:

· Cut lemons, limes or oranges into crosswise slices; stud edge with cloves.

· Slit thin crosswise slices from center to edge; twist.

· Cut fruit in half; with sharp knife, carve scalloped or serrated edge.

FROSTED GRAPES: Dip clusters of grapes into slightly beaten egg white to coat; dip in granulated sugar. Dry on wire rack.

FRUITED ICE CUBES: When making ice cubes, add a maraschino cherry, strawberry, or lemon or lime twist to each compartment. Fill with water or fruit juice; freeze.

SUGARED OR SALTED GLASSES: Dip rim of glass in lemon or lime juice, then in granulated sugar or coarse salt.

CHOCOLATE CURLS: Shave room-temperature semisweet or milk chocolate with a sharp knife or vegetable peeler.

CUTOUT SHAPES: Use hors d'oeuvre cutters or sharp knife to cut foods into fancy shapes. Cut from thin slices of carrot, turnip, pimento, aspic, luncheon meat, citrus peel, fruit-flavored gelatin, kiwi fruit or toast.

HARD-COOKED EGGS:

· Use chopped whites, yolks or whole egg, depending on desired effect. Or press egg yolks through sieve for more delicate pieces.

· Slice eggs or cut into wedges

FRUIT AND VEGETABLE CONTAINERS:

Tomatoes, green peppers, melons, squashes, eggplants, pineapples, citrus fruits and other fruits and vegetables make stunning, practical containers for food. Simply cut off the top third of the fruit or vegetable and remove the pulp, leaving enough thickness in the shell to hold its shape. Leave shell with straight edge or, with small, sharp knife, cut scallops or serrations. Fill with dips, spreads or other foods.

INDEX